AUTHORITY IN EUROPEAN
BOOK CULTURE 1400–1600

Material Readings in Early Modern Culture

This series provides a forum for studies that consider the material forms of texts as part of an investigation into early modern culture. The editors invite proposals of a multi- or interdisciplinary nature, and particularly welcome proposals that combine archival research with an attention to the theoretical models that might illuminate the reading, writing, and making of texts, as well as projects that take innovative approaches to the study of material texts, both in terms the kinds of primary materials under investigation, and in terms of methodologies. What are the questions that have yet to be asked about writing in its various possible embodied forms? Are there varieties of materiality that are critically neglected? How does form mediate and negotiate content? In what ways do the physical features of texts inform how they are read, interpreted and situated?

Consideration will be given to both monographs and collections of essays. The range of topics covered in this series includes, but is not limited to: History of the book, publishing, the book trade, printing, typography (layout, type, typeface, blank/white space, paratextual apparatus); technologies of the written word: ink, paper, watermarks, pens, presses; surprising or neglected material forms of writing; print culture; manuscript studies; social space, context, location of writing; social signs, cues, codes imbued within the material forms of texts; ownership and the social practices of reading: marginalia, libraries, environments of reading and reception; codicology, palaeography and critical bibliography; production, transmission, distribution and circulation; archiving and the archaeology of knowledge; orality and oral culture; the material text as object or thing.

Authority in European Book Culture 1400–1600

Edited by

POLLIE BROMILOW
University of Liverpool, UK

LONDON AND NEW YORK

First published 2013 by Ashgate Publishing

2 Park Square, Milton Park, Abingdon, Oxon OX14 4RN
711 Third Avenue, New York, NY 10017, USA

Routledge is an imprint of the Taylor & Francis Group, an informa business

First issued in paperback 2016

British Library Cataloguing in Publication Data
A catalogue record for this book is available from the British Library

The Library of Congress has cataloged the printed edition as follows:
Authority in European book culture 1400-1600 / edited by Pollie Bromilow.
    pages cm. -- (Material readings in early modern culture)
  Includes bibliographical references and index.
  ISBN 978-1-4724-1010-8 (hardcover)
1. Books--Europe, Western--History--1450-1600. 2. Manuscripts,
Medieval--Europe, Western--History. 3. Manuscripts, European--
History--16th century. 4. Transmission of texts--Europe--History--16th century.
5. Transmission of texts--Europe--History--To 1500. 6. Authorship--History--16th
century. 7. Authorship--History--To 1500. 8. Book industries and trade--Europe--
History--16th century. 9. Book industries and trade--Europe--History--To 1500. 10.
Authority--History. I. Bromilow, Pollie.
  Z8.E9A98 2013
  002.094--dc23

                                                                      2013003627
ISBN 978-1-4724-1010-8 (hbk)
ISBN 978-1-138-25705-4 (pbk)

Contents

List of Figures

Notes on Contributors

Adrian Armstrong is Centenary Professor of French at Queen Mary University of London, UK

Pollie Bromilow is Lecturer in French at the University of Liverpool, UK

Catherine Emerson is Lecturer in French at the National University of Ireland, Galway, Eire

Jane Finucane is Lecturer in History at the University of Glamorgan, UK

Robert Aleksander Maryks is Associate Professor of History at Bronx CC of the City University of New York, USA

Brian Richardson is Emeritus Professor of Italian Language at the University of Leeds, UK

Massimo Rospocher is a researcher at the University of Leeds, UK and Institute for Italian and German Historical Studies in Trent, Italy

Albert Schirrmeister is a researcher on the 'Transformations of Antiquity' project based at the Humboldt-Universität in Berlin, Germany

Tracey A. Sowerby is the Centre for Medieval and Renaissance Studies Career Development Fellow in Renaissance History at Keble College, University of Oxford, UK

Helen Swift is University Lecturer in Medieval French and Fellow of St Hilda's College at the University of Oxford, UK

Samuel Willcocks is a literary and academic translator based in Cluj, Romania

Acknowledgements

This volume originated in a conference 'Authority in European Book Culture 1400–1600', held at the University of Liverpool in June 2006 and co-organised with Godfried Croenen. The conference is grateful to the Conference Office of the University for its help in planning and organising the event. Several speakers and attendees at the conference are not represented here, but all contributed significantly to making it a valuable forum for the discussion of the themes and ideas pertinent to the essays included in this volume and more general related issues. I wish particularly to thank Honor Aldred, Christopher Allmand, Vasily Arslanov, Jos Biemans, Emma Cayley, Mark Crane, Rebecca Dixon, Alex Drace-Francis, Martha Driver, Wim François, Ines Jerele, Jaska Kainulainen, Barry McKay, Kathleen O'Neill, Florent Noirfalise, Dirk Schoenaers, Sonja Svoljšak, Jane Tylus, Esther Villegas de la Torre and Julia Walker. The conference was generously supported by the British Academy and the Department of Cultures, Languages and Areas Studies of the University of Liverpool.

Introduction

Pollie Bromilow

Many critical works which address the notion of authority, whether within the confines of literary authorship or in its political manifestations, perceive it to be a universal notion that transcends the constraints of the particular historical moment and does not require explicit definition.[1] However, this reliance on authority as a value that has predominantly universal qualities is unsatisfactory as pre-modern definitions of authority can differ strongly from their modern counterparts. It is true that the overarching mechanism by which authority is conferred upon works remains constant: writing must converge with a predominant value system, which can be supported by political, religious, civic, aesthetic or commercial imperatives.[2] What changes is the agency of the different stakeholders in the process of textual production and dissemination. Patrons, scribes, authors, printers, editors, booksellers, audiences and readers must all be considered here, as should the religious, civic and political powers that work with or against them. It is because of the nature of authority as at once a value attached to the individual work as authorship, yet also generated and propagated in a more diffuse and less precise way by institutional structures that critical studies have frequently favoured one aspect of this relationship over the other. Some studies have focused on intrinsic authority as the range of practices adopted by authors during the process of textual creation.[3] Others have centred instead on the wider institutional structures and conditions that have governed the production and dissemination

---

[1] Although this study concerns the publication of works in Latin and European languages, its arguments may be of interest to those working on other language areas. For this reason, contributors have translated all references to foreign-language works into English, while primary works have been cited in their original language with a translation given in English. All translations of secondary works are the contributors' own, while translations of primary works refer to translations by other scholars unless otherwise stated. See, for example, Derek Cohen, *Searching Shakespeare: Studies in Culture and Authority* (Toronto: University of Toronto Press, 2003).

[2] Albert Russell Ascoli has outlined the ways in which authority is generated by the coincidence of, on the one hand, the individual work and on the other, 'impersonal' or institutional networks of knowledge. *Dante and the Making of a Modern Author* (Cambridge: Cambridge University Press, 2008), p. 5.

[3] See, for example, Kevin Dunn, *Pretexts of Authority: The Rhetoric of Authorship in the Renaissance Preface* (Stanford, CA: Stanford University Press, 1994); David F. Hult, *Self-fulfilling Prophecies: Readership and Authority in the First 'Roman de la Rose'* (Cambridge:

of texts and images and their integration into cultural memory.[4] This latter might also include the problematics of textual transmission and the ways in which a text is authenticated as an original and reliable source.[5] In certain respects it is not difficult to see why scholars have sometimes preferred to view authority as an enduring value that has the same presumed sources, agency and effects in the pre-modern period as in the twenty-first century, as to attempt to redefine it in a more historicised way requires an almost forensic reconstruction of all of the different elements at play.

Furthermore, not all of the factors that combine to create authority are necessarily easy to grasp. While it is straightforward to see the ways in which authority has, broadly speaking, been created through the same processes throughout the centuries (for instance, through the action of royal or religious power), what are evidently more difficult to discern are the instances when the origins and agents of authority subvert modern expectations. These include, for example, the twenty-first-century tendency when approaching texts to construct the author as a privileged touchstone of knowledge and experience that is, in fact, at odds with pre-modern perceptions where this seemingly straightforward relationship was far from assured. This problem becomes even more pronounced when one leaves the realm of the textual to engage with the issues that arise from material transmission. Readers and audiences would have taken many material aspects for granted, leaving no trace of the ways in which presentation to the audience (whether orally or textually) shaped reception. Analysis of material authority therefore requires rigorous contextualisation, but this poses yet further questions. In a period when so many different aspects shaped the presentation of the written word, how do we reconstruct the forces acting on the reader that were refracted through so many ideological, stylistic and material factors?

Twentieth-century critics, such as Roland Barthes, encourage us to construct the meaning of the text as a kind of afterlife that follows the so-called 'Death of the Author'. In order to understand authority in book culture in the pre-modern period, Alberto Ascoli has argued that we must also interrogate it during the moments before the 'birth' of the text and challenge many underlying assumptions that construct authority as a necessary pre-condition for textual creation.[6] Among the most significant of these is the assumption that authority is 'always already' there

Cambridge University Press, 1986); Susan Sniader Lanser, *Fictions of Authority: Women Writers and Narrative Voice* (Ithaca, NY: Cornell University Press, 1992).

[4]   See, for example, Lu Ann Homza, *Religious Authority in the Spanish Renaissance* (Baltimore, MD: Baltimore University Press, 2000); Louis Montrose, *The Subject of Elizabeth: Authority, Gender, and Representation* (Chicago, IL: University of Chicago Press, 2006).

[5]   See, for example, *Rewriting Chaucer: Culture, Authority and the Idea of the Authentic Text 1400–1602*, ed. by Thomas A. Prendergast and Barbara Kline (Columbus, OH: Ohio State University Press, 1999).

[6]   One of the most important aspects of this is the revision of the modern expectation

in the text's genesis, whereas many texts were created in conditions that did not automatically construct them as authoritative.[7] Furthermore, scholars must not be distracted by the veneer of authority that has built up around the pre-modern text during the centuries of its reception.[8] To understand the value added to the text by authority is firstly to acknowledge that we as modern readers have a tendency to construct ancient and canonical texts as authoritative. To attempt to overcome this, we must see the text as the medieval author would have seen it in the stages of its composition in its natural, original state, stripped bare of centuries of critical reaction, displaced from its pedestal within the canon and distanced from the place assigned by history to its powerful patron or author.

Having disabused ourselves of the expectation that authority has a primarily universal value, further questions regarding the nature of authority remain. The first of these is the complicated matter of how authority relates to one of its cognates: power.[9] Do these two terms connote the same collection of cultural practices or can a clear distinction be made between them? Scanlon has sought to interrogate the relationship between authority and power by tracing the relationship between the concepts back to their Roman constitutional usage.[10] For Scanlon, the relationship between *auctoritas* and *potestas* in late Antique Rome gestures forwards to their cultural value in the Middle Ages when they eventually come to signify the split between spiritual authority assured by the Church through its exclusive link to God as the original *auctor* and the much weaker *potestas* wielded by the laiety.[11] In order to present itself as authoritative to the audience, Scanlon argues, medieval textual culture had to position itself as the rewriting and thus continuation of Latinate clerical culture. The Roman and ecclesiastical history of the concepts prepares the way for an institutionalisation of *auctoritas* or, at least, a stable connection between institutions of political power and authority.[12] Thus, the shift from the Middle Ages to the Renaissance is characterised by the movement

---

that the 'auctor' is necessarily the source of 'auctoritas': an authoritative figure in both the process of textual production and in the cultural reception of his or her own works.

[7]   Ascoli, *Dante*, p. 4.

[8]   It is precisely this veneer which Ascoli argues must be stripped away if we are to appreciate the work as it would have been received in the pre-modern period. Ascoli, *Dante*, pp. 4–5. However, few author's works can have acquired such a veneer as those which form the focus of Ascoli's study: the works of Dante.

[9]   For a study of the effects of power on print culture during this period see *Print and Power in France and England 1500–1800*, ed. by David Adams and Adrian Armstrong (Aldershot: Ashgate, 2006).

[10]   Larry Scanlon, *Narrative, Authority and Power: The Medieval Exemplum and the Chaucerian Tradition* (Cambridge: Cambridge University Press, 1994), esp. chapter 3, '"Auctoritas" and "Potestas": A model of analysis for medieval culture'.

[11]   Scanlon, *Narrative, Authority and Power*, pp. 38–9.

[12]   I am grateful to Albert Schirrmeister for his help in formulating this point.

away from authority as uniquely divinely ordained, towards an appreciation of it as a human reality.

Critical studies of authority have tended to confuse, or conflate, the two categories of 'authority' and 'power'. This is a particularly noticeable feature of studies that assess the representational value of authority in literary texts, where power and authority are sometimes used interchangeably as synonyms for each other.[13] Many descriptions of the relationship between power and authority construct the former as essential and original and the latter to be analogous to the discursive. Brenda Bolton and Christine Meek have proposed that 'power without authority was little more than brute force, while claims to authority without the power to make them effective were in the long run unsustainable'.[14] This suggests that authority was a set of discursive practices that legitimated power wielded by political, social and religious institutions. In his analysis of representations of Elizabeth I, Louis Montrose has similarly suggested that, while power was a positive value which might be projected and manipulated by a monarch, her authority was cast into doubt by the cultural discourses which interrogated the nature of her queenship.[15] Thus while Elizabeth's political power was not openly contested, her authority was constantly undermined by representations that sought to mediate the rupture between her monarchal status and the prevailing cultural expectation that authority was the preserve of men.

We can probe this further by using the definitions of power and domination formulated by Max Weber:

> A. "Power" (Macht) is the probability that one actor within a social relationship will be in a position to carry out his own will despite resistance, regardless of the basis on which this probability rests.

> B. "Domination" (Herrschaft) is the probability that a command with a given specific content will be obeyed by a given group of persons.[16]

---

[13]   See, for example, Mark Thornton Burnett, *Masters and Servants in English Renaissance Drama and Culture: Authority and Obedience* (Basingstoke: Macmillan Press, 1997), esp. 'Power and Resistance', pp. 5–10.

[14]   'The relationship of power and authority was fundamental in the Middle Ages, since power without authority was little more than brute force, while claims to authority without the power to make them effective were in the long run unsustainable.' 'Introduction' in *Aspects of Power and Authority in the Middle Ages*, ed. by Brenda Bolton and Christine Meek. *International Medieval Research*, vol. 14 (Turnhout: Brepols, 2007), p. 2.

[15]   Louis Montrose, *The Subject of Elizabeth: Authority, Gender and Representation* (Chicago, IL: University of Chicago Press, 2006).

[16]   Max Weber, *Economy and Society: An Outline of Interpretive Sociology* (Berkeley, CA: University of California Press, 1978), p. 53.

In this configuration, all kind of signs of domination – the crown, the throne, ceremonies, rituals or, in literary culture, precepts and genres – are also signs of authority. How these signs are validated and in what contexts they are given prominence is a constant process of negotiation. These dynamics may be easier to detect in political spheres than in literary contexts. Nevertheless, power will never be actualised in a single way. It will always have multiple agents and be further challenged, stressed and transformed by the heterogeneity of hierarchical structures.[17] What this collection is to a large extent exploring, therefore, is what happens when power and the signs of domination (authority) converge in the form of the text.

Where power and authority differ is in the way in which the latter retains a semantic link back to the process of textual creation and, in the modern era, the author. This means not only that the question of authority can take on a more explicitly literary dimension, but also that the question of authenticity and origins is constructed as more central to its concerns.[18] Scanlon has conceptualised authority as an 'enabling past reproduced in the present':

> For it involves not just deference to the past but a claim of identification with it and a representation of that identity made by one part of the present to another. In this way the constraint of authority can also be empowering. The power to define the past is also the power to control the constraint the past exerts in the present. Authority, then, is an enabling past reproduced in the present.[19]

This triangular definition of authority emphasises the need for agency in the process of appropriating the past so that it may act as a touchstone of experience in the present. This has the consequence of creating an almost seamless interface between its textual and political dimensions: each can be used to inform analysis of the other because the two cannot easily be differentiated.

Authority is a concept that invites us both to reflect on its beginnings and to observe its cumulative effects. In this sense, authority can be conceptualised in terms of Derrida's 'supplement', as an entity which:

---

[17] These interpretations are at odds with Michel Foucault's definition of power, which is more easily seen as equivalent to authority. According to Foucault, power not only incorporates the relationship that holds the privileged in an advantageous position over their subordinates, but also extends to include a network of agents from all levels of the social spectrum, including those who might be considered to be the 'victims' or recipients of its actions. Michel Foucault, *Discipline and Punish: The Birth of the Prison*, trans. by Alan Sheridan (Harmondsworth: Penguin, 1979), pp. 26–7.

[18] For an exploration of authority that explicitly addresses the question of authenticity with regard to the literary counterfeit see *Discourses of Authority in Medieval and Renaissance Literature*, ed. by Kevin Brownlee and Walter Stephens (Hanover, NH: University Press of New England, 1989).

[19] Scanlon, *Narrative, Authority and Power*, p. 38.

adds to itself, [it] is a surplus, a plenitude enriching another plenitude, the fullest measure of presence. It cumulates and accumulates presence. It is thus that art, *technè*, image, representation, convention, etc., come as supplements to nature and are rich with this entire cumulating function.[20]

Although the original work can be seen to be in Derrida's terms 'full', the cultural discourse that is added to it over time supplements its value. At its most extreme, in the process of institutionalisation, the authority conferred upon a work may come to compete with and replace the significance of its primary manifestation.[21] In the late medieval and early modern period, the conceptualisation of authority as a kind of 'supplement' provides us with a new way of understanding the multiplicity of textual practices which became simultaneously more explicit, more widespread and more diverse following the invention of moveable type. It highlights the way in which numerous texts come to enjoy fame, not for the interest of their original manifestation, but for the ways in which they could be adapted through re-printing, editing or re-writing at a later date. Although these possibilities had always existed, the technological advances that the period saw increased the possibilities for re-presenting a text across temporal or geographical boundaries such that its primary authority might be overlooked, ignored, called into question or bolstered at the service of its new embodiment.[22]

This volume presents 11 studies of the role of authority in the production and distribution of texts across Europe from 1400 to 1600, a period which saw numerous radical changes in the way in which books were produced and disseminated. The essays included here all reflect to a greater or lesser extent on the issue of the emergence of the author, a development related to authority that is

---

[20]   Jacques Derrida, *Of Grammatology*, trans. by Gayatri Chakravorty Spivak (Baltimore, MD: Johns Hopkins University Press, 1976), pp. 144–5.

[21]   As Ralph Flores has observed: 'The concept of *auctoritas* has, after all, the feel of secondariness: it denotes a supplementation by senatorial elders of a projected course of action. The *auctor* offers "more than advice but less than command", almost as if trying to become the *archē* he never is. By definition he augments, guiding but not controlling the development of any putative offspring. Ideally a public *auctor* connects present communal values with a shared past and future, but his work is implicitly doubtful because it merely points.' *The Rhetoric of Doubtful Authority: Deconstructive Readings of Self-Questioning Narratives, St Augustine to Faulkner* (Ithaca, NY: Cornell University Press, 1984), p. 22.

[22]   As Kevin Dunn has noted, the rise of the printing press consequently saw the transformation of authority and its relationship to textual production: 'If humanism quickly made its peace with autocracy and courtly culture, it nonetheless had its origins in the Italian bourgeoisie and took its strength from the growing market for books that was created by the printing press. This double-sided humanism – in service to monarchical and aristocratic interests but at its core part of market culture – thus contains both systems of authorization and representation I described above. Yet if it contains both, it also remains to a certain extent aloof from both, not fully committed to the representations of power or to the diffusion of the representations in the marketplace.' Dunn, *Pretexts of Authority*, p. 9.

often assumed to have taken place during the pre-modern period and is most often considered to have been chronology-led. Indeed, if one considers a solely literary corpus, one might find much evidence to support this thesis. The appearance of printed collected works during the sixteenth century, for example, would appear to attest to a growing market for books that were attractive to buyers because of their association with a particular author. This would seem to imply that over time it was the author that became the single most important factor in determining which books were selected by buyers and consequently produced and stocked by printers and booksellers. In this series of case studies of a much wider corpus of texts, there is much to challenge these assumptions. What the essays collectively show is that the status of the author is subject to great variability across the fifteenth and sixteenth centuries without necessarily confirming the thesis that any clear emergence of the author figure took place. This variability arises because of aspects including medium, genre, national or regional tradition, intellectual trends, place of publication, claimed audience, ideological purpose and institutional influence. Work remains to be done on how the so-called emergence of the author might be revisited in the literary corpus in light of these competing aspects.

Brian Richardson starts by exploring the role of authority in a wide range of published texts in Renaissance Italy. To what extent did the medium of the text, whether oral, manuscript or print, contribute to the authority that it commanded in the eyes of the reader? How might the authority of the works have been transformed at the moment when it was actualised by its audience? Richardson addresses these questions from four different perspectives: firstly, the rise to prominence of paratexts, particularly dedications, where publishers and authors sought to ensure that their text or edition was viewed as the most authoritative and as a consequence made an appeal to the reader who in turn came to be defined as an authority who was not only worthy of such an important work, but also apparently especially able to judge its value; secondly, the revision of a work, whether in scribal transmission or in print by an editor other than the original author, which could be undertaken to make the work fit more closely the moral requirements of the day or to ensure that its linguistic qualities kept up with norms of usage and corresponded to contemporary taste; thirdly, the inscription of a work in a particular medium, where choices of the script used by the scribe, the font used by the printer or the quality of the performance in recitation or song play a key part in how authority is created by the reader; and lastly, Richardson considers the transmission of texts in its social context, whether by the author in person, via a regularly used messenger, a mutual friend or acquaintance or through the intermediary of an accompanying letter. These strategies for presentation might all confer authority on the work, especially if it was a printed rather than a more exclusive manuscript gift.

The volume continues with a theorisation of the different manifestations of authority in book culture during the period. Adrian Armstrong approaches the question of authority in light of Foucault's notion of 'capillary power': the acknowledgement that power rarely exerts its influence from a single unified source, but more commonly results from multiple interrelated factors.[23] From this he develops a typology of 'viral authority' which recognises that authority enjoys a certain amount of autonomy from its hosts and manifests itself in a number of ways. Aesthetic authority would appear to be bestowed upon the text by its author, who lavishes rhetorical embellishment or narrative technique upon it, so that it may correspond to the most sought-after reading experience of its time. Discursive authority reflects the desire of authors to present themselves as suitably qualified in the subject matter at hand to pen a persuasive and useful work. Pragmatic authority seeks to influence the reader's reception of the work by advising on particular reading strategies or offering specific guidance. It is distinct from discursive authority because of the ways in which it seeks directly to engage the reader, through prefatory material, for example. Editorial authority is exercised over the text during the processes of its dissemination to prevent amendments and alterations. In an age when textual instability reigned, the need to retain this type of authority was a constant preoccupation for authors, who were brought into conflict with scribes, editors, printers and other book producers. Lastly, there is proprietorial authority, a range of strategies adopted by writers and book producers in order to bolster what Foucault has described as the 'author function', that is to say, the value added to the meaning and commercial success of a work because of its association with a particular author.[24]

Numerous critical studies have already traced the unsure yet still perceptible emergence of the author figure from within the text as the primary site of authority to a cultural construct that was able to command authority in its own right.[25] Changes in the way the author constructed his or her own identity had been afoot even before the advent of the new technology of the printing press. Helen Swift examines this issue by looking at the competing roles of the patron and the author in authorial design. She takes as her example *La Complainte du livre du 'Champion des dames' a maistre Martin le Franc son acteur*, a mid-fifteenth-century debate poem that stages exchanges between the Book (the previously published *Le Champion des dames* to which the *Complainte* functions as a kind of sequel) and its Author. During the poem the Book laments its unfavourable reception by the Burgundian court, claiming that it was spurned by courtiers and was left to gather dust. The reasons why the work may indeed have provoked such a reception are connected to both its moral content and its material presentation. A protagonist in the debate (Lady Holy Church) appears to promote the ecclesiastical reform to which the

---

23   Michel Foucault, *History of Sexuality*, I, trans. by Robert Hurley (Harmondsworth: Penguin, 1981), p. 84.

24   Michel Foucault, 'What is an author?', in *The Foucault Reader*, ed. by Paul Rabinow (Harmondsworth: Penguin, 1984), pp. 101–20.

25   See, for example, David F. Hult, *Self-Fulfilling Prophecies: Readership and Authority in the First Roman de la Rose* (Cambridge: Cambridge University Press, 1986); Maureen Quilligan, *The Allegory of Female Authority: Christine de Pizan's 'Cité des dames'* (Ithaca, NY: Cornell University Press, 1991).

work's patron (Philip the Good) was opposed, and the manuscript contains only two illustrations and no rubrics, making it a poor relation to its contemporary counterparts. However, Swift calls into question whether, after all, the *Champion* was negatively received in the manner that it claims. Could its representation of its audience reaction have been merely a fictional device designed to boost interest in the author's previous work? A comparison with the work's classical antecedent would seem to suggest that this is, in fact, the case. Whereas Ovid's *Tristia* seeks forgiveness for his notorious *Ars amatoria*, the *Complainte* offers no such apology for its predecessor. Furthermore, the second presentation copy of the *Champion*, which is accompanied by the *Complainte*, reflects this assertive tone. It is a much more lavish affair than the earlier copy of *Le Champion des dames*, including 66 miniatures, the last of which can be read as both a celebration of the peace achieved at Arras in 1435 and an exhortation by Le Franc for Philip to seek further reconciliation with France. The textual and material aspects of the manuscript are therefore seen to be inextricably intertwined with the author's sometimes audacious desire for self-promotion vis-à-vis a wealthy and powerful patron.

Authority was established through many different forms of publication, which crossed the boundaries of what we would understand as 'high' and 'low' communications. Massimo Rospocher's study of Pope Julius II explores this aspect of the pontiff's management of his own image through the lesser-known vernacular representations such as songs and poetry as well as more widely studied oratory and art. Propagandist discourse was disseminated not only through cheaply printed pamphlets, but also through their related oral tradition. Even if the means of circulation may have been 'popular', the essential ideological messages remained the same: the association of Julius's image with the 'golden age' of the Renaissance intended to signify a renewal of papal power, the appropriation of the imagery of Caesar to evoke the pontiff's projects of financial power and territorial expansion and military force. From this case study, we see the early signs of a Habermasian 'public sphere' in which public opinion could be formulated and developed, not only in Italy, but also across Europe as the influential role of both print and oral transmission were increasingly recognised.

The process of textual editing was also one in which the authority of the source text could be called into question. Catherine Emerson's account of the career of the editor Denis Sauvage demonstrates this clearly. Over time his works became increasingly dependent on manuscript rather than printed sources. On the one hand, this return to the manuscript was viewed (as in modern editorial practices) as a revisitation of anterior and thus more authentic and authoritative sources. At the early stages of his career Sauvage appeared to concur that the author's original version of the text would be superior. However, as his confidence in text editing increased, Sauvage felt the need to intervene orthographically so that the works he produced reflected his own interests in spelling and punctuation and were better suited to circulation in Lyon, a city with a vibrant intellectual community. This is evidenced by the fact that Sauvage's amendments were so numerous that his printed editions of La Marche's *Mémoires* cannot be traced back to manuscript sources with any certainty. His later edition of Froissart takes these adaptations a stage further. It contains so many added paratextual elements that many of them were relegated to the end of the volume and the value that he added to the work through his editing was recognised by the privilege that was accorded jointly to him and the printer Jean de Tournes.

The author figure saw an inexorable, if doubtful and uncertain, rise during the early modern period.[26] This is as true for the authorship of religious and political texts as it is for literary ones. Indeed, the status of the author played an especially important part in the dissemination of texts within religious communities. This is illustrated in the case study presented by Robert Maryks, who examines the fortunes of a sixteenth-century Jesuit penitential manual: Juan Alfonso de Polanco's *Short Directory for Confessors*. The work was widely disseminated during the author's lifetime, enjoying the largest number of editions in the year of his death (1576). However, Polanco's work was not the most comprehensive text on confession, nor did it reflect important socio-economic shifts taking place in the late sixteenth century. Its publishing success must therefore have stemmed from reasons other than its usefulness. Letters by Polanco widely distributed in Jesuit schools at the time state that it was written by a group from the Jesuit headquarters in Rome at the request of the Jesuit Superior General, Loyola. These letters also indicate that the work was then attributed to Polanco, partly because of the need to name a single author to avoid censorship and also because of his position as Secretary of the Society of Jesus. This strategy of naming Polanco as the author was adopted to assure both readers and the censors of the work's credibility. Thus, the authority of the book and that of its author became inevitably conflated and the work which was the most widely disseminated penitential text quickly fell from favour with printers once Polanco had relinquished his influential role.

The composition and distribution of texts was also shaped by the most authoritative cultural models of the day, spawning works that would in time have authority conferred upon them by a reading public keen to find a message that suited their ideological outlook. This dynamic is explored by Samuel Pakucs Willcocks in his examination of the fortunes of the German narrative of the travels of Johann Schiltberger, who served as a captive soldier in Asia for over 30 years from 1394 to 1426 before returning to Bavaria and compiling his memoirs. Schiltberger's account attracted interest after he was captured at Nicopolis in 1396 and sought to reinforce the contemporary public's notion of Islam as a cruel and barbarous religion. However, the text that was circulated was far from the first-person eye witness account that could be expected from such a remarkable experience. Everywhere the extraordinary journey is recast in familiar terms to appeal to the courtly audience or reader. The narrative underwent several transformations through the medium of print during the course of the sixteenth century, to emerge

---

[26]   On the notion of authority in book production in late medieval France, see Cynthia J. Brown, *Poets, Patrons and Printers: Crisis of Authority in Late Medieval France* (Ithaca, NY: Cornell University Press, 1995).

at the end of it as a pamphlet that made explicit the relevance of Schiltberger's text for the political and doctrinal climate of the day. In spite of the mutations the text had undergone, which distanced it from the real travels of its narrator, the narrative fitted the aspirations of a readership that sought assurance that the threat of the Turk could be brought under control, most notably through the 'prophecy' that the Turks would be vanquished by the Christians. This prophecy had in all probability not been witnessed by Schiltberger, but was 'borrowed' from Sir John de Mandeville's *Book* and woven into the narrative when it first took textual form.

In late medieval and Renaissance culture, the models of antiquity formed the basis for many claims to authority, particularly in historiography, the focus of Albert Schirrmeister's chapter. His study of Erasmus Stella, Johannes Cuspinian and Robert Gaguin explores different national traditions of humanism and how they manifested themselves in book culture. Erasmus Stella's history of Prussia not only adapted classical texts in its content, but was also printed in Basel by Froben, who had become famous for his printing of the works of a much more celebrated humanist: Erasmus of Rotterdam. Johannes Cuspinian's *Oratio protreptica* captured the military struggles of Hungary against the Turks through his claimed rediscovery of the country's ancient heritage in monuments and inscriptions that he had read himself. The French author Robert Gaguin adds a different perspective to this issue. He strove for his *Compendium* to distinguish itself from medieval historiographical traditions such as chronicles by ensuring that his first-person account corresponded to the principles of 'fides et eloquencia' ['fidelity and eloquence'].

Nowhere are the multiple effects of authority more apparent than in Tracey Sowerby's contribution, which traces the international distribution of tracts written to bolster the reputation of Henry VIII following his repudiation of papal authority. Sowerby examines the way in which Henrician polemic established itself in texts such as the early *A Glasse of the Truthe* (1532) as an authority surpassed only by the Scriptures themselves. The credibility of this attack on the power of the papacy was paramount in the task of justifying Henry's new position as Supreme Head of the English church. In order to further this aim, the *Glasse of the Truthe* was translated into both French and Latin, which suggests an intended circulation within both the Holy Roman Empire and Italy. This practice of disseminating polemical texts across Europe was to continue with works such as Edward Foxe's *De vera differentia* (1534), both through the provision of tracts to English ambassadors who travelled abroad and through the distribution of texts to foreign ambassadors at the English court, a strategy that could have achieved only partial success given that English was not a prominent diplomatic language at the time. However, by the mid-1530s the extensive role of ambassadors in producing and distributing these tracts ensured that they were not seen simply as polemical texts that reflected on the King's situation, but as books which were validated by and sought to augment his authority.

Numerous studies have established the extent to which questions of authority during this and other periods are linked to the sex of the author. Pollie Bromilow explores these issues with respect to a woman writer, Hélisenne de Crenne, who was active in Paris during the 1530s and 1540s. Crenne is a remarkable figure from this early period as she appears to have chosen the path of professional writer at a time when print rather than manuscript circulation was a relatively new and potentially challenging venture for women authors in sixteenth-century book culture. In order to maximise the appeal of her works to the readership, Crenne and her printer Denis Janot adopted numerous strategies that were designed to imbue her works with authority. Foremost amongst these were the positioning of her first work, the *Angoysses douloureuses qui procedent d'amours*, as an exemplum of lived experience for female readers to avoid. Crenne also conflated her authorial identity with that of the protagonist of three of her works in order to strengthen the impact of her textual 'brand' and ensure that her writing persona stayed in the reader's mind. However, the case of Crenne demonstrates the fragility of the author's position in the sixteenth century, as she could not protect her works from later editorial intervention that supplanted her authority by bringing a new version of the text into circulation.

Jane Finucane examines the tensions involved when two different types of authority, those of the Lutheran Church and imperial power, need to be reconciled in order for polemical writings to achieve their desired effect. She takes as her example the texts penned by Erasmus Alber relating to the Magdeburg Interim. In around 1550, the city of Magdeburg was besieged by Maurice of Saxony and his armies. During this time, the inhabitants of the city used the medium of print to spread the word throughout Germany concerning their battle, which had sprung from a dispute over whether the imperial power had the authority to instigate religious reform. This had arisen after the victory of Charles V against the Schmalkaldic League of Protestant princes and powers in 1547, which had led the Emperor to decree a settlement, known as the 'Interim', which he hoped would one day lead to the reunion between the Lutheran Church and Rome. Even though the publication of texts critical of the settlement was actually prohibited by the Interim itself, nevertheless the town council and church issued tracts encouraging citizens to resist the Interim and Magdeburg became a centre for intellectuals and dissident theologians who sought to ally themselves with this cause. Alber's distinctive contribution to this cause includes short works such as songs and verses, which may have been transmitted orally and by manuscript and destined for a local audience rather than one located further afield.

The concerns of the studies presented here extend even beyond the realms of authorship and textual authority to embrace the ways in which, as Scanlon has suggested, authority might be understood not solely in textual terms, but also as a cultural discourse that is politically enabling. They seek collectively to explore the ways in which authority was at play in the practices of producing and distributing books during this period of ebb and flow between understandings of authority as both clerical and Latinate and humanistic culture, which more frequently conceived of authority as connected to the individual and vernacular. What these chronologically-arranged studies highlight is that, despite the variation in the ways that texts were produced and circulated across Europe during this period, numerous similarities emerge that take our understanding of authority beyond the literary text to embrace the materiality of its manifestations in discourses of historiography and religious and royal power. In an era when the author figure was only one amongst several agents in the process of textual production, authority was at least as likely to be constructed through the authentification of the text's origin, its relationship to existing authoritative textual models, the quality of its editing or its appropriate and high-quality transmission through manuscript, print, recitation or song.

Chapter 1

Manuscript, Print, Orality and the Authority of Texts in Renaissance Italy

Brian Richardson

The theme of authority in relation to book culture in our period could be approached in at least two ways. One would be to consider authority as an outside agency – the means by which entities such as the state or the Church sought to influence the process of communication, positively or negatively, overtly or discreetly. A second approach would be to consider the authority of the word itself as manifested to others in its published form. My essay will explore this latter aspect. Dante, writing his *Convivio* at the start of the fourteenth century, saw authority as closely linked with the term 'author':

> "Autore" … si prende per ogni persona degna d'essere creduta e obedita. E da questo viene questo vocabulo del quale al presente si tratta, cioè "autoritade"; per che si può vedere che "autoritade" vale tanto quanto "atto degno di fede e d'obedienza".

> ("Author" … applies to every person worthy of being believed and obeyed. From this comes the word we are now discussing, that is, "authority": hence one can see that "authority" means "act worthy of faith and obedience".)[1]

An author, in Dante's sense, was intrinsically deserving of respect and hence so, too, was what the author said. Mary Carruthers, though, writing on memory in the Middle Ages, reminds us that 'there are two distinct stages involved in the making of an authority – the first is the individual process of "authoring", and the second is the matter of "authorizing", which is a social and communal activity'.[2] In this

---

[1] Dante Alighieri, *Convivio*, IV. 6. 5, in *Opere minori*, vol. I, part 2, ed. by Cesare Vasoli and Domenico De Robertis (Milan and Naples: Ricciardi, 1988), p. 584. A useful outline of the significance of *auctor* and *auctoritas* in the Middle Ages is provided by A.J. Minnis, *Medieval Theory of Authorship: Scholastic Literary Attitudes in the Later Middle Ages* (London: Scolar Press, 1984), pp. 10–12.

[2] Mary J. Carruthers, *The Book of Memory: A Study of Memory in Medieval Culture* (Cambridge: Cambridge University Press, 1990), p. 189. A related point is made, apropos of glossing, by Suzanne Reynolds: '*Auctoritas* is not a cultural monolith …; it is forged in practice out of the interaction of texts and readers, and, therefore, reinvented for each of the

stage of collective authorising, we might ask, what role is played by the form taken by the author's text? I wish to attempt an overview of how, in Renaissance Italy, the authority of a text could be said to be increased by its actualisation during the process of publication. Putting the question another way, what was the potential 'value added' of the medium through which a text was diffused, with regard to the esteem in which the text was held and its power to influence the opinions of others?

The term 'actualization' is used by Roger Chartier when he reminds us of the role played by form in the construction of the meanings of texts:

> To reconstruct this process of the "actualization" of texts in its historical dimensions first requires that we accept the notion that their meanings are dependent upon the forms through which they are received and appropriated by their readers (or hearers). Readers and hearers, in point of fact, are never confronted with abstract or ideal texts detached from all materiality .... Against a purely semantic definition of the text ..., one must state that forms produce meaning and that a text, stable in its letter, is invested with a new meaning and status when the mechanisms that make it available to interpretation change.[3]

The term embraces, then, both the production of texts in writing, to be read either in manuscript or in print, and their production for listeners, to be heard through the spoken or sung word. It is important to consider all these categories of actualisation – not just print, but also manuscript, because even in the sixteenth century handwriting continued to be used throughout Europe for the circulation of many kinds of texts, such as lyric poetry or texts that challenged orthodox views of politics or religion. In addition, not just the written word must be considered, but also orality: in our period, some texts were performed as well as being transcribed, or were even performed without being written down. This applies not merely to obviously performed or performable texts such as plays, speeches or sermons, but also to other kinds of poetic and prose texts, whether they originated at the author's desk or were improvised.

I wish, therefore, to consider, within all the forms that texts could take, how verbal and non-verbal resources could be used in order to raise the status of texts or to confer added legitimacy on them. I shall be considering texts throughout their life-cycle, from the point when they were still under the control of the author, to

---

various purposes it is made to serve.' See her essay 'Inventing authority: Glossing, literacy and the classical text', in *Prestige, Authority and Power in Late Medieval Manuscripts and Texts*, ed. by Felicity Riddy (Woodbridge: York Medieval Press, 2000), pp. 7–16 (p. 16).

[3]   Roger Chartier, *The Order of Books: Readers, Authors, and Libraries in Europe between the Fourteenth and Eighteenth Centuries*, trans. by Lydia G. Cochrane (Cambridge: Polity Press, 1994), p. 3. Stanley Fish draws attention to the temporal dimension of the actualization of texts in *Is There a Text in This Class? The Authority of Interpretive Communities* (Cambridge, MA: Harvard University Press, 1980), pp. 2–3.

later phases when other people might become involved in the process of diffusing them. I shall examine four primary ways in which authority might be added: through the accretion of paratexts, including both authorial and non-authorial texts or images added during publication; through the revision of the text by someone other than the author (so that the texts discussed here are not always 'stable in their letter', in Chartier's phrase); through the 'inscription' of the text in a broad sense, both in writing on a material support (which would then be available for as long as the medium survived) and fleetingly in spoken or sung performance, through the physical but invisible medium of air; and finally through the process of transmission of the text as a social act, from person to person. In the first two categories, I shall look at the media of manuscript and print; when we come to the third and fourth categories, we can add the medium of orality. (It is probable that oral performance involved the accretion of paratextual material, such as an introduction to the performance, and that it involved some variation of the author's text, but we cannot be sure of the extent of these processes.)

The Accretion of Paratexts

Already in the Middle Ages, written texts acquired *auctoritas* by being presented together with commentaries and glosses, and a similar process occurred through the use of paratexts in the Renaissance. Further, these paratexts regularly acted as types of metadiscourse, in other words features that explicitly refer to and comment on the discourse itself, and one of their functions could be to assert the authority of the text in the eyes of the reader. Here I must be selective, and I shall comment briefly on just three of the various uses of paratexts in this respect in Renaissance Italian manuscript and printed books.

In the course of this period, dedications addressed to a named individual increasingly coexist with, or are replaced by, another kind of liminal matter: prefaces or letters addressed to the unnamed singular reader or to readers in general. This development was a result of the ability of print to reach a wider readership and of the power that, consequently, the readers themselves wielded in respect of the critical and commercial success or failure of the printing venture.[4] How far did dedications to named individuals and letters to the unnamed reader use similar strategies of authorisation, and how far did they have to use different approaches? Both could praise the text, of course, pointing for example to the excellence of the author, the importance of the subject matter, the diligence of its editors or printers, and so on. Both also sought, explicitly or implicitly, to associate the text with the prestige of the person or persons being addressed, often suggesting that the person writing had had the work printed at the request of these others. However,

---

[4]   On the reading of the texts of authority in early modern England and on the growing authority of readers, see Kevin Sharpe, *Reading Revolutions: The Politics of Reading in Early Modern England* (New Haven, CT: Yale University Press, 2000), pp. 27–62.

the two kinds of paratexts had to justify that prestige in rather different ways. In the case of a dedication to a specific individual, the source of authority was usually the social status of the dedicatee, which would be given prominence in the heading and sometimes, too, on the title page. However, in the address to readers in general, how was *their* authority asserted? One stratagem was to identify their prestige with right thinking, with a correctness of judgement that was shared of course with the writer. Letters to readers are not always, in fact, addressed to all readers, in spite of appearances; rather, they tend to construct a preferred audience, a subset of readers that is defined by values that are also those of the producer of the text and that are identified as authoritative ones. In a sense, then, the reading (and purchasing) public now comes to play the role of the dedicatee.

An example of this process of authorisation is provided by a letter addressed to readers by Nicolò Garanta, a bookseller–publisher who operated in Venice in the early sixteenth century, in his edition of Boccaccio's *Decameron* printed in 1525. Garanta's task was to give authority to his text in two respects. First and more generally, he needed to persuade readers that they should follow the new trend towards considering the fourteenth-century Florentine of Boccaccio as the best Italian prose of past or present and as a worthy object of study and imitation, in preference to using some contemporary variety of the vernacular. Second, Garanta needed to persuade readers to buy *his* edition and not one of the rival editions that were then on offer from Venetian and Florentine presses. His letter therefore makes a series of claims to authority. Garanta begins by talking of the judgement of others: of the many Italian men of letters who hold the *Decameron* in high esteem and of the other noble persons who have begged him to publish the work in a small (that is, octavo) format. He then claims that he himself has had the text edited according to the highest possible standards, so that it is as correct as it could be. However, he appeals to the standing of those who will use his edition, not just to that of the edition itself. He suggests that his readers are pure, and he expresses the hope that Boccaccio's writing, in this now similarly unsullied state, will reach the hands of the virtuous and well-intentioned. Thus the readers, as well as the book, are made an integral part of the authorising process:

A gli candidi lettori, Nicolò Garanta. … Là onde, candidissimi lettori, appresso questi così honorevoli maestri et sovrani giudici del volgar idioma, molte altre nobilissime persone sonomi all'incontro sovragiunte, dalle quali fui non solamente pregato, ma con gli loro istretti prieghi sospinto per commodo et piacer universale, a dover in questa picciol forma le predette cento Novelle Boccacciane ridurre. Per la qual cosa veggendo anchor io il splendore di essa lingua thoscana molto più hoggi dì che per lo tempo davanti in favore et gratia di tutta Italia trovarsi, con li migliori testi, che per me poterono essere trovati, habbiamo posta ogni possibile diligenza in dar fuori essa opera lucida, et in tutte le sue parti castigatissima. Spero che la varietà dell'inventione, l'acuità dell'ingegno, et ultimamente la nativa dolcezza nel comporre del scientiato Boccaccio intiera et sanza macola perverrà alle mani di qualunque virtuosa et honorevole persona, la qual per ammaestramento et commodo della vita humana tai Novelle in thosca lingua composte con ardentissima affettione legger disidera.[5]

(To the pure readers, Nicolò Garanta. … Whence, purest readers, after these honourable masters and sovereign judges of the vernacular, many other most noble people came to see me. I was not merely asked by them but pressed with their insistent prayers to turn these hundred Tales of Boccaccio into this small format, for the advantage and pleasure of all. Thus since I, too, can see that the splendour of this Tuscan language is in much higher favour in the whole of Italy than in the past, we have taken the greatest pains to publish this work polished and completely emended in all its parts, using the best texts I could find. I hope that the variety of invention, the sharpness of wit and lastly the natural sweetness of style of the learned Boccaccio will reach, entire and spotless, the hands of any virtuous and honourable person who with the most ardent affection wishes to read, for the instruction and advantage of our human life, these Tales written in Tuscan.)

A further use of paratext that is relevant here is that of the figurative elements through which authors might seek to reinforce, directly or obliquely, the views expressed in their works. One instance concerns the poet Ludovico Ariosto, who wished to stress his independence, or his desire for independence, from the court of Ferrara, to which he owed service, but which he considered did not appreciate poets sufficiently. He transmitted this message within the text of his epic, the *Orlando furioso*, but he backed up his claim to a higher status than that of other courtiers by using visual elements. In the first two editions, of 1516 and 1521, he included a woodcut emblem of bees being smoked out of a log, together with the biblical phrase 'Pro bono malum' ('Evil in return for good'). Image and words referred to the ingratitude of the world, while bees also acted as a traditional symbol of the process of authorship and of eloquence. In the third edition, of 1532, the text of the poem was followed in the first copies printed by a woodcut of a ewe suckling a wolfcub, alluding again to the theme of ingratitude. After a few copies of the final sheet had been printed off, Ariosto had this woodcut removed and inserted the phrase 'Pro bono malum'.[6] He thus used woodcuts and

---

[5]   Giovanni Boccaccio, *Il Decamerone* (Venice: per Gregorio De Gregori, 1525), fol. +8ᵛ; see, too, Neil Harris, 'Nicolò Garanta editore a Venezia 1525–30', *La Bibliofilìa*, 97 (1995), pp. 99–148 (p. 116). Another example of this approach is found in the letter 'Agli studiosi della regolata volgar lingua' in Giovan Francesco Fortunio, *Regole grammaticali della volgar lingua*, ed. by Brian Richardson (Rome and Padua: Antenore, 2001), pp. 3–11: here Fortunio sets up an opposition between 'us' (himself and other students of the regulated vernacular) and 'them' (critics of their position).

[6]   Conor Fahy, *L''Orlando furioso' del 1532: Profilo di una edizione* (Milan: Vita e Pensiero, 1989), pp. 107–18, Plates I and IX. For the commonplace of the author as a

words in metadiscursive acts of self-authorisation, in order to refer obliquely to the frustrations of the system of patronage and to justify and enhance his own independent status as author.

As the title pages of printed books became more elaborate in the course of the sixteenth century, they could act increasingly as another means of imposing authority, through their wording and through their imagery. Their descriptions of the book could draw attention to the same kind of points that Nicolò Garanta was making, reassuring the reader about the accuracy of the text. A claim that was often made was that the contents were fresh in some way, newly revised or at least newly printed; for instance, the quarto *Decameron* printed in 1542 by Gabriele Giolito was proclaimed to be 'Nuovamente stampato et ricorretto'. Non-verbal techniques might include classicising architectural motifs that acted as a grandiose portal to what was by implication an equally imposing interior. An example is the engraved title page of the Venetian *Orlando furioso* printed in 1584 by Francesco De Franceschi. In sixteenth-century Italian editions in general, it becomes increasingly common to see visual representations of the author and his or her values that add authority in more direct ways than those used by Ariosto. One of the techniques used was to add classicising elements to the portrait of the author; thus, for instance, Boccaccio and Dante were portrayed with laurel wreaths on the title pages of two Venetian editions, respectively the quarto *Decameron* just mentioned and the folio *Commedia* printed in 1564 by the Sessa firm.[7]

An example that brings together the author's use of figurative elements and the use of the title page is that of the edition of a chivalric romance by Francesco de' Lodovici, the *Triomphi di Carlo*, printed in Venice by Francesco Bindoni and Maffeo Pasini in 1535. In a woodcut on the title page, the literary status of Lodovici is represented by means of a depiction of him in the act of presenting his work to its dedicatee. On his left, seated above him on a raised throne, is the doge, Andrea Gritti; on the right, on a still higher level, is the sun, from whose countenance a ray, no doubt symbolising poetic inspiration, reaches out to touch Lodovici. He and his work are thus positioned strategically between the two sources on which they depend: his patron and his poetic skill. The work itself, it is suggested, is both worthy of presentation to the head of state and touched by the quasi-divine gift of poetry.[8]

---

bee, see Carruthers, *The Book of Memory*, pp. 191–2. St Ambrose's future eloquence was supposedly presaged when a swarm of bees descended on his head in his infancy: John Moorhead, *Ambrose: Church and Society in the Late Roman World* (London: Longman, 1999), pp. 19–20.

[7]   Ruth Mortimer, 'The author's image: Italian sixteenth-century printed portraits', *Harvard Library Bulletin*, n.s. 7, no. 2 (Summer 1996), pp. 1–87 (pp. 35–52).

[8]   On this and similar images, see Mortimer, 'The author's image', pp. 63–76.

Revision

The revision of a text, carried out by a person other than the author, could occur during scribal transmission, but it was likely to be more radical in the medium of print, where professional or amateur editors could undertake a task of 'correction' that paradoxically tended to make the text less authentic. Changes could be made to the content of a work, in order to bring it into line with current orthodoxies. During the Counter-Reformation, for instance, the Church would not permit the *Decameron* to be printed at all without expurgation, and thus the tales had to be stripped of any compromising references to the misbehaviour of the clergy or of any potentially heretical doctrine. However, after the first expurgated edition of 1573 successive editors sought to enhance the esteem of the work by making more radical interventions: for instance, the adulterous couple of Ricciardo and Catella in Day III story 6 was made to die of remorse in Lionardo Salviati's editions of 1582, while in Luigi Groto's edition, printed in 1588, ser Ciappelletto, a merchant who made a false confession on his deathbed (Day I story 1), was locked in a box and burned alive. Another and more common kind of revision that was intended to raise the standing of a work was linguistic 'correction'. In Italy, the language of vernacular works that lay outside the canon of the best fourteenth-century texts was often made to conform with what was regarded as best practice. Even canonical authors could be affected: for instance, when the Venetian scholar and poet Pietro Bembo was preparing his edition of Petrarch's vernacular verse for printing in 1501, he was fortunate enough to have on his desk a copy of Petrarch's autograph copy of his verse; yet he still felt it necessary to make stylistic 'improvements' in order to regularise Petrarch's usage and thus make his edition even more authoritative as a model for lyric poetry.[9] Petrarch, it is worth remembering, had himself had some involvement in elevating the texts of others when he imposed a revision of both content and language on the last tale of Boccaccio's *Decameron*, the story of patient Griselda, by translating it 'upwards' into Latin.

Inscription

With our third category, the inscription of the text in a particular medium, we begin to move over the elusive border between what was being said, by word or sign, and the techniques used to make meaning visible or audible.

The choice between the medium of manuscript and that of print could itself sometimes have been perceived as having a strong bearing on the standing of what was being read. For a number of reasons, print in the sixteenth century still had somewhat negative connotations in the eyes of some people. A few authors avoided using it if they could, preferring their works to circulate in manuscript,

---

[9]   Brian Richardson, *Print Culture in Renaissance Italy: The Editor and the Vernacular Text, 1470–1600* (Cambridge: Cambridge University Press, 1994), pp. 49–51.

and then sometimes only within a limited circle of friends. For example, the exclusivity of scribal culture was important, in the first half of the century, in preserving the prestige of two upper-class women who were venturing into the writing of lyric poetry, Vittoria Colonna in southern and central Italy and Veronica Gambara in the north.

Once a text had been actualised, one of the first impressions to be made on the audience would have been that of the status of the person who had created its visible or audible form, if that person was identifiable. Within the range of possible modes of inscription of texts, it has been plausibly argued by Harold Love that an authorial holograph has what he terms the strongest 'presence', because it is closer to 'an assumed source of validation in the movement of the author's fingers'.[10] A curious attempt to make use of the power of autography in a printed edition is the engraved facsimile of the handwriting of the editor, Lionardo Salviati, in one of his editions of Boccaccio's *Decameron* (Venice: Giunti, 1582, fol. oo5^v), to present a statement that he had checked the text personally: 'Io Lionardo Salviati ho riscontrato questo dì 29 d'Aprile 1582, e soscritto di man propria.'[11] When an author published in manuscript, however, he or she often preferred to ask a scribe to make a fair copy. This could even be the case when verse was being sent to someone very close; thus on 4 January 1501 Pietro Bembo sent a letter to his lover Maria Savorgnan with some poems of his that were evidently in someone else's hand, since he added that he would have sent further writings to her if he had had time to have them copied.[12] In such instances the sense of the author's 'presence' would have been diminished, but the elegance of a skilled scribe's hand and the fact that the author had commissioned the transcription would have provided another and perhaps greater source of authority.

With texts other than holographs, the identity of the producer or producers of the text, and hence their status, might or might not be explicitly proclaimed. Those responsible for printed texts often identified themselves by name and represented their values emblematically through the printer's devices that could be displayed prominently on title pages. On the other hand, the work of scribes and illuminators remained anonymous more often than not. Peter Beal has commented that the reason for this was probably a desire to maintain the privileged and select nature of scribal culture: manuscripts would have lost their sense of exclusivity if they

---

[10] Harold Love, *The Culture and Commerce of Texts: Scribal Publication in Seventeenth-Century England* (Amherst, MA: University of Massachusetts Press, 1998), p. 145.

[11] Marco Bernardi and Carlo Pulsoni, 'Primi appunti sulla rassettatura del Salviati', *Filologia italiana*, 8 (2011), pp. 167–200 (p. 170 and Fig. 1).

[12] 'Altre cose vi manderei ancora se a me non mancasse il tempo di farle trascrivere' ('I would send you other things, too, if I did not lack the time to have them copied'): Pietro Bembo, *Lettere*, ed. by Ernesto Travi, 4 vols (Bologna: Commissione per i testi di lingua, 1987–93), no. 123 (I, p. 117).

had advertised themselves as printed books did.[13] One can compare this desire to conceal the provenance of a manuscript, in spite of the prestige that could have been derived from it, with the anti-economic and visibly disinterested behaviour that, as Pierre Bourdieu has shown, is necessary when cultural goods are aimed at an audience of other producers of cultural goods. In this sector there is room for the accumulation of what he calls symbolic capital, 'economic or political capital that is disavowed, misrecognised and thereby recognised, hence legitimate, a "credit" which, under certain conditions, and always in the long run, guarantees "economic" profits'. This process is essential where success depends on authority alone:

> In short, when the only usable, effective capital is the (mis)recognized, legitimate capital called "prestige" or "authority", the economic capital that cultural undertakings generally require cannot secure the specific profits produced by the field – not the "economic" profits they always imply – unless it is reconverted into symbolic capital.[14]

In the fashioning of a written text as a material object, authority could be derived from a combination of other factors, including the script used by the copyist or the font chosen by the printer; the support on which the text was transcribed or printed, with vellum at the top of the scale, followed by larger sizes of paper, allowing more generous margins; for texts covering more than one leaf, the format chosen (in general, the larger the format, the greater the perceived authority of the volume, but small formats could add prestige if books were elegant in other respects); the spaciousness or otherwise of the layout of the text; and any decoration added to individual copies by illuminators or rubricators. A further potential source of prestige in the sixteenth century was the inclusion of a text as part of a series or anthology. Grouping texts in this way could raise the status of those that were not uniformly recognised as authoritative, by associating them with texts by canonical authors or better-known ones; or it could create a body of texts whose critical mass gave them a collective importance. The relationship between the texts might be implicit, based simply on a physical resemblance, as in the case of the octavo editions that Aldus Manutius began to print in 1501, but from the 1560s onwards the Giolito firm in Venice made the link explicit by using metaphors such as a 'necklace' or 'garland' of texts.[15]

As suggested earlier, the term 'inscription' could be extended to encompass the representation of a text in sound: during the Renaissance, vocalisation was

---

[13]   Peter Beal, *In Praise of Scribes: Manuscripts and their Makers in Seventeenth-Century England* (Oxford: Clarendon Press, 1998), pp. 14–19.

[14]   Pierre Bourdieu, *The Field of Cultural Production*, ed. by Randal Johnson (Cambridge: Polity Press, 1993), p. 75.

[15]   Angela Nuovo and Christian Coppens, *I Giolito e la stampa nell'Italia del XVI secolo* (Geneva: Droz. 2005), pp. 113–15.

a not uncommon alternative to written representation and sometimes the only medium in which a text was actualised. Just as admiration for the skill with which a text was written on a durable surface could enhance the standing of the text, by association, so could admiration for the quality of its realisation in recitation or in song. In 1537, a manuscript copy of a dialogue on love was sent by its author, Sperone Speroni, to one of the speakers, Niccolò Grazia (or Grassi), in Venice. Pietro Aretino recounted how he and another writer listened to Grazia reciting the work to them over two days, and the harmony to which Aretino refers in his description of this performance seems to owe as much to the reading voice as it does to what Speroni had written:

> il Grazia con la graziosa maniera ha recitato in casa mia graziosissimamente il vostro Dialogo, a la cui armonia, senza più respirare, due dì, uno doppo l'altro, stetero appese le caste e dote orecchie del buon Fortunio e le mie, quali esse si sieno.[16]

> (Niccolò Grazia with his graceful manner has recited in my house most gracefully your Dialogue, on the harmony of which the chaste and learned ears of the good Fortunio [Spira] and my own, whatever they are worth, hung transfixed for two consecutive days.)

Singing was considered to add both to the persuasive force and to the pleasurability of the text. A speaker in Baldesar Castiglione's *Libro del cortegiano* (first printed in 1528) described how an accompaniment enhanced the words of poetry: 'Ma sopra tutto parmi gratissimo il cantare alla viola per recitare: il che tanto di venustà ed efficacia aggiunge alle parole, che è gran maraviglia' ('But above all, singing with the viol for recitation seems to me most pleasurable: it is marvellous how much beauty and effectiveness it adds to words').[17] A more general belief in the powers of song to heal and to lift the spirit upwards was expressed by the late fifteenth-century Neoplatonic philosopher Marsilio Ficino. For him, although sight was the supreme sense, music had a more powerful effect on man than anything else perceived through the other senses, because the medium of air, in which music is transmitted, is of the same kind as the human spirit.[18] Ficino wrote in his *De vita*

---

[16]   Pietro Aretino, *Lettere*, ed. by Paolo Procaccioli, 6 vols (Rome: Salerno Editrice, 1997–2002), no. 139 to Speroni (6 June 1537), I, pp. 209–11. On the parallels between written texts and oral performance, see John Dagenais, 'That bothersome residue: Toward a theory of the physical text', in *Vox intexta: Orality and Textuality in the Middle Ages*, ed. by A.N. Doane and Carol Braun Pasternack, pp. 246–59 (pp. 252–6).

[17]   Baldesar Castiglione, *Il Libro del cortegiano con una scelta delle Opere minori*, ed. by Bruno Maier, 2nd edn (Turin: UTET, 1964), II.13 (pp. 208–9).

[18]   D.P. Walker, *Spiritual & Demonic Magic: From Ficino to Campanella* (University Park, PA: Pennsylvania State University Press, 2000), pp. 3–11.

(III. 21) that song imitates the intentions and passions of the soul and imitates words, and links our spirit with the celestial:

> Memento vero cantum esse imitatorem omnium potentissimum. ... Eadem quoque virtute quando coelestia imitatur, hinc quidem spiritum nostrum ad coelestem influxum, inde vero influxum ad spiritum mirifice provocat.

> (But remember that song is a most powerful imitator of all things. ... By the same power, when it imitates celestial things, it also wonderfully arouses our spirit upwards to the celestial influence and the celestial influence downwards to our spirit).[19]

Transmission

So far we have been considering the inscription of the text as a kind of performance in search of an audience. We need to look, finally, at the transmission of a text as a social act, and to consider some of the ways in which the process of communicating it to others might be used to bestow authority.

The gift-giving of handwritten or printed texts offered clear opportunities to enhance the sense of authorial 'presence' that, as we saw earlier, could seem to validate a work. The author might present the text to a dedicatee or other recipient in person. If it were not possible to do this, then the text could be sent with an accompanying letter or, in the case of scribal diffusion, within the body of a letter. While a manuscript was by its nature unique, special care was needed in ensuring that a gift copy of a printed book had greater value than copies that were on sale to the general public. A common means of doing this was to have the book bound before presentation. We know, for instance, from Pietro Bembo's correspondence that in the mid-1530s he had bound, probably in Venice, several copies of his new edition of the Latin letters that he had written as papal secretary in the second decade of the century, so that these copies could be presented as gifts. He wrote to his close friend Carlo Gualteruzzi on 17 October 1536 that the Venetian printer of the edition was sending to Rome, as well as 100 copies for sale, two volumes in the best possible bindings, one in red for the pope, Paul III, and another in blue for the pope's young grandson, Cardinal Alessandro Farnese, plus 11 others 'legati semplicemente' ('bound simply'). The letter goes on to list the receivers of these 11 copies. At the bottom of the list, and in the minority, were a few close personal friends; higher up were key figures in the papal court.[20] Bembo's main concern at this late point in his career was to become a cardinal. Any copy of the edition would have demonstrated Bembo's skill in writing Ciceronian Latin, but these 13

---

[19]   Marsilio Ficino, *Three Books on Life*, ed. and trans. by Carol V. Kaske and John R. Clark (Binghamton, NY: Medieval and Renaissance Texts and Studies, 1989), pp. 358–9.

[20]   Bembo, *Lettere*, no. 1792 (III, pp. 674–5).

copies did something more: they created a personal link between the author and those whose favour he most needed to win.

These and other copies of Bembo's *Brevi* were presented on his behalf by intermediaries. This was a means of presentation that was commonly preferred to the use of a regular messenger. A typical example of the sending of an individual poem via a go-between is seen in Torquato Tasso's letter of 21 June 1584 to Marcello Donati in Mantua. Tasso was sending a poem to the Duke of Mantua, Vincenzio Gonzaga, in celebration of his recent wedding; it was to reach Donati through the scribe who had copied it out, Giulio Mosti. Tasso would have wanted to arrange matters this way so that Donati could choose the most opportune moment and present the poem to the Duke with words that would enhance the value of what the author had written:

> Mando al signor principe una canzona per lo signor Giulio Mosti che se ne viene a Mantova, la qual vorrei che gli fosse appresentata da Vostra Signoria con quelle parole che gli posson fare il poema altrettanto grato, quanto la volontà con la quale l'ho composta.[21]

> (I am sending to the prince a *canzone* via Giulio Mosti who is leaving for Mantua. I would like this to be presented to him by you with those words that can make the poem as welcome to him as the goodwill with which I composed it.)

The transmission of a text to select readers, whether as a gift or not, was one of the areas where the exclusivity of manuscript culture gave it an advantage over print. Handwritten texts were, in sixteenth-century Italy at least, passed between individuals known to one another more often than they were sold over the counter in the way that most printed books were. Manuscript culture thus flourished in 'scribal communities' with shared interests, to use a term illustrated by Harold Love (pp. 177–84). We have already noted that recipients of works in manuscript form would have felt privileged to have access to them if they were not normally available through the commercial market. Because the readership of handwritten texts might be restricted, and was in some cases deliberately restricted by their authors and owners, copies of the texts were more valued possessions.

Scribal communities were often interested in texts expressing ideas that were outside or even challenged mainstream political or religious opinion. An example is the body of texts that expressed heterodox religious views in Cinquecento Italy. Many of these texts were printed, either clandestinely in Italy or abroad, from where they could be imported across the Alps. However, some were circulated partly or solely in manuscript. The most obvious reason for this was that scribal production and circulation made it easier to avoid censorship, since by the middle of the century printed texts had to be approved by the Church. However, another

---

[21]   Torquato Tasso, *Le lettere*, ed. by Cesare Guasti, 5 vols (Florence: Le Monnier, 1852–55), no. 289 (II, pp. 277–8).

factor could have been that transmission in manuscript had the advantage of adding prestige to a text because its readers in this medium would feel that they belonged to an exclusive circle of like-minded people. One writer from outside the mainstream who preferred to circulate some of his works to a restricted readership was the Dominican friar Battista da Crema, whose doctrine was later condemned by the Roman Inquisition. Already when he had his *Via de aperta verità* printed in Venice in the 1520s, he apologised to his imaginary reader if he was revealing certain ideas to too wide an audience: '[A]nchora pregoti, che mi habbi per iscusato, se forse ritrovi alcune cose pubblicate a molti, le quali a pochi se dovriano manifestare' ('I also ask you to excuse me if perhaps you find some things made public to many that should be shown to few'). A later work, his *Specchio interiore*, was composed by 1531 for a very select group, the 12 governesses of a hospital for incurables in Venice, and was not printed until 1540, after Fra Battista's death; before then, it circulated solely in manuscript, among his closest followers.[22] A related case is that of the Benedictine monk Giorgio Siculo, executed for heresy in 1551. Some but not all of his writings were printed; others were read only in manuscript. How did he or his followers choose which to have printed and which to circulate in handwritten form? Adriano Prosperi has suggested that Don Giorgio used these two circuits of diffusion for different purposes: print in order to transmit to an undifferentiated public the part of his message that was compatible with official religion, but manuscript to transmit his true heretical message, through private channels, to a select group of followers.[23] Don Giorgio's key heterodox text, the so-called *Libro grande*, was not printed during his lifetime. Nor was it made easily available even to the monk's followers. It was dispensed to the Ferrarese physician Francesco Severi in a calculated and gradual way, three or four handwritten fascicules at a time; it seems that he had to earn the right to pass on to the next instalment.[24]

Finally, effective transmission through recitation or singing in social gatherings could bring its own kind of authority to a text. An anecdote that illustrates this point is recounted by Torquato Tasso in explaining how his father Bernardo came to rewrite his chivalric romance *Amadigi*. The plot of the first version of the poem followed the rule of unity of action. Bernardo initially published parts of this redaction by reading it aloud to Ferrante Sanseverino, prince of Salerno, and a number of courtiers. However, the recitation proved both an artistic and a social failure: by the time his father had finished, the audience had slipped away. Bernardo

---

[22]   Orazio Premoli, *Fra' Battista da Crema secondo documenti inediti: contributo alla storia religiosa del secolo XVI* (Rome: Desclée, 1910), pp. 105, 113–14; Gabriella Zarri, 'Note su diffusione e circolazione di testi devoti (1520–1550)', in *Libri, idee e sentimenti religiosi nel Cinquecento italiano* (Modena: Panini, 1987), pp. 131–54 (pp. 142–3).

[23]   Adriano Prosperi, 'Opere inedite o sconosciute di Giorgio Siculo', *La Bibliofilia*, 87 (1985), pp. 137–57 (p. 140), and *L'eresia del Libro Grande: storia di Giorgio Siculo e della sua setta* (Milan: Feltrinelli, 2000), p. 142.

[24]   Prosperi, 'Opere inedite o sconosciute', p. 142, and *L'eresia del Libro Grande*, p. 271.

therefore decided to abandon Aristotelian precepts and rewrite the *Amadigi* with a greater variety of action, in order not to lose favour within courtly society. Torquato's description shows that the reputation derived from Bernardo's social use of his text as a courtier, performing it to his peers, was more important than the merely literary reputation that could be derived from pedantically following the rules of Aristotle:

> [P]er non perder il nome di buon cortigiano, non si curò di ritener a forza quello d'ottimo poeta; e udite come. ... Leggeva alcuni suoi canti al principe suo padrone; e quando egli cominciò a leggere, erano le camere piene di gentiluomini ascoltatori; ma nel fine, tutti erano spariti: da la qual cosa egli prese argumento che l'unità dell'azione fosse poco dilettevole per sua natura, non per difetto d'arte che egli avesse.[25]

> (In order not to lose the reputation of being a good courtier, he did not care about keeping by force that of being a very good poet; and here is how. ... He was reading some cantos of his to the prince his master, and when he began to read, the rooms were full of gentlemen listening; but by the end they had all disappeared. From this he was persuaded that unity of action gave little pleasure through its nature, not through any lack of skill on his part.)

It was not just a matter of Bernardo's personal standing in court circles. The authorising of his *Amadigi*, he realised, was ultimately dependent on the response of its audience (of readers as well as listeners); it would be, in other words, the result of what Carruthers called 'a social and communal activity'.

I conclude with two general reflections that arise from these cases. The first is that the three types of diffusion that we have been considering – manuscript, printed and oral – contribute to the creation of authority in ways that sometimes differ to a greater or lesser extent between the media concerned but that are sometimes similar. The activities of adding paratexts and of revising the author's text are least relevant to the oral medium. They are found frequently in both scribal and print diffusion, but their use is more prominent in print than in manuscript. On the other hand, the processes of inscribing texts and of transmitting them socially have a great deal in common in all three media, beneath the obvious superficial differences. This common ground shows, I believe, that in our period one should consider oral diffusion as an integral part of the history of the circulation of literature alongside the history of the material book. The second reflection is that, in evaluating how authority might be achieved by a text in this period, we need to consider the social and commercial contexts in which texts were diffused. Although Dante saw authority as deriving, not only etymologically, from an individual author, authors were rarely if ever alone in making their texts authoritative. The process

---

[25]   Torquato Tasso, *Apologia in difesa della Gerusalemme liberata*, in his *Prose*, ed. by Ettore Mazzali (Milan and Naples: Ricciardi, 1959), pp. 411–85 (pp. 416–17).

of authorisation depended also on the others who were involved in different ways, as producers or as receivers, in the actualisation of texts.[26]

---

[26]   Some of the points discussed in this essay have been developed in Brian Richardson, *Manuscript Culture in Renaissance Italy* (Cambridge: Cambridge University Press, 2009) and 'Autografia e pubblicazione manoscritta nel Rinascimento', in *'Di mano propria': gli autografi dei letterati italiani. Atti del Convegno internazionale di Forlì, 24–27 novembre 2008*, ed. by Guido Baldassarri and others (Rome: Salerno Editrice, 2010), pp. 269–85.

Chapter 2

Books on the Bridge: Writing, Printing and Viral Authority

Adrian Armstrong

My title has a double resonance, appropriate to the matter in hand. On the one hand, the 'bridge' is an image of transition, reflecting the process of partial, fragmented, variously paced evolution from manuscript to print on which I focus below. On the other hand, the bridge recalls an important twentieth-century novel, which points towards a productive way of considering the parts that authority played in that evolution. In 1945, the Yugoslav novelist Ivo Andrić published his best-known work, *The Bridge Over the Drina* (*Na Drini ćuprija*), which chronicles the Bosnian town of Višegrad through the life on and around its bridge, completed in 1571 and partially destroyed in 1914. This period is almost completely encompassed[1] by two key moments. The first is the public execution, by impalement, of a workman who had disrupted the bridge's construction. The second occurs after Bosnia becomes an Austro-Hungarian protectorate in 1878, when officials of the Dual Monarchy take the first steps towards establishing the infrastructure of the modern state:

> They measured out the waste land, numbered the trees in the forest, inspected lavatories and drains, looked at the teeth of horses and cows, asked about the illnesses of the people, noted the number and types of fruit-trees and of different kinds of sheep and poultry.[2]

What is more generally significant about these two moments is that they allow us to chart a shift in the ways in which power has been exercised in society. Indeed, Andrić's novel reads almost like an allegory of the historical processes that have been identified as taking place – over a shorter period, due to different socio-political conditions – in early-modern Western culture. The classic statement of these processes is Michel Foucault's *Discipline and Punish*, which traces an evolution from the display of spectacular power, which punishes the criminal 'as a glorification of its strength', to what Foucault calls 'a micro-physics of power', a set of discourses and practices that permeate innumerable, apparently trivial,

---

[1]   In respect of chronology, if not of narrative space: the second moment occurs less than half-way through the novel.

[2]   Ivo Andrić, *The Bridge Over the Drina*, trans. by Lovette F. Edwards (London: Harvill, 1995), p. 135.

aspects of everyday life.[3] In Andrić's narrative as in Foucault's, we witness a movement towards what Foucault elsewhere calls 'a power organised around the management of life rather than the menace of death'.[4]

The implications of this movement for late medieval and early modern book culture lie at the level of micro-physics, in what Foucault scholars widely call 'capillary power'.[5] Capillary power is not monolithic, nor is it purely oppressive; it consists of multiple, interrelated, constantly evolving relations of force. The techniques of capillary power existed well before the period in which they became generalised: Foucault himself notes more than once that the rules of monastic orders are an important example of this power's prehistory.[6] Whatever we might think of Foucault, and indeed Andrić, as historians – and this is not an issue I shall consider – the notion of capillary power is useful for the present purpose. For book historians, authority in manuscript and early print culture is manifested in the most variegated ways. It thus seems worth exploring the extent to which we can productively consider these manifestations through Foucault's model, understanding it very broadly and heuristically as an encouragement to seek out plural, local, shifting, competing sources of authority. For capillary power, we might substitute the image of *viral authority*: an authority that spreads in ways that are not necessarily hierarchical, nor even predictable (we might talk in Deleuzian terms of rhizomatic, deterritorialised operations); an authority that can mutate according to local conditions, that can pass from one host to another, that can affect those hosts in different ways. This study attempts an inevitably partial, provisional pathology of the virus, outlining and reflecting on some of the ways in which authority was deployed in this period, with examples drawn mainly but not exclusively from Francophone areas. By teasing out different forms of authority, identifying their interplay and indicating their wider resonances for textual production and transmission, I shall gesture towards a strategy of 'reading for authority' in texts of this period.

An initial point that may seem obvious, but that is all too easily forgotten, is that 'authority' even in a narrow sense, the sense of social control over book culture, was exercised in different ways in different regions, and sometimes even within regions: what was possible in one northern Italian city-state or German dukedom might be unthinkable in another. The bourgeois classes, which constituted such important markets for early printers, developed at varying rates across Europe. Academic institutions had widely differing relationships with other power centres. These variables can surface in intriguing ways, for instance, in the contrasts between the Indices of forbidden books published in the mid-sixteenth century by,

---

[3]   Michel Foucault, *Discipline and Punish*, trans. by Alan Sheridan (Harmondsworth: Penguin, 1979), pp. 9, 26.

[4]   Michel Foucault, *History of Sexuality*, I, trans. by Robert Hurley (Harmondsworth: Penguin, 1981), p. 147.

[5]   Foucault, *History of Sexuality*, I, p. 84.

[6]   Foucault, *Discipline and Punish*, pp. 137, 149.

among others, the Universities of Paris and Louvain; the ecclesiastical authorities in Venice, Portugal and Spain; and the Papacy itself.[7] In the same period, questions of gender could be framed in unexpected fashion in particular spaces: it has been suggested that for historical, cultural and infrastructural reasons, Lyon and Venice offered by far the widest opportunities for publishing women's writing.[8] Generalisations are inevitably vexed.

If one examines the effects on printing of 'authority' in this very specific sense, it soon becomes clear that print culture is not simply a democratising influence, as various commentators have suggested, struggling against a repression emanating from one or more centres of political power. The interplay between media technologies and mechanisms of control cannot be reduced to such terms. Printing can produce techniques of power to be exercised over itself: the sixteenth-century Indices emerge precisely as a response to the new methods of dissemination, which indeed are easier to police – because the means of production are more difficult to hide – than manuscript copying.[9] If one considers a different kind of 'authority', the social control that could be exercised *through* printing rather than *over* it, this takes a range of forms that is not always adequately acknowledged. Printed diffusion can extend not only the visibility of traditional, spectacular power, through illustrated accounts of royal festivities and the like,[10] but also the influence of more capillary forms of power, in the shape of cheaply produced conduct books and manuals of procedure. Both kinds of power were, of course, already promoted in manuscript culture, and continued to figure in manuscripts throughout the period in question. Authors continued to present lavish copies of their work to illustrious patrons, while Francesco Barbaro's conduct book *De re uxoria* (*On Wifely Duties*, 1416) survives in more than 50 manuscripts – almost all from the fifteenth century – in Italian libraries alone.[11] However, the stakes are obviously different once this kind of text is printed; the virus spreads in new ways. In the case of propagandist literature or reportage, for instance, the audience of a presentation manuscript is likely to have been small, and to have exercised social authority over the author (most obviously in the form of patronage). The audience of a printed version is not only much larger, more culturally diverse and

---

[7]   *Index des livres interdits*, ed. by J.M. de Bujanda, 11 vols (Geneva: Droz, 1985–2002), I, pp. 11–18.

[8]   Ann Rosalind Jones, *The Currency of Eros: Women's Love Lyric in Europe, 1540–1620* (Bloomington, IN: Indiana University Press, 2000), pp. 155–200.

[9]   For reflections on these issues, see David Adams and Adrian Armstrong, 'Introduction', in *Print and Power in France and England, 1500–1800* (Aldershot: Ashgate, 2006), pp. 1–11.

[10]   See, for example, Alison Saunders, 'Spreading the word: Illustrated books as political propaganda in seventeenth-century France', in *Print and Power*, pp. 69–84.

[11]   *The Earthly Republic: Italian Humanists on Government and Society*, ed. by Benjamin G. Kohl and Ronald G. Witt with Elizabeth B. Welles (Manchester: Manchester University Press, 1978), p. 186.

geographically distant; it also stands in a different relationship to the authority glorified in the text. Whereas the presentation manuscript reflects an image of authority back upon its source, the edition diffuses that image to new recipients; whereas the recipient of the manuscript regards the author as subservient, for the reader of the printed version the author partakes of the authority he celebrates – at least on a discursive level, if not necessarily on a social one. However, this image of printing and its implications is all too familiar, schematic and simplistic; it must be refined. What, for instance, can be said about readers of non-presentation manuscripts? Their relationship with social and discursive authority may be much more like that of the print audience than that of the author's patron; it is not a relationship determined solely, or even primarily, by a particular technology of textual dissemination. Yet these very refinements make it all the more obvious that we cannot talk of authority in book culture as if it were some universal currency. It slips all too easily from one meaning, one owner, one site, to another.

The diverse relationships of publishers to authority illustrate this slippage vividly. Probably the most obvious such relationship is that between publishers and institutions that wield power. The workings of censorship, whether religious or political, position publishers as objects of authority – and, in extreme cases, as actors in a display of spectacular power no less memorable than Foucault's or Andrić's: the best-known example is the scholarly author, translator and printer Étienne Dolet, hanged and burnt along with his publications in 1546.[12] Yet many publishers resemble authors, in courting rather than fearing institutional authority: this attitude is materialised in the luxury, hand-finished, parchment copies produced by the important Parisian publisher Anthoine Vérard, individualised versions of his printed output for presentation to royal and other noble patrons.[13] When individualising these copies, Vérard often incorporates paratextual elements additional to, or different from, those of the standard print run; in doing so, he becomes a subject rather than an object of authority. By intervening in the texts in whose commercial success he had a stake, Vérard implies that publishers enjoy more authority over the works they disseminate than their authors. This authority is manifested not only over *books*, but also over *texts*, not only over the financial proceeds of publication, but also over the integrity of the semiotic structures that are reproduced in print. This latter form of publisher's authority has long been acknowledged as characteristic of the other technology of reproduction in this period: textual instability is endemic in manuscript culture. Of course, not all instances of *mouvance* or *variance*, to use the recent coinages of Paul Zumthor

---

[12]   On Dolet's execution, see Richard Copley Christie, *Étienne Dolet, The Martyr of the Renaissance: A Biography* (London: Macmillan, 1880), pp. 454–7.

[13]   On all aspects of Vérard's luxury copies, see Mary Beth Winn, *Anthoine Vérard, Parisian Publisher, 1485–1512: Prologues, Poems, and Presentations* (Geneva: Droz, 1997).

and Bernard Cerquiglini,[14] are manifestations of scribal authority, conscious or otherwise – very often, scribes simply misread their exemplars. However, numerous manuscript variants testify to the phenomenon that Elspeth Kennedy labelled 'the scribe as editor'.[15] One of the best examples of scribal editing considerably predates the period covered by the present volume, but is sufficiently rich and complex to be worth adducing here. Thomas Becket's secretary, Herbert of Bosham, coordinated the production of a four-volume set of Peter Lombard's *Magna glossatura* on the Psalms and Pauline Epistles, commissioned by Becket himself.[16] The original enterprise of composition already has interesting implications for authority: as with any major Biblical gloss, the ultimate authoritative text is interpreted by a scholar who will himself become an *auctor* [author], an intellectual reference point for future scholars, and who cites *auctoritates* [authorities], in other words statements by existing *auctores*, in the service of his interpretation. However, Herbert adds a further dimension, in that he produces a critical text. To the Gallican text of the Psalms, on which Lombard commented, he appends St Jerome's version, and where Lombard wrongly attributed particular *auctoritates*, he adds corrections in the margins, and signals the errors through marginal images. At the top right of one page, St Augustine is depicted pointing with a lance at a passage ascribed to him, and disclaiming his authorship by stating in a phylactery: '*Non ego*' [not me].[17] Hence authority passes from one text, or person, to another, and undergoes a number of shifts in the process. Biblical discourse is the point of departure for the *auctores*, whose theological assertions inform Lombard's gloss, whose contribution to doctrine motivates a powerful cleric to commission a prestigious set of manuscripts, whose conceptualiser wields a philological authority of his own. Both manuscripts and printed books, then, are sites where viral authority is apt to spread, to mutate, and on occasion to be contested.

It is entirely symptomatic of the virus that particular kinds of host are difficult to isolate: publishers, authors and political institutions infect each other all too readily. Yet some forms of authority are more apt than others to travel between different hosts. It is therefore crucial to identify, if only provisionally, the ways in which viral authority can manifest itself, and the areas in which it is more or less

---

[14]   Paul Zumthor, *Essai de poétique médiévale* (Paris: Seuil, 1972), p. 507; Bernard Cerquiglini, *Éloge de la variante: Histoire critique de la philologie* (Paris: Seuil, 1989), pp. 62, 111–12.

[15]   Elspeth Kennedy, 'The scribe as editor', in *Mélanges de langue et de littérature du Moyen Age et de la Renaissance offerts à Jean Frappier*, 2 vols (Geneva: Droz, 1970), I, pp. 523–31.

[16]   See *The Cambridge Illuminations: Ten Centuries of Book Production in the Medieval West*, ed. by Paul Binski and Stella Panayotova (London: Harvey Miller, 2005), pp. 92–4.

[17]   Cambridge, Trinity College, MS B.5.4, fol. 135ᵛ; reproduced in *The Cambridge Illuminations*, p. 93.

likely to be transmitted outside the strictly literary field.[18] Accordingly, in what follows I revisit, broaden and refine a typology of different forms of authority which I previously outlined in a study of authorial strategies in late medieval France.[19] The five types of authority that I distinguish are not by any means autonomous; they very often overlap. Nevertheless, it is useful to approach them in isolation in the first instance, so as to shed a more precise light on questions of power, transmission and the relationship between authors and other agents.

The first kind of concern for authority, the mastery of form and language, might be called *aesthetic authority*. It is perhaps the most specifically literary manifestation of authority – although even here some kind of institution, or community, is an essential precondition. The virtuoso control of rhetoric, versification or narrative technique bestows authority in an aesthetic sense, but only as long as this ability can be recognised by other writers, readers or critics. External criteria of some sort are always operative, whether or not these are explicit and codified – as they were in French poetry of the late fifteenth and early sixteenth centuries, when a number of manuals of versification, the so-called 'arts of second rhetoric', were influential enough to be printed.[20] Book producers may not display this sort of authority themselves, but they can and do advertise that they know it when they see it – and on these occasions, the virus mutates from an aesthetic to a more discursive strain, underpinned not by the expressive exploitation of formal conventions but by the evaluation, or at least the acknowledgement, of that exploitation. At a low level of intervention, this may involve scribes punctuating lines of verse in ways which demonstrate that they have spotted internal rhymes or other refinements; at a higher level, the conceptualisers of a manuscript or edition can signal formal devices through paratextual features such as titles or metadiscursive prefaces. In so doing, book producers adopt a practice often used by authors of the period, especially those authors accustomed to printing and its implications for transmission and reception.[21] The sixteenth-century French didactic and historical author Jean Bouchet exemplifies this tendency: he paid great attention to the prefatory material in early editions of his work, sometimes using it to indicate key formal features

---

[18]   While most of my examples are 'literary' in the narrow sense, I use the term much more broadly, to cover all kinds of writing.

[19]   'Paratexte et autorité(s) chez les Grands Rhétoriqueurs', in 'L'Écrivain editeur, 1: Du Moyen Age à la fin du XVIIIᵉ siecle', *Travaux de Litterature*, 14 (2000), pp. 61–89.

[20]   See especially Pierre Fabri, *Le Grand et vrai art de pleine rhétorique*, ed. by A. Héron, 3 vols (Rouen: Société des Bibliophiles Normands, 1889–90); Jean Molinet, *L'Art de Rhétorique*, in *Recueil d'arts de seconde rhétorique*, ed. by Ernest Langlois (Paris: Imprimerie Nationale, 1902), pp. 214–52. The market for these manuals suggests that the ability to recognise such aesthetic authority, if not necessarily to reproduce it, was on some level socially desirable.

[21]   The practices of various French authors and book producers in this respect are outlined in Adrian Armstrong, *Technique and Technology: Script, Print, and Poetics, 1470–1550* (Oxford: Clarendon Press, 2000).

in verse texts.[22] Hence, while aesthetic authority may be specific to authors, it depends on assumptions shared by a community of readers. Moreover, it has a double-edged relationship to book producers. On the one hand, scribes or printers can tacitly display their cultural competence by signalling their understanding of what aesthetic authority is based on; on the other, these signals, by facilitating the recognition of this authority, help authors acquire it.

The second item in my typology might be called *discursive authority*: the display of knowledge, or of conformity with orthodox doctrine, which indicates that authors are suitably qualified to talk about their chosen field of discourse. This might appear as a debt to respected texts or *auctores*, as in Lombard's glosses – and indeed Herbert's amendments to them – in which case authority is transmitted relatively straightforwardly from one writer to another. Elsewhere, establishing discursive authority might involve reliance on institutional endorsement; Jean Bouchet again provides a fascinating example. For his *Triumphes de la noble et amoureuse dame* (1530), an allegory that charts the soul's journey through life and condenses a large body of learned religious writing into a vernacular narrative, Bouchet had the text checked for orthodoxy by two theologians of the University of Poitiers, whose laudatory assessments he has included among the liminary pieces accompanying the first edition.[23] Yet discursive authority should not be considered as having two branches, one textual and the other institutional: these two sources are very often intertwined. The materials which writers adduce as *auctoritates* may owe their canonical status to institutions of some sort, whether ecclesiastical bodies, universities or princely courts. At the court of the dukes of Burgundy in the late fifteenth century, for instance, the work of the official poets and historians, or *indiciaires*, enjoyed a discursive prestige greater than that of the 'freelance' authors who moved in the same circles, even though the *indiciaires* often had less close contact with current affairs than their contemporaries.[24] Equally, institutions may derive their legitimacy from texts: the Church is the most obvious example. Book producers may advertise the discursive authority of writers – as when the first printers of Bouchet's *Triumphes* reproduce the theologians' certificates – or indeed their own contribution to this authority, for instance by signalling on a title-page that their edition of a well-known text has been corrected. Such advertising is of course a commercial strategy, but it also affects perceptions of the producers' relationship with discursive authority. If a printer can present his publications as authoritative, in respect either of their content or of the accuracy with which they have been reproduced, some of the prestige associated with these works is bound to be transmitted to him, and perhaps in turn attract future authors and readers who value this kind of authority. There may be scope for illuminating research

---

[22]   For examples, see Armstrong, 'Paratexte et autorité(s)', pp. 67–8.

[23]   Jennifer Britnell, *Jean Bouchet* (Edinburgh: Edinburgh University Press, 1986), p. 221.

[24]   On the role of the *indiciaires*, see Jean Devaux, *Jean Molinet, Indiciaire bourguignon* (Paris: Champion, 1996), pp. 25–42.

from this perspective into the early publishers of women's writing. An impeccably scholarly and accurate printer such as Jean de Tournes, in mid-sixteenth-century Lyon, may prove to have earned a more illustrious reputation for the female authors he published – Louise Labé, Pernette du Guillet and Marguerite de Navarre – than the earlier Parisian printer Denis Janot, less highly regarded in philological terms, achieved for Hélisenne de Crenne. Certainly the subsequent critical reception of Hélisenne has been much more lukewarm than that of the authors published by de Tournes.[25]

A third area in which authors can show a concern for authority is the guidance of readers: highlighting key arguments or strategies, blocking inappropriate interpretations and other attempts to assert authority over a text's reception. This form of authority often helps underpin aesthetic or discursive authority, but differs from these in that it involves a direct engagement with the audience: a suitable designation might be *pragmatic authority*, pragmatics being that branch of linguistics that considers the relationship of language to its context. Pragmatic authority tends to be exercised through metadiscourse, in particular through prefatory material, although it can also be an effect of anthologisation: in manuscript or print, the juxtaposition of texts can draw attention to what they have in common, foregrounding certain themes at the expense of others. Broadly speaking, explicit metadiscourse is more common in print than in manuscript culture. The audience opened up by printing is more distant from an author – culturally as well as geographically – than the initial public of a work transmitted in manuscript form; it is less likely that readers will share the author's assumptions, more likely that they will misread him. Consequently, authors attuned to printing often take pains to clarify their approach, to limit the possibility of misinterpretation. Bouchet, like many of his contemporaries, invests heavily in the potential of the preface as 'user guide'.[26] However, it is perhaps when this potential is *not* realised that the role of pragmatic authority becomes clear. The best-known example is the preface to Rabelais's *Gargantua*, which has exercised generations of scholars seeking to reconcile its apparently incompatible messages about meaning, reading and interpretation.[27] Are we to look below the surface so we can discover a 'doctrine

---

[25]   On these printers, see Alfred Cartier, *Bibliographie des éditions des de Tournes, imprimeurs lyonnais*, 2 vols (Paris: Editions des bibliothèques nationales de France, 1937–8 ; repr. Geneva: Slatkine Reprints, 1970); Stephen P.J. Rawles, 'Denis Janot, Parisian printer and bookseller (*fl.* 1529–1544): A bibliographical study' (unpublished doctoral thesis, University of Warwick, 1976). On the issues informing the selection of publishers by French female authors, see Susan Broomhall, *Women and the Book Trade in Sixteenth-Century France* (Aldershot: Ashgate, 2002), pp. 112–17.

[26]   See Armstrong, 'Paratexte et autorité(s)', pp. 74–7.

[27]   See especially Edwin Duval, 'Interpretation and the "Doctrine absconce" of Rabelais's Prologue to *Gargantua*', *Etudes Rabelaisiennes*, 18 (1985), pp. 1–17, and an important scholarly debate: Gérard Defaux, 'D'un problème l'autre: herméneutique de l'*altior sensus* et *captatio lectoris* dans le prologue de *Gangantua*', *Revue d'histoire*

plus absconce' ['abstruse teaching']?[28] Or are we to exercise suspicion, since the author claims that 'n'y pensasse en plus que vous, qui par adventure beviez comme moy' ['I gave no more thought to the matter than you, who were probably drinking at the time, as I was']?[29] A more productive reading might be that this preface does not *exercise* pragmatic authority so much as *thematise* it. In supplying a profusion of interpretative cues, which do not all appear to lead in the same direction, Rabelais is in a sense parodying the 'user guides' so common in serious literature of the early 1530s. Parodying, but also transcending; the preface does guide the reader, but by resembling the text it introduces rather than by commenting on it. Like the novel that follows it, the preface is challenging, dialogical, centrifugal: it does not entirely resist interpretation, but it constantly reminds us of how provisional and selective our interpretations are. Broadly in line with humanist educational theory, the answers are not supplied at the outset; rather, readers are obliged to come to their own conclusions on the basis of the evidence in front of them, and on the assumption that they have the requisite intellectual skills and personal qualities to assess that evidence properly, 'en la perfectissime partie' ['in the most perfect sense'].[30] However, pragmatic authority is not the exclusive privilege of authors: publishers and editors have boundless opportunities to direct readerly interpretations, in the same way as has become commonplace in modern critical editions. Sylvia Huot's study of the manuscript reception of the *Romance of the Rose* illustrates admirably the ways in which copyists and conceptualisers subject this 'protean text' to a multitude of selective readings, through editorial interventions of various kinds.[31] Similarly, in the first half of the sixteenth century, when works by the Burgundian *indiciaires* are printed in France for a public with different values, the political charge of these publications is carefully minimised. When a major collection of poems by Jean Molinet, the most consistently anti-French of the *indiciaires*, was published in Paris in 1531 under the title *Les Faictz et dictz*, its contents were selected and ordered, briefly described in an editorial preface, and even discreetly reworked, in ways that privilege Molinet's

---

littéraire de la France, 85 (1985), pp. 195–216; Terence Cave, Michel Jeanneret and François Rigolot, 'Sur la prétendue transparence de Rabelais', *Revue d'histoire littéraire de la France*, 86 (1986), pp. 709–16; Gérard Defaux, 'Sur la prétendue pluralité du Prologue de *Gargantua*', *Revue d'histoire littéraire de la France*, 86 (1986), pp. 716–22.

[28]   François Rabelais, *Gargantua*, ed. by Ruth Calder and M.A. Screech (Geneva: Droz, 1970), p. 14. English translation from François Rabelais, *Gargantua and Pantagruel*, trans. by J.M. Cohen (Harmondsworth: Penguin, 1955), p. 38.

[29]   *Gargantua*, ed. Calder and Screech, p. 17; *Gargantua and Pantagruel*, trans. Cohen, p. 39.

[30]   *Gargantua*, ed. Calder and Screech, p. 18; *Gargantua and Pantagruel*, trans. Cohen, p. 39.

[31]   Sylvia Huot, *The 'Romance of the Rose' and its Medieval Readers: Interpretation, Reception, Manuscript Transmission* (Cambridge: Cambridge University Press, 1993), p. 323.

didactic and religious writing over his more politically tendentious output.[32] The anthology's presentation powerfully indicates the range of ways in which book producers could wield pragmatic authority.

The possibility of such interventions – and the textual instability, typical of manuscript and early print culture, which permits them – sometimes elicit counter-strategies on the part of authors. In these instances, authors are staking their claim to a fourth type of authority, *editorial authority*: control over a text's stability, including the right to revise or recontextualise it on one's own terms. François Villon's *Testament* thematises the difficulty of asserting this control in manuscript culture: it alludes to the dissemination of Villon's previous major poem, the *Lais*, in ways which he was unable to influence, and to the likelihood that the Testament will undergo similar alterations in the process of transmission, alterations that are duly manifested in the diverse avatars of Villon's work now available to us, in both manuscripts and editions, from Pierre Levet's of 1489 to Claude Thiry's half a millennium later.[33] However, authors who involved themselves in the printing of their work could resist such erosion, at least to some extent. A number of French writers of the early sixteenth century recognised this possibility. Jean Lemaire de Belges, successor to Jean Molinet as Burgundian *indiciaire*, tended to revise his work for print publication after an initial presentation manuscript was produced, and to liaise – albeit not always very closely – with printers in both Paris and Lyon.[34] Bouchet frequently revised and republished his work, to take account of new historical circumstances or changing conventions of versification, or simply to reaffirm his authority over material that had previously appeared in unauthorised editions.[35]

In this respect, editorial authority comes close to the fifth and final manifestation of authority with which writers of this period are concerned: *proprietorial authority*. A broader phenomenon than the other types, this form of authority relates closely to another concept of Foucault's, the 'author function'.[36] Foucault's

---

[32]   Jean Molinet, *Les Faictz et dictz* (Paris: Jean Longis and the widow of Jean Saint-Denis, 1531). On this edition's presentation, see Armstrong, *Technique and Technology*, pp. 56–70; Adrian Armstrong, 'Cosmetic surgery on Gaul: The printed reception of Burgundian writing in France before 1550', in *Print and Power*, pp. 13–26 (pp. 19–22).

[33]   François Villon, *Le Grant Testament Villon et le Petit. Son Codicille. Le Jargon et ses Balades* (Paris: Pierre Levet, 1489); *Poésies complètes*, ed. by Claude Thiry (Paris: Librairie Générale Française, 1991). On the transmission of Villon's work, see Nancy Freeman Regalado, 'Gathering the works: The *Oeuvres de Villon* and the intergeneric passage of the medieval French lyric into single-author collections', *L'Esprit Créateur*, 33 (1993), pp. 87–100; Mary B. Speer, 'The editorial tradition of Villon's *Testament*: From Marot to Rychner and Henry', *Romance Philology*, 31 (1977), pp. 344–61.

[34]   Armstrong, 'Paratexte et autorité(s)', p. 78.

[35]   Armstrong, 'Paratexte et autorité(s)', p. 80–81.

[36]   The notion is presented in Michel Foucault, 'What is an author?', in *The Foucault Reader*, ed. by Paul Rabinow (Harmondsworth: Penguin, 1984), pp. 101–20.

term covers not only the attribution of a text to a named author, but also the twin readerly assumptions that a text's authorship influences its meaning, and that a single author's works are on some level coherent. It is often tempting to regard the author function as an effect of printing, and certainly technological changes seem to have fostered the development of embryonic notions of literary property. Cynthia Brown has noted that, in early-sixteenth-century France, authors are acknowledged in lawsuits as having a stronger claim than printers to dispose of their work as they see fit, and that various writers of the period – Molinet, Lemaire de Belges, Bouchet, Pierre Gringoire and André de La Vigne – adopt increasingly proprietorial attitudes towards their work, not only involving themselves in publication but also more frequently referring to themselves by name and talking about their authorial activity.[37] However, we must not forget the important, albeit relatively isolated, instances of a prominent author function in manuscript contexts: Christine de Pizan's production of manuscripts of her own work is perhaps the best-known example.[38] Indeed, in print as well as in manuscript, book producers can grant authors rather too much proprietorial authority. In the sixteenth century, printed anthologies of work by particular authors often include pieces wrongly ascribed to them: this is the case in England with editions of Chaucer, and in France with editions of Villon, Clément Marot and Alain Chartier.[39] Whether or not these misattributions reflect a commercial agenda, they indubitably attest to the power of the author function. Yet the author–text relationship can be manifested in many ways, not only through explicit attributions. Any overt indication of an author's investment in a text – formal virtuosity, metadiscourse, revisions – contributes to some extent to proprietorial authority. It follows that the techniques that assert proprietorial authority are, to a large extent, the same techniques that assert the other types of authority previously outlined. However, these are not equally accessible to all authors: genres, periods and locations all influence an author's selection of techniques. There is considerable potential for valuable comparative research into this issue, as the following brief and culturally specific example should make clear. In late-medieval French didactic literature, an especially prominent technique for establishing proprietorial authority is the use of a first-person narratorial voice which appears to coincide with the historical author. This

---

[37] Cynthia J. Brown, *Poets, Patrons, and Printer: Crisis of Authority in Late Medieval France* (Ithaca, NY: Cornell University Press, 1995); the lawsuits are discussed on pp. 1–5.

[38] See James C. Laidlaw, 'Christine de Pizan – A Publisher's Progress', *Modern Language Review*, 82 (1987), pp. 35–75. On the author function in manuscript culture more generally, see Roger Chartier, *L'Ordre des livres: Lecteurs, auteurs, bibliothèques en Europe entre XIVe et XVIIIe siècle* (Aix-en-Provence: Alinéa, 1992), pp. 60–67.

[39] See Alice Miskimin, *The Renaissance Chaucer* (New Haven, CT: Yale University Press, 1975), pp. 227–28, 241–6; Freeman Regalado, 'Gathering the works', p. 98; Clément Marot, *Œuvres poétiques complètes*, ed. by Gérard Defaux, 2 vols (Paris: Bordas, 1990–93), I, pp. 9–11; Alain Chartier, *The Poetical Works of Alain Chartier*, ed. by James C. Laidlaw (Cambridge: Cambridge University Press, 1974), p. 143.

conflation can be achieved by simply using the author's name to designate the narrator, or by making apparently autobiographical allusions. It inevitably has different local effects in different works, whatever the surface similarities between narratorial personas. When, for instance, the homodiegetic narrator of Christine de Pizan's *Chemin de Longue Étude* (1402) talks of her bereavement in ways that recall the experience of the historical Christine, this pseudo-autobiography helps the author develop an argument concerning the relationship between knowledge and Fortune in the context of sublunary human activity.[40] A century later, when the narrator of Lemaire de Belges's *Plainte du Désiré* (1504) refers to the author's own recent work, this is one of a panoply of techniques by which the text explores questions of æsthetics, especially the value of poetry.[41] In both cases, however, proprietorial authority is enhanced; author and text become inextricably linked.

The various examples adduced above reveal the viral nature of authority in the literary and publishing cultures of this period. Authority passes between authors and publishers, and from one author or publisher to another; it assumes different forms, which may reinforce or at least complement each other. All these shifts resist any generalising overview: it is in the particular combinations of texts and intertexts, and of these texts' physical manifestations, that viral authority takes its various shapes. If it is impossible to predict what these shapes might be, the typology I have sketched out may at least provide a way of describing them and their implications. Between the Foucauldian concept of capillary power on the one hand, and what Don McKenzie called the sociology of texts on the other,[42] it is possible to think of a methodological bridge: a political virology of the book.

---

[40]   Christine de Pizan, *Le Chemin de Longue Étude*, ed. by Andrea Tarnowski (Paris: Librairie Générale Française, 2000). This edition reproduces the rubrics from Christine's autograph manuscript (London, British Library, MS Harley 4431), which likewise designate the narrator as 'Cristine'. On the relationship between the autobiographical and the universal in the *Chemin*, see Sarah Kay, *The Place of Thought: The Complexity of One in Late Medieval French Didactic Poetry* (Philadelphia, PA: University of Pennsylvania Press, 2007), pp. 150–76.

[41]   Jean Lemaire de Belges, *La Plainte du Désiré*, ed. by Dora Yabsley (Paris: Droz, 1932). On æsthetic issues in the *Plainte*, see Adrian Armstrong, 'La *Plainte du Désiré* de Jean Lemaire de Belges: du manuscrit illustré aux marges de l'imprimé', in *Actes du IIème Colloque international sur la Littérature en Moyen Français (Milan, 8–10 mai 2000)*, ed. by Sergio Cigada, Anna Slerca, Giovanna Bellati and Monica Barsi, *L'Analisi linguistica e letteraria*, 8 (2000), pp. 139–56 (pp. 140–42).

[42]   See Don F. McKenzie, *Bibliography and the Sociology of Texts* (London: British Library, 1986).

Chapter 3

Competing Codes of Authority in mid-Fifteenth Century Burgundy: Martin Le Franc and the Book that Answers Back

Helen Swift

Item y a ung staple ouquel a ung livre de balades que, quant l'en y vault lire,
les gens se treuvent tous broulliez de noir et tantost qu'ilz regardent dedans
aussi sont ils moulliez d'eaue quant on veult.

A book of ballads lies on a desk but, when you try to read it,
you are squirted with soot, and, if you look inside it,
you can be sprayed with water.[1]

It would be easy to approach the question of patronal authority with a series of straightforward assumptions: that it operates within strict and restricted parameters of what is deemed acceptable; that the mechanics of the process are a simple given, in that an author presents a book that the patron receives; and that authority in this process is a unilateral affair, with the humble writer submitting himself to the powerful dedicatee. Existing studies of late-medieval French manuscript production have already considerably nuanced such an image and begun to explore the complexities that concrete realisations of poet–patron relations introduce to any abstract model. Recent work on the prolific and well-documented writers Guillaume de Machaut and Christine de Pizan, for example, has demonstrated the multifaceted role of the author as an influential agent in shaping the presentation of her/his work, whether through strategic development within the texts of the manuscript of narrator personae whose identities subtly intersect with that of the

---

[1]   Extract from the accounts of 1433, detailing the mechanical contrivances installed in Philip the Good's trick rooms within his palace at Hesdin: *Inventaire sommaire des archives départementales du Nord. Série B*, ed. by André Le Glay et al., 10 vols (Lille: 1863–1906), IV (1877), pp. 123–4. The English translation is Richard Vaughan's: *Philip the Good: The Apogee of Burgundy* (Harlow: Longmans, 1970; repr. Woodbridge: Boydell, 2002), pp. 137–9 (p. 138). See also Jutta Huesmann's commentary on the castle's chambers in her study of 'Hospitality at the Court of Philippe le Bon, Duke of Burgundy (c.1435–67)' (Oxford: unpublished DPhil thesis, 2001), pp. 193–6.

historical author, or through careful organisation of the ordering and decoration (miniatures and rubrication) of the works to operate as part of the manuscript's rhetoric, its persuasive power.[2] Such studies have, however, largely focused on situations of harmony, where a writer supports her/his work and encounters a favourable reception by its targeted patron. The present article addresses a case study characterised by competition and conflict between all parties in the process, in order further to disrupt any easy assumptions about the stakes and agents at play in poet–patron communications.[3]

In a mid-fifteenth century verse debate between a Book and its Author, *La Complainte du livre du 'Champion des dames' a maistre Martin Le Franc son acteur*, Martin Le Franc's pro-feminine debate poem, *Le Champion des dames*, revisits its author in a dream-vision to complain of its distinctly unfavourable reception in *c.* 1442 at the court of Philip the Good, whose prestigious Burgundian patronage it had sought to secure:

> Tant a l'en fait qu'il m'a falu
> Demourer seulet en la mue,
> De mousse et de pouldre velu
> Comme ung viez aiz qu'on ne remue.[4]

> ('As a result of their [= the courtiers'] actions I was locked up on my own, and had to stay there gathering mould and dust, like an old abandoned axe'.)

On the authority of his courtiers' advice, the book has reportedly been consigned to oblivion on a dusty shelf. However, the *Complainte* itself reveals that that was far from the end of the story. In this short, 500-line sequel to the *Champion*, the Book, *Livre*, has apparently resurrected itself in order to return to its Author and argue over who is imputable for its failure. In the above quotation, the image of the abandoned axe perhaps suggests ominously that the work has a further blow to wield if it picks itself up, dusts itself off and starts all over again. An enigmatic little poem in its own right, the *Complainte* more broadly raises important

---

[2]   Deborah McGrady, *Controlling Readers: Guillaume de Machaut and His Late Medieval Audience* (Toronto: University of Toronto Press, 2006); *Christine de Pizan: The Making of the Queen's Manuscript (London, British Library, Harley MS 4431)*, <http://www.pizan.lib.ed.ac.uk>, accessed 2 August 2010.

[3]   For a comparative approach to the problematisation of author-patron relations in *querelle des femmes* texts, see Helen J. Swift, '"Des circuits de pouvoir": un modèle pour la relecture des rapports poète-mécène dans les apologies du sexe féminin de la fin du moyen âge', *Études françaises*, 47 (2011), pp. 55–69.

[4]   *La Complainte du livre du Champion des dames a maistre Martin Le Franc son acteur*, in Gaston Paris, 'Un poème inédit de Martin Le Franc', *Romania*, 16 (1887), pp. 383–437, ll. 145–8. Subsequent references to the *Complainte* will be incorporated into the text; all translations are my own.

questions about the dynamics of patronal authority, for instance, asking how, according to what criteria and what agency the acceptability or inadmissibility of a particular work is determined, given that the poem's tale increases the number of parties exercising influence in the process – not only foregrounding the book as an apparently autonomous entity, and thereby implying the significance of a work's materiality as well as its delivery before its court audience,[5] but also highlighting the role played by court advisors in affecting the outcome of a work's reception. It is already clear that nothing is a given in the intriguing case of manuscript presentation recounted by the *Complainte* (that of the *Champion* in Brussels, Bibliothèque Royale, MS 9466), not to mention the further case represented by the poem itself in its own codex, Paris, Bibliothèque nationale, fonds français, MS 12476. Competing authorities are evidenced both within the text, as Author and Book jostle responsibility for a work's reception, and without, as the poem's presentation in manuscript serves as a vehicle for communication between poet and patron. The present article anchors its study of authority in an examination of the Book's assertion of its failed reception. It will first consider possible reasons for the *Champion*'s rejection, matters of both textual content and artistic presentation that might have displeased a Burgundian audience. Second, it will ask whether, indeed, the book *was* spurned; if the *Complainte* is purely a fiction, might this locate the greater authority with the author, whose lively debate thereby constitutes a strategy to boost interest in the original *Champion* manuscript, now BR, 9466? Third, it will examine the subsequent presentation copy, BN, f. fr. 12476, that *was* accepted by Philip some nine years later, and which is the sole surviving witness of the juxtaposed *Complainte*.[6] Does this second manuscript bear signs of concessions to an intractable patron, or, on the contrary, of shrewd manoeuvrings on the part of its compiler (plausibly Le Franc himself) which enabled him to reinforce rather than retract the message that the *Champion* originally wanted to address to the Burgundian duke – and what exactly was that message? Lastly, I shall propose two new optics through which the enterprise of Le Franc's *Complainte* may be viewed in the context of contemporary Burgundian cultural practices. Overall, we shall see emerging a more flexible, intricate and interactive model for reading author–patron communication, one which can lead us to a more culturally and politically

---

[5]   For discussion of the Book's self-presentation and manner of delivery, see Helen J. Swift, 'Martin Le Franc et son livre qui se plaint: une petite énigme à la cour de Philippe le Bon', in *L'écrit et le manuscrit à la fin du moyen âge*, ed. by Tania Van Hemelryck and Céline Van Hoorebeeck (Turnhout: Brepols, 2006), pp. 329–42.

[6]   Nine manuscript copies of the *Champion* survive, of which five are illustrated with between two and 182 miniatures; two printed versions, a Lyons incunable from 1485 and a Paris edition from 1530, are also extant. For a full description of the medieval manuscript and print tradition of the *Champion*, see Helen J. Swift, *Gender, Writing and Performance: Men Defending Women in Late Medieval France* (Oxford: Oxford University Press, 2008), pp. 250–51.

embedded approach to literary authority, and which may even bring us to question the truth of the very communication scenario we are apparently presented with.

The *Champion* depicts a lengthy debate, across five books, between the pro-feminine Champion, Free Will, and a series of anti-feminine adversaries, delegates of the arch-misogynist Ill Speaking. Various additional personifications intervene on the pro-feminine side, notably Lady France, Lady Holy Church and Lady Nature. The poem concludes with Free Will's victory. Amongst the little attention that its short sequel, *La Complainte*, has received, there has evolved a consensus view of the rejection it recounts, which takes the Book at its word: it is a matter of inflammatory politico-religious content, as flagged up by Livre when it first accosts the authorial persona l'Acteur:[7]

Tu as parlé de sainte eglise
Je ne sçay en quele maniere. (Complainte, ll. 209–10)[8]

(You have spoken about Holy Church in I-don't-know-what manner.)

The particular controversy to which Livre alludes is that of conciliarism – the movement of ecclesiastical reform being promoted, in the 1430s and 1440s, at the Council of Basel,[9] from whose discussions Philip the Good had withdrawn his

---

[7]   The term 'acteur' is used by medieval French writers to denote the first-person fictionalised narrator, although playing to a greater or lesser degree on potential intersections between the fictional *acteur* and the historical *auteur*. The full title of the *Complainte* may be seen to promote such slippage: Le Franc was the author of the *Champion*, which also featured a narrator designated *l'Acteur*; in the *Complainte* he features within the dream fiction as the dreaming *Acteur*'s projection of himself as author of the *Champion*. See also Cynthia J. Brown, *Poets, Patrons, and Printers: Crisis of Authority in Late Medieval France* (Ithaca, NY: Cornell University Press, 1995), pp. 197–205.

[8]   The most significant commentary on the *Complainte* hitherto has been provided by Pascale Charron, 'Les Réceptions du *Champion des dames* de Martin Le Franc à la cour de Bourgogne: "Tres puissant et tres humain prince ... veullez cest livre humainement recepvoir"', *Bulletin du bibliophile*, 2000, 9–31. Other interesting remarks, situating the poem in the context of fifteenth-century poetics, have been offered by Jacqueline Cerquiglini-Toulet, 'L'Imaginaire du livre à la fin du moyen âge: pratiques de lecture, théorie de l'écriture', *Modern Language Notes*, 108 (1993), pp. 680–95. See also below, n. 17.

[9]   As Antony Black explains, a distinction arose in the latter stages of Basel (1437–49) between support for conciliarism in principle and support for Basel in its current circumstances, namely its more radical arguments for conciliar supremacy and its initiation of schism, having deposed Eugenius IV (whom most major powers continued to support or, alternatively, declared neutrality) and appointed Felix V as anti-pope (who commanded support from only minor European powers, together with universities, notably Paris): *Council and Commune: The Conciliar Movement and the Fifteenth-Century Heritage* (London/Shepherdstown, WV: Burnes & Oates/Patmos, 1979), pp. 110, 113. More

prelates in early 1438 as he came increasingly overtly to side with Pope Eugenius IV.[10] Livre fulminates:

> Item, tu as esté a Basle;
> Pour tant, comme a Basilien
> Condempné a la triquebale,
> On m'a rompu bas et lyen. (*Complainte*, ll. 229–32)[11]

> (Item, you were at Basel; and on account of this, as if punishing a Basilian by torture, they tore me to shreds.)

Le Franc's particular connection with the council's activity derived from his office as secretary to Amadeus VIII of Savoy, who had been elected anti-pope Felix V in 1439 after the Council's decision to depose Eugenius in late 1438;[12]

---

generally, as Heribert Müller observes, with reference to Thomas de Courcelles's role as redactor of Basel, 'il y a autant de conciliarismes que d'auteurs': '"Et sembloit qu'on oÿst parler un angele de dieu": Thomas de Courcelles et le Concile de Bâle ou le secret d'une belle réussite', in *Académie des inscriptions et belles-lettres: comptes-rendus des séances*, 1 (2003), pp. 461–84 (p. 471).

[10]   Joachim W. Stieber, *Pope Eugenius IV, the Council of Basel and the Secular and Ecclesiastical Authorities in the Empire: The Conflict over Supreme Authority and Power in the Church* (Leiden: Brill, 1978), p. 41; Vaughan, *Philip the Good*, pp. 211, 213. The political reality of Burgundian relations with Basel was, of course, far more complex than this simple statement suggests. The duke's ambassadors found fault with the Council's procedures and hierarchies from their first arrival: Vaughan, *Philip the Good*, pp. 206–07. Philip himself appeared at first to adopt a position of (strategic) neutrality, which, over time, turned into overt support for Eugenius; there were significant benefits to be gained from his collaboration with the pope: *Philip the Good*, pp. 213–16. See also Joseph Toussaint, *Les relations diplomatiques de Philippe le Bon avec le Concile de Bâle (1431–1449)* (Louvain: Bibliothèque de l'Université, 1942), pp. 106–79.

[11]   Le Franc's analogy for his book's violent treatment is, unless intended purely metaphorically, curious, since one of the singular defining features of Basel is that it operated as an arena for working through dispute with the word rather than the sword; as Black notes, the use of force was rejected and there were no martyrs: 'Popes and Councils', in *The New Cambridge Medieval History, Volume VII c. 1415–c. 1500*, ed. by Christopher Allmand (Cambridge: Cambridge University Press, 1998), pp. 65–86 (p. 85).

[12]   Amadeus arrived at Basel on 24 June 1440, presumably with Le Franc accompanying him; his coronation as Felix V took place on 24 July. Amadeus was Philip the Good's uncle (having married Philip the Bold's daughter, Mary of Burgundy), and it is thus interesting to consider relations between the two dukes following the former's election as anti-pope while the latter supported his opponent. Burgundy and Savoy affirmed a treaty of alliance in the early 1440s, in spite of Philip's refusal to support Felix V. Surviving (Burgundian) chronicle accounts of the Savoyard visit to Philip's court that precipitated this treaty agree on the amity sustained between the two parties: the memorialist Olivier de La Marche concludes that, although 'sur caste matiere ne firent les deux ducz aucune conclusion; mais

Le Franc is attested as having been incorporated at Basel on 1 July 1440.[13] In fairness to Livre's accusations, it is true that an explicit promotion of 'mes saincts conciles' is promulgated in the *Champion* by Lady Holy Church;[14] however, Le Franc anticipates her polemical discourse by including in the preface to the poem a *nota bene* on the accepted rhetorical code of propriety which licenses a given personification to speak in a particular way according to the quality it represents:[15]

> Se en cest livre est trouvee parolle desplaisante ou trop legiere ou trop aigre ou trop obscure, on doibt considerer la nature du personage qui parle. (*Champion*, p. 6)

> (If, in this book, speech is found that is displeasing or too reckless or too biting or too obscure, one must take into account the nature of the character who utters it.)

---

en alliance d'amour et de paix se partirent' (*Mémoires d'Olivier de La Marche*, ed. by Henri Beaune and J. d'Arbaumont, 4 vols (Paris: Renouard, 1883–88), I, p. 264), and specifies that Burgundian support of Eugenius over Felix was not straightforward and universal (La Marche, *Mémoires*, I, p. 262). Discrepancy seems to occur, however, regarding the personnel and timing of this meeting: La Marche has Amadeus and his wife visiting Philip at Chalon-sur-Saône in July 1443 (La Marche, *Mémoires*, I, p. 257), whereas the account in Urbain Plancher's *Histoire générale et particuliere de Bourgogne* (4 vols (Dijon: Antoine de Fay, 1739–41)), has Amadeus's son, Louis, visiting in July 1442 (IV, pp. xx, 25).

[13]   *Concilium Basiliense: Studien und Quellen zur Geschichte des Concils von Basel*, ed. by Johannes Haller, 8 vols (Basel: 1896–1936), VII (1910), p. 194: Le Franc is identified as a master of arts, 'domini nostri pape secretarius'. His involvement in the Council's discussions is mentioned on 7 August 1441 (*Concilium Basiliense*, VII, p. 404). Aeneus Silvius Piccolomini, a prominent humanist and pro-conciliar commentator on Basel (who would, however, later come to support the papal cause and eventually become Pope Pius II), includes Le Franc as a character (Martinus Gallus) in his *Libellus dialogorum de auctoritate concilie generalis ac des gestis Basiliensium et Eugenii papae contradictione* in November 1440: Marc-René Jung, 'Situation de Martin Le Franc', in *Pratiques de la culture écrite en France au XVᵉ siècle*, ed. by Monique Ornato and Nicole Pons (Louvain-la-Neuve: Fédération internationale des instituts d'études médiévales, 1995), pp. 13–30 (pp. 15–17). Piccolomini was employed as secretary by a number of significant dignitaries in the 1430s and 1440s, but from 1440 to 1442 he was, like Le Franc, in the service of Felix V (Cecilia M. Ady, *Pius II (Aeneas Silvius Piccolomini): The Humanist Pope* (London: Methuen, 1913), pp. 68–71); it is thus credible that the friendship represented in the *Libellus*'s dialogues had some grounding in actuality.

[14]   Martin Le Franc, *Le Champion des dames*, ed. by Robert Deschaux (Paris: Champion, 1999), l. 9923. Subsequent references to the *Champion* will be incorporated into the text; all translations are my own.

[15]   See the lengthy caveat and disclaimer offered by La Marche regarding the dangerous enterprise of speaking against Philip the Good and against Holy Church: *Mémoires*, I, p. 261.

I flag up Le Franc's use of his prologue to set the ground-rules for reading as I shall return to it later, when we shall see evidence for a certain provocativeness underpinning the author's apparently defensive statements.[16]

Received opinion regarding the *Champion*'s rejection thus centres on questions of moral content.[17] One may also broach, however, a material or aesthetic dimension to this refusal to do with the manner of the book's presentation. The *Complainte*'s debate itself arguably points us in this direction, in two respects: first, in the attention it accords to Livre's existence as material object, as witnessed in this article's first quotation; second, in the extent to which its debate about culpability for the *Champion*'s failure addresses the question of the work's rhetorical construction. Livre strives to attribute failure to poor *inventio* or *elocutio* on its author's part:

Se bouté m'eusses en mon sain
Maint brocard et mainte sentence
Dont on a entendement sain,
Gaignié j'avoye l'audience. (Complainte, ll. 201–204)

---

[16]   In addition to the speech by Dame Sainte Église (in book II), the greater part of book V of the *Champion* is devoted to a defence and celebration of the Council of Basel's endorsement of the dogma of the Immaculate Conception (at its thirty-sixth session on 17 September 1439). Introducing a series of articles addressing nine councils of the fifteenth and sixteenth centuries, Nelson H. Minnich observes that the Council of Basel, in particular the reforms it enacted and its rulings in the area of doctrine, such as the Immaculate Conception, stand in need of much further research: *Councils of the Catholic Reformation: Pisa I (1409) to Trent (1545–63)* (Aldershot: Ashgate, 2008), pp. 11, 15. There has, however, been important work by Joachim Stieber (*Pope Eugenius IV*), Gerald Christianson (e.g. 'Annates and Reform at the Council of Basel', in *Reformation and Renewal in the Middle Ages and the Renaissance: Studies in Honor of Louis Pascoe, S.J.*, ed. by Thomas M. Izbicki and Christopher M. Bellitto (Leiden: Brill, 2000), pp. 193–209), and, with particular regard to the Immaculate Conception, Thomas Izbicki: 'The Immaculate Conception and ecclesiastical politics from the Council of Basel to the Council of Trent: The Dominicans and their foes', in *Reform, Eccesiology, and the Christian Life in the Late Middle Ages* (Aldershotn: Ashgate, 2008), pp. 145–70.

[17]   It should be noted that a further passage seen to have caused controversy concerns the *Champion*'s support of Joan of Arc, whom Philip the Good had captured and sold on to the English: 16809–40; 16905–17000: in BN, f. fr. 12476; six of these stanzas (vv. 16921–68) have been excised, but 10 remain. The case of Joan is not examined in the present article mainly because the *Complainte* does not flag up this polemic (although doubtless an argument for the significance of the 'non-dit' could be proposed), but also because it has already received critical attention: see Gertrude H. Merkle, 'Martin Le Franc's commentary on Jean Gerson's treatise on Joan of Arc', in *Fresh Verdicts on Joan of Arc*, ed. by Bonnie Wheeler and Charles T. Wood (New York: Garland, 1996), pp. 177–88.

(If you'd stuffed me with lots of healthy commonplaces and palatable sayings that are readily accepted, I'd definitely have won over my audience/gained a hearing.)

L'Acteur, on the other hand, shifts blame onto the book on account of an alleged deficiency in *actio* when called upon to present itself to the court:

Or comme poi endoctriné
Tu as volu trop haut parler. (Complainte, ll. 165–6)[18]

(So, like an unskilled orator, you wanted to speak too loudly.)

This emphasis on the importance of presentation may also be read into Livre's fulmination 'Item, tu as esté a Basle'; its grievance may well be not its author's religious preferences, but simply his absence from the Burgundian court when the Book needed his support to ensure it gained a hearing and was successfully promoted.[19] Livre's disgruntlement may thus be seen to evoke the competitive nature of bids for literary patronage in fifteenth-century court society.

Hints at formal inadequacy within the text of the *Complainte* may point to actual deficiencies in the presentation of BR, 9466, and there are at least two grounds for finding this manuscript of the *Champion* physically unattractive to Philip in 1442. First, although the text is over 24,000 lines long, there are only two illustrations punctuating it, and no marginal rubrication to serve as paratextual guides for navigating the work. According to Burgundian standards of sumptuousness, this manuscript may have seemed a *parent pauvre*, a poor offering.[20] The second point is a question of timing: Philip, it seems, did not begin to cultivate as it were bibliophilic tendencies until he was in his fifties;[21] therefore, in 1442, it is quite conceivable that his sphere of interests did not yet include

---

[18]   As Jung notes, it may be possible to deduce a particular importance of eloquence to Le Franc from Piccolomini's *Libellus*, where, in the seventh dialogue, Martinus Gallus laments the contemporary decline in rhetorical skill such that ambassadors do not *orare* so much as *arare*: 'Situation', p. 17.

[19]   For more detailed analysis of how the Book and its Author dispute responsibility for the work's failed reception, see Swift, 'Martin Le Franc'.

[20]   In brief examination of the *Champion* as a gift that failed to fulfil its intended goal (in the broader context of gift-giving at the Valois courts), Brigitte Buettner considers material shortcomings to be the cause of the first copy's failed reception, and also makes interesting mention of the 'wishful thinking' dimension of so-called '"presentation" images': 'Past presents: New year's gifts at the Valois Courts ca. 1400', *The Art Bulletin*, 83.4 (2001), pp. 598–625 (pp. 616–17).

[21]   See Scot McKendrick, 'Reviving the past: Illustrated manuscripts of secular vernacular texts, 1476–1500', in *Illuminating the Renaissance: The Triumph of Flemish Manuscript Painting in Europe*, ed. by Thomas Kren and Scot McKendrick (Los Angeles, CA: J. Paul Getty Museum, 2003), pp. 59–78 (p. 68).

contemporary literature which marketed itself, according to Le Franc's prologue, as 'poesie et fiction amoureuse' dedicated to the honour of 'la querelle des dames singulierement recommandee' (*Champion*, p. 3).[22]

Therefore a case can clearly be marshalled, on grounds of both content and form, to support Livre's tale of the *Champion*'s rejection. However, its tale is, after all, just another *fiction*, and a dream-encased one at that, so what if, in fact, Le Franc is fibbing? What if his intentions in juxtaposing the *Champion*, for its second presentation, with this sequel did not involve humble grovelling, but rather a desire for self-promotion with a duke who had, perhaps, received the first presentation copy, but not paid it much attention, such that a more striking follow-up was needed for Le Franc to impose himself as a mover-and-shaker at the Burgundian court and get his message across? The physical form of the second presentation copy is obviously an important factor in entertaining this hypothesis, but before moving to address this, I want first to consider textual grounds as well as two further, extratextual reasons for proposing this alternative approach to the *Complainte*. Within the text of its debate, it is clear that l'Acteur is in no way offering an apology for the *Champion*: he retracts nothing, is unrepentant and, in fact, concentrates on bolstering the timorous Livre's confidence to re-enter the fray at court and compete again for attention:

> Ainsy se tu veulx conquester
> Nom souef longuement tenant,
> Laisse fronchier et quaqueter
> Les envieux de maintenant. (*Complainte*, ll. 377–80)

> (Thus, if you want to win long-lasting and sweet renown, be content to leave today's ill-willed/jealous souls to their frowning and backbiting.)

The emphasis on time in l'Acteur's pep-talk is striking, and can perhaps be seen to suggest some significance in the timing of the 1451 presentation. A little earlier in the poem, casting his book as an organic figure of virtue, l'Acteur comments:

> Tu es planté pour raverdir
> …
> Tout est a Vertu transitoire;
> Vertu passe tout et endure
> Pour acquerir honneur et gloire
> Et renon lequel toujours dure. (*Complainte*, ll. 317–20)

---

22   Philip's first official commission as bibliophile, seeking to extend the already impressive library inherited from his father, is generally held to be his request for Jean Wauquelin's *Chroniques de Hainaut* translation; payment for the first volume was made in 1448, and the entire work completed in 1453.

(You have been planted to flower again .... Compared with Virtue, everything is transient; Virtue outlasts everything and endures in order to gain honour, glory, and renown which lasts forever.)

The author seems to be making some distinction between immediate, ephemeral response and later, lasting reputation, perhaps, in a sort of nod-and-a-wink way, highlighting to Philip how the ecclesiastical issues that were a hot potato in 1442 have now cooled: Basel disbanded in 1449 after the abdication of Felix V. The *Champion*'s reformist controversy therefore acquires the safer status of criticism *après coup* at the time of the poem's second presentation in 1451. The *Complainte* thus does double duty, spicing up the *Champion* as a scandalous work in order to attract an audience, but proposing this sensation in the safety net of coming after the event.

Looking outside the texts of both works, there is a further significant event occurring between 1442 and 1451 that connects Le Franc to the Burgundian duke and suggests that the author was not in Philip's black books during this time. In 1447–48, the duke commissioned from him a new work, *L'Estrif de Fortune et de Vertu*. The *Estrif* presents a prosimetrum debate between Fortune and Virtue concerning which of them exerts the stronger force in controlling human life. Reason arbitrates, and decides in favour of Virtue. The *Estrif* evidently experienced significant contemporary popularity, surviving in more than 20 fifteenth-century manuscripts.[23] I have suggested elsewhere that the *Complainte*, through its insistent figuration of the Book, that is, the *Champion*, as Vertu, opens up an intertextual dialogue with the *Estrif*.[24] Early on in the *Estrif*, it becomes clear that Virtue, who voices a vehement defence of poetic writing, is aligned with the position of a poet. In the *Complainte*, l'Acteur predicts the ultimate victory of Vertu and the honours it will receive; thus, he suggests that Vertu represents both the lasting reputation of the poet and the literary work that will accord him this renown. Le Franc's aim in contriving this intertextual *rappel* is not just a self-congratulatory indulgence in textual dexterity, but a strategic manoeuvre intended to improve the prospects for the second presentation of his *Champion*. Forging this connection potentially enables the *Estrif* to act as a sort of paratext or commentary in relation to the *Champion*: through the figure of Vertu the *Complainte* provokes recollection of the more successful and highly esteemed commissioned work in order to promote the earlier poem that experienced far less initial success. Through a sort of literary nod-and-a-wink from poet to patron, this recollection gives weight to the argument advanced by l'Acteur in the *Complainte*'s debate that Vertu, that is, his book, *Le Champion des dames*, *will* triumph in the end, since Virtue has already been shown to have triumphed within the *Estrif*.

---

[23]   See the editorial introduction to *L'Estrif de Fortune et de Vertu*, ed. by Peter F. Dembowski (Geneva: Droz, 1999), pp. xxi–xxviii.

[24]   Swift, 'Martin Le Franc', pp. 339–40.

The second extratextual reason for doubting the sincerity of the *Complainte*'s claim of failure stems from perhaps the most significant literary precedent for forging some sort of dialogue between an author and a spurned book, namely Ovid's *Tristia*.[25] The *Tristia* consist of letters that Ovid supposedly wrote during his exile, having been banished from Rome in the wake of his infamous *Ars amatoria*.[26] The first chapter of the first book of the *Tristia* is constructed around the poet's address to his work, while the first chapter of the third book may be seen as a sort of response from the work itself. The poet's letter in *Tristia* I.i is intended to accompany the transmission of some new elegies that Ovid has composed in the hope of reconciling himself to the Emperor. The advice that he offers his work in this letter, the conduct he counsels before the imperial court and, later, the repentance he manifests, invite comparison between the *Tristia* and the *Complainte*. The former begin with a letter being dispatched to Rome:

> Parve – nec invideo – sine me, liber, ibis in urbem,
>   ei mihi, quod domino non licet ire tuo! (*Tristia,* I.i.1–2)

> (Little book, you will go without me – and I grudge it not – to the city. Alas that your master is not allowed to go!)

The author emphasises how his book 'veni[t] magnam peregrinus in urbem' ('enter[s] into the great city as one from foreign lands') (I.i.59). This may be seen to reflect Le Franc's position as portrayed in the *Complainte*, where l'Acteur thinks it best that his Book should advance independently of its author. Livre is reportedly greeted by the Burgundian court as a figure entirely foreign to the courtly milieu which consequently refuses him entry:

> ... Le prince a fait edit
> Qu'en sa chambre n'entre estrangier. (*Complainte*, ll. 109–10)

> (... the prince [= Philip] has ruled that no foreigner/stranger should enter his chamber.)[27]

---

[25] For French humanist interest in this work, see Ann Moss, *Ovid in Renaissance France: A Survey of the Latin Editions of Ovid and Commentaries Printed in France Before 1600* (London: Warburg Institute, 1982), pp. 19–22.

[26] The narrator refers to two crimes: 'carmen et error': *Tristia*, II.207, in Ovid, *Tristia; Ex ponto*, ed. and trans. by Arthur Leslie Wheeler (Cambridge, MA/London: Harvard University Press/Heinemann, 1965). Subsequent references will be incorporated into the text; all translations are the editor's own. The 'song' is identifiable as the *Ars*, while the particular 'mistake' is much debated.

[27] The spatial logistics and protocol for audiences with the duke are evoked in Huesmann, 'Hospitality', pp. 17–47. See also Olivier de La Marche's account of public

The Book's status as 'estrangier' is reinforced, and related to the condition of exile, towards the end of the *Complainte*, when l'Acteur identifies his Book – and by extension himself as its author – with the figure of Vertu:

> Mais Vertu est trop fortunée
> Trop est sa proesse notoire:
> Batue ou en exil menée,
> Il fault enfin qu'elle ait victoire. (*Complainte*, ll. 305–308)

> (But Virtue's auspices are most fortunate, her prowess is most famous: whether beaten or sent into exile, her ultimate victory will certainly come to pass.)

Might Le Franc be alluding here to his personal situation, writing this poem in France, in other words 'in exile' in relation to the boundaries of the duchy of Burgundy? The narrator of the *Tristia* counsels prudence and propriety in *actio*:

> ne, quae non opus est, forte loquare, cave!
> …
> tu cave defendas, quamvis mordebere dictis. (*Tristia*, I.i.22, 25)

> (And take care that you chance not to say what you should not! … Do you take care to make no defence though attacked with biting words.)

He expresses a concern for delivery that accords with the advice offered by l'Acteur to Livre when he instructs the Book not to be goaded by provocation: 'Aux horyons ne te retourne' ('Do not respond to their blows', *Complainte*, l. 385). In the same vein as l'Acteur, Ovid recommends humility and cautions against overweening ambition:

> ergo cave, liber, et timida circumspice mente,
>   ut satis a media sit tibi plebe legi.
> dum petit infirmis nimium sublimia pennis
>   Icarus, aequoreas nomine fecit aquas. (*Tristia*, I.i.87–90)

> (Therefore be careful, my book, and look all around with timid heart, so as to find content in being read by ordinary folk. By seeking too lofty heights on weak wings Icarus gave a name to waters of the sea.)

Both *je*-narrators encourage their books to seek out a champion from amongst the imperial or ducal entourage, someone who may serve as broker to ensure the book

---

audiences at the court of Charles the Bold, Philip's son by Isabel of Portugal and successor as duke: *Mémoires*, vol. IV (1888), pp. 4–6.

reaches, and is successfully received by, its target audience. Ovid does not make explicit the identity of such a guarantor when he conjectures:

> siquis erit, qui te dubitantem et adire timentem
> > tradat, et ante tamen pauca loquatur, adi. (*Tristia*, i.i.95–6)

> (If there is anybody, while you are hesitating in fear to approach, who will hand you to him [= the Emperor], introducing you with but a few brief words – then approach him.)

Le Franc, for his part, nominates two individuals as his protectors whose identities are well known: Philip the Good's wife, Isabel of Portugal ('du sang de Portugal semée'; *Complainte*, l. 434) and Jean de Créquy ('le seigneur de Crequy'; l. 456), a Burgundian bibliophile who favoured contemporary works and, most pertinently, served as literary advisor to Philip. The appointment of these individuals fits perfectly with the theory of the *Champion*'s rejection; for example, within the *Champion* itself, Le Franc congratulates Isabel for her role in securing the Arras Peace Treaty of 1435 between France and Burgundy, two enemy factions;[28] in his *Complainte*, he thus begs her to intervene on his behalf with the duke in order to bring about a similar peace between two antagonistic parties, the writer and his (hoped for) patron. Comparison between the *Tristia* and *Complainte* is equally provoked by the third book of the *Tristia*, where Ovid's book speaks out; like Le Franc's *Livre*, timorous about returning to court, it expresses his fears and anxieties,

> me miserum! vereorque locum vereorque potentem,
> > et quatitur trepido littera nostra metu.
> aspicis exsangui chartam pallere colore?
> > aspicis alternos intremuisse pedes? (*Tristia*, iii.i.53–6)

> (Wretched me! I fear the spot, I fear the man of power, my script wavers with shuddering dread. See you my paper pale with bloodless colour? See you each alternate foot tremble?)

This book recounts its fate as a material object in a manner that anticipates the isolation and dilapidation detailed in the *Complainte*:

---

[28]   For Isabel's diplomatic role, see Monique Sommé, *Isabel de Portugal, duchesse de Bourgogne: une femme au pouvoir au quinzième siècle* (Villeneuve d'Ascq: Presses universitaires du Septentrion, 1998), p. 385. Philippe Contamine asserts that Le Franc, 'dans sa pièce intitulée *Le Traictié de paix fait à Arras l'an M.IIII^c.XXX.V*, insiste sur son rôle de pacificatrice': 'Aperçus nouveaux sur *Toison d'or*, chroniqueur de la paix d'Arras (1435)', *Revue du nord* 88 (2006), pp. 577–96 (p. 583, n. 20); I have not been able to locate this play.

… custos me sedibus illis
praepositus sancto iussit abire loco.
…
interea, quoniam statio mihi publica clausa est,
privato liceat delituisse loco. (*Tristia*, III.i.67–8, 79–80)

(… from that abode the guard who presides over the holy place commanded me
to depart. … In the meantime, since a public resting-place is closed to me, may
it be granted me to lie hidden in some private spot.)

Having been rejected, Ovid's book laments how its own fate has – unjustly – been
intertwined with that of its author:

in genus auctoris miseri fortuna redundat,
    et patimur nati, quam tulit ipse, fugam. (*Tristia*, III.i.73–4)

(The fate of our unfortunate sire overflows upon his offspring, and we suffer at
our birth the exile which he has borne.)

He evokes a similar genealogical stain to that described in the *Complainte* where
Le Franc's persona fears that the sins of the father are being visited upon his
literary son ('mon filz'; l. 62):

En despit de moy, je n'en doubte,
On te regarde de travers. (*Complainte*, ll. 333–4)

(It's doubtless out of spite towards me that they're eyeing you suspiciously.)

Thus far my comparative analysis has focused on the similarities between the
Complainte and its Classical antecedent, with such similarities supporting the view
that a sincere appeal for reconciliation is represented in both texts. However, the
key difference between these two scenarios arises in the extent to which they each
constitute apologies, expressing repentance for offences committed previously
in an earlier work. Ovid, for his part, appears to seek forgiveness for his *Ars
amatoria*; he strives, in the *Tristia*, to distance himself from this earlier, notorious
work, acknowledging some wrongdoing ('mea poena'; II.578). He underlines the
distinction separating Ovid the man from the content of his literary work:

crede mihi, distant mores a carmine nostro –
    vita verecunda est, Musa iocosa mea –
magnaque pars mendax operum est et ficta meorum:
    plus sibi permisit compositore suo.
nec liber indicium est animi, sed honesta voluntas
    plurima mulcendis auribus apta ferens. (*Tristia*, II.353–8)

(I assure you, my character differs from my verse (my life is moral, my muse is gay), and most of my work, unreal and fictitious, has allowed itself more licence than its author has had. A book is not an evidence of one's soul, but an honourable impulse that presents very many things suited to charm the ear.)

By contrast, we have already seen how Le Franc retracts nothing from his *Champion* in the course of the *Complainte*. He sees nothing for which he need apologise, and thus addresses his Book:

Toutes fois n'as tu riens porté
(Soyes en seur, je le te jure)
Blechant aucune auctorité
Ou faisant a personne injure. (*Complainte*, ll. 249–52)

(However, you have carried nothing (be quite sure of this, I promise you) which may tarnish someone's authority or offend anyone.)

L'Acteur also proposes a theory of poetic composition quite contrary to that espoused by the narrator of the *Tristia*:

Or saches, fieulx, que ma science
N'est pour oreilles affoler:
Je n'en eulx oncq experience;
Ains est pour langues affiler. (*Complainte*, ll. 245–8)

(Now take heed, my son, that my science is not intended to delight the ear: I've no experience of that; rather it is intended to sharpen the tongue.)

His words do not aim at 'charming', at pleasing everyone, but at provoking his audience. It thereby follows that l'Acteur should emphasise, rather than diminish or deny, the close connection between man and work, father and son. Close comparison between Ovid's and Le Franc's respective animations of the relationship between an author and his work may thus be used to suggest the irony present in the latter's apparent suit for reconciliation. Indeed, the Classical antecedent provides a further, at least implicit, dimension of authority to the poet–patron negotiations being worked out in the *Complainte*: Le Franc manipulates a Latin *auctoritas* to align his own project, on the surface, with a famous plea for forgiveness, when what he is actually proposing is an unchanged script brandished as a challenge rather than withdrawn with apology.

We may now turn to address the physical *cadre* which frames the juxtaposition of the *Champion* and the *Complainte*, namely the second presentation copy, now BN, f. fr. 12476. How might this codicological context support or counter my alternative reading of the *Complainte* as a promotional strategy rather than an apologetic account of actual failure? Whether its compiler was trying to redeem Le

Franc's reputation or simply boost it, it is clear that BN, f. fr. 12476 was carefully designed to be more visually impressive than BR, 9466. First, it boasts a programme of 66 miniatures, which are regularly inserted to punctuate the *Champion*'s two columns of text; these miniatures offer vivid, often lurid snapshots of the famous women whose case is defended by the text, such as the bloody suicide of Dido, or the rape of Lucretia. Marginal notes and visual labels provide further aids to navigation. There is also evidence, as Pascale Charron has noted, for some of these images being specifically tailored towards currying favour with Philip.[29] As well as the presentation miniature and opening page of text being awash with emblems and heraldic images referring to Philip or to his chivalric Order of the Golden Fleece, certain images of the poem's pro-feminine hero protagonist, the eponymous Champion, assimilate him to the duke through his black-cloaked attire: a further gesture of flattery to the patron whom the prologue vaunts as a 'tres excellent et tres humain prince' with a 'singuliere devocion' (*Champion*, p. 8) to the cause of women. This iconographic arrangement thus seems a fairly conventional, if somewhat gushing expression of a compiler–author's perhaps desperate desire to impose his work and ensure its acceptance.[30] Yet why was Le Franc so bothered about gaining the Burgundian ear and eye? I should like to suggest that there is something else going on in this illustrative programme that shifts the balance of authority between poet and patron, putting the former in a more assertive, less defensive position. This 'something else' brings back into play the political dimension of the *Champion* – a dimension that its prologue appeared to play down in favour of *fictions amoureuses*, but that the *Complainte* flags up, although in a 'safe' way, and that is still present in the text in its second presentation copy. The sort of political dimension I allude to here is not the pageantry politics of emblems and heraldic display, nor, in fact, is it related to the ecclesiastical reformist polemic highlighted in the *Complainte*. It is related, instead, to another of Le Franc's personal campaigns, namely the restoration of peace between France and Burgundy, which brings us back to his position as 'basilien': as Joycelyne Gledhill Dickinson emphasises,

> From the first, the council of Basle had been particularly concerned with peace in Europe ... It is ... important [to] stress the tenacity with which the council clung to its chosen role of peacemaker: in the struggle with Eugenius IV over the

---

[29]   Charron, 'Les Réceptions', pp. 21–3.

[30]   Beyond the conventional gesture of incorporating a patron into a manuscript's illustrative programme (especially in presentation miniatures), we may also see this strategy to have been designed to play to a particular Burgundian interest in personal display: 'the display of the princely person ... was one of the Burgundians' most cherished representational devices': Peter J. Arnade, *Realms of Ritual: Burgundian Ceremony and Civic Life in Late-Medieval Ghent* (Ithaca, NY: Cornell University Press, 1996), p. 17.

dissolution, the council's work for peace was declared to be an essential reason for its continued existence.[31]

A significant event in its course of work were the peace negotiations at Arras in the summer of 1435.[32] Dickinson proposes that:

> to place the Congress in its rightful diplomatic setting, it should be treated as one incident in the long history of papal mediation between the states of Europe, and in that of the parleys which punctuated the Hundred Years War.[33]

Representatives of both Pope Eugenius and the Council acted as mediators at Arras, responding to two imperatives: those of securing general peace and, separately, of restoring harmonious relations between France and Burgundy in the wake of the Treaty of Troyes of 1420, which had allied Burgundy with England.[34] Le Franc presents a poetic vision of the congress's concluding rites in the Abbey of St Vaast through a precious allegory of conjoined ruby hearts being offered up to Amour during a ceremony in the Chapel of Love:[35]

> Tantost devant l'autel alerrent
> Ou, par grande devocion,
> Deux cueurs de rubis presenterent
> De tant noble condicion

---

[31]   Joycelyne Gledhill Dickinson, *The Congress of Arras 1435: A Study in Medieval Diplomacy* (Oxford: Clarendon Press, 1955), pp. 86–7.

[32]   Dickinson explains how successful conduct of the Council's embassy was a matter of prestige in affirming Basel's validity: *Congress*, p. 93.The congress officially commenced at the start of July, but, as records show, most of the protagonists did not appear until the end of the month; discussions continued until the agreed terms of the treaty were publicly declared in St Vaast on 21 September. As Mark Warner in particular points out, the discussions of 1435 were the culmination of a much longer process, and one in which similar terms of peace to those eventually agreed had already been on the table over ten years earlier: 'The Anglo-French dual monarchy and the House of Burgundy, 1420–1435: The survival of an alliance', *French History*, 11 (1997), pp. 103–30 (p. 112).

[33]   Dickinson, *Congress*, p. ix.

[34]   Dickinson, *Congress*, p. 84. They succeeded in the latter, if not in the former (*Congress*, p. 198). As Malcolm Vale describes, 'the war continued, despite the moral victories of the Valois cause': 'France at the end of the Hundred Years' War (*c.* 1420–1461)', in *The New Cambridge Medieval History, Volume VII c. 1415–c. 1500*, ed. by Christopher Allmand (Cambridge: Cambridge University Press, 1998), pp. 397–403 (p. 397).

[35]   Le Franc's presence at Arras has been accepted by critics as a given (e.g. *Champion*, p. viii), although corroborating documentary evidence for this is not cited; there is, however, beyond the general caveat that a narrator is a fictionalised first-person projection of the author, no particular reason to challenge the idea that the *Champion* Acteur's statement of his personal witness was informed by Le Franc's own experience of the congress.

…
Assez paroit que dessoudez
Eussent esté moult rudement.
Neantmains furent ils ressoudez
Ensemble si estroitement
Qu'il sembloit veritablement
Qu'on ne les peu deslier. (*Champion*, ll.1761–4; 1769–74)[36]

(They [= ambassadors representing Duke Philip and King Charles] went straight to the alter, on which, in a gesture of great devotion, they presented two ruby hearts of very noble condition … It was very clear that they had been torn asunder most brutally; however, they were now joined back together so neatly that it truly seemed impossible for anyone to separate them [again].)

This allegory befits the term 'precious' because it is quite conceivable that Le Franc is wanting to evoke the artifice, perhaps even a suspected speciousness,

---

[36]   For an overview of the documentary sources, see Dickinson, *Congress*, pp. xii–vxi. Surviving chronicle accounts of the ceremony of 21 September 1435 offer varying degrees of detail (and, indeed, differences in detail) regarding its events, order, and personnel: see, from the French perspective, Jean Chartier (*Chroniques de Charles VII, roi de France*, ed. by Vallet de Viriville, 3 vols (Paris: Jannet, 1858), I, pp. 193–208); for Burgundian vantage points, see Jean Le Fèvre (the herald 'Toison d'Or': *Chronique de Jean le Fèvre, siegneur de St-Rémy*, ed. by François Morand, 2 vols (Paris: Renouard, 1876–81), II (1881), pp. 327–61), La Marche (memorialist, though not official *indiciaire*), *Mémoires*, I (1883), pp. 196, 203–41), and Enguerran de Monstrelet (active in Burgundy, but not employed by the court: *La Chronique d'Enguerran de Monstrelet en deux livres avec pieces justificatives 1400–1444*, ed. by L. Douët-d'Arcq, 6 vols (Paris: Renouard, 1857–62), V (1861), pp. 151–83). The most meticulous detail is furnished, not unsurprisingly, by Antoine de La Taverne, provost of St Vaast (*Journal de la paix d'Arras*, ed. by André Bossuat (Paris: l'Avenir, 1936), pp. 79–82). On the evidence of all extant sources, the ruby hearts are entirely of Le Franc's own invention; however, a golden cross was involved in proceedings. It was held by the Cardinal of Sainte-Croix, Niccolò Albergati (the papal legate who had been acting as one of the mediators at Arras), for the two parties to touch as a sign of repentance for and forgiveness of the assassination of John the Fearless, Philip the Good's father, in 1419 (which had precipitated the Treaty of Troyes) (Monstrelet, *Chronique*, V (1861), p. 183; Dickinson, *Congress*, p. 180). Additionally, La Taverne makes interesting mention of the conclusion to a sermon pronounced the following day on the theme of Galatians 5:22 *Fructus spiritus: caritas, pax et gaudium*. The preacher, a Carmelite friar, ends with God's instruction to Ezekiel to take two tablets ('tablez de bos'), to write Juda on one and Joseph on the other, and to join them together as one (Ezekiel 37:15–19); he presents this as a metaphor ('raporta a moralité') for the reconciliation of the king and duke (*Journal*, p. 83). The motif of the heart desirous of peace was a commonplace in diplomatic rhetoric of the period: Nicolas Offenstadt, *Faire la paix au moyen âge: discours et gestes de paix pendant la guerre des cent ans* (Paris: Odile Jacob, 2007), pp. 103–5.

of this peace.[37] Political tensions between France and Burgundy were far from definitively resolved by the declaration of the treaty's terms on 21 September 1435, however much its ceremonial conclusion suggested perfect and lasting harmony and amity.[38]

One may thereby suggest that at least part of Le Franc's project in promoting the *Champion* was an attempt to impress upon Philip a need for further, more thoroughgoing reconciliation with France, and such a conclusion may be drawn from the miniature that features at the very end of the poem in BN, f. fr. 12476. I commented above how this manuscript's images are mostly interested in illustrating the *exempla* that the pro- and anti-feminine debaters enlist to amplify their arguments, but also represent the debaters themselves at certain points. In both cases, the miniatures adhere very closely to the text; the penultimate image, showing the ultimate triumph of the Champion, Free Will, as he is crowned victor by Lady Truth, is equally precise in its visual translation of textual activity. The final miniature, however, departs from the poem by adding an image to suggest what activity might have followed this crowning: it shows Free Will riding in a horse-drawn chariot being guided by Lady Reason towards two figures of noble bearing who are labelled the god of Love and Lady Peace. What political message may this image be seen to mobilise? The Champion, once again understood to represent Philip, is being physically directed towards Peace and Love to reflect the conduct exhorted of the duke as the proper response to, or *mise en pratique* of, a reading of the *Champion*: an exhortation to move for a more general and definitive peace with France under the auspices of Amour. One might see in this image a potential visual allusion to the phenomenon of ceremonial entries, whose political significance was carefully marshalled by the Burgundians, and often centred on the duke's person.[39] The final miniature showing Philip as Champion could, in

---

[37]   For an overall reassessment of Philip's motives to make peace in 1435, see Warner, 'The Anglo-French dual monarchy'.

[38]   Discussion of how to implement the treaty continued long after its proclamation: Anne-Brigitte Spitzbarth records that 40 percent of franco-burgundian meetings between 1435 and 1444 concerned the application of Arras's terms, amongst other issues: 'De la vassalité à la sujétion: l'application du traité d'Arras (21 septembre 1435) par la couronne', *Revue du nord*, 85 (2003), pp. 43–72 (p. 45, n. 5). Vaughan elaborates upon the uneasy alliance between France and Burgundy in the same period (*Philip the Good*, pp. 98–126) and also notes the particular example of the succession struggle in Tournai from 1433 to 1438 (pp. 219–20). La Marche describes breakdown of discussions at Nevers in 1442 that were attempting to arrange an amicable meeting between Philip and Charles VII (*Mémoires*, I, p. 250).

[39]   Arnade proposes that aristocratic posture and gesture, rather than actual speech, were the mainstay of such ceremonials: *Realms of Ritual*, p. 18. An entry ceremony habitually began with the duke and his company being met outside the city by a delegation. In BN, f. fr. 12476 this would be represented by Raison, here shown leading the duke into the city. Mime plays and *tableaux vivants* took place on the parade route offering what Hurbult calls a 'mythico-ritual performance' with a cultural function: both proclaiming and

fact, be read as a joyful ducal entry.[40] An entry ceremony habitually began with the duke and his company being met outside the city by a delegation. In BN, f. fr. 12476 this would be represented by Raison, here shown leading the duke into the city. Mime plays and *tableaux vivants* took place on the parade route, offering what Hurbult calls a 'mythico-ritual performance' with a cultural function: both proclaiming and re-establishing the cultural beliefs (rights, privileges, obligations) binding duke and city. Allegorical figures were used similar to those featured in Le Franc's poem representing Peace and Love. When the duke entered a city for the first time, he swore an oath, promising to uphold the city's established rights, privileges and customs. Is this effectively what Raison is seeking of the Champion/duke in BN, f. fr. 12476, that he vow anew to commit, indeed humbly submit, to love and peace as routes to political stability? One may also relate this image back to the ceremonial dimensions of Arras in 1435: not only, or even primarily, to the splendour and order of Philip's arrival procession, led by trumpeters, kings at arms, heralds and poursuivants,[41] but rather to the symbolic and didactic function of the various sermon themes ('theumes' – quotations from the Bible) selected by preachers at the congress's various masses, in especially that on 21 September, for example, the Bishop of Auxerre, Philip's confessor,

> fist une solempnelle predication ... [et] prist son theume: *Ecce quam bonum et quam jocundum*. Lequel theume demena moult haultement en remonstrant aux dessusdis prinches le bien de union fraternelle ... Item demena moult fort sondit sermon et predication sur ce que Abraham dist a Loth comme est contenu ou Livre de Genese, c'est assavoir: *Non sit jurgium inter me et te, neque pastores meos et pastores tuos, fratres enim sumus*. Sur quoy allegua amiable reconciliation, doulce communication et pluseurs aultres belles paroles servans oudit propos.[42]

> (gave a solemn oration ... [and] took as his theme: *Behold, how good and how pleasant it is for brethren to dwell together in unity!* He discussed the aforesaid

---

re-establishing the cultural beliefs (rights, privileges, obligations) binding duke and city. Allegorical figures were used similar to those featured in Le Franc's poem representing Peace and Love. When the duke entered a city for the first time, he swore an oath, promising to uphold the city's established rights, privileges and customs. Is this effectively what Raison is seeking of the Champion/duke in BN, f. fr. 12476, that he vow anew to commit, indeed humbly submit, to love and peace as routes to political stability?

[40]   According to at least one account of this ritual's *déroulement*: Jesse Hurbult, 'The city renewed: Decorations for the *joyeuses entrées* of Philip the Good and Charles the Bold', *Fifteenth Century Studies*, 19 (1992), pp. 73–84.

[41]   See, for example, Monstrelet, *Chronique*, V (1861), p. 135.

[42]   La Taverne, *Journal*, p. 81. The theme corresponds to Psalm 133:1, and the later reference is to Genesis 13:8. The English translation is my own, quoting *The Holy Bible: King James Version* (Cambridge: Cambridge University Press, 1995).

theme at great length, demonstrating to the above-named princes the merits of fraternal union ... He also elaborated substantially in his sermon and oration on what Abram said to Lot as is found in the Book of Genesis, that is to say: *Let there be no strife, I pray thee, between me and thee, and between my herdmen and thy herdmen; for we be brethren.* He evinced by this amicable reconciliation, peaceful communication and many other fine words serving the aforesaid subject matter.)

In the same way that a textual analogue to the fifteenth-century political situation is deployed by the preacher to reinforce the congress's imperative to its audience of secular princes, so, in BN, f. fr. 12476, is an analogous visual narrative introduced by the manuscript compiler to shore up the *Champion*'s underlying directive to its ducal dedicatee.

Earlier in this article it was suggested that the *Champion*'s prologue may not be as platitudinous as first appears in its flattery of Philip, its promotion of amorous fictions and its modesty topoi. A further passage from this same prologue seems singularly pertinent to my proposed interpretation of the poem's final miniature in BN, f. fr. 12476. The author presents his motivations for composing the poem:

aussy que l'onneur deu aux dames doibt estre soustenu et gardé et publié au gré de Verité, laquelle en fin en tenebres reluist et en prison est franche et les bouches closes desclost et les oreilles sourdes ouvre, j'ay jugié que, sans encourir crime de lese majesté, la victoire et le triumphe d'Amours et des dames celer ne devoye meismement, car Verité vouloit que j'en fusse herault. (*Champion*, p. 3)

(just as the honour due to ladies must be supported and protected and proclaimed at the behest of Truth, who in the final reckoning lights up the darkness, knows freedom when imprisoned, unlocks closed lips and opens deaf ears, I decided that, in the same way, without incurring any crime of treason, I must not conceal the victory and triumph of Love and ladies, for Truth wanted me to be its/her herald.)

With a parenthetical self-exculpation against causing offence, the poet declares himself to be the herald of Truth who opens the way to the victory of Love by promoting action. Le Franc does not 'hide' the triumph of Love and ladies – it is the explicit verdict of the poem's fictional narrative. What his mention of 'hiding' triggers, though, is a sense of something being concealed within this personified tale, or, more precisely, of the poet garnering the resources of *fictions amoureuses* to present through fabular fiction an allegory of political instruction. In other words, to go back to the quote with which this article opened, the *Champion* is an axe that still has a force to wield.

When discussing above an appropriate political context in which to interpret BN, f. fr. 12476, I mentioned pageantry politics as a propagandistic tool wielded by Burgundian dukes. By way of conclusion, it is interesting to consider this cultural dimension of contemporary political authority as a resource that may be exploited by the poet in respect of the patron, as if trumping the duke at his own game. If we assume Le Franc to have been the compiler of BN, f. fr. 12476, he may be seen in this manuscript to harness the double-edged nature of the importance of symbolic representation in the Burgundian political economy. As Arnade comments, 'ritual made the duke, the duchess, and ... courtiers politically supreme yet eminently malleable: it constantly fashioned them from one thing into another'.[43] In the concluding miniature of the *Champion*, Le Franc thus plays to the duke's fondness for powerful images of his princely person, but also profits from the flexibility of such representation and its potential for ambiguity. A more 'innocent', uncontroversial reading of the final miniature would see it as a further celebratory reinforcement of the particular peace achieved at Arras, as opposed to the more polemical exhortation to a general peace. Carrying this intersection between cultural and literary authority further, one may note that, while the Burgundian court dressed themselves in mythical and literary clothing, evoking the world of medieval romance, Le Franc puts the shoe on the other foot, having his amorous fictions take on, as expediency requires, historical identities. Finally, invoking a second cultural context, and enlisting the quotation that features as this article's epigram, one may liken Le Franc's hermeneutic enterprise of symbolic manipulation to the deceptive powers of those artificial devices and twisted mirrors found in the trick rooms of the ducal residence of Hesdin.[44] He turns on duke Philip the theatrical properties of such contrivances, presenting a seemingly innocuous book of poems which, when studied more closely, squirts political soot that may tarnish the apparently blemish-free prince. Le Franc thereby establishes himself the servant poet, rather than his powerful patron, as master narrator.

This brief exploration of the apparent change in fortune experienced by Le Franc's *Champion* is intended to serve as a case study for probing new possibilities in the workings of poet–patron relations in mid-fifteenth century Burgundy. Whatever our understanding of the tale of rejection recounted in the *Complainte*, the poem itself, offered as a commentary on, rather than simple supplement to, the earlier *Champion*, complicates our reading of the *Champion* and its previous presentation, raising questions of polemical content and material design which entail potentially rather subtle and shifting negotiations between the authorities of poet, compiler and patron, not to mention, within the *Complainte*, the voice of the Book itself. The very debatability of the Book's tale of woe incites a more

---

[43]   Arnade, *Realms of Ritual*, p. 29.

[44]   These trick rooms, originally installed in the thirteenth century, were elaborately refurbished in 1433; an account entry detailing how £1000 was spent on upgrading the mechanical contrivances describes with relish the devices of illusion and deception established therein (Vaughan, *Philip the Good*, pp. 137–9); see Arnade, *Realms of Ritual*, pp. 30–31. Huesmann discusses the role of these chambers to function as spectacular demonstration of ducal control: 'here, Philippe le Bon showed himself as a host who was lord over simulation, mechanics and nature' ('Hospitality', p. 194).

interrogative approach to every aspect of a work's presentation, starting with the basic question of whether or not it was accepted and how one should evaluate the evidence offered by a manuscript for its own reception. The simple event of presentation is rendered multiple and contestable; Le Franc shrewdly exploits the pronounced fictionality of his poetic sequel, with its dream vision framework, to manipulate the reality of the original poem's presentation. The *Complainte's* intertextual connections demonstrate the complex layering of a work's authority through dialogue with antecedent *auctoritas* as well as with the didactic message of a contemporary text by the same poet. The role of paratextual materials, here proposing particular interaction between the prologue and final miniature, is shown to afford strategic possibilities to the compiler of a manuscript (whether or not this agent may be identified with the author) to re-cast the poem in a new didactic mould, one of political counsel or even, in certain lights, satire.[45] Finally, the manuscript's cultural context is identified as providing at very least a pungent parallel to its own dynamic power-play, a set of specific concrete practices against which to view the issue of patronal authority in a more challenging, flexible and interactive light.

Did the *Champion* end up achieving its longed-for *renom lequel tousjours dure*? It survives to us in a further seven manuscripts, of which three boast lavish programmes of illustration and are thought to form a family with the second presentation copy; two printed editions, one from Lyons and one from Paris, suggest circulation until the early 1530s. Moving from the fifteenth to the twenty-first century, there still seems to be a valid case for taking the *Champion* and *Complainte* off their dusty shelf and listening attentively to what this Book has to say: the *Champion* may proclaim overtly in its prologue to deliver a message as benign, derivative and comfortably clichéd as that professed by the minstrel in a Donald Reilly cartoon in *The New Yorker*:[46] however, just as the minstrel's exaggerated innocuousness discloses 'between the lines', the *Complainte* reveals a much more dynamic, interesting and multi-faceted set of negotiations between poet and patron in late medieval culture.

---

[45]   Jung's preliminary analysis of elements of the poem's prologue points up Le Franc's satirical intentions as an imitation of Roman poets. He notes the prologue's explicit naming of Perseus and Juvenal together with its implicit evocation of Horace through mention of the principle of conversational poetic language: 'Le Franc se présente ainsi comme le Horace français' ('Situation', p. 21). Ennius is also named (*Champion*, p. 4).

[46]   Donald Reilly, *The New Yorker Collection*, <http://www.cartoonbank.com> (Image ID: 15261) [accessed 23 March 2013].

Chapter 4

Authority through Antiquity – Humanist Historiography and Regional Descriptions: The Cases of Erasmus Stella, Johannes Cuspinian and Robert Gaguin[1]

Albert Schirrmeister

From 1500 onwards humanism quickly spread from its birthplace in Italy throughout European countries. Owing to the diverse social and cultural conditions of its reception and use, however, different regions developed very different approaches to humanistic practices. Sometimes, in the case of Germany, these differences have been interpreted as the most important elements of this scholarly habitus, and there has even been a tendency to interpret German humanism as an autochthonous movement.[2] Nevertheless, a more or less complete set of practices can be discerned, which can be used to characterise what I mean when I speak about 'humanism', making way for a comparison of the different European humanistic cultures.[3]

---

[1]   This contribution forms part of the Project A4: 'Transformations of the writing of national and regional history through the reception of antiquity in European humanism' within the Collaborative Research Centre 644 'Transformations of Antiquity' at the Humboldt University, Berlin. Research for this project was financed by the German Research Foundation. I have much profited from discussions with my colleagues Stefan Schlelein and Patrick Baker and the head of our project, Johannes Helmrath.

[2]   For a short and concise overview of German humanism see Noel L. Brann, 'Humanism in Germany', in *Renaissance Humanism*, ed. by Albert Rabil, 3 vols (Philadelphia, PA: University of Pennsylvania Press, 1988), II, pp. 123–56 (pp. 123, 136); Lewis W. Spitz, 'The course of German Humanism', in *Itinerarium Italicum: The Profile of the Italian Renaissance in the Mirror of its European Transformations. Dedicated to Paul Oskar Kristeller on the Occasion of his 70th birthday*, ed. by Heiko A. Oberman and Thomas A. Brady Jr (Leiden: Brill, 1975), pp. 371–436.

[3]   Robert Black, 'Humanism', in *The New Cambridge Medieval History, Volume VII c. 1415–1500*, ed. by Christopher Allmand (Cambridge: Cambridge University Press, 1998), pp. 243–77 (p. 252): 'A humanist is thus someone who acts like other humanists; this is how contemporaries would have identified humanism, and such a definition, stripped of historical paraphernalia, will work equally for us.'

First of all, humanists established a normative image of antiquity, especially of Roman antiquity. This was then combined with an ontological view of language, whereby only a classical use of the Latin language was considered acceptable for discussions of moral, ethical or scholarly matters. In addition to this close tie to ancient culture, humanism's foundation in rhetoric was decisive for its scholarly practices. A clear example of the difference between humanist and established university praxis can be found in the preference for the *declamatio*, or rhetorically polished oration, over the *disputatio*, along with a predilection for a decidedly unceremonious, less formal and less strict form of the (written) dialogue. This basic understanding of scholarly standards was also closely linked with other practices of an explicitly social nature. For humanists, all knowledge had to be useful for politics and ethical choices. This understanding of a fundamental practical use of scholarly knowledge also defined the social role that humanists hoped to attain. Their aim was to establish themselves at a court and – if possible – at a university. Because the humanists were up against considerable competition among the various actors in these social configurations, it was necessary to find patrons who could help them in their attempts to establish themselves in these positions. There was a tendency to establish networks of actors interested in humanistic culture – networks of literary actors in a broader sense. Hence, they did not only have to establish themselves and to promote their careers, but also to promote the humanistic idea of the usefulness of their specific forms of erudite knowledge. With this intention, the humanists acted in contrast to and conflict with traditional aristocratic and scholastic forms of social and cultural distinction.

I

One of the major fields in which humanists attempted to obtain a dominant position at the European courts was historiography.[4] With their works of history – and, to a certain extent, geography – humanists tried to legitimate the power of their princely governance and to represent the pre-eminence of their nation in the European concurrence of power by constructing a national 'community of honour'.[5]

---

[4]   Johannes Helmrath, 'Probleme und Formen nationaler und regionaler Historiographie des deutschen und europäischen Humanismus um 1500', in *Spätmittelalterliches Landesbewußtsein in Deutschland*, ed. by Matthias Werner, Vorträge und Forschungen, 61 (Stuttgart: Thorbecke, 2005), pp. 333–92; *Diffusion des Humanismus. Studien zur nationalen Geschichtsschreibung europäischer Humanisten*, ed. by Johannes Helmrath, Ulrich Muhlack and Gerrit Walther (Göttingen: Wallstein Verlag, 2002).

[5]   Caspar Hirschi, *Wettkampf der Nationen: Konstruktionen einer deutschen Ehrgemeinschaft an der Wende vom Mittelalter zur Neuzeit* (Göttingen: Wallstein Verlag, 2005).

In this paper, I would like to examine three humanists, Erasmus Stella, Johannes Cuspinian and Robert Gaguin, who used humanistic practices in different social, political and cultural contexts, and to show how these different contexts influenced their work. Because the first two lived in the Holy Roman Empire, and the third in France, these three authors differ substantially in terms of social, national and cultural identity.

Erasmus Stella (Stuler)[6] wrote a history and description of Prussia.[7] He was born in Leipzig around 1460, and received his bachelor's and master's degrees at the University of Leipzig in 1480 and 1482. In all probability, he studied medicine at the University of Bologna since he referred to the medical professor Giovanni Garzoni as his teacher. In 1500, he worked as a physician in Zwickau, a town in Electoral Saxony. He apparently enjoyed a good reputation at the electoral court of Frederick the Wise since he was affiliated to its council. This affiliation helped him to advance in his career, later becoming a personal physician of the Grandmaster of the Teutonic Order in Königsberg, Frederick of Saxony (the cousin of Frederick the Wise), who was Grandmaster from 1498 until his death in 1510. Frederick and Erasmus Stella went to Prussia at a time of acute conflict between the Order and Poland. Frederick had not previously been a Teutonic knight; he based his power and his political actions on his secular council instead of the Order's chapter, as was usually the case for the grandmasters before him. Although Erasmus Stella was well respected at the Grandmaster's court, he returned early to Zwickau, where he worked as a physician until his death. On several occasions, he was the town's representative at the Electoral-Saxon parliament. In addition to the description of Prussia, he also wrote some miscellanies on Zwickau's local history. In addition, we know of another printed book, a *Libellus eximius de gemmis*, printed in 1517 at Nuremberg. This treatise on gemstones is important for an understanding of his position at the Grandmaster's court in Königsberg. It was dedicated to the Bishop Hiob von Dobeneck, the same man who challenged him to write his description of Prussia.[8]

The second example is Johannes Cuspinian, who was an imperial diplomat in approximately the same period, and who began a description of Austria in 1527,

---

[6] Hans Joachim Schönborn, *Lebensgeschichte und Geschichtsschreibung des Erasmus Stella: Ein Beitrag zur Geschichte des gelehrten Fälschertums im 16. Jahrhundert* (Düsseldorf: Nolte, 1938).

[7] Erasmus Stella, 'Erasmi Stellae Libonothani De Borussiae Antiquitatibus Libri duo', in *Scriptores Rerum Prussicarum oder Die Geschichtsquellen der preussischen Vorzeit*, ed. by Theodor Hirsch and others, 5 vols (Leipzig: Hirzel, 1861–74), IV (1870), pp. 275–98.

[8] Stella, *De Borussiae Antiquitatibus*, p. 285. 'Ego autem hanc scribendi provinciam non tam mea sponte quam iussu venerandi antistis Jobi Pomesaniensis a nullo antea tentatam accepi' ('I accepted to write about this province not of my own accord, but following the challenge of the venerable Hiob Pomesanius').

which remained unfinished.[9] Cuspinian was born in December 1473 at Schweinfurt in Franconia, and he died in 1529 in Vienna. Like Erasmus Stella, Cuspinian was also a physician. Rather than Italy, he studied in Leipzig and Würzburg before moving to Vienna, where King Maximilian crowned him as Poet Laureate in 1493.[10] In Vienna, he came into contact with the flourishing humanistic circles. In 1499, he became a professor at the university there. After the death of the German 'arch-humanist' Conrad Celtis in 1508, he became a professor of poetry and was considered the most important humanist in Vienna. After 1510, he spent many years in the diplomatic service of the Emperor, especially in Poland and Hungary. His most important diplomatic success was the so-called First Viennese Congress in 1515 with the Polish and the Hungarian kings, who acceded to an agreement about a double marriage that would establish the Austro-Hungarian Monarchy. Especially for his edition of the most important German historiographical source of the Middle Ages, Otto von Freising's chronicles, he received considerable recognition among German humanists. In addition, he edited several antique texts and wrote histories of the Roman consuls and the Roman emperors, including the emperors of the Holy Roman Empire (*De Caesaribus atque imperatoribus romanis* and *Consules*).[11]

The French author Robert Gaguin was one of the first humanists to write national histories that rivalled those of the Italian humanists.[12] Born in 1433 in Calonnes (Artois), he is the oldest of the three authors, and he is distinct from the two German authors since he was the Minister General of the Trinitarian order from 1473 until his death in 1501 and therefore a cleric. Like Cuspinian, he also taught at a university (he was Dean of the Faculty of Arts at the University of Paris from 1483 until 1500), and was entrusted with a number of diplomatic missions by the French Kings Louis XI and Charles VIII: to Germany in 1477, Italy in 1485 and 1486, and England in 1489 and 1490.[13] In addition to his *Compendium de*

---

[9]   Hans Ankwicz-Kleehoven, *Der Wiener Humanist Johannes Cuspinian. Gelehrter und Diplomat zur Zeit Kaiser Maximilians I.* (Graz: Böhlau, 1959). *Austria* was first printed in 1553 in Basel with the other historiographical texts.

[10]   Albert Schirrmeister, *Triumph des Dichters: Gekrönte Intellektuelle im 16. Jahrhundert*, Frühneuzeitstudien, NF 4 (Cologne: Böhlau, 2003).

[11]   Elisabeth Klecker, 'Extant adhuc in Pannonia monumenta Severi: Historia-Augusta-Rezeption und humanistisches Selbstverständnis in Cuspinians Caesares', in *Medien und Sprachen humanistischer Geschichtsschreibung*, ed. by Johannes Helmrath, Albert Schirrmeister and Stefan Schlelein, Transformationen der Antike, 11 (Berlin: de Gruyter, 2009), pp. 77–98.

[12]   Franck Collard, *Un historien au travail à la fin du XVe siècle. Robert Gaguin* (Geneva: Droz, 1996), p. 301.

[13]   Henri-Jean Martin and Jean-Marc Chatelain, *La Naissance du livre moderne (XIVe–XVIIe siècles): Mise en page et mise en texte du livre français* (Paris: Éditions du Cercle de la Librairie, 2000), p. 146.

Francorum origine et gestis, first published in 1495, he also translated Caesar's *Commentarii de Bello Gallico* for the French king that was published in 1485.[14]

These three authors handle literary techniques in very different ways, and their involvement within humanist circles and with powerful political connections was also different. These social and cultural differences influenced the successful recognition of authority claimed by all of them.

In comparing these three authors, I would like to examine their more or less distinctive philological (semantic and narrative) practices and to show how they imitated and continued the antique models in terms of both style and content. This will be followed by some brief remarks concerning their typographical claim to authority, which should be interpreted as closely connected to these philological forms since the material form strongly influenced the way in which their texts were meant to be perceived. By including social elements of the claim to authority – the dedications to political authorities and the poetic elements from other humanists in their books – I shall sum up with the reason for the success or failure of the actions of these humanists.

II

Despite the considerable differences between the authors, there are still several common starting points that make a comparison of their literary output possible: the literary claims to authority are generally marked by the interplay between antique authority, signs of authorship and questions of literary genre.

Especially in the case of humanistic historiography, the allusion to Roman antiquity was important in two different areas that referred to one another in a reciprocal way. Roughly since Petrarch and his coronation as Poet Laureate, Roman antiquity, considered as part of their own French or German history, promised, for humanists, participation in Roman imperial history.[15] Only Roman imperial history merited the name of 'history', while other stories were considered merely stories about barbarians.[16] The success of this conception was based on the older medieval concept of the *translatio imperii*, the transferral of the Roman

---

[14]   Frédéric Duval, 'Le Livre des commentaires Cesar sur le fait des batailles de Gaule par Robert Gaguin (1485) ou de l'art de la transposition', *La Figure de Jules César au Moyen Âge et à la Renaissance* (= *Cahier de Recherches médiévales*), 13 (2006), pp. 167–82.

[15]   Joseph Burney Trapp, 'The Poet Laureate: Rome, Renovatio and Translatio Imperii', in *Rome in the Renaissance: The City and the Myth*, ed. by Paul A. Ramsey, Medieval and Renaissance Texts and Studies, vol. 18 (Binghamton, NY: Centre for Medieval and Renaissance Studies, 1982), pp. 93–130.

[16]   Anthony Grafton, 'Invention of traditions and tradition of invention in Renaissance Europe: The strange case of Annius of Viterbo', in *The Transmission of Culture in Early Modern Europe*, ed. by Anthony Grafton and Ann Blair (Philadelphia, PA: University of Pennsylvania Press, 1990), pp. 8–38.

Empire to the French or the German kingship. Rome remained the stable point of orientation for all historiography because of the given eschatological status of the Roman Empire and the possibility of combining this concept with the claim to political authority. On the other hand, and with some conceptual difficulties, certain German humanists combined Roman antiquity with the very pressing concept of the indigenous and undefeated German people. In this case, the Roman authors were considered eyewitnesses of German participation in normative Roman antiquity.[17]

Erasmus Stella

This initially seems to have been the case for Erasmus Stella. However, he negotiated certain difficulties by making a few conceptual changes. In striking contrast to the image of the 'noble savage' propagated by the German humanists for the Germanic peoples, he drew a picture of the imperial German cultivators of barbarian Prussia. His account ends with the establishment of a new political order by the Teutonic Knights. Erasmus Stella used etymological techniques to demonstrate the continuity from the Germanic era to the German era in Culmerland (Chełmno Land). He attempted to compose a complete and consistent representation of the German history of Prussia.[18]

As sources of his description, Stella mentioned among others, Pliny, Tacitus and Caesar, using both open citation and dissimulated allusion to establish the image of an initially quite primitive Germanic order in contrast to the indigenous but barbarian and ferocious Prussian peoples. Stella described the Teutonic Order as a source of a salutary order after Prussia's revolts against and disputes with the 'new Caesar', Emperor Frederick I Barbarossa. In Stella's account, Emperor Frederick Barbarossa is described as the legitimate successor of the Roman Caesar. He is seen as having brought peace to Prussia in the same way as Caesar arbitrated the quarrels of the Gallic peoples.[19]

Stella used some semantic techniques to point out the legitimacy of the German power in Prussia.[20] For example, he described Prussians explicitly as '*ferox*'

---

[17] Dieter Mertens, 'Die Instrumentalisierung der "Germania" des Tacitus durch die deutschen Humanisten', in *Zur Geschichte der Gleichung 'germanisch-deutsch': Sprache und Namen, Geschichte und Institutionen*, ed. by Heinrich Beck (Berlin: De Gruyter, 2004), pp. 37–101.

[18] Schönborn, *Lebensgeschichte*, p. 76.

[19] Gaius Iulius Caesar, *C. Iuli Caesaris commentarii*, vol. I. *commentarii belli Gallici*, ed. by Alfred Klotz (Leipzig: Teubner 1921), *lib. Vii.*

[20] The analysis of the semantic structure and the characteristic, distinctive semantic elements of the humanistic historiography represent a major part of the research of our project. We have now established a database to study the different semantic elements of the humanist histories and their relation to antique models. What I can mention here are no more than the first observations.

(ferocious), as opposed to the Germanic peoples for whom he emphasised the term 'cultor', since only the Germanic peoples cultivated Prussia agriculturally. In the juridical discourse of the time, this kind of cultivation was considered an act of legitimate appropriation rather than an oppressive and usurping occupation.[21]

Because Greek ethnological and geographical literature was inadequate to serve as a basis for descriptions of nations and regions in northern Europe, humanistic historiography tended to draw on Roman authors. Nevertheless, it does not seem to have been only the lack of information in the case of Greek literature that brought about the predominance of Roman literature. Klaus Müller has pointed out that Roman geographical and ethnographical literature, and especially Varro and Tacitus, was written for use in cases of war and for administration.[22] If we can agree with these analytical conclusions, these texts might have had a special attraction for sixteenth-century historiography, which was always a historiography at the service of political power.

It has been shown that, although Erasmus Stella occasionally followed medieval models to define the Prussian frontiers, he was also the first to add some elements of antique ethnographical literature when he defined the eastern frontier of *Borussia* with the region of the Alans, and the southern frontier with the Amaxobian Mountains.[23] In this way, Stella followed Tacitus' example in *Germania* – also in the text's structure. The first chapter of Tacitus' account begins with a description of the geographical frame; he used ethnic groups, rivers and mountains to define *Germania*'s frontiers before resuming a discussion of the (mythological) origin of the Germanic peoples. Tacitus' text focuses on everything that differed from a Roman point of view and was thus typical of the Germans.[24] According to this model, Stella's narration seems to be a good example of Stephen Greenblatt's thesis that cultural knowledge is frequently used to designate and arrange experience. Perhaps, in this sense, we should understand – at least partially – the characteristic tendency of the humanistic regional descriptions to combine ethnological, historical and geographical details. After the first steps, made in the case of Prussia by Enea Silvio Piccolomini, it was Erasmus Stella who

---

[21]   Daniel Damler has demonstrated the importance of these semantic denotations for the discussion between Columbus' inheritors and the Spanish crown in his article: Daniel Damler, 'Pars pro toto. Die juristische Erfindung der Entdeckung Amerikas', *Zeitsprünge*, 10 (2006), pp. 424–71.

[22]   Klaus E. Müller, *Geschichte der antiken Ethnographie und ethnologischen Theoriebildung: Von den Anfängen bis auf die byzantinischen Historiographen*, 2 vols, Studien zur Kulturkunde, 29 and 52 (Wiesbaden: Steiner, 1972/1980).

[23]   Norbert Kersken, 'Aspekte des preußischen Geschichtsdenkens im 16. Jahrhundert', in *Preußische Landesgeschichte: Festschrift für Bernhard Jähnig zum 60. Geburtstag*, ed. by Udo Arnold, Mario Glauert and Jürgen Sarnowsky, Einzelschriften der Historischen Kommission für ost- und westpreußische Landesforschung (Marburg: N.G. Elwart Verlag, 2001), pp. 439–56 (p. 444f.).

[24]   Müller, *Geschichte der antiken Ethnographie*, Studien zur Kulturkunde, 52, p. 82.

complemented his description with considerations of Prussia's flora and fauna, especially the notes on amber and the wisent.[25] Stephen Greenblatt has argued that the description of cultural institutions and cultural practices can be used to enforce an imaginative order of exclusions in society. He therefore attached considerable importance to the power of anecdotal narration.[26] The anecdote may be understood as a kind of case study, and it may be understood in the form of an *exemplum* as a historical narration *par excellence.*[27] The concrete power of the example helps to bring about the humanistic ideal of *historia magistra vitae.*

Johannes Cuspinian

This was Johannes Cuspinian's ideal, too. In his printed oration, he combined actuality and perpetuity. He wrote his *Oratio protreptica* after the Hungarian defeat against the Turks in 1526, in which the young Hungarian King Ludwig died. The text included a description of Hungary as a part of an *exhortatio*, which was intended to engage the German princes in the struggle against the Turks. The description of embattled Hungary was meant to demonstrate the legitimacy of the struggle. Thus Cuspinian described Hungary's participation in Roman civilisation. Elsewhere, in a dedicatory letter to the imperial treasurer, Jacob Villinger, he explained the importance of historiography for the cultural identity of an individual and a social community:

> But among our people, there is no one with so little understanding that he would not want to explore with pleasure the customs and traditions and deeds of other kingdoms or countries, should he have the chance. I am of the same opinion as Plutarch that man flees nothing more than ignorance and obscurity, to which we fall prey should we live in such a way that no one remembers us once we are gone. If possible, we should leave a few monuments to bear witness to our lives. One man leaves children, another books, another land, another possessions,

---

[25] Kersken, 'Aspekte des preußischen Geschichtsdenkens', p. 445: 'A closer examination of the nature of the state cannot be found in earlier state historiographies. First Piccolomini added an observation regarding the nature and culture of the state with an allusion to the *locus amoenus*. Erasmus Stella then commented on single aspects of the nature of the state. He pays particular attention to amber, based on Pliny's observations, but without mentioning anything about the contemporary amber trade.'

[26] Stephen Jay Greenblatt, *Marvelous Possessions. The Wonder of the New World* (Chicago, IL: University of Chicago Press, 1993), p. 3: 'If anecdotes are registers of the singularity of the contingent ... they are at the same time recorded as representative anecdotes, that is, as significant in terms of a larger progress or pattern that is the proper subject of a history perennially deferred in the traveller's relation of further anecdotes.'

[27] *Fallstudien: Theorie – Geschichte – Methode*, ed. by Johannes Süßmann, Susanne Scholz and Gisela Engel, Frankfurter kulturwissenschaftliche Beiträge, 1 (Berlin: trafo Verlag, 2007).

another estates, another a good name. We all try to leave behind a good name; otherwise death prevails.[28]

Thus, compared with Erasmus Stella, Cuspinian found another way of incorporating a kind of antiquity into his texts. Since Austria and Hungary took part in the Roman civilisation, he integrated many antique sources into his texts. He not only quoted Roman authors, but also mentioned antique inscriptions and monuments. This was particularly the case in his *Austria*, where he announced a list of the texts he used as sources; and to enforce his argument, he pointed out what he had observed himself in antique monuments and texts, and that he had read these antique inscriptions.[29]

Cuspinian and other humanists combined this emphasis on their 'autopsy' of testimonials with a more or less systematic imitation of Roman antique models. They not only collected antique inscriptions but also fabricated inscriptions and coins to document the cultural identity of their own group or their own personality. Hence, the list of the sources used in Cuspinian's *Austria* mentions Pliny, Livy and Roman inscriptions next to medieval documents and texts of Cuspinian's friends. It is well known that this tendency also led to the extreme case of Annius of Viterbo, who buried and found inscriptions he had produced himself with the sole intention of bearing witness to the Etruscan past of his native city Viterbo.[30]

These practices are integrated in nearly all humanistic historiography.[31] One could argue that the humanists perceived the distance between their own time and

---

[28]   Johannes Cuspinian, *Johann Cuspinians Briefwechsel*, ed. by Hans Ankwicz-Kleehoven, Humanistenbriefe, 2 (Munich: Beck, 1933), no. 32, pp. 68–70 (p. 69). A letter to Jakob Villinger, Vienna, August 20, 1515 reads: 'Sed ex plebe nemo est tam excors, qui non velit aliorum regnorum ac provinciarum non libenter indagare et ritus et mores et res gestas, si habere copiam possit. Ob id cum Plutarcho sentio hominem nihil omnium aeque refugere, ac ignorantiam et tenebras atque ideo non esse vivendum, ut nemo nos vixisse senciat. Sed ita potius vivere, ut aliquo monimento, si fieri potest, nos vixisse testemur. Hic post se liberos, hic libros relinquit, hic praedia, hic possessiones, hic aedificia, hic bonam famam, omnes bonum nomen conemur post nos relinquere, alioquin vita nostra mors potius est.'

[29]   Johannes Cuspinian, *Austria Ioannis Cuspiniani cum omnibus eiusdem marchionibus, ducibus, archiducibus, ac rebus preclare ad haec usque tempora ab iisdem gestis* (Frankfurt: Wechel, 1601), p. 611: 'annexa tabula, quae scriptis … testabatur [missed]'; p. 651: 'sicut ex vetustissimis monumentis & annalibus observavi …; aspexi et legi hanc in eo inscriptionem.'

[30]   Anthony Grafton, *Forgers and Critics: Creativity and Duplicity in Western Scholarship* (London: Collins & Brown, 1990), pp. 28, 55.

[31]   See Dieter Mertens, 'Landeschronistik im Zeitalter des Humanismus und ihre spätmittelalterlichen Wurzeln', in *Deutsche Landesgeschichtsschreibung im Zeichen des Humanismus*, ed. by Franz Brendle et al. (Stuttgart: Steiner, 2001), p. 56: 'New is the inclusion of antique remains. Real objects in the form of Roman coins and inscriptions became the subject of practical as well as literary collections, but they were also included in

normative Roman antiquity, but that they tried to transcend this distance through their practices. To understand this better, we might consider an observation made recently by Frank Wittchow reading Livy. He argues that the city 'Rome' is so important for Roman identity not because the Romans lived there, but because of the monuments, the memorial sites. Wittchow has revealed that Camillus needed to represent the city to the Romans in his famous oration after Rome's destruction by the Gauls (Livy, 5, 51–4) in a way that could represent Roman identity.[32]

Yet however the humanist authors used the Roman models, they gave their narration a special point of view that was very distinct from classical texts, as Frank Wittchow has recently pointed out. Even if Johannes Cuspinian alluded to the famous *sine ira et studio* from the annals of Tacitus, he replaced these words with *odium* and *favor*. Cuspinian gave the ideals of historiography a completely new sense, since *favor* and *odium* had been used to write unfairly about *Austria*. Johannes Cuspinian wanted – as opposed to Tacitus in the case of Rome – to write a positive account of Austria.[33] The aim of humanistic historiography was to structure memory and to form identity on the basis of legitimate power, as Cuspinian wrote in the above-quoted letter. In this sense, Cuspinian enforced the genealogical legitimacy of the Habsburg family and combined their history with the antique history of *Austria* and the account of Saint Leopold.

Robert Gaguin

Robert Gaguin referred to the same antique authority when he conceived his *Compendium de origine et gestis de Francorum*. In this, he was concerned to distinguish his *historia* from a chronicle, since, owing to the predominant confusion and inelegance, this literary genre was not generally appreciated.[34] For Gaguin, the *Compendium* is not only a narration but also an oration. He took into account the theoretical efforts made by the Italian humanists, who also referred to the antique models, and therefore took Livy and Leonardo Bruni as points of orientation.[35]

---

the historiographical presentation. Furthermore, the Roman epigraphical sources also leant the recent epigraphy a special historiographical dignity. Beatus Rhenanus wrote epigraphs about a recent event in his hometown Schlettstadt and about its earlier history. He took care of their arrangement, and he also fixed them historiographically when he included high- and late-medieval inscriptions in the long Sélestat chapter of his *Rerum Germanicarum libri tres*.'

[32] Frank Wittchow, 'Von Fabius Pictor zu Polydorus Vergil: Zur Transformation narrativer Modelle der antiken römischen Geschichtsschreibung in der Humanistenhistorie', in *Medien und Sprachen humanistischer Geschichtsschreibung*, ed. by Johannes Helmrath, Albert Schirrmeister and Stefan Schlelein, Transformationen der Antike, 11 (Berlin: de Gruyter, 2009), pp. 47–76 (p. 62).

[33] Wittchow, 'Von Fabius Pictor zu Polydorus Vergil', p. 48.

[34] Collard, *Un historien au travail*, p. 70.

[35] Collard, *Un historien au travail*, p. 70.

Hence, Gaguin intervened in his narration; he provided an introduction and a commentary, and wrote in the first person. He spoke openly about his selective account of history: 'selecting those things that are most useful from the series of things' and he admitted that he was not convinced about the origins of the French people – 'To me, the true origin of the Franks is not at all surely known.'[36] With these remarks, he responds to two of the most important principles of humanist historiography: *'fides et eloquencia'*.[37]

In Gaguin's *Compendium*, the second point, the eloquent narration of history, forms the basis of his attempt to bring about a renovation of French history. Of course, there is also the tendency to disprove legends and to establish a certain basis for historical narration, and this tendency seems to be more present in the Latin version of Gaguin's text, as Michael Randall has recently shown in his study of the conversion of the French Royal heraldic symbol from a toad to lilies.[38] However, the effort to re-establish classical Latin, the ideal of clarity, which Gaguin claimed in opposition to the medieval obscurity of the more or less official *Grandes Chroniques*,[39] left numerous traces in such diverse linguistic elements as syntax and lexis or the linking of the narrative elements and the inclusion of the orations. It has been observed that Gaguin took considerable care throughout the many re-editions of the *Compendium* to modify these elements, to ultimately attain variety, and always with the classical ideal of *utilitas et delectatio* in mind.[40] He did not only avoid employing unusual words, but also, when writing about French medieval political institutions, translated the vocabulary into classical Latin.[41]

III

In the sixteenth century, humanistic texts generally circulated in the form of printed books. At the same time, however, there were many manuscripts in circulation, which were borrowed, copied and discussed in humanistic circles. One of the major applications of these manuscripts – one for which they still seem to have been preferred to printed books – was dedication as a splendid

---

[36]   Elizabeth A.R. Brown, 'The Trojan origins of the French. The commencement of a myth's demise, 1450–1520', in *Medieval Europeans: Studies in Ethnic Identity and National Perspectives in Medieval Europe*, ed. by Alfred P. Smyth (New York: St Martin's Press, 1998), pp. 135–79 (p. 154).

[37]   Franck Collard, 'Formes du récit et langue historique dans le Compendium de origine et gestis Francorum de Robert Gaguin', *Bibliothèque d'Humanisme et Renaissance*, 57 (1995), pp. 67–82 (p. 69).

[38]   Michael Randall, 'On the evolution of toads in the French Renaissance', *Renaissance Quarterly*, 57 (2004), pp. 126–64.

[39]   Collard, *Un historien au travail*, pp. 72–3.

[40]   Collard, *Un historien au travail*, p. 247.

[41]   Duval, 'Le Livre des commentaires Cesar', p. 180.

gift to a patron. Nearly all texts, however, were meant to become printed books, since only this form enabled the text's circulation beyond a limited geographical space and – more importantly – a restricted personal network. In this period, only printed books provided a way of partially controlling the external form of the circulating texts. This was particularly important for the authors because the appearance of the text guided the perception and attention of the potential readers. Roger Chartier has pointed out that, for all texts, there is always a space for interpretation created by the gap between the text written by the authors and the printed (or otherwise transformed) product.[42] The humanist authors tried to limit this interpretative freedom by guiding the reader in a specific way. This tendency started very soon and long before the advent of print with Petrarch and his wish to control his text, as Armando Petrucci has analysed.[43] The humanistic scholars extended and intensified the aim to establish a common and clear orthography and palaeography in their printed books. To achieve this, they approximated all their texts, and especially the printed books, to antique models. The humanists attached considerable importance to the choice of font; for their own texts and for antique roman texts they preferred *Antiqua*. Already in the late fifteenth century, the clarity of this font gave it its authoritative character. The different status of Roman antiquity and Greek antiquity for the humanists may be indicated by the radical difference between the Greek font and the Latin font of the most illustrious printing press of the time: the Manutiana. Aldus Manutius used an extremely clear Latin *Antiqua*; the Greek font on the other hand demonstratively simulated the appearance of a manuscript, and even specialists have difficulty deciphering it.

This is why Erasmus Stella's description of Prussia was not printed in Leipzig or even Zwickau, which would have been nearer, but was sent to Basel, where the best printer could be found for printing texts in a humanistic manner. In my

---

[42]   Chartier, 'Communities of Readers', in *The Order of Books*, pp. 1–25 (p. 10): 'True, authors do not write books: they write texts that become written objects, which may be hand-written, engraved, or printed (and, today, electronically reproduced and transmitted). The space between text and object, which is precisely the space in which meaning is constructed, has too often been forgotten, not only by the traditional sort of literary history that thinks of the work as an abstract text whose typographic forms are without importance, but also by the "aesthetic of reception" that, in spite of its desire to historicise the readers' experience, postulates a pure and immediate relationship between the "signals" emitted by the text (which play with the accepted literary conventions) and the "horizon of expectation" of the public to which those signals are addressed. In this perspective the "effect produced" in no way depends upon the material forms that operate as a vehicle for the text. Still, those forms also fully contribute to fashioning the reader's expectations and to calling for a new public or novel uses.'

[43]   Armando Petrucci, *Writers and Readers in Medieval Italy: Studies in the History of Written Culture*, ed. and trans. by Charles M. Radding (New Haven, CT: Yale University Press, 1995), esp. 'Reading and writing Volgare in Medieval Italy', pp. 169–235; unlike Petrucci, I am not convinced that this tendency to enforce authorship is characteristic of vernacular poets.

opinion, it was Erasmus Stella himself who in 1518 decided to give the text to the printer Johannes Froben, since all accompanying texts, such as the dedication or poem, referred only to Stella and to the situation in Prussia. Even though Froben, who worked as printer for the much better known Erasmus of Rotterdam, did not pay much attention to this 'book on demand' and its appearance, Stella's book drew on Froben's reputation. Froben was best-known for his well-made editions of antique and contemporary texts, a reputation that all readers could identify as soon as they saw Stella's book and the clear *Antiqua* that had been chosen to print the description of Prussia.[44]

In Germany, there was also a tendency among humanists to use a different font to clearly distinguish between German and Roman texts. Henri-Jean Martin has described the tendency to use a 'gothic' font as a form of German resistance to *Antiqua*. He mentions the Emperor Maximilian, whose search for a national font led him to establish the example of the famous prayer book made in Nuremberg and illustrated by Albrecht Dürer.[45] Consequently, Johannes Cuspinian's *Austria* used *Antiqua* for the entire text except the quotations of German medieval documents. Because a Romanisation might have dissimulated the real German quality of these documents of German political power, these texts required another form of typographical authorisation.

Interestingly, it is not possible to identify a similar concern regarding the choice of the font in the different editions of Robert Gaguin's *Compendium*. Even if he paid considerable attention to the so-called *Manutian blank*, different editions of his text are known that are printed with a kind of *Rotunda* – for example, the first edition in Lyon.[46] It seems that in France there was no strict distinction between fonts used for humanistic texts and those used in a national context.

IV

Even if Erasmus Stella, Johannes Cuspinian and Robert Gaguin all participated in different but similar ways in the political affairs of their princely or royal

---

[44]   Erasmus of Rotterdam expressed the prestige of Froben's printing office in the prefatory epistle to Froben's edition of Thomas More's *Utopia* (the letter is dated 25 August 1517; the printing date is 1518): 'Quando ea est tuae officinae autoritas, ut liber vel hoc nomine placeat eruditis, si cognitum sit e Frobenianis aedibus prodisse.'

[45]   Martin and Chatelain, *La Naissance du livre moderne*, pp. 62, 74.

[46]   Some examples of different fonts used for the *Compendium* by the different editors: Robert Gaguin, *Compendium de Francorum origine et gestis* (Paris: Andreas Bocard, 1497) <http://catalogue.bnf.fr/ark:/12148/bpt6k52876x> [accessed 31 March 2009]; Robert Gaguin, *Compendium de Francorum origine et gestis* (Lyon: [s. pub.], 1497) <http://catalogue.bnf.fr/ark:/12148/bpt6k52897w> [accessed 31 March 2009]; Robert Gaguin, *Compendium de Francorum origine et gestis* (Paris: Thielman Kerver, 1500) <http://diglib.hab.de/wdb.php?dir=inkunabeln/289-7-hist-2f> [accessed 31 March 2009].

authority, their social success and the success of their historiographical attempts differ substantially.

Again, it is especially Robert Gaguin who differs from the two German authors. Franck Collard summed up the fruits of his diplomatic services to the French king as follows: 'les missions diplomatiques n'étaient payées ni de succès ni de deniers',[47] and he added that these failures also obstructed a successful literary integration into courtly life. Neither Gaguin's attempt to elevate the glory of the French monarchy and nation above that of Rome[48] nor the translation of his *Compendium* and the assimilation of the vernacular version to other narratives[49] helped him to attain a durable success at the royal court. In addition to this diplomatic disappointment, there is another reason for this failure: Robert Gaguin had a successful Italian rival who wrote a *De rebus gestis Francorum* for the French king and thus claimed to have constructed French history.[50] Nevertheless, Robert Gaguin's concept of a French-Gallic history received a certain authority in later times. In the late sixteenth and even seventeenth centuries, it was not only historians who drew on his conception of France as the successor of the Gauls, as Philippe Desan has shown.[51] However, it seems that Gaguin's version of French history needed this detour to finally have real political influence, since it was in proximity to the most powerful Cardinal-Minister Richelieu that the Jesuit Philippe Labbé wrote in the apocryphal *Testamentum christianum*, published with the feigned authorship of Richelieu himself, that it was always his aim to reconstruct France within the frontiers of the ancient Gaul and to bring together these two different historical entities.[52]

Indeed, it was much easier for Erasmus Stella to establish himself as a historian in the very small courtly configuration of the Teutonic knights at Königsberg and the court of the bishop of Dobeneck at Riesenburg. I am also convinced that his relative success also depended on the political circumstances of his time. While Stella was in Prussia, the Grandmaster tried to reinforce his political situation against the Polish king. Stella's description of the Germanic civil superiority

---

47   Collard, *Un historien au travail*, p. 81.

48   Collard, 'Formes du récit', p. 69.

49   Randall, 'On the evolution of toads in the French Renaissance'.

50   Franck Collard, 'Paulus Aemilius' *De rebus gestis Francorum*: Diffusion und Rezeption eines humanistischen Geschichtswerks in Frankreich', in *Diffusion des Humanismus: Studien zur nationalen Geschichtsschreibung europäischer Humanisten*, ed. by Johannes Helmrath, Ulrich Muhlack and Gerrit Walther (Göttingen: Wallstein Verlag, 2002), pp. 377–97.

51   Philippe Desan, 'Nationalism and history in France during the Renaissance', *Rinascimento*, 24 (1984), pp. 261–88 (p. 275).

52   [Philippe Labbé,] *Testamentum christianum; testamentum politicum, epitaphium sorbonicum Armandi Richelii cardinalis* (Lyon: [s. pub.], 1643), p. 5: 'Hic igitur ministerii mei scopus, restituere Galliae limites quos natura praefixit, reddere Gallis regem gallum, confundere Galliam cum Francia, et ubicumque fuit Gallia ibi restaurare novam.'

compared with the Prussians and their Polish allies,[53] the Germanic 'institution building' understood as a kind of 'nation building', and the 'peacemaking mission' of the German emperor and the Teutonic knights could serve as an argument in the actual political and diplomatic negotiations. It should also perhaps be emphasised that this was the case because of the range of the vocabulary used, and not because of the special humanistic claim to antique authority. It seems that the narrative structure of the circumscription that Stella borrowed from Tacitus and Caesar was rather more important. This structure can be understood as a literary variation of the mounted processions through the dominion (German: *Umritt*), which was a medieval technique of governance that was revived in 1516 and 1518 to establish who should make up part of Prussia. These processions were not ceremonial actions, but at each station, a representative of the dominion made a judgement concerning local conflicts and thus established their power.[54] Yet even if Stella's geographical and ethnographical description had political importance at the time, this would only have been in manuscript form. The printed version of the text arrived too late to be used in the political discussion. However, only this printed version would have effectively actualised the antique authority, and it was this version that later had a certain impact in the scholarly context. It is significant that Stella's *De Borussiae Antiquitatibus libri duo* not only became a major source for later Prussian historiography, but was also reprinted in one of the most important collections of geographical descriptions in the sixteenth century. Stella's description of Prussia is the last in Simon Grynaeus' *Novus orbis*, printed in 1532 in Basel.[55] On examining the contents of this book, it might seem surprising to find Stella's text among descriptions of the new world, as a part of the history of Peter Martyr d'Anghiera, a letter from Amerigo da Vespucci and others. What all texts have in common, however, is the reference to antique models – in a narratological sense as well as in their discussion of antique sources.

Whereas Gaguin and Stella's claims to authority took some time to develop their effects, and both in distinct ways, it seems prima facie that Cuspinian was more successful in establishing himself and his historiographical view of Austrian history as a real authority. However, we must distinguish carefully. It is correct that he had some success in terms of his career and his political and diplomatic efforts, but the success of his historiographical writings required time. He was not able to find a printer to print his *Consules* and his *Caesares*, and, together with his *Austria*, they were not printed until 1553 – thus 24 years after his death.

---

53   Kersken, 'Aspekte des preußischen Geschichtsdenkens', p. 450.

54   Marian Biskup, 'Die herrschaftlichen Umzüge im Ordensland Preußen in den Jahren 1516 und 1518', *Jahrbuch für die Geschichte Mittel- und Ostdeutschlands*, 46 (2000), pp. 113–38.

55   Simon Grynaeus, *Novus orbis regionum ac insularum veteribus incognitarum una cum tabela cosmographica et aliquot aliis consimilis argumenti libellis quorum omnium catalogus sequenti pagina patebit* (Basel: Herwagen, 1532).

V

Since only a printed edition could assure a text's impact within humanistic circles, it might be concluded that the immediate success of a text could only typically occur within a limited scholarly context, either owing to the fact that the specific humanistic claim to authority through antiquity could be controlled before a printed edition or because this claim to authority was recognised in relation to social criteria: the author needed to be approved as a real humanist author.

Otherwise, it seems that the success of the historiographical texts in an actual political context did not depend on the perfect application of humanist techniques but on the possibility of applying humanistic narratives to the actual situation, as in the case of Erasmus Stella. The cases of Robert Gaguin and Johannes Cuspinian may show that in the long run humanistic techniques could help establish a specific view of history, which could be exploited in political contexts.

In both contexts, in the erudite discussions among humanists as well as the political debates among European monarchies, the humanists' claim to authority had better chances of being recognised in the long term, while short-term authority was limited to much smaller social groups. Authority within a broader group was a question of time.

Nevertheless, these erudite connections to antiquity were not indispensable for effective and authoritative historiography, as can clearly be seen in the early-sixteenth-century *Grandes Chroniques de Bretaigne*, by Alain Bouchart. Bouchart wrote this work relying only on the vernacular translation of Robert Gaguin's chronicle and thirteenth-century French versions of Caesar.[56] Even learned historiography could dispense with a reliance on classical antiquity. Johannes Sleidan, for example, considers the Bible the most authoritative historiographical model for his own work. In his *Commentarii* of his own times, which as such made no pretence to the title of *Historia*, he relies on a theologico-historical scheme to order events, a scheme that is apocalyptic and oriented by the history of salvation.[57]

The authors treated here base their claims to authority on more than just their historiographical argumentation. The shortest formulation for this principle in the sixteenth century is 'locus antiquitatis' (respectively 'locus ex antiquitate'). Markus Völkel has shown the importance in the context of church history, but it is as important for national historiography, too: this formula signifies that all dogmas

---

[56]   Alain Bouchart, *Grandes croniques de Bretaigne: Texte établi par Marie-Louise Auger et Gustave Jeanneau sous la direction de Bernard Guenée*, 3 vols (Paris: Editions du CNRS 1986–98); Jean Kerheve, 'Aux origines d'un sentiment national: Les chroniques bretons de la fin du Moyen Age', *Bulletin de la Societe Archéologique du Finistere*, 108 (1980), pp. 165–206.

[57]   Matthias Pohlig, *Zwischen Gelehrsamkeit und konfessioneller Identitätsstiftung: Lutherische Kirchen- und Universalgeschichtsschreibung 1546–1617*, Spätmittelalter und Reformation, Neue Reihe, 37 (Tübingen: Mohr Siebeck, 2007).

are falsified if they cannot be derived from the origins and if they do not have a permanent validity.[58]

Instead, it has been possible to show how they construct stylistic, narrative and formal connections with normative models from antiquity. Yet these claims to authority are based on specific practices that have validity in particular contexts. They can be informed by content, form or social setting; they can be contradictory, and they are not bound lastingly to the text. Through new social, literary or material gestures of authority, the texts can be transported to other contexts with a claim to authority. Nevertheless, such a claim is rarely accorded validity without some conflict. On the contrary, as the various validation strategies show, one can properly speak of a constant, continually renewed struggle for authority.

---

[58]   Markus Völkel 'Wie man Kirchengeschichte schreiben soll: Struktur und Erzählung als konkurrierende Modelle der Kirchengeschichtsschreibung im konfessionellen Zeitalter', in *Die Autorität der Zeit in der Frühen Neuzeit*, ed. by Arndt Brendecke, Ralf-Peter Fuchs and Edith Koller. Pluralisierung & Autorität, 10 (Berlin: LIT Verlag 2007), pp. 455–89 (p. 457).

Chapter 5
Schiltberger's Travels, 1396–1597

Samuel Willcocks

This article follows one text through the two centuries of our topic, looking at the text's transition from manuscript book to printed book, and from book to printed pamphlet. At each stage material, both textual and visual, was incorporated from elsewhere, and repurposed from the original contexts. This contribution examines the German narrative of the travels of Johann Schiltberger in Muslim Asia, its probable oral composition, subsequent compilation, expansion, abridgement and embellishment with woodcut images.[1] Schiltberger's travels are one strand in a strong German tradition of works about the Turkish world. The manuscript transmission of the work in the fifteenth century gave rise to printed editions in Augsburg around 1480. In these early forms, the work was classed with other travel narratives and purported to offer eye-witness accounts of the Muslim world, complete with tales of wonder and prophecy. The Augsburg edition formed the basis for further printed books in the mid-sixteenth century, expanded with a printer's preface that was more sceptical of the wonders related and advised caution to the reader. At the end of the sixteenth century came radically abridged pamphlets that bore Schiltberger's name on the title page but used only one chapter, and returned to the more fantastic material, offering a prophecy that the Turks would be defeated. This final moment in the process of publication shows that the Schiltberger name had become an authority in its own right, from beginnings in which the work borrowed heavily from earlier texts, although as we shall see, these late pamphlets merely used the Schiltberger name to present material from much earlier sources. Although Schiltberger went through fewer editions than many other texts on Turkish matters, it provides a useful case study as a relatively early text that was reprinted and adapted through the entire period.

Paul Zumthor treats the early modern travel text especially as a touchstone of attitudes to authority in an era which he characterised as one of increasing sceptical empiricism: 'from the fourteenth to the sixteenth century, sight gradually replaces hearing in its function as source of knowledge'.[2] Schiltberger's travels through book history reveal that prophecy in particular was an unexpectedly

---

[1]   *The Bondage and Travels of Johann Schiltberger, a native of Bavaria, in Europe, Asia, and Africa, 1396–1427*, ed. and trans. by J. Buchan Telfer (London: Hakluyt Society, 1879). For the general reader this remains a good introduction.

[2]   Paul Zumthor, 'The medieval travel narrative', trans. by Catherine Peebles, *New Literary History*, 25 (1994), pp. 809–24 (p. 817).

stubborn trope of authority in this period; what is spoken of but not yet seen to happen is invoked alongside eye-witness testimony. Schiltberger the man travelled for only 30 years in Asia, but his text returned at crucial moments in the history of the book in the early modern era.

By his own account, Johann Schiltberger had been away from his native Bavaria for 32 years by the time he returned in 1426 and wrote or dictated his memoirs. Most readers and printers were not interested, however, in the first two years of his travels, spent attending assemblies that planned war against the Turks. Only once a crusading army was raised and battle was joined at Nicopolis in September 1396 did Schiltberger's tale become worth telling: what happened at Nicopolis ensured that his story would still be worth printing 200 years later. The battle was a painful defeat for Europe's chivalric armies, and set back crusading efforts in the Balkans by 50 years. The victorious Sultan Bayezid had several thousand defeated Christians killed on the battlefield and several thousand more taken prisoner, mostly younger pages and foot soldiers; among these was Schiltberger, who served as a captive for 30 years before returning to Bavaria with tales of the Muslim East. Bayezid was defeated in turn by Tamburlane at Ankara in 1402, and Schiltberger served with the warlord and his successors in Central Asia. Many of his stories reinforced established European ideas about the cruelty of Islam, as when he relates the slaughter of women and children in a city which had surrendered too late to Tamburlane.

When these stories were written down in Munich, the scribe bolstered Schiltberger's own memories with topographical descriptions from pilgrim handbooks of the Holy Land, including details of places that Schiltberger had not visited. These intrusions of scribal literacy exemplify the 'double account, narrative and descriptive' which Zumthor notes as characteristic of travellers' tales: 'For the one who narrates his voyage, this narrative (by pen or by mouth) achieves his reintegration into the familiar world from which he set off'.[3] Yet a parallel drive requires that the text talk of the unfamiliar, and allow some abstraction from the particular to the general even in episodes which rest entirely on personal observation. When Schiltberger sees other crusaders killed, his text describes how they met their deaths in a Christian manner and reinforced the values of his Bavarian homeland. When his own life is spared, the text explains that 'none under twenty years of age were killed' and discusses the Turkish treatment of captives.[4] After he is forced into Tamburlane's service and travels ever further from Europe, the text becomes less able to draw comparisons with Christendom or to discover the rules of conduct that obtain in Asia. Fantastic anecdotes and descriptions of fabulous beasts also begin to feature.

The German scholarship on Schiltberger has been concerned with this first-stage recension of his experiences into a manuscript version. Hans-Jochen Schiewer suggests that descriptions of military cruelty are relayed in an emotionally

---

[3]   Zumthor, 'Medieval travel narrative', p. 812.

[4]   Telfer, *Johann Schiltberger*, p. 5.

detached tone because Schiltberger was reluctant to admit to his participation in these events as a slave soldier, and therefore adopted a neutral chronicler's stance.[5] It is equally conceivable that the affectless tone is due to a scribal concern to pass over personal aspects in favour of more universally valid information, or as Gert Melville suggests, that Asiatic warfare was not even regarded as particularly cruel and that siege and slaughter were reported as business as usual.[6] Regardless of how his past as a slave may have been viewed, Schiltberger became a valued member of the Bavarian aristocracy once more on his return, serving as chamberlain to the Wittelsbach Duke Albrecht III at the court in Munich. This completed his reintegration into the world he had left; while he had not 'travelled' in the full and free sense of the word while a slave soldier in Asia, his return to Germany made him a 'traveller'.[7]

The fifteenth-century manuscript transmission is detailed by the German editor Langmantel and by Telfer; the most likely candidate for the original MS came from the Munich court.[8] Around 1488 Mattheus Brätzl, Receiver of Revenues to Duke Albrecht IV, had this manuscript bound up in a geographic compendium alongside the voyages of Marco Polo, St Brendan, Oderic of Pordenone and Sir John Mandeville; according to Brätzl's note on the fly-leaf, he also embellished the book with a map showing where each of these travellers had ventured. The map was missing by the time the book was seen by bibliographers in the early nineteenth century, and the book itself vanished shortly thereafter; however, that all these voyages could be mapped together onto one space illustrates a medieval attitude giving equal authority to texts which modern readings categorise either as fabulous (Brendan, Mandeville) or as historical testimony (Polo, Schiltberger). Similarly typical is the scribal process whereby other authoritative texts were interpolated into Schiltberger's narrative to assimilate it to tradition; of particular interest here are the borrowings from the widely read *Book* of Sir John Mandeville, a fantastic travel narrative compiled from several sources.

Schiewer has raised the question of whether the Schiltberger text might even itself be a Mandevillean fabulation put together from other sources, but dismisses

---

[5] Hans-Jochen Schiewer, 'Leben unter Heiden: Hans Schiltbergers türkische und tartarische Erfahrungen', *Daphnis: Zeitschrift für mittlere deutsche Literatur*, 21 (1992), pp. 159–78 (p. 170).

[6] Gert Melville, 'Die Wahrheit des Eigenen und die Wirklichkeit des Fremden: Über frühe Augenzeugen des osmanischen Reiches', in *Europa und die osmanische Expansion im ausgehenden Mittelalter*, ed. by Franz-Reiner Erkens (Berlin: Duncker & Humblot, 1997), pp. 79–101 (p. 89).

[7] See Schiewer's remark that 'Schiltberger reiste nicht, er war unterwegs.' Schiewer, 'Leben unter Heiden', p. 159.

[8] See Valentin Langmantel, *Hans Schiltbergers Reisebuch nach der Nürnberger Handschrift herausgegeben* (Tübingen: Literarischer Verein, 1885), pp. 148–59; Telfer, *Johann Schiltberger*, pp. vii–x.

the possibility.[9] In a study of the medieval reception of Mandeville, Rosemary Tzanaki enumerates the specific episodes taken over into Schiltberger and suggests that where the latter shows such debts to established narratives this is due to a 'ghost writer'.[10] Among other details the writer of Schiltberger's story took over from Mandeville the tale of the Castle of the Sparrowhawk, where a fairy lady will grant a wish to any virtuous knight who watches a vigil for three nights. Various knights make the attempt, but are brought down by fatigue or their own base desires; the lady of the castle curses one knight who wishes for an ever-full purse by prophesying his order's downfall. 'Schiltberger's passage is a very close retelling of the *Book*'s tale, with minor variations and additions: the lady of the castle is a virgin but not explicitly a fairy; the hawk screams at the end of the vigil to summon her; the knight who keeps watch is now a Hospitaller rather than a Templar.'[11] When the Mandeville author wrote in the mid-fourteenth century, a prophecy against the Templars was no great feat of prediction, since that Order had been condemned and dissolved some 40 years previously; an episode that is presented as a prophecy reveals itself to be a caustic joke about the fate of a knightly order that was condemned for its greed and involvement in banking practices. The author who included this anecdote into the Schiltberger text was more audacious in telling the tale, and the substitution of the Hospitallers is more than a minor variation, since this Order was not definitively defeated by the Turks until driven from Rhodes in 1522. This shifts the episode from the humorous back into the prophetic genre and may later have added to the text's aura of authority, even partly ensuring its survival in the sixteenth-century book market. The re-identification of the lady of the castle from a fairy to a mere virgin may also represent an attempt to make her prophecy more seriously plausible. In the context of manuscript composition, these alterations might represent Schiltberger's own memories of the Hospitallers' part in the defeat at Nicopolis, or a scribe's attempt to revitalise an old tale. It is even possible to imagine that Schiltberger read or heard the Mandeville story after his return to the ducal court, and made the story part of his memory of his time in the East. The Castle of the Sparrowhawk becomes a landmark in his travels, with details adjusted to fit his own life story. We may even speculate about a common source for both Mandeville's and Schiltberger's versions of the story, although the weight of textual evidence supports Tzanaki's conclusion that the borrowings are direct.

The use of Mandevillean material probably indicates an amanuensis who, in taking down the traveller's tales, cast them in familiar terms. If Schiltberger was telling the truth of his own life story, he is unlikely to have been widely read himself, yet his experiences had to be reworked to be comprehensible to the courtly audience or reader. Andrea Klein's study of literary activity at the

---

[9]　Schiewer, 'Leben unter Heiden', pp. 163–4.

[10]　Rosemary Tzanaki, *Mandeville's Medieval Audiences: A Study in the Reception of the 'Book' of Sir John Mandeville* (Aldershot: Ashgate, 2003).

[11]　Tzanaki, *Mandeville's Medieval Audiences*, p. 116.

Munich court shows that Central Asia was adapted to Bavarian concerns, as in several chapters describing the Christian kingdom of Armenia. Klein relates these chapters to a Wittelsbach household myth tracing the lineage back to a supposed Armenian ancestor Bavarus.[12] Neither Klein nor Tzanaki venture to name the literatus who interviewed Schiltberger and took down his tale, but even without an explicit identification we can read the traces of this mediation of experience to known texts.

Another narrative of crusade and Turkish captivity from later in the fifteenth century shows a similar process of mediation. Michael Beheim's song on the battle of Varna explicitly states that it recounts the experiences of the captive soldier Hans Magest, who was with the Turks for 15 years before returning to Germany.[13] Here the mediator names himself, and by the act of naming indicates to the audience that this text will conform to certain traditions; Beheim was a singer who supported the crusade polemic of the day, thus he tells the story in verse and celebrates the Christian princes who fought at Varna, passing over Magest's captivity in two lines as irrelevant to the song's main purpose. The paradigmatic instance of such mediation may be Rusticiano's recension of Marco Polo's travels; Zumthor has remarked that the last fifth of the *Travels* seems to be a chivalric fabulation unconnected to Polo's experience but typical of the romance genre in which Rusticiano had previously worked.[14] Schiltberger's Munich amanuensis marked his text by citation and interpolation, Beheim adapted Magest by working in verse and Rusticiano used generic tropes. We have also seen that Mattheus Brätzl assigned 'Schiltberger' a certain authority by choosing to bind it up with other texts and creating a common map.

As well as citation, genre and linguistic form, illustration can also affect how a text is read. The fifteenth century saw the incorporation of woodcut illustrations into printed books, as in three editions of Schiltberger from the Augsburg printer Anton Sorg between 1478 and 1493. These woodcuts showed battle scenes featuring the Christian and Muslim armies of the narrative, although the armies are not distinguished from one another by dress, armour or weaponry. At most, two armies in a scene will carry different banners, and a woodcut for the chapter relating the Christian defeat at Nicopolis is not substantially different from a picture purporting to show two Muslim armies in Central Asia later in the text. Sorg printed more than 100 illustrated books from 1475 to 1493 and employed several woodcut artists, one of whom designed blocks for the Schiltberger book, for Sorg's edition of the St Brendan journey and for the popular epic *Herzog Ernst*.[15] Like Matthaeus

---

[12]   Andrea Klein, *Der Literaturbetrieb am Münchner Hof im fünfzehnten Jahrhundert* (Göppingen: Kümmerle, 1998), pp. 203–4.

[13]   Song 104 in *Die Gedichte des Michel Beheim*, ed. by Hans Gille and Ingeborg Spriewald, 3 vols (Berlin: Akademie-Verlag, 1968–72), I, pp. 328–56.

[14]   Zumthor 'Medieval travel narrative', p. 814.

[15]   Elisabeth Geck, *Buchkundlicher Exkurs zu Herzog Ernst, Sankt Brandans Meerfahrt, Hans Schiltbergers Reisebuch* (Wiesbaden: Guido Pressler, 1969), pp. 11–18.

Brätzl at the Munich court around the same time, Sorg and his artist treat the
slave's voyage as seriously as the saint's, but they also assimilate him to a tradition
of chivalry. Although the illustrations do not distinguish Muslim armies from a
somewhat idealised notion of European soldiery, the text does offer some account
of the strength and tactics of the Turks. This includes the cheering news that they
could be defeated, even if this required an opponent as pitiless as Tamburlane. We
have already encountered the suggestion that service with Tamburlane's forces
was personally and psychologically stressful for Schiltberger, and that this may
have influenced the neutral chronicler's tone in which he reported his experiences.
Sorg's woodcuts reduce yet further the trauma of captivity and battlefield atrocity
by assimilating the Asian episodes to known chivalric imagery.

The theme of crusade against the Turks is strongly represented in incunabular
book history, and was discussed in moral as well as in military terms. The first
printed book from a European press, an eight-page *Türkenkalender* of 1454,
called for crusade and exhorted European princes to abandon their feuds and show
Christian unity.[16] Since Nicopolis, war against the Turks had been unsuccessful;
Varna in 1444 was a further demoralising defeat, Constantinople fell in 1453 and
only 1456 offered some consolation when Mehmet II's army was turned back from
Belgrade. These events are the historical background for Sorg's edition of 1479,
and it is conceivable that the reprints of the following years were in part motivated
by the Turkish capture of Otranto in 1480. The Christian response to this incursion
displayed the unity which crusade literature demanded, when Italian princes and
cities set aside their own feuds to expel the invaders the following year.

By the mid-sixteenth century such unity was a thing of the past. Turkish
advances had taken Rhodes from the Hospitallers in 1522 and had fragmented
the medieval kingdom of Hungary following the victory at Mohács in 1526, even
laying siege to Vienna in 1529. A pashalik was established in Buda in 1541, and
what the Turks had not conquered was divided under Christian rule between the
house of Habsburg and the Zápolya dynasty. Norman Housley has traced the
figures of the 'internal' and 'external' Turk in European political discourse in this
century, where Protestant and Catholic each believed that the other did more to
harm 'Christendom' than the actual Ottoman Turk.[17] We shall see that, by the end
of the century, some communities would ask whether they could not lead a more
peaceful Christian life under Turkish rule. A much-printed polemic against this
tendency was the *De afflictione* of Bartolomej Georgijevic, a later captive than
Schiltberger, a soldier at Mohács who spent 13 years with the Turks; this went
through 43 editions in various languages between 1544 and 1600.[18]

---

[16]   Ferdinand Geldner, 'Bemerkungen zum Text des 'Türkenschreis' von Balthasar
Mandelreiß, des 'Türkenkalenders' (1454) und der 'Ermanung ... wider die Türken' von
Niclas Wolgemut', *Gutenberg-Jahrbuch 1983* (1983), pp. 166–71.

[17]   Norman Housley, *Religious Warfare in Europe, 1400–1536* (Oxford: Oxford
University Press, 2002), esp. pp. 131–59.

[18]   Housley, *Religious Warfare*, p. 137.

The standard bibliography of German sixteenth-century printed works disagrees, in its listing of mid-century Schiltberger editions, with the more specialist study of *Turcica* by the Transylvanian scholar Carl Göllner.[19] Nevertheless both studies agree that the Schiltberger text appeared in at least two full editions, from the Nuremberg printers Johann vom Berg and Ulrich Neuber around 1549 and the Frankfurt house of Weigandt Han in 1553 and thereafter.[20] Berg and Neuber in Nuremberg also published sermons by the influential Lutheran preacher Veit Dietrich, and the Frankfurt house of Han published Luther's own *Vom Krieg wider den Türcken*: despite these confessional links, their editions of Schiltberger did not explicitly engage Reformation polemic. Both editions have lengthy titles: the Nuremberg edition advertised itself as 'a wonderful and diverting history'; the Frankfurt reprint was even 'very entertaining to read'.[21] These are unusual plaudits for a book whose protagonist first faces execution on a battlefield and then offers cold-blooded accounts of slaughter. The fantastic and entertaining aspects of the text, mostly interpolations from Mandeville and other wonder-literature, are further emphasised by a more diverse set of woodcuts than Anton Sorg's battle scenes.

The Nuremberg edition also opens with an unsigned printer's introduction on the utility of the text for moral improvement. Citing the examples of Polybius, Herodotus and Xenophon, this foreword explains how historians discern the useful truth behind credulous stories from an unlettered witness such as Schiltberger. 'When somebody once said that it is not good to have a hare run across your path, he doubtless meant that it would be better to catch it and cook it: but this led to a silly saying among simple, superstitious folk.'[22] Thus the use of the word *Histori* in the title and the sceptical methodology of the foreword assign interpretative authority to the reader, who must unravel the sense of an imperfect observer.

It is an irony of textual history that Schiltberger had said much the same to the scribe who had first written down his experiences, and who in writing had

---

[19]   *The Verzeichnis der im deutschen Sprachbereich erschienenen Drücke des XVI. Jahrhunderts* (Stuttgart: Hiersemann, 1983) or VD16, is compiled by the Staatsbibliothek in Munich and the Herzog-August-Bibliothek in Wolfenbüttel; Carl Göllner's *Turcica: die Europäischen Türkendrucke des 16. Jahrhunderts*, 3 vols (Berlin and Bucharest: Editura Academei and Akademie Verlag, 1961–78) was the work of a single scholar.

[20]   The VD16 lists three editions from Han before 1570 where Göllner lists only that of 1554.

[21]   Johann Schiltberger, *Schiltberger. Ein wunderbarliche/und kurtzweylige/Histori/ wie Schiltberger/eyner auß der Stadt Muenchen/in Bayern/von den/Tuercken gefangen/ in die Heydenschafft gefueret/unnd wider heim kommen.* (Nuremberg: Johann vom Berg and Ulrich Neuber, c. 1549). The Frankfurt editions bore an almost identical title with the further phrase 'sehr luestig zu lesen'.

[22]   'Also hat auch etwa einer gesagt: Es sey nicht gut/wenn ein haß ueber den wege lauff/und on zweyffel gemeint/es were besser das der selbige gefangen/und gebraten werden moecht/Darauß aber ein leichtfertige auffmerckung bey den liderlichen aberglaubigen erfolget.' Schiltberger, *Schiltberger*, fol. Aivr.

expanded them with the unlikely tales that these later editors now rejected. 'All that I saw in the land of the Infidels, of wars, and what was wonderful, also what chief towns and seas I have seen and visited, you will find described hereafter, perhaps not quite completely, but I was a prisoner and not independent.'[23] If we tentatively identify the authors of the foreword as Berg and Neuber, we may rate them alongside Johan Eichmann, who printed the sailor Hans Staden's memoirs of Brazil in 1557, as a model of the sixteenth-century endeavour identified by Zumthor: 'how to distinguish the true?'[24] It is a method that has no place for the uncertainties of prophecy, and the selection of fantastic woodcut illustrations underlines the need for scepticism even as it makes good on the title's promise of entertainment and diversion.

A radical reversal of editorial emphasis and practice came with pamphlet editions printed in Frankfurt and Vienna from 1595 to 1597. These are much slimmer than the mid-century editions of 60 or 80 pages, using only one chapter of the Schiltberger text to fill four to eight pages. This chapter is another interpolation from Mandeville, although not a fantastic episode: rather it offers an account of Muslim belief and doctrine, which the Mandeville author had taken in turn from the thirteenth-century tractate of William of Tripoli.[25] There is no reason to suppose that the printers were aware of the genealogy of the chapter, or that they used Schiltberger's name in conscious preference to Mandeville's: the name was simply already attached to the text that they wished to use. Although the original material was uncommonly tolerant in its account of Muslim belief, redaction over the centuries added negative details. Among these was an expectation that Islam would last only 100 years and that what the prophet Mohammed had founded would fail under the 'next Machomet'; in the later sixteenth century this was supposed to mean the emperor Mehmed III (reigned 1595–1603). All this was certainly a part of the reason for a ripple of anti-Turkish propaganda at the end of the sixteenth century, but the military situation on the Hungarian frontier is at least as important for an informed reading of these pamphlets.

In 1593 an Austrian alliance had begun a new campaign to retake the lands lost at Mohács for the Habsburg rump of Royal Hungary. Habsburg and papal diplomacy spread the financial costs of the campaign and the imperial diet of the Holy Roman Empire voted subsidies for the war beginning in 1594.[26] The Frankfurt house of Weigandt Han had published the full text of the travels in the mid-century, and in 1595 issued an eight-page pamphlet of 'Schiltberger prophecies' of which the front page bears the title 'Of the Turks and Mahomet. A true, thorough report from the historian Johan Schiltberger' and a selection of verses from the Book

23   Telfer, *Johann Schiltberger*, p. 1.

24   Zumthor, 'Medieval travel narrative', p. 813.

25   Ian Macleod Higgins, *Writing East: The 'Travels' of Sir John Mandeville* (Philadelphia, PA: University of Pennsylvania Press, 1997), p. 113.

26   Jan Paul Niederkorn, *Die europäischen Mächte und der 'Lange Türkenkrieg' Kaiser Rudolfs II* (Vienna: Akademie der Wissenschaften, 1993), pp. 53–7.

of Daniel.[27] Overleaf are couplets calling Islam a Satanic corruption of Christian doctrine, and only on the third page does the text from Schiltberger/Mandeville begin. This abridges the original chapter to make Islam appear more bloodthirsty, omitting William of Tripoli's mention of the prohibition on carrying weapons in the mosque. On the final page is a newly written hymn exhorting faithful readers to take up arms, and the whole pamphlet accords with the Regensburg imperial diet's support for the Habsburg war. The use of the word *Geschichtschreiber*, which I have provisionally translated as 'historian', is perhaps less important than the continuing authority attached to Schiltberger's name to unite these diverse texts.

After initial victories the war took a turn for the worse, occasioning peasant uprisings in Austria in 1596–97 which demanded an end to military conscription.[28] The Vienna pamphlets were thus printed at a moment when the costs of the 'Long War' were becoming a matter of open dispute. In 1596 Gregor Hübner printed the 'Schiltberger prophecies' and an eight-page news-sheet enthusiastically reporting recent Habsburg victories and Turkish defeats.[29] Such booklets contributed to the dominant discourse of Christian unity and Turkish danger, and Hübner's 'Schiltberger pamphlets' are aggressively polemical. The version described here is the printing of 1596, which seems to have been reprinted virtually unchanged the next year.[30]

In this context the printer was no longer interested in acknowledging that Schiltberger was an unfree agent, or that his observations need a sceptical reading. Instead he is cited as an authority in doctrinal and political matters, and even credited with prophetic authority. Hübner had not printed any full edition of the travels, and his creation is different enough from the earlier Schiltberger to merit quoting at length. This is the full text of the title page of the 12-page pamphlet:

> Erzehlung eines Bürgers Sohn aus der Stadt München im Beyerlandt Hans Schielborg genandt.

> So von dem Türcken 32. Jahr gefangen/in Eysen umbher gangen/und mitler zeit des Machomets anfang/Türcken Ceremonien in Kirchen/Schulen/und Heusern erfahren/nach seiner erledigung/zur trewen warnung an alle gleubige geschrieben/

---

[27] 'Vom Turcken und Machomet/Ein warer gruendtlicher bericht/aus dem Geschichtschreiber/Johan Schiltberger ...'; cf. Göllner, *Turcica*, II, no. 2063 a., 548.

[28] Otto Brunner, *Land and Lordship: Structures of Governance in Medieval Austria*, trans. by Howard Kaminsky and James van Horn Melton (Philadelphia, PA: University of Pennsylvania Press, 1992), p. 287; Niederkorn, *Die europäischen Mächte*, pp. 61–2.

[29] 'Narratio oder gründliche Erzehlung aller gedenkwirdigen sachen so sich in Ober und nieder Ungern, Podolien, Walachey Siebenbürgen, Crabaten und Steuermarck zu Wasser und Lande zugetragen, vom 8. October 95. bis auff den 1. Januarij 96. Stylo novo'; cf. Göllner, *Turcica*, II, no. 2245, 632.

[30] See note 14 for the confusion over editions and years. Here I describe the booklet held as Flugschrift 1596/6 in the incunabular cabinet of the Berlin Staatsbibliothek.

so da sprechen/das der Türcke die Christen ihres glaubens frey unter seinem Tribut
wohnen lesset.

1596.

Auch mit was List ehr eine gar Alte Türckische Propheceyung bekommen/
welche sie mit beschwerten Hertzen offt heimlich gedencken/und itzo unter dem
andern Keyser/Machomet vollenden sol Anno. 1603. welche Prophecey in ihrer
eigener Sprach so wol Latein als Deutsch hierbey gedruckt worden

Gedruckt zu Wien bey Greger Hübner.[31]

There are several innovations here. 'Schielborg' is a *Bürger* rather than a nobleman
and his military service is elided; although kept in chains, he is enterprising
enough to spy on the Turk; he has got hold of a prophecy 'by cunning'. After this
appearance on the title page Schielborg does not feature in the pamphlet at all;
he is simply the guarantor for the prophecy, and this absence of narrator is neatly
marked by the blank verso of the title page.

Blank pages are slightly unusual in a polemical work of this length, more so
in the Hübner pamphlet since it is made up of two gatherings with one blank page
in each. The first gathering of eight pages contains the title page, a selection of
Biblical verses, and the history of Machomet familar from the William of Tripoli
material. The second gathering of four pages gives the 'old Turkish prophecy'
in three languages, with a blank final page. The first page bears a separate title,
suggesting that the four pages may have been sold or distributed on their own
without the Schielborg material, although Göllner's bibliography does not know
of any such separate booklet. The prophecy is printed in three typefaces with the
Turkish text in plain Roman type, the Latin translation in Italic and the German in a
Gothic typeface; the Latin and German texts are glossed with dates. The text itself

---

[31]   'Narrative of a burger's son from the city of Munich in Bavaria called Hans Schielborg.

Who was captured by the Turk 32 years/went in irons/and in that time learnt of
Machomet's origin/the ceremonies of the Turk in churches/schools/and houses/after
his release/written as a true warning to all those faithful/who say/that the Turk allows
Christians to live under his tribute free in their faith.

1596.

Also with what cunning he took a very old Turkish prophecy/which they often think
of with heavy hearts in private/and now will be fulfilled under the second emperor/
Machomet in the year. 1603. Which prophecy is printed here in their own language as
well as Latin and German.

Printed in Vienna at Greger Hübner.' Translation mine; der ander Machomet is Mehmet III.

is a version of a prophecy given by Bartolomej Georgijevic in 1545, and Göllner's entry on this item discusses the early use of Latin characters to transcribe Turkish words.[32] The more elaborate layout of parallel texts in Hübner's pamphlet typifies the European impulse to appropriate Oriental knowledge into its own discourse. The blank pages could even be seen as a space into which each reader or owner of the booklet inscribes the uses which 'Schielborg' must now serve.

The prophecy in both versions recounts that the Ottomans will conquer the *kuzul almai*, which is translated as the 'red apple', but not further identified or glossed even in the more extensively annotated Vienna pamphlet. After 12 years of peaceful occupation, during which the Turks plant orchards and build roads and schools, Christendom will reconquer the region and the Ottoman empire will fall. In an essay on the prophetic sub-genre of Turcica, Göllner interprets the *kuzul almai* as a symbol for empire in general, while allowing that early printers sometimes sought to identify it with Constantinople or Rome.[33] Hübner may have chosen to leave the term unspecified in order to make the prophecy more plausible: whatever region was understood or implied, the actual conquests and territorial changes of the Long War were so minimal that the print history of the war is almost of more interest than the military history. The Ottoman empire did not collapse; indeed it remained vigorous enough to lay siege to Vienna in 1683.

The fifteenth and sixteenth centuries were the height of Turkish power, when Europe felt threatened by Islam and readers felt a need for captive narratives or travellers' tales. Since Schiltberger's story dates back to such an early moment in the encounter between cultures, it is silent on many aspects of Ottoman life and government, saying nothing of the conquest of Constantinople and its role as capital, of the naval struggles in the Mediterranean or the *millet* system of self-government for religious minorities. What printers offered was not knowledge but reassurance: that the Turks could be resisted by a chivalrous Christian soldier, or by a sceptical European observer, or at the last by a prophecy.

---

[32] Göllner, *Turcica*, I, no. 853, p. 401.

[33] Göllner, 'Der Mythos über die Zukunft des Osmanischen Reiches', *Turcica*, III, pp. 334–50.

Chapter 6

Print and Political Propaganda under Pope Julius II (1503–13)

Massimo Rospocher

Julius II, the 'warrior pope', was one of the most controversial figures of the early modern period,[1] the judgements about him by his contemporaries ranging from bitter criticism to lavish praise.[2] Specialists are well aware of attacks on Julius II and of his uncanny ability to trigger the visceral opposition of figures such as Erasmus, epitomised by the anonymously issued *Iulius Exclusus e coelis*.[3] Here I intend to examine a lesser-known facet of this pope's image: the positive side, which he himself took an active part in managing with his protean quality of generating a huge range of activities whose collective object was to exalt his figure and his role in contemporary affairs. Partly because of this contested image, Giuliano della Rovere was a pontiff highly aware of the forms and modes of his own self-representation. He understood the communicative power of art, architecture, music and oratory to uphold his image as 'sovereign pontiff'.[4] The purpose of this present study is to show how this exercise in persuasion was expressed not solely via the great communicative media of art or of oratory but also at a 'low' level of political communication, represented by poetry and other printed material in the vernacular, inspired by the same pontifical authority. This 'popular' representation of the pontiff is a neglected aspect of the historiography of Julius II, which has traditionally concentrated on 'high' elements of papal propaganda: the iconography of Michelangelo and Raphael's works, the ambitious

---

[1]   Christine Shaw, *Julius II: The Warrior Pope* (Oxford: Blackwell, 1993).

[2]   See Bram Kempers, 'Julius inter laudem et vituperationem: Ein Papst unter gegensätzlichen Gesichtspunkten betrachtet', in *Hoch-renaissance im Vatikan: Kunst und Kultur im Rom der Päpste I (1503–1534)* (Citta del Vaticano: Biblioteca Apostolica Vaticana, 1999), pp. 15–29. See also Massimo Rospocher, 'Propaganda e opinione pubblica: Giulio II nella comunicazione politica europea', *Annali dell'Istituto Storico Italo-Germanico*, 33 (2007), pp. 59–99.

[3]   Erasmus of Rotterdam, *The 'Julius Exclusus' of Erasmus*, trans. by Paul Pascal; ed. by Jesse Kelley Sowards (Bloomington, IN: Indiana University Press, 1968).

[4]   Ingrid D. Rowland, *The Culture of the High Renaissance: Ancients and Moderns in Sixteenth-century Rome* (Cambridge: Cambridge University Press, 1998), pp. 141–92 (pp. 158–9). Paolo Prodi, *The Papal Prince. One Body and Two Souls: the Papal Monarchy in Early Modern Europe* (Cambridge: Cambridge University Press, 1988).

architectural projects of Bramante, the elaborate prose of the pontifical orators and the Latin poems of the panegyrists.

The themes developed by Julian propaganda were conceptually linked to the great *topoi* of humanistic Renaissance culture: the classical myth of the golden age based on *pax* et *concordia*, the reminiscence of Roman antiquity, the whole perspective of the *plenitudo temporum* (fulfilment of time) and of the *renovatio imperii* (intended as the restoration and renewal of the ancient Roman Empire). These *topoi* were not abstractions without links to contemporary reality but concepts reworked in a political and religious vein, to legitimate Julius II's temporal aspirations. The combination of political and cultural aspects and Christian and pagan ideals was symptomatic of an overall ideology in which political and religious elements could not be dissociated from cultural ones. In addition to being Roman pontiff, Julius II was in fact a great patron of the arts and a politician. Even in vernacular form, hundreds of poems conveyed the same concepts, circulating in print or performed by travelling singers (*cantastorie*), intended for a large and diverse audience.

The arguments put forward in large-circulation printed material reached a wide audience. However, it would be difficult to define them as popular from the point of view of production because of the closeness of their links with the world of political and artistic high culture. This was the sphere in which ideas and concepts were originally developed and then adapted for a wider public. The propaganda images conveyed consisted of a political vocabulary that was common to producers and receivers. Communication was not mono-directional as, via the mediating work of various figures, there emerged a political discourse shared equally by the lower as well as upper social groups. During the Renaissance, in fact, public political discourse, whether 'high' or 'low', could be expressed in different registers, but was based on a shared set of arguments and concepts.[5] Julian ideology projected itself in different modes, but what was conveyed to different audiences contained a common message.

It is appropriate to summarise here the main points that the following pages seek to develop. At the beginning of the early modern period when the aim was to reach a wide audience, poetry was the favoured language of political communication.[6] If poetry was the language, popular printed material, along with oral performance, were the instruments for spreading political discourse. The combination of poetry

---

[5] '… The supposedly "high" and "low" cultures of Renaissance political discourse in fact share an enormous amount of common ground'. Margaret Meserve, 'The news from Negroponte: Politics, popular opinion and information exchange in the first decade of the Italian press', *Renaissance Quarterly*, 59 (2006), pp. 440–80 (p. 472).

[6] Lauro Martines, *Strong Words: Writing and Social Strain in the Italian Renaissance* (Baltimore, MD: John Hopkins University Press, 2001), pp. 232–48. See also Rospocher, 'La Poesía como lenguaje de comunicación política en los espacios públicos de las ciudades italianas del Renacimiento', in *Opinión pública y espacio urbano en la Edad Moderna*, ed. by James Amelang and Antonio Castillo Gómez (Gijón: Trea, 2010), pp. 185–210.

and cheap printed material and the intermediality between orality and print became fundamental elements of political communication. Lastly, the *auctoritates* to which Julian propaganda referred were the major *topoi* of humanistic Renaissance culture. Interpreted in its historical context the political claims this propaganda made can account for its popular success and wide circulation.

Cheap Prints and 'Wars of Verses'

Historical research has recently brought to light the role of printing, from its very beginnings, in the spreading of political information in Italy in the early modern period. The capture by the Turks of the Venetian outpost of Negroponte, in 1470, represents a turning point in the circulation of news and political comment in printed form.[7] During the Italian wars, when political and military events were following one another at a breathless pace, the demand for ever faster information by a socially heterogeneous public arose. The need for immediacy and the large number of recipients required the printing of short and economical texts that could be quickly reproduced in large numbers. Produced by the presses of printers large and small, a flood of 'popular prints' engulfed the peninsula between the end of the fifteenth and the beginning of the sixteenth centuries.[8]

The prints contained primarily poetic writings, very rarely prose, concerning the dramatic events of contemporary history. They were distributed in public, politically charged spaces like the squares and markets of Italian cities,[9] by itinerant figures such as *cantastorie* (street singers) and *cerretani* (ambulant sellers – *cerretani* can also be singers).[10] They were very cheap: 'e perché ognun ne possa comperare/solo tre quatrini vi averà costare' ('and so that each one of you can buy it/it will cost you only three pennies'), as a mountebank from Ferrara declared.[11]

---

[7] See Meserve, 'News from Negroponte'.

[8] See the important compilation of sources: *Guerre in ottava rima*, 4 vols, ed. by Amedeo Quondam and others (Modena: Panini, 1989).

[9] On the notion of 'political space' in early modern Europe, a reflection of the current 'spatial turn' in historiography, see *Political Space in Pre-industrial Europe*, ed. by Beat Kümin (Aldershot: Ashgate, 2009).

[10] Concerning these travelling singers, see Susan Noakes, 'The book market in Quattrocento Italy', *The Journal of Medieval and Renaissance Studies,* 11 (1981), pp. 23–55 (p. 45); Paolo Toschi, *Stampe popolari italiane* (Milan: Electa, 1964); Dale V. Kent, *Cosimo de' Medici and the Florentine Renaissance: The Patron's Oeuvre* (New Haven, CT: Yale University Press, 2000), pp. 43–52; Rospocher and Rosa Salzberg, 'Street singers in Italian Renaissance: Urban culture and communication', *Cultural and Social History*, 9 (2012), pp. 9–26; Salzberg, 'In the mouths of charlatans. Street performers and the dissemination of pamphlets in Renaissance Italy', *Renaissance Studies*, 24 (2010), pp. 638–53.

[11] Bighignol, *Li horrendi e magnanimi fatti de l'ilustrissimo Alfonso duca di Ferrara contra l'armata de Venetiani* (Ferrara: Baldassare Selli, 1510), fol. 2ᵛ.

The elements contained in these booklets belonged to an oral, unwritten poetic tradition. Through the narratives of the travelling singers, oral delivery became therefore another means of distribution of this ephemeral textual production, which the illiterate sections of society could also enjoy. Via this new printed medium and the related oral tradition, people in the cities were informed of the evolution of the wars that were raging for supremacy in Italy. The 'horizon of expectations'[12] of the public included not only the demand for news but also the wish to receive it in familiar narrative forms. This explains the prevalence of poetic laments, short chivalric epics and *capitoli*, the traditional genres of popular political poetry.

The information conveyed was not neutral; the narrative structure and the form of the text, in particular in the short chivalric epics in octaves, meant taking up a position in favour of one or other of the factions at war.[13] Additionally, the sale of pamphlets and the performance of compositions required the consent of the local political authorities. It was unthinkable that a cantastorie, or a pamphlet seller, would peddle poems hostile to the ruling powers of the place in which he wished to work. Even if one cannot always speak of a direct political commission, the authorities during the Italian wars exercised control over the circulation of information and political comment in poetic form, in some cases removing from sale political poems contrary to their position and in others permitting the circulation of verses in their favour. This occurred in Venice at the time of the war of the League of Cambrai (1509–17), when in November 1509 two poems circulating against Emperor Maximilian I were sequestered by the agents of the Council of Ten – the government body concerned with state security and social order.[14] Simultaneously, this same authority encouraged the diffusion of three compositions in verse against their current enemy, the duchy of Ferrara.[15]

---

[12]   Concerning this concept, see Hans R. Jauss, 'Literary history as a challenge literary theory', *New Literary History*, 2 (1970), pp. 7–37.

[13]   As Amedeo Quondam has remarked: 'The speed of response to events, the extension of their presence in the network of communication thanks to printing and their own narrative effectiveness, combined as integral elements of a general message underlying the surface text: a political message of self-promotion and propaganda by the parties to the conflict'. 'Materiali per un nuovo cantiere documentario e testuale', in *Guerre in ottava rima*, I, p. 15.

[14]   'Era stampado una canzon si chiama *La gata di Padoa* con un'altra in vilanescho di Tonin, *E l'è partì quei lanziman*, qual per non offender il re di Romani, cussì chome si vendevano un bezo l'una, fo mandato a tuorle per li capi di X, *adeo* più non si vendeteno. ... vene fuora altre canzon fate contra Ferara numero tre, e fono lassate vender'; Marin Sanuto, *I Diarii*, 58 vols (Venice: Visentini, 1879–1903), IX, col. 335.

[15]   On this episode and in general on attempts to control the printing press by political authorities during the Italian Wars, see Rospocher, 'Stampe e versi pericolosi: Controllo delle opinioni e ricerca del consenso durante le guerre d'Italia', in *From Florence to the Mediterranean and Beyond: Essays in Honour of Tony Molho*, ed. by Diogo Curto et al. (Florence: Olschki, 2009), pp. 381–407.

Poetry proved itself more effective than prose in putting across clear moral and political messages, by its ability to interact with the emotions of the reader–listener and to create negative stereotypes of the enemy. The political authorities sensed the possibility to influence the opinion of the audience via this phenomenon, and to this end they used the new communicative resources made available by printing. Sometimes, it was the same political figures who commissioned and distributed the texts free of charge, on the occasion of public civic ceremonies of particular importance. Such was the case during the entry of the papal legate, Cardinal Francesco Alidosi, into Bologna on 8 May 1510: poetic works were showered down from the windows in the main streets along the route of the Cardinal's procession, and distributed free of charge in crucial public spaces like the central market and the piazza.[16]

Such products might be printed with commercial intent, to respond to the public's demand and the growing market for information; they might also be produced for direct political ends, on commission of political authorities. Mass-produced printed material became another piece in the jigsaw of moods, voices, opinions and judgements that among the Italian urban population formed a common 'public opinion'.[17] Obtaining the favour of this *vox populi* became essential for political actors seeking to foster consensus during periods of conflict.[18]

The main features of this type of publishing can be summarised thus: cheapness and speed of production, use of the vernacular and of the language of poetry, wide distribution and a direct link with contemporary political reality. An indisputable protagonist in this historical period, and one of the main fomenters of the wars that were being fought then, Julius II was also a central figure in the sphere of this production, not only because he was the object of violent attacks from the opponents of his political plans, but above all because a large number of texts in his favour were circulated during the span of his pontificate. A war of print and a 'war of verses' accompanied the real wars promoted by the pontiff. The pro-Julian production developed the function of fostering the *consensus populi* and of celebrating the image of Julius II among his contemporaries.

---

[16] 'Nota che per Stra Mazore e per el Marchà di Mezo e per Piaza fu trato zoxe da le fenestre molti soniti in laude del dito chardinale di questo tenore'; Friano Ubaldini, *Cronica*, Bologna, BU, ms. 430, vol. III, cc. 842ᵛ–843ʳ.

[17] Ottavia Niccoli, *Rinascimento anticlericale: Infamia, propaganda e satira in Italia tra Quattrocento e Cinquecento* (Rome-Bari: Laterza, 2005), pp. 14–15.

[18] On the role of the *vox populi* in political debate see Sandro Landi, *Naissance de l'opinion publique dans l'Italie moderne: Sagesse du peuple et savoir de gouvernement de Machiavel aux Lumières* (Rennes: Presses Universitaires de Rennes, 2006), pp. 22–4.

The 'Golden Age'

The classical myth of the golden age was one of the recurrent metaphors in Renaissance culture, often used for promotional purposes on the part of political authorities.[19] In the view of contemporary humanists, their period had seen the return of the golden age, after the periods of decline known as the ages of silver, bronze and iron. Following the interpretation given by Virgil in the fourth Eclogue, the new golden age prophesied by the Sibyl of Cumae was to be marked not so much by the dimension of a rural pastoral idyll but more by a new flowering of culture, the arts and political institutions. The proponents of the culture of the Roman Curia represented the whole Julian pontificate in the perspective of a secular rebirth of the papacy. The metaphor suited the political project pursued by Julius II, directed towards the *renovatio imperii*. According to this political interpretation of the *aetas aurea* (the golden age), Roman cultural circles around the court of the Della Rovere intended to add a Christian vision of revival to the new age. They wished to associate the figure of Julius II with the spirit of the age.

The theme of the golden age found its best theoretical formulation in the Latin pamphlet *De Aurea Aetate* of Giles of Viterbo, the papal orator who played a key role in representing the intellectual, political and religious vision of Julius's Rome.[20] Four golden ages had followed one another in human history, of which the present one, brought to completion by Julius II, was considered the ultimate and the most glorious. Its focal point was the link established between *incrementum Ecclesiae* – to be intended as the expansion of the pontifical state – and *aetas aurea*.[21] Giles made his prophetic vision match directly the political and religious events of contemporary reality, so that his conception of the golden age fitted the political aims of the pontiff. The Augustinian Prior General reworked Roman Platonism into a philosophy of history that legitimated spiritually the temporal action of the papacy as a Christian empire. The link with contemporary reality is the essential interpretive element for understanding how the philosophical and theological ideal of the golden age could be used in the realm of political propaganda.

In poetic production intended for a heterogeneous public, the theme of the new age took on a promotional value in support of papal authority. Julius II's first military feat, which resulted in the reconquering of Bologna in 1506, was accompanied by an outpouring of verses of praise in the vernacular, printed and circulated to exalt Julius's pontificate as a new age of prosperity, freedom and justice. A *Barzelletta nova in laude di papa Julio II* (*New Barzelletta in Honour of Pope Julius II*), composed by a Servite friar from Rimini, celebrated the conquest

---

[19]   Concerning a propagandistic and political use of the myth, see Ernest H. Gombrich, 'Renaissance and the Golden Age', *Journal of the Warburg and Courtauld Institutes*, 24 (1961), pp. 306–9.

[20]   John W. O'Malley, 'Fulfillment of the Christian Golden Age under Julius II: Text of a discourse of Giles of Viterbo, 1507', *Traditio*, 25 (1969), pp. 265–338.

[21]   See Luca D'Ascia, *Erasmo e l'umanesimo romano* (Florence: Olshki, 1991), p. 180.

Barzelletta noua in laude di papa Julio ij. composta per frate Matheo Maria da Rimino delsacro Ordine di Serui.

Gaude mundi gran Pastore
de la chiesa alto Augumento
poi chel Ciel e ogni elemento
te obedisse e rende honore
Del Remuleo sceptro volse
subiugare Italia a Roma
lustricento se riuolse
consudore e tua persona
inmomento la incorona
con prudentia del suo fiore
Gaude mundi.
Uirtu nel sublime scano
sol te ha posto a residentia
vitij: fraude ogni tirano
fuge dala tua presentia
tu sei ornato di excellentia
piu chel Sol di chiar splendore
gaude mundi.
Quanto fa tua Quercia lombra
tanto stato ha lhonestate
el politico se adombra
cincto el baltheo di pietate
pace: amore e caritate
frondansi da lalto arnore
gaude mundi.
Gloria sei del sacro ceto
signor iusto: pio e sincero
facto e il clero per te lieto
dogni menda insonte e mero
certamente a dire il vero
fu accadente il tuo feruore
gaude mundi.
O magnanimo e clemente
per la chiesia almondo nato
per te Roma alta e souente
se rralegra che hai tornato
al deifico senato
le herbe del piscatore

Figure 6.1 Frontispiece of Matteo Maria da Rimini

of Bologna and of the Romagna, foretelling the beginning of a new golden age for a new province.[22] This short work was accompanied by a woodcut representing Julius II seated on a throne and surrounded by two groups of prelates in an attitude of submission to his authority (Figure 6.1). From a publishing point of view, this constituted the typical form of this sort of production: few pages, an initial illustration and a text in verse. A work of similar format – *Lamento di Bentivoglio* (*Bentivoglio's Lament*) – was circulated and posted up in the city's public places to denigrate the Lord of Bologna driven out by Julius II and to convey the message that a new political era of freedom had begun, after the tyranny of the Bentivoglio.[23] The literary genre was that of a lament, traditionally employed to convey political messages.[24] In his monologue, the protagonist – in this case the former Lord of Bologna Giovanni Bentivoglio – described himself in a tragic situation, in order to highlight his own wrongdoings and then to take the side of his opponent, whose merits were illustrated by contrast.

A poetic miscellany in the vernacular published in Bologna by the popular press represented a *summa* of the rhetorical arguments that typified the political use of the myth of the golden age during Julius's pontificate.[25] The dominant theme was renewal and the end of decline, coinciding with the coming of Julius II. 'Bologna hor per te nasce et se rinova' ('Thanks to you [Julius] Bologna is now born and renewed') declared the anonymous author of the first sonnet, while another echoed him by predicting that the city's troubles were now over and that in the future only years of happiness lay ahead.[26]

The destiny of Bologna was likened to that of Rome, for which was prophesied a return to its ancient splendour, in the context of a general renewal that would involve the whole Christian empire. Rome would become again the temporal as well as spiritual centre of the world, taking on once more the role of *caput mundi* (literally 'head of the world'). The allegorical language of poetry lent itself to giving voice to such celebratory events. The myth of the Arabian phoenix that was reborn of its own ashes was adapted to fit a political purpose for the city of Rome, as an omen for the rebirth of a stronger state:

---

[22]   Matteo Maria da Rimini, *Barzelletta nova in laude di papa Julio II composta per frate Matheo Maria da Rimino del sacro Ordine di Servi* (Bologna: Giustiniano da Rubiera,1506/1507).

[23]   Anonymous, *Lamento di Bentivogli* (Bologna: A. Lippus, 1506/1507).

[24]   On the political use of this poetical genre, see Martines, *Strong Words*, p. 244; see also *Lamenti storici dei secoli XIV, XV, XVI*, ed. by Antonio Medin and Luigi Frati, 3 vols (Bologna: Romagnoli, 1969).

[25]   Florian Zanchin and others, *Sonetti, capituli in laude de papa Iulio* (Bologna: Giovanni Antonio de'Benedetti, 1506/1507).

[26]   'Pò che Iulio secondo il ciel ti presta/requie e riposo al tuo passato affanno;/di che felice sia ogni tuo anno'. *Sonetti*, fol. 1ʳ.

Roma, seben non sei uccel Phenice,
del tuo rinovar è giunta l'hora:
d'un stato più glorioso et più felice.[27]
(Rome, even if you are not the Phoenix,
now is the time for your renewal
as a more glorious and happier state.)

A piece by Florian Zanchin, a student and later professor of medicine and philosophy in Bologna,[28] contained a bombastic description of the bucolic life, in which peace, concord and wealth prevailed while the earth gave forth its fruits without being cultivated. This egalitarian vision of the golden age, valid as much for the people as for the powerful, found its cultural roots in Ovid's *Metamorphoses* (I, 89–112). Julius II was presented as the artisan of this social palingenesis.

The contents of the verses were unquestionably the product of 'high' and elite culture, but their ideological meaning also reached the popular spheres of the urban community. This occurred thanks to the work of cultural mediation by non-professional poets, such as the anonymous versifier who flaunted his mythological learning, or of young students such as Zanchin, or else of clerics such as Fra Matteo Maria of Rimini.

Beneath their laudatory and allegorical surface, the texts reveal an ideology and a very clear political message: the contents presaged an age of splendour to be understood historically and politically. In an absolute sense for the pontifical state, this age represented a general renewal of papal temporal power. In the context of Bologna – the place of production and distribution of the verses – it meant a new age of freedom and good government after the tyranny of the Bentivoglio family, hence a legitimation of the new papal domination that would guarantee the 'common good'.

The argument of the new age that was beginning with Julius II was not used solely in circumstances of triumph but became a common thread running through the whole of Julius's papacy even in times of political and social crisis. One of these occasions was that of the distribution of a short vernacular work in verse – *Epistola di Roma a Julio pontifice maximo* (*Letter from the city of Rome to Julius the greatest pontiff*) – published in Rome between 1510 and 1511.[29] The city was going through a difficult period; the prolonged absence of the papal court owing to the pontiff's military campaigns was having a negative effect on its atmosphere. In this case, too, the author was not a professional poet but a Florentine doctor working in Rome for the Curia, Giovanni Jacopo de' Penni. He was a well-known figure in

---

27   *Sonetti*, fol. 1ʳ.

28   Concerning Florian Zanchin, see Francesco Saverio Quadrio, *Della storia e della ragione d'ogni poesia* (Milan: Francesco Agnelli, 1741), II, 675; see also Antonio Rossi, *Serafino Aquilano e la poesia cortigiana* (Brescia: Morcelliana, 1980), p. 141.

29   Giovanni Jacopo de'Penni, *Epistola di Roma a Julio pontifice maximo con la risposta del pontefice a Roma* ([Étienne Guillery(?)]: Rome, c. 1511).

Epistola di Roma a Julio Pontifice maximo
con la risposta del Pontifice a Roma.

Roma a Julio secondo pontifice maximo S. P. D.

La miseranda Roma derelitta
a te Julio pastor conuien che scriua
con cocenti sospiri mesta & afflitta
Se mal mie carmi a tua orechi arriua
non pensar senza causa mi muoua
quando penso che teco ero si diua
Di mesta piango & ognior si rinnoua
qualche nouella causa a dolermi
Cose che mal si sanno a chi sol proua

Veggo e mia plebei e ciul infermi
dolersi & io sol sento e lor sospiri
ch' bé no voglia ácor conuien dolermi
Albula ancor tal hor par che sadiri
e tumefatta va del termin fora
p che nonal pastor piu che lamiri
La gia Florida via patisce ancora
e de limini sua qualche arbor secha
per chel pastor suo fa troppo dimora

Figure 6.2　　Frontispiece of Giovanni Jacopo de'Penni

court circles and had strong links with Roman printer–publishers, for whom, on other occasions, he supplied poetic works in the vernacular celebrating Julius's pontificate.[30] This short work contained a lament in which the personification of Rome turned to Julius, despairing of his absence. The basic iconography of the publication reflected the symbols of Roman antiquity: the city presented itself in fact clad in Roman attire, while at its feet lay a shield bearing the inscription S.P.Q.R. (Figure 6.2).

The literary formula was that of an exchange of letters, the pope's reply following the lament of Rome. The latter accused Julius directly, since, after he had abandoned the city, its sacred buildings were falling into ruin, the magnificent palaces built in the new century becoming inns and taverns, agriculture was suffering and sovereigns and ambassadors were no longer visiting the city – in other words, a state of general decadence.[31]

To paraphrase the meaning of these verses, one of the indirect effects of the expansionist aims of Julius II was the political, social, religious and urban decline of Rome. What was the political message that the Florentine doctor wished to put across to the Roman people? The answer was in Julius's reply. After listing his own secular and spiritual merits, the pontiff asserted that his absence was justified by the fact that by his wars he wished to restore Rome to its former glory. With Julius's pontificate a new era would begin, which would re-establish Rome, and with it the Church, at the peak of its temporal power. The promise made by Julius was that Rome would become once more *caput mundi*.

Although shaken by contemporary events, belief in the golden age, developed in humanist circles and spread among the population, became vital as a propaganda message and also proved to be a conceptual perspective open to other themes. The ideal of the golden age recalled in fact a period of power that had typified ancient Rome, with its heroes well imprinted on the popular collective imagination and to which the papacy of Julius II claimed to be the heir, within the context of the *renovatio imperii*.

The Comparison with Caesar and the Appeal to Ancient Rome

The martial traits that the figure of Julius II assumed on the occasion of his military conquests made him resemble a great character from the Roman past: Julius Caesar. Such a comparison was not only a polemical argument used by the

---

[30]   See, for example, Giovanni Jacopo de'Penni, *La magnifica festa facta dalli Signori Romani per el carnevale MDXIII: Novamente composta per Io. Ia. De Pennis* ([Étienne Guillery(?)]: [Rome(?)], 1514).

[31]   'Molti templi pariete in terra … /Né imbasciador cercon mio confino/e regi più non scrivono a me versi/ … Le gran case e palazi che già apersi/con tanta boria del secul novello/stanno locande chome può vedersi'. de'Penni, *Epistola di Roma a Julio pontifice maximo*, fol. 1ᵛ.

pontiff's opponents – such as Erasmus or Hutten – but also, in a positive vein, by the propaganda that praised him.[32]

In 1507, a Latin panegyric by Giovanni Nagonio represented Julius as a classical *Triumphator* and an *Alter Caesar*.[33] A Latin sermon by the apostolic notary Cristoforo Marcello, delivered and printed in 1511, exalted the figure of Julius II for his work in protecting ecclesiastical freedom and his action aimed at increasing the temporal domains of the Church of Rome. According to the papal orator, he had truly conducted himself 'like a second Julius Caesar', via his fight against the barbarians and his defence of Italy against enslavement to foreign domination.[34] The likening of Julius II to Caesar, together with the recalling of the Roman past, were rhetorical formulae that found their source in the heart of pontifical cultural circles, and then spread outwards, into the periphery – both geographical and socio-cultural – of the Papal State.

The myth of Rome was rooted in the collective memory of Italian society, on all social levels, whether 'high' or 'low', representing the *auctoritas* on which to found a promotional message. Many promotional writings emphasised the parallel between Julius II and Julius Caesar. 'A un Julio Roma, a l'altro la Romagna/è destinata per ragion al mondo' ('As the first Julius conquered Rome, the destiny of Julius II is to dominate the region Romagna'), argued an anonymous sonnet circulated in Ferrara in the autumn of 1506, with the aim of strengthening the inevitability of papal action in Romagna.[35] In the verses of a Servite friar, the latter rejoiced because it was henceforth clear that Rome had returned to the ancient splendours of the time of Caesar and indirectly the Church saw its own authority being reborn. In his cyclical view of history the negative cycle of decadence had been completed and he seemed now to hear once more the trumpets of 'Caesare

---

[32]   Erasmus compared the two Juliuses in his satiric *Epigramma in Iulium II*; see Erasmus of Rotterdam, *Iulius exclusus e coelis*, ed. by Giorgio Maselli (Bari: Palomar, 1995), pp. 152–5. Concerning Hutten, see for example the Latin epigram *De Iulio Allusio*: 'Iulius est Romae, qui abest? Date, numina, Brutum!', *Ulrichi Hutteni Opera*, ed. by Eduard Böcking, 5 vols (Leipzig: Teubner, 1859–62), III (1862), p. 265.

[33]   Giovanni Nagonio, *Ad divum Iulium II et Franciscum Mariam nepotem libri I–VIII* (1507). Rome, Biblioteca Apostolica Vaticana: ms. Vat. Lat. 1682. Nagonius wrote celebratory verses like these for many European monarchs, often celebrating them by the comparison with Caesar. See Paul Gwynne, '*Tu Alter Caesar eris*: Maximilian I, Vladislav II, Johannes Michael Nagonius and the *Renovatio Imperii*', *Renaissance Studies*, 10 (1996), pp. 56–71.

[34]   Cristoforo Marcello, *Oratio ad Iulium II pont. max. in die omnium Sanctorum* (Rome: M. Silber, 1511); on this oration see John W. O'Malley, *Praise and Blame in Renaissance Rome: Rhetoric, Doctrine, and Reform in the Sacred Orators of the Papal Court, c. 1450–1521* (Durham, NC: Duke University Press, 1979), p. 66; see also Charles L. Stinger, *The Renaissance in Rome* (Bloomington, IN: Indiana University Press, 1998), p. 242.

[35]   The sonnet was copied by Sanuto, see Sanuto, *Diarii*, VI, col. 463.

imperatore'.[36] 'You were Julius the second, but now you are Julius the first', was how the pope was praised in another eulogistic composition of 1507, which compared the taking of Bologna with the great conquests of Roman history achieved by Julius Caesar and Scipio.[37] In the same poetical miscellany the biographies of the two figures were placed alongside one another, establishing an analogy between the life of Julius II and that of Caesar. The reference was to the forced exile in France that Della Rovere endured during Alexander VI's pontificate and Caesar's campaigns in Gaul: after being forced to leave Rome behind, both returned there in triumph, reaching the apogee of their power.[38]

The similarity was explicit in the symbology of the triumphal rite celebrated by Julius II in Bologna in 1506. A medal struck for the occasion bore the effigy of the pontiff accompanied by the inscription IULIUS CAESAR PONTIFEX II,[39] while a triumphal arch carried an inscription with an unmistakable reference to the figure of Caesar: *Veni, Vidi, Vici*.[40]

In this climate of recalling the symbols of Imperial Rome, members of the consistory also sometimes enjoyed similar treatment. In 1509, after the victory of the papal troops at Agnadello against the Venetians, the return to Bologna of the cardinal legate Alidosi was greeted by anonymous tercets that depicted him as the executor of the pontiff's great military designs. Thanks to their actions the pontiff and the cardinal deserved the same glory as the ancient Romans. While Julius II had acted to eliminate the nepotistic power of Cesare Borgia in Romagna and to depose the local tyrants, Alidosi had triumphed militarily along the Via Flaminia. The words of the motto with which the author described the cardinal's undertakings left no doubt as to whom his reference to antiquity was intended:

> Domò i nipoti, e i fieri tiranni estinse
> Giulio Ligure invitto e glorioso,
> L'altro in Flaminia *venne, vide e vinse*.[41]

---

[36]   Matteo Maria da Rimini, *Barzelletta nova in laude di papa Julio II*, fol. 1ᵛ.

[37]   *Sonetti*, fol. 1ʳ.

[38]   'Cesar partisse e tornò cum victoria', and 'Iulio scacciato fu cum molto torto/hor vive in sedia cum triompho e gloria'. *Sonetti*, fol. 1ᵛ.

[39]   Luigi Frati, *Delle monete gettate al popolo nel solenne ingresso in Bologna di Giulio II per la cacciata di Gio. II Bentivoglio*, Estratto dagli Atti e memorie della R. Deputazione di storia patria per le provincie di Romagna, III serie, I, fasc. VI (Modena: Tipografia Vincenzi, 1883), pp. 1–15; see also Roberto Weiss, 'The medals of Pope Julius II (1503–1513)', *Journal of the Warburg and Courtauld Institutes*, 28 (1965), pp. 163–82.

[40]   See Sanuto, *Diarii*, VII, col. 64.

[41]   Anonymous, *In Franciscum Alidosium Cardinalem Papiensem Italiae totius Legatum, post felicem de Venetis victoriam, Bononiam redientem Encomion*; in Giovan Francesco Negri, *Annali della patria*. Bologna: Biblioteca Universitaria, MSS 1107, t. VII/1 (1500–28), fols. 83ᵛ–84ʳ. I wish to thank Dr Giorgio Forni for drawing my attention to this poem.

(Julius of Liguria undefeated and glorious
with nephews subdued and tyrants extinguished,
the other[42] to Flaminia *came, saw* and *conquered.*)

Alidosi was a figure hated by the people of Bologna, and so the propaganda operation launched at the moment of his entry into the city was not only justified but necessary. It was therefore prepared very carefully by the pontifical authority. On the occasion of his entry more than 500 propagandistic prints were distributed among the population, as the chronicler Giovan Francesco Negri recorded.[43] The vernacular verses served a promotional function of consolidating the local authority of papal government in a situation in which its prestige was seriously questioned. When – after 1510 – the pope challenged militarily the King of France, Louis XII, in the context of his political project of freeing Italy from the 'barbarians', the figure of Julius Caesar and the memory of his successes in Gaul were amply exploited by popular political poetry to foment anti-French sentiments. The appeal to the figure of Caesar was intended as a promotional presage for the papal undertaking, which would result in a similar success. An anonymous travelling singer invited the Italian townspeople to remember the exploits of Caesar against the Gauls:

su riportate a memoria
Iulio Cesar quel Augusto
che ottenne così grande victoria
contra el Gallo tanto robusto.[44]
(Remember
that glorious Julius Caesar Augustus
who achieved such a great victory
against the strong Gaul.)

It is probable that Julius II did not consider himself as Julius Caesar's heir and did not even hope to actually revive the imperial Roman tradition. He did, however, have a political interest in encouraging the spread of this type of representation and he never denied his own support for those very humanist circles that encouraged such comparison. The references to the myth of ancient Rome and to the figure of Caesar represented a political allegory of Julius II's temporal conception of the papacy. This was not only a rhetorical and propagandistic expedient but also the

---

    42   The cardinal Alidosi.

    43   'Si dispensarono per la città alle genti in honor del Cardinale alcuni cartelli stampati, dei quali se ne gettarono dalla Ringhiera de gl'Anziani più di cinquecento'. Negri, *Annali della patria*, fol. 83ᵛ.

    44   Anonymous, *Barzelletta in laude de tutta l'Italia et la liberatione sua contra francesi* ([n.p.]: [n. pub.] c. 1512).

pragmatic expression of a real and personal programme, driven by great financial power, military force and territorial expansion.

The renewed Julian empire differed from that of the past by being a Christian *imperium*. The eternal mission of Rome gave a sacred and prophetic dimension to the political cum religious activity of Julius II in defence of *Dignitas Ecclesiae*.[45] This vision found expression in the verses of a sonnet by Matteo Maria of Rimini. With the coming of Julius the Church was at last freeing itself of the yoke that had long oppressed it and had forced it to remain 'nuda di costumi e di stato' (naked of culture and of a state). Thanks to the exploits of the 'gran pastore' ('the great pastor'), extolled as a new Augustus and a divinity on earth, the Church – understood as synonymous with Rome – was returning to its ancient splendours after a long period of moral and political decadence.[46]

Tranquillitatis Largitori: Julius as a Peace Keeper

The definition of Julius II as a 'warrior pope' has now become a tautology, for the very nature of his political and military activity fully justifies such an appellation. Many symbols and representations of Julius's power could indeed be traced back to an ideology of domination and military force. However, in an apparently sharp contrast to the traditionally bellicose image associated with him, one of the modes of self-representation most often employed by the pontiff was the image of one who had restored peace, harmony and justice.[47]

In 1513, in the funeral oration that he delivered for the recently deceased pontiff, the orator Tommaso Inghirami pointed out the characteristic merits of the figure of Julius II. Inghirami, one of the key figures in the cultural entourage of the Roman court, exalted the conciliatory role played by Julius during his pontificate. Among Della Rovere's qualities, the Lateran canon particularly emphasised in his eulogy Julius's prudence and amongst the pope's achievements those of having overthrown tyrants, ended civil discord and internal feuds in the cities, and having done so not through force of arms but thanks to his authority and judgement.[48]

---

45   D'Ascia, *Erasmo e l'umanesimo romano*, p. 183.

46   'Godi de nostra etate o summo Augusto,/Sacro signore magnanimo e cortese/ … Per te la Chiesa del iugo vetusto/se svelle e mira compensar le offese'. 'Sonetto' in Matteo Maria da Rimini, *Barzelletta nova in laude di papa Julio*, fol. 2ᵛ.

47   'In Julius's pontificate there was no room for symbols of power linked to peace, abundance or justice, notions tied to projects of internal pacification'. Irene Fosi, 'Court and city in the ceremony of the *Possesso*', in *Court and Politics in Papal Rome (1492–1700)*, ed. by Gianvittorio Signorotto and Maria Antonietta Visceglia (Cambridge: Cambridge University Press, 2002), pp. 31–52 (p. 42).

48   'Bone Deus! Quod illius ingenium fuit, quae prudentia, quae regendi, administrandique imperii peritia? … tyrannides exintinxisset, civiles dissensiones, intestinaque odia, *non armis, sed consilio*, atque auctoritate sua absolvisset'. Tommaso

Similar peace-giving representations of Julius II were also to be found in contemporary large-circulation publications. Among these texts was a short work printed in Bologna in 1507, a short chivalric epic in octaves recounting the reconquering of the city by the pope: *Historia come papa Iulio ha prese la città de Bologna* (*The history of how Pope Julius took the city of Bologna*).[49] The author was a travelling singer who made no secret of his allegiance to Julius II – surely the same Giacomo de' Sorci who had celebrated the pontiff's exploits on other occasions.[50] This short poem conveyed the image of Julius as a great bringer of peace to the cities of the Papal State, which were being torn apart at the time by violent internal factional strife. The ballad singer sought to put across the providential nature of Julius II's undertakings, which was response to a real sense of urgency felt by the local population, a demand for political and social peace.

The pontiff's ceaseless striving for peace, in the course of the march that led him from Rome to Bologna, was described by the travelling singer according to a decidedly repetitive narrative pattern: Julius II travelled through the papal lands, stopped in a city divided by internal struggles and restored to it a climate of peace. This happened first in Viterbo;[51] then in Perugia;[52] again in Cesena;[53] and lastly in Bologna, the final goal of the papal expedition.[54]

Despite the apparent inconsistency, a pope known in history for his outstanding feats of arms and his warrior image was celebrated as the defender of peace and justice. It was in this peace-bringing light that he was portrayed in one of the apologetic compositions produced after the reconquering of Bologna. This was no longer a time for war but for peace – this was the message communicated to make the Bolognese population accept the change of government imposed upon it:

Inghirami, *Thomae Phaedri Inghirami Volaterrani orationes duae altera in funere Galeotti Franciotti Card. Vicecancellarii altera item funeris pro Julio II Pontifice Maximo*, ed. by Pietro Galletti (Rome: [s. pub.], 1777), p. 96.

[49]   Giacomo de' Sorci ('il Cortonese'), *Historia come papa Iulio ha prese la città de Bologna* (Bologna: Benedetto di Ettore Faelli, 1507).

[50]   See, for example, Giacomo de' Sorci ('il Cortonese'), *Historia dele guerre, dela beatitudine de Papa Iulio secondo* (Bologna: Giustiniano da Rubiera, 1532).

[51]   'Perché era quella terra in divisione,/ ... e presto ha quel popul congregato/e finalmente lo pacificane'. Cortonese, *Historia come papa Iulio ha prese la città de Bologna*, fol. 1ᵛ.

[52]   'La quale sentiva affanni e graveze/con suo bel parlar e careze/ ... fe far a tutto quanto el populo pace'. Cortonese, *Historia come papa Iulio ha prese la città de Bologna*, fol. 1ᵛ.

[53]   'La quale era divisa in mantinente/e Iulio presto la cavò de pena,/pacificò quel populo humilmente'. Cortonese, *Historia come papa Iulio ha prese la città de Bologna*, fol. 1ᵛ.

[54]   'Dove ciaschuno si serà pacificato/ ... el papa ve metterann a bon porto/e ve farano bona signoria'. Cortonese, *Historia come papa Iulio ha prese la città de Bologna*, fol. 2ᵛ.

Viva Iulio el gran pastore,

...

de iustitia tutto ornato

e della pace protectore.[55]

(Long live the great pastor,

...

adorned with justice

and protector of peace.)

There were many similar examples of the image of the pope as peace-maker in papal propaganda, not only in popular publications but also in other promotional media. In the triumph celebrated for his entry into the city of Bologna, the inscriptions written on the triumphal arches created for the parade and the civic festivity left no doubt as to the message that the papal entourage wished to convey to the citizens: IULIO II. TYRANNORUM EXPULSORI, TRANQULLITATIS LARGITORI; LIBERATORI PATRIAE; BONOMIA A TYRANNIDE LIBERATA; ECCLESIASTICI STATUS REPARATOR; DONATOR LIBERTATIS BONOMIAE.[56] In the procession that took place for his re-entry into Rome, in March 1507, the inscriptions were in the same vein: DIVO IULIO II, PONTIFICI MAXIMO, LIBERTATIS ASSERTORIS, AUCTORIS PACIS, JUSTITIAE PROPUGNACULO, CUSTODI QUETIS, TRANQUILLITATIS FUNDATORI.[57]

The short printed works circulated at the same time as Julius's entrance and triumph were an integral part of a vast ceremonial programme, the organisation of which was delegated to the pontifical master of ceremonies Paride de' Grassi, in direct consultation with the pontiff. In the plan of the celebratory rituals, the image of the pope as peace-keeper had a central role. It is difficult to show what degree of control the master of ceremonies could also exercise over the minor publications, but it is certain that their message was perfectly consistent with the programme he had conceived. The papal authorities used printed matter, also communicated in oral form, as an instrument to make the central meaning of an event accessible to the people, comprehensible to different levels of readership. This was a common practice, employed for most public festive events in the early modern period.[58]

For people of the time the term 'peace' could take on various meanings: concrete and political on the one hand, universal and religious on the other. In a less abstract and more understandable sense for the inhabitants of the Italian cities of that period, it meant the ending of the wars that since 1494 had been afflicting the peninsula. The topical appeal to peace was conceptually linked to the dominant theme of papal propaganda, the myth of a new golden age dominated

---

[55] *Sonetti*, fol. 3ʳ.

[56] Sanuto, *Diarii*, VI, coll. 492–3.

[57] Sanuto, *Diarii*, VII, coll. 63–5.

[58] Christian Jouhaud, 'Nota sui manifesti e i loro lettori (secoli XVI–XVII)', *Annali della Scuola Normale Superiore di Pisa*, 23 (1993), pp. 411–26 (p. 416).

by concord and prosperity. The connection was evident in a short poem in octaves produced in perhaps the most violent period of the Italian wars, that preceding the dramatic battle in Ravenna between the confederates of the Holy League, formed by Julius II, and the French. However, the anonymous travelling singer conferred a pragmatic value on the theoretical ideal of a new golden age, identifying it with the widespread hope among the Italian population for an end to the wars.[59] The figure who embodied this yearning for peace was none other than the 'Great Pope' Julius II: 'Eccoti in nostro aiuto quanto po' Iulio gran pastor' ('here he is to help us as much as he can: Julius the great pastor').[60]

The explosion of the Italian wars had made all of the peninsula's population aware of the political and social crisis affecting it, not only the highest levels, and it was on these shared feelings and fears that Julius's propaganda sought to build. In this socio-historical situation the call for the defence of Italy was expressly linked to the aspiration towards peace and political order. In 1510, the Roman printer Joan Belpin published a short work containing a poem in octaves composed by a cleric and poet from Romagna, Giraldo Podio of Lugo. In this poem he lamented Rome's past, a time when it dominated the whole of the known world. Rome was understood as being synonymous with Italy, both of which Podio referred as one and the same 'patria' ('homeland').[61] The author reviewed the events of the recent past, from the descent of French King Charles VIII until his own day, describing how Italy had now lost its independence and its ancient power.

In harmony with the policy pursued by Julius II at that time, the romagnol bard asserted that peace in Italy was linked to its liberation from domination by foreign powers. In addition Podio likened the destiny of the Church – defined as an 'errante barca' ('wandering ship') on a stormy sea – to that of Rome and the whole of Italy, for which the hope of salvation, peace and freedom was always represented by Julius II.[62]

The *Lamento de Italia* (The Lament of Italy) by the poet Giacomo Rossetto, in which the personification of Italy entrusted its own fate to the secular force of the papacy, was also dedicated to 'beatissimo Papa Giulio secondo' (the most holy pope Julius II).[63] Italy was represented on the frontispiece by the image of a woman, kneeling between two groups of soldiers holding out their weapons

---

[59]   'Ritornando l'aurea nostra etade/regnarà amore, pace e charitade'. Anonymous, *La vera nova de Bressa de punto in punto com'è andata. Novamente impressa* (Venice: Alessandro Bindoni, c. 1512), fol. 2ʳ.

[60]   Anon., *La vera nova de Bressa*, fol. 2ʳ.

[61]   Giraldo Podio da Lugo, *Continentie de tutte le guerre de franzosi in Jtalia* (Rome: J. Belpin, [1510(?)]).

[62]   'Ma tu pastore delle celesti chiavi/che sei in terra unico Monarcha/ ... fai felice il tuo sacro Tevere/metti Italia in pace e suo paese libero'. Giraldo Podio, *Continentie de tutte le guerre de franzosi in Jtalia*, fol. 4ᵛ.

[63]   Giacomo Rossetto, *Lamento de Italia diviso in capituli septe composito per Jacobo Rossetto Darthonese al beatissimo Papa Julio Secundo* ([n. p.]: before October 1512).

Lamento de Italia diuiso in capituli septe:com posito per Jacobo Rossetto Darthonese: al Beatissimo Papa Julio Secundo.

Ital dolce fonte/o ql benigno fiume
dara tanta aqua a qsti occhii doleti
che pianger possa/e mantenere el lume
Qual aura suaue /o quai piatosi uenti
daran tal fiato al mio palato exausto
che esca la uoce infra la lingua e i denti
Qual elleganza o qual facundo fausto
dara de ornato pur una sintilla
tal chel mio canto sia grato holocausto
Italia son che piu non ho fauilla
che sia lucente unde mi lagno e doglio
chio fui Regina/e son uenuta ancilla
Perho Minerua piu inuocar non uoglio
ne Dio/ne Apollo/ne Romul/ne Iano
piu non essendo quella che esser soglio
Inuocar uoglio ogni deserto strano
qual per pieta del mio dolore amaro
ascoltar uoglia el mio lameto humano
Ma narraro qualche tempo mio chiaro
prima che i danni e le ferite conti
a cui non so como piu sia riparo
Audite silue/e uuy riuere/e monti
isole/boschi & aride spelonche
tiui/torrenti/fiumi/lachi e fonti

Audite scogli/e uuy marine conche
antri/e deserti che natura mostra
uuy uirtu perse/ e uuy speranze tronche
Region lotane oue el mio nome giostra
ficre/ucelli/aque/terra/aiere/e foco
audite el mal dela regina uostra
Quella man santa riuerita poco
qual se del mondo tutte le prouincie
me die bel sito/e deleteuol loco
Tal che nulla altra di belta mi uince
ben che per longa uetusta grauata
troppo consompta a indebilir comince
Son pur la terra ben posta e fondata
sotto le stelle fortunata e chiara
e de gli ben de la natura ornata
Son di circuitu e di grandeza rara
larga e diffusa quanto porta el sito
e de ogni fructo a ben uiuer preclara
Da un cato ho lalpe e il gra mote munito
che parton Fracia/ e Lalamagna prope
da laltra il piano/e la marina/e il lito
De amenitate i non mi trouo inope
ho laier dolce/e temperato il cielo
piu che i Britanno, e piu che Lethiope

Figure 6.3   Frontispiece of Giacomo Rossetto

Spauento de Italia

F . M . S . ad Lectorem .
Depofto haueuo giu larco : e la cetra
la pēna : il calamar : linchioftro:e carte
piu non uolendo exercitar queftarte
batter uolea la lyra : in uña pietra
Quando chio uidi uña dongella tetra
uenir contra di me : daftrana parte
un gallo la feguia con lale fparte
lei grida : e fugge : e quanto po farietra
Stupefatto : mirando tal fciagura
mi feci audace : adomandar chi lera
la mefchina rifpofe : Italia obfcura
Chi tha condutta diffi : in tal maniera
Marco : che ftato meffo in fepultura
pero mi fegue il Gallo : e uol chio pera
Alhor turbai la cera
Domandando pur come/e lei fofpira
tal che fu forza a ripigliar la lyra

Figure 6.4   Frontispiece of Francesco Maria Sacchino da Modigliana

(Figure 6.3). Rossetto's lament consisted of a verse summary of the history of Italy, from the founding of Rome up until the present. The first two chapters explained the link with the Roman past, described as a golden age for the peninsula, via the enumeration of the political and cultural glories of ancient Rome. The third and fourth dealt with the decline characterised by the barbarian invasions, while the fifth evoked the dramatic events of the Italian wars, presenting a peninsula divided and torn apart by war. The sixth chapter described an Italy from which the ancient golden age had now vanished and contained an urgent topical appeal to Julius II to restore peace and concord, ushering in a new golden age. Thus would the pope have honoured the memory of the ancient Julius.[64]

The verses of this travelling singer represented a synthesis of the main themes that typified the rhetoric of Julian ideology so far discussed: the golden age, the appeal to Caesar and to ancient Rome, and the image of Julius as a bringer of peace and defender of Italy. Like the woman in the frontispiece of the *Spavento de Italia* (Fear of Italy), the destiny of Italy was also inextricably tied to the oak tree of the Della Rovere family (Figure 6.4), the only hope of peace and salvation for the destiny of the peninsula.

Conclusion

There was no shortage of discordant voices to speak out against the glowing picture of the Julian papacy painted by pontifical propaganda. In periods of dispute with the papacy, poets and travelling singers were encouraged by other institutional political players to publish polemical messages and disparaging writings against the pontiff.[65] Venice and Ferrara were the main centres of this adversarial propaganda, which sought to deny or overturn the arguments of papal rhetoric. The communicative process analysed here for Italy and for Julius II's papacy was not therefore an isolated phenomenon but can be placed within a wider European framework. It is well known that in the German-speaking area with the coming of the Reformation, the production of *Flugschriften* (literally flying sheets) made use of the power of images and printing to spread a message of religious propaganda among the illiterate members of the population.[66] However, even earlier, in the years of Julius's pontificate, similar phenomena were to be found in other European contexts, in the realms of both political communication

---

[64] 'Sotto te spero un triumphante premio/qual mostra el nome del antico Iulio'. Rossetto, *Lamento*, fol. 5ᵛ.

[65] 'The Church hierarchy was often the target of fierce attacks in verse, a risky exercise; but these were most likely to be handed around in learned circles, except in times of war with the papacy, when poets and *cantimbanca* were protected by their cities or by the prince in conflict with the Church'. Martines, *Strong Words*, p. 243.

[66] Robert W. Scribner, *For the Sake of Simple Folk: Popular Propaganda for the German Reformation*, 2nd edn (Oxford: Clarendon Press, 1994).

and publishing. In France, Louis XII orchestrated publicity campaigns by means of the printing press to promote his own political actions. The first of these was directed against Venice at the time of the League of Cambrai;[67] the second was aimed against Julius II himself with the purpose of justifying to the French public the war undertaken by the *très chrétien* (most Christian) king against a Roman pontiff.[68] The war initiated by Louis XII was one of communication, fought via the use of the printing press, by the publication on royal command of a heterogeneous mass of anti-Julian texts: pamphlets, poetical works, vignettes and printed matter of every kind.[69] The majority of them were works in verse distributed by means of cheap print and in oral form via readings and public performances.

In England, Henry VIII's decision to ally himself militarily with Julius II and therefore to wage war against Louis XII was the source of a printed propaganda campaign directed towards the English people, who had to bear the economic brunt of the war. A dense Latin prose treatise was written by the humanist James Whytstons to legitimate, using the weapons of law and theology, the political decisions of Henry VIII in the eyes of a cultivated public.[70] The same text was translated into English verse by an anonymous poet and consequently given wide printed circulation in various editions and re-editions. The result was a poetical and allegorical synopsis of a prose work, a short and accessible text that extracted the meaning of the initial work and made it suitable to a wider and less cultivated public, conveying a propagandistic message.[71]

In the whole of Europe, therefore, published material that was inferior in quality but significant in quantity came to play an important role in political debate. This prompts general reflection on the role of the printing press in the realm of political

---

[67]   Michael A. Sherman, 'Political propaganda and Renaissance culture: French reactions to the League of Cambrai, 1509–1510', *The Sixteenth Century Journal*, 8 (1977) Supplement, pp. 97–128.

[68]   Michael A. Sherman, 'The selling of Louis XII: Propaganda and popular culture in Renaissance France, 1498–1515' (unpublished doctoral thesis, University of Chicago, 1974).

[69]   According to Cynthia J Brown: 'Ce moment marque le vrai début de la guerre pamphlétaire de Louis XII, par laquelle il cherchait à contrôler l'opinion publique en France'. Pierre Gringoire, *Œuvres polémiques rédigées sous le règne de Louis XII*, ed. by Cynthia J. Brown (Geneva: Droz, 2003), p. 125.

[70]   James Whytstons, *De iusticia & sanctitate belli per Iulium pontificem secundum in scismaticos et tirannos patrimonium Petri invadentes indicti allegationes* (London: Richard Pynson, 1512).

[71]   Anonymous, *The Gardyners Passetaunce: Touchyng the outrage of Fraunce* (London: Richard Pynson, 1512). Concerning this poem, see *The Gardyners Passetaunce*, ed. by Franklin B. Williams (London: printed for presentation to members of the Roxburghe Club, 1985) and Rospocher, '"Il passatempo del giardiniere": La giusta guerra di Enrico VIII in difesa della Chiesa cattolica', in *Famiglia e religione nella prima età moderna. Saggi in onore di Silvana Seidel Menchi*, ed. by Giovanni Ciappelli, Serena Luzzi and Massimo Rospocher (Rome: Edizioni di Storia e Letteratura, 2011) pp. 129–44.

communication, its potential to influence the formation of public opinions and its relation to political power. It is certainly anachronistic to speak of a 'public sphere' in the Europe of the early sixteenth century, since large-circulation printing was not yet an instrument able to foster an informed and critical popular participation in political life, but rather a tool of political communication in the hands of authorities. However, the attempts made by political authorities to condition the political discourses of an early modern form of public opinion via the printing press are witness to the fact that the conditions for the emergence of a 'public sphere' of political debate, although far from being fully realised, were already present in the first half of the sixteenth century.[72]

---

[72]   The historiographical debate originated by the seminal work of Jürgen Habermas (*The Structural Transformation of the Public Sphere: An Inquiry into a category of Bourgeois Society* (Cambridge: Polity Press, 1989) is too broad to be summarised here. On the Habermasian notion of the 'public sphere', see *Habermas and the public sphere*, ed. by Craig Calhoun (Cambridge, MA: MIT Press, 1992) and, more recently, *Beyond the Public Sphere: Opinions, Publics, Spaces in Early Modern Europe*, ed. by Massimo Rospocher (Berlin/Bologna: Dunker & Humblot/Il Mulino, 2012).

Chapter 7

Denis Sauvage – Renaissance Editor of Medieval Manuscripts

Catherine Emerson

The path that Denis Sauvage (1520?–87?) took to becoming the editor of medieval French historiography almost reads like a caricature of the career of a Renaissance man. An examination of his subsequent evolution tells us much about his – and his century's – attitude to authorities, whether textual or historical. Historiographer by appointment to four successive French monarchs, Henri II, François II, Charles IX and Henri III, Sauvage's early work was, like that of his mentor and friend, Jean Martin dedicated to the transmission of Latin and Italian culture to an impoverished France.[1] Between 1546 and 1553 he published at least seven such works, beginning with a translation of Plutarch before moving onto Italian authors such as Bocaccio and the works of writers of history, Paul Jove and Pandolfo Collenuccio. At some point he seems to have become convinced, along with many of his contemporaries, that mere translation of Italian works would not be sufficient to rescue France from the state of post-classical desuetude into which it had fallen, and that what was necessary was the creation of a competing French tradition equally aware of its classical ancestry. This decision may have had a personal motivation: he had spent a short period in Geneva and appears to have flirted with Protestantism and, on his return, was seeking to prove his orthodox credentials by acquiring aristocratic patronage.[2] Flattery of France and of its royal family was one way to do this, but Sauvage suggests that he has other disinterested

---

[1] Sauvage's close relationship with Martin, who was over a decade his senior, means that he appears in a peripheral role in accounts of the other man's career. See *Jean Martin: Un traducteur au temps de François Ier et de Henri II*, Cahiers Saulnier, 16 (Paris: Presses de l'École Normale Supérieure, 1999). Indeed, it was Sauvage who wrote Martin's biography when he died. However, the fact that Martin was above all else a translator means that many accounts of Sauvage's activity focus on this aspect of his work, and on the editorial assistance he provided to Martin, rather than on his editions of French texts. For an appraisal of Sauvage's role as royal historiographer, see Paul-Martin Bondois, 'Henri II et ses historiographes', *Bulletin Philologique et historique (jusqu'à 1715) du comité des travaux historiques et scientifiques* (1925), pp. 135–49.

[2] A biography of Sauvage, including a discussion of his stay in Geneva, the motives for which remain to be uncovered, is given in Cristian Bratu 'Denis Sauvage: The editing of medieval chronicles in sixteenth-century France', *Studies in Medieval and Renaissance History*, 3rd series, 7 (2010), pp. 256–78.

and patriotic motivations for his choice. For example, in a prologue dedicated to Henri II prior to his acquisition of the title of royal historiographer, Sauvage claims that he began compiling an account of the deeds of earlier kings of France, a work that he hoped would be both pleasurable and profitable 'à tous les Seigneurs & peuples de Frāce' ('to all the Lords and peoples of France') and fulfil the 'commun deuoir de proffiter à la patrie' ('the common obligation to benefit the nation').[3] Whether this account ever actually existed, or whether it was simply a pretext for his editing activities, is a matter for debate, but it seems clear that his own history never saw the light of day. Instead, he claimed that, in the course of writing it, he came across the work of other historians who had been ill-served by earlier editors and he interrupted his own historiography to work on editions that would do them justice. His first edition, of the work of Nicole Gilles, appeared in 1549, and this was followed three years later by the *Mémoires* of Philippe de Commynes, whom he believed would be revealed as 'le plus excelent [des] Historiographes François, voire egal aux meilleurs de toutes autres langues' ('The most excellent of the French historians, equalling even the best of those writing in other languages'),[4] given an adequate edition. In the years that followed, Sauvage subjected the work of other late medieval historians to the same treatment: his edition of the history of Jean Froissart appeared in four weighty volumes between 1559 and 1561, that of Olivier de La Marche in 1562 and that of Enguerrand de Monstrelet in 1572. Extracts from the latter three authors' works also appeared in his continuation to the *Chronique de Flandres*, published, like the anonymous *Chronique* itself, in 1562. This year also signalled a break with his previous methodology, for while he had worked largely from printed editions for his translations and for his editions of Gilles, Commynes and Froissart, La Marche's *Mémoires* and the *Chronique de Flandres* were previously unpublished and Sauvage was obliged to establish his texts from manuscript sources.

That is not to say that Sauvage had not previously used manuscripts. His editions of Froissart and of Commynes had both employed manuscript witnesses alongside printed editions. However, in each of these cases the manuscripts used had only contained a part of the text to be edited and Sauvage's primary point of reference had been to printed editions. With La Marche's *Mémoires* and the *Chronique de Flandres* this approach had to change but, when it did so, it was

    3   Denis Sauvage, 'Au Treschrestien Roy Henry' in *Les Memoires de MESSIRE PHILIPPE DE Cōmines, Cheualier, Seigneur d'Argenton: sur les principaux faicts & gestes de Louis onziéme & de Charles huictiéme, son fils, Roys de France. Reueus & corrigez par Denis Sauvage de Fontenailles en Brie, svr vn Exemplaire pris à l'orignal de l'Auteur, & suyuant les bons Historiographes & Croniqueurs. Auec distinction de liures, selon les matieres, estans aussi les chapitres autrement distinguez que par cy deuant, & brief, le tout mieux ordonné: ainsi que les Lecteurs pourront voir par l'auertissement à eux addrecé, apres l'Epistre au Roy* (Paris: Iean de Roigny, 1552). Hereafter this edition will be referred to as Commynes, *Mémoires*, ed. by Sauvage.
    4   Sauvage, 'Au Treschrestien Roy Henry', in Commynes, *Mémoires*, ed. by Sauvage.

in unexpected ways that provide insight into a complex relationship between the sixteenth-century editor, the modern reader and the question of the authority to be accorded to a manuscript.

We cannot neglect the role of the modern reader in this interaction because it is in part our assumptions about Sauvage's modernity that condition the expectations that we bring to his manuscript editing – expectations that are, as we shall see, far removed from his actual practice. Sauvage is considered to be a modern editor partly because his editions look like modern critical editions: they contain marginal notes and extensive commentaries at the end of the volumes. This is not the case in earlier printed editions – where they exist – of the same works. In earlier editions the text had been presented alone, without any editorial gloss. The innovation of Sauvage's editions is to distinguish visually between the editor and his material. Since the pattern adopted by Sauvage is the one followed by subsequent editors, the tendency to regard Sauvage's edition as 'modern' in contrast to earlier 'medieval' versions is great. Moreover, it is inevitably heightened by the fact that, unlike earlier editors, Sauvage did not employ gothic script but had his books set in humanist typefaces. All these things taken together lead modern commentators to adopt attitudes such as that displayed by Jean Dufournet, who is currently working on an edition of Commynes's *Mémoires*, and who refers to Sauvage's edition (the fourth to be published of the work) as 'la première édition critique' ('the first critical edition').[5] Nevertheless, it would be wrong to assume that, just because Sauvage's editions look like modern critical editions, his attitude to the primacy of the manuscript was that of a modern author.

Recent research has made it increasingly clear that, although Sauvage uses the rhetoric of the modern editor of medieval texts, sifting through variant and corrupted readings in an attempt to establish an 'original text', his idea of what constitutes this ideal text is somewhat removed from modern approaches. Cristian Bratu has shown that, despite his criticism of the intervention of editors in his translations, Sauvage relies upon their editions to establish the text from which he works, and does not return to a manuscript source.[6] This produces the incongruous situation where a translator purports to present a text that is closer to the author's original than any edition in the original language, despite the fact that the translator is only working from these published editions. Of course, it could be objected that the constraints placed on travel in the sixteenth century may have made access to manuscripts difficult, but an examination of the way that Sauvage treated manuscripts he did have access to – especially when manuscripts were his only source – suggests that his attitude to them and to the sort of authority that they represented was somewhat different from what one might expect from his rhetoric.

---

[5]   Jean Dufournet, 'Denis Sauvage et Commynes. La première édition critique des *Mémoires*', in *Convergences médiévales: Épopée, lyrique, roman. Mélanges offerts à Madeleine Tyssens*, ed. by Nadine Henrard, Paola Moreno and Martine Thiry-Stassin (Paris: De Boeck, 2001), pp. 161–72 (p. 161).

[6]   Bratu, 'Denis Sauvage', pp. 268–9.

One of the first observations that must be made in this regard is that terminology in the sixteenth century appears to have been more developed in the realm of printing than in that of codicology. Specialist terms for manuscripts, including that designating the object itself, appear to have been lacking or underused and the terminology that existed was drawn from the world of printing. Sauvage consciously applies typographical vocabulary to handwritten documents when describing the manuscript he used to compile Commynes's *Mémoires*, with its 'grandes lettres, que les Imprimeurs nomment Capitales & Versales' ('large letters, which printers call capitals and initials'). The word *manuscrit* itself is not attested to prior to 1594 and was not used as a noun until La Fontaine's *Fables* in 1668.[7] Perhaps as a consequence, Denis Sauvage does not appear to have had an exact terminology to describe manuscripts themselves. Where the manuscript source is partial, as is the case for his edition of Froissart, he uses the term 'abregé'. Otherwise, he uses 'exemplaire' and 'copie' but does not distinguish between the two terms and does not restrict the use of either to manuscript sources. For instance, in his introductory 'Advertissement aux lecteurs' to the *Mémoires* of Philippe de Commynes, Sauvage details the 'Exemplaires ou Copies, que i'aye peu recouurer, pour m'aider à la correction' ('the exampla or copies which I have been able to retrieve, to aid me in my correction')[8] of his source manuscript, before detailing the four earlier printed editions of the work. He does not count the manuscript which he has consulted to prepare this edition as one of these 'Exemplaires ou Copies', but he calls it too an 'Exemplaire'. Sometimes he signals a distinction between printed sources and manuscripts by employing the definite article when talking about the manuscript, saying 'l'Exemplaire' or 'le viel Exemplaire', but he is not consistent in this usage. In other editions where he has referred to a manuscript Sauvage employs the same terminology, suggesting that the manuscript is a source to be consulted but only one amongst others. In a sense, the situation could not be otherwise when the manuscript used contains just a section of the complete text – as was the case for Sauvage's editions of Commynes and Froissart. On the other hand, the use of the definite article suggests that Sauvage regards the manuscript as a more authoritative witness to the text. The addition of the adjective 'vieil' intimates that this additional authority arises from the belief that it represents an older reading. The antiquity of the manuscript version leads in turn to a presumption that its version is closer to the author's original than subsequent printed editions, as Sauvage suggests in the title he gives to Commynes's *Mémoires*: *Les Memoires de MESSIRE PHILIPPE DE Cõmines, Cheualier, Seigneur d'Argenton: sur les principaux faicts & gestes de Louis onziéme & de Charles huictiéme, son fils, Roys de France. Reueus & corrigez par Denis Sauvage de Fontenailles en Brie Exemplaire pris à l'orignal de l'Auteur, & suyuant les bons Historiographes & Croniqueurs* (*The Memoires of My Lord Philippe de Commines, Knight, Lord of Agenton: on the principal acts and achievements of Louis XI and Charles VIII, his*

7　Centre National de Ressources Textuelles et Lexicales.

8　Sauvage, 'Advertissement aux lecteurs', in Commynes, *Mémoires*, ed. by Sauvage.

son, Kings of France, Reviewed and Corrected by Denis Sauvage of Fontenailles en Brie, according to an exemplum based on the author's original and following good authors of histories and chronicles).

This presumption that the manuscript text is anterior to – and therefore to be privileged over – printed versions is not too different from that displayed in modern text editing, but Denis Sauvage's conclusions are somewhat different from those of many of today's editors. Realising that the manuscript reading must represent at least some departure from the authorial version, Sauvage sought to correct the text, not to return it to a pristine authorial state, but to make it fit more exactly with the linguistic conventions of his own epoch. In keeping with many of his contemporaries, especially in a town such as Lyons with a very active printing industry, questions of linguistic rectitude were very important to Sauvage, as we shall see. In addition, such questions appear to have become more of a preoccupation as he became increasingly experienced as an editor so that, while he was initially content to theorise that he might publish an authorial manuscript as a testimony to antique linguistic conventions, the closer he came to identifying an original manuscript, the further he moved from this non-interventionist stance. Thus, when faced with a partial recension of Froissart's texts, Sauvage tells his reader that:

> Touchant le stile & anciéne maniere d'escrire de nostre Auteur, ie ne doute point qu'il n'ay este quelques fois changé, & aucunément renouuelé, selon les temps: mais ie fay tant de scrupule de rien innouer en tels Auteurs, que si i'eusse eu la propre copie, qu'il escriuit, ou feit escrire, ie l'eusse fait imprimer en son entier, pour faire apparoir du language d'alors à celuy de maintenant.[9]

> (As regards the style and antiquated manner of writing of our Author, I have no doubt that it has been altered on a number of occasions and somewhat updated, according to the fashions of the day: but I pride myself on not introducing any innovations to such authors to the extent that, if I had his own copy, that he himself had written or dictated, I would have printed it in its entirety in order to make apparent the difference between today's language and that of the past.)

However, when discussing a manuscript containing a version of Commynes's *Mémoires* that he considered to be 'copié sur le vray Original de l'Atheur' ('Copied from the Author's true original'), Sauvage says that he has decided not to restore many of the manuscript readings which differed from versions found in printed editions and, further, to correct and update some of the outmoded vocabulary of those editions, but at the same time not to correct others 'pour ne faire trop de

---

[9]   Denis Sauvage, 'Aduertissement aux Lecteurs', in *Premier volume de l'histoire et chronique de Messire Iehan Froissart Reueu & corrigé sus diuers Exemplaires & suyuant les bons Auteurs, par DENIS SAVVAGE de Fonteinailles en Brie, Historiographe du Trescrestien Roy HENRY IIᵉ de ce nom* (Lyons: Jean de Tournes, 1559).

compte de l'Antiquité, & pour ne la desestimer ainsi plus que de raison' ('So as not to give too much credit to ancient things, and so as not to underrate them any more than is reasonable').

It is important to bear this in mind when attempting to evaluate the use that Denis Sauvage makes of the manuscripts to which he refers: the editor does not necessarily intend his edition to be a faithful reproduction of his manuscript, nor does he see his role as to produce an authorial version of the text. Moreover, he appears to have been operating under constraints or with criteria that he does not discuss with his readers. He tells us that three of the manuscripts that he uses (one of the Froissart manuscripts, and the sources for La Marche's *Mémoires* and the *Chronique de Flandres*) have the same provenance: the 'maison de la Chaux'. This origin is cited with approval: Sauvage tells us that he has had access to its manuscripts through the good services of a Burgundian nobleman.[10] However, Sauvage does not tell us what it was about this household or its manuscripts that made them such important witnesses and it is difficult to say whether his approval arose out of a feeling of gratitude at having been given access to any manuscript whatsoever or whether he believed that the particular manuscripts of this collection were of especially high quality.

Moreover, it is impossible for the modern critic to make a judgement as to the calibre of the manuscript witnesses consulted by Sauvage, since in no case can a source manuscript be uncontroversially identified. Georges Durville has demonstrated that the manuscript used by Sauvage to correct previous printed editions of Commynes's *Mémoires* was similar, although not identical, to a manuscript in the Musée Dobrée in Nantes, since Sauvage cites emendations that are not to be found in the Dobrée manuscript.[11] In the case of his edition of Froissart, Sauvage claims that he has supplemented his reading of previous printed editions with reference to two manuscript fragments, but Godfried Croenen has found that there is no passage where the influence of a manuscript can be proved conclusively and that neither of the two manuscripts that Sauvage describes appears to have survived.[12] For the *Chronique de Flandres* and Olivier de La Marche's *Mémoires*, which were previously unedited and where a manuscript was perforce the sole source, Sauvage not only gives his reader exact details as to where his manuscript came from (once again the library of Jean de Poupet, son of Charles de Poupet, Seigneur de la Chaux), but he also provides an extract of each of the manuscript texts in its unedited state in the prologue to the work. He does this ostensibly to give his readers some idea of the vast difficulty he has encountered in producing

---

[10]   '*par la courtoisie d'vn grand Signeur de Bourgongne*', Denis Sauvage, 'Advertissement aux lecteurs', *Chronique de Froissart*, vol. 1.

[11]   Georges Durville, *Catalogue de la bibliothèque du musée Thomas Dobrée. Tome premier: Manuscrits* (Nantes: Musée Thomas Dobrée, 1904), pp. 484–501.

[12]   Godfried Croenen, 'La Tradition manuscrite du Troisième Livre des Chroniques de Froissart', in *Froissart à la cour de Béarn: l'écrivain, les arts et le pouvoir*, ed. by Valérie Fasseur (Turnhout: Brepols, 2009), pp. 15–59 (p. 53, n. 64).

a readable text, but it has the consequence of facilitating an identification of the manuscript in question. However, in the instance of La Marche's *Mémoires* in any case, it actually serves to complicate the question. From the nineteenth century Sauvage's source has been considered to be a Bibliothèque nationale de France, ms fonds français 2869. Indeed, this manuscript is now called manuscript *S*, because of its long-standing association with Sauvage. It bears an annotation on its first folio to the effect that this was the one used by him. However, there are problems with accepting this identification, despite the extensive transcription which Sauvage gives of its opening passage.

Part of the difficulty in accepting *S* as Sauvage's source lies in the fact that at some time the first 16 folios of the manuscript were damaged. This damage had certainly taken place before 1888, when it was noted by Henri Stein, but there is no record of precisely when it occurred.[13] Indeed, the documentary evidence relating to this manuscript is surprisingly scarce, considering that its provenance seems well attested from shelfmarks given on the first folio. From the collection of Samuel Guichenon in the seventeenth century, it passed into that of Philibert de la Mare and thence into the Royal Library, which in turn became the Imperial Library and the Bibliothèque nationale. However, it does not appear to have been described prior to its appearance in the catalogue of the Bibliothèque nationale and even then the description is fairly limited in its scope. As a consequence, the date at which the damage occurred is not known. Similarly, although Sauvage tells his reader where he obtained the manuscript that he used, the history of manuscript *S* prior to its acquisition by Guichenon cannot be proven. Nor are textual indications unambiguous. Manuscript *S* is alone in wording the closing words of La Marche's first volume in the way that Sauvage says that his source does, but there are some features of the manuscript that do not fit with the text presented in his edition. For example, the presence of two figures of the court, 'monseigneur de Pons et madame la chanceliere' at the famous Banquet of the Pheasant in 1454 is noted by all surviving manuscripts of the *Mémoires* except manuscript *S*, but the phrase nevertheless occurs in Sauvage's edition.[14] Moreover, the feature of Sauvage's edition which might be expected to resolve the question – his transcription of the opening chapter of his source – does not accord completely with the surviving text of manuscript *S*. It is true that, of all known manuscripts of La Marche's *Mémoires*,

---

[13] Henri Stein, *Olivier de la Marche: Historien, poète et diplomate bourguignon* (Brussels: Hayez, 1888), p. 129.

[14] BnF ms f. fr. 2869 fol. 316ᵛ, *Les Memoires de Messire Olivier de La Marche, Premier Maistre d'hostel de l'archeduc Philippe d'Austriche, Comte de Flandres: Nouvellement mis en lumiére par Denis Sauvage de Fontenailles en Brie, Historiographe du Treschrestien Roy Henry, second de ce nom* (Lyons: Rouillé, 1561), p. 279. For further details on some correspondences and divergences between Sauvage's text and ms *S*, see Catherine Emerson 'Five Centuries of Olivier de La Marche: The Rhetoric of the *Mémoires* in the Hands of Scribes, Editors and Translators', *Revue belge de philologie et d'histoire*, 83 (2005), pp. 1103–31 (pp. 1125–7).

it is the most similar and the only one to contain no substantial departures from the wording presented by Sauvage, but it differs substantially from Sauvage's rendering in matters of both spelling and especially punctuation.

Normally, this variation might be considered trivial, but there are good reasons for taking it seriously in this instance. Sauvage explains his lengthy excerption from the preface:

> de laquelle vous aurez ici Copie, telle, qu'elle estoit, de mot à mot, auec son orthographie & punctuation, tant pour tesmoingnage de ce que nous vous disons, comme pour vous monstrer quelle raison nous a induits à nommer cette premiére partie Introduction, & non pas Premier volume de ses Memoires.[15]

> (the copy of which you have here, exactly as it was, word for word, with its spelling and punctuation, partly as a testimony to what we have told you and partly to demonstrate to you what reasons impelled us to call this first section the Introduction and not the first volume of his Mémoires.)

If part of the purpose of Sauvage's transcription is to illustrate spelling and punctuation, it would be surprising if it was inaccurate on precisely these points. All the more so, indeed, since Sauvage had a particular interest in these matters: he was the inventor of two novel punctuation marks – the *entrejet* and the *parenthésine*[16] – and intervened in contemporary debates surrounding orthographic practice. Indeed, according to Paul-Martin Bondois, Sauvage's most original work was in the realm of spelling and punctuation.[17] He was the author of an unpublished treatise on the spelling of the French language, which, although now

---

[15]   La Marche, *Memoires,* ed. by Sauvage, 'Aux lecteurs'.

[16]   Ferdinand Brunot, *Histoire de la langue française des origines à 1900: Le Seizième Siècle,* 2nd rev. edn (Paris: Colin, 1922), p. 111, n. 1 cites Sauvage's preface to his translation of Paul Jove as the occasion on which these novel marks were introduced. However, according to Brunot he was not very rigorous in the way in which he employed his own punctuation and, indeed, Sauvage explains that he has seen fit to introduce them and given them names 'nonobstant que ie les aye fait seruir l'vne pour l'autre quelquefois : n'ayant encores voulu ⁖ nonplus qu'en l'orthographie ; tenir ce qu'il m'en semble : iusques à ce que i'en aye mis mes raisons en-auant : apres celles de tant de doctes personnes, qui en ont escrit' ('despite the fact that I have sometimes made one of them do the work of the other: still not wishing ⁖ no more than I do in matters of spelling, pronounce on what I think : until I have set out my reasons : following the example of so many learned figures, who have written on the topic'). *Histoires de Paolo Iovio ⁖ Comois; Evesque de Nocera ; sur les choses faictes et avenues de son temps en tovtes les parties dv monde, tradvictes de Latin en François, & reueües pour la seconde edition, par DENIS SAVVAGE Signeur du Parc-Champenois, Historiographe du Roy.* Premier Tome (Lyons: Rouillé, 1558), fol. *3ʳ. Attentive readers will note that one of the marks – the entrejet – appears in both Sauvage's title and in his justification for using it cited here.

[17]   Bondois, 'Henri II et ses historiographes', p. 142.

lost, may have formed the basis of a section in the second volume of Peletier's *Dialogue de l'orthografe*, published in 1555, where Sauvage himself appears as a character debating matters of correct spelling. Three years before this, in the prologue to his edition of Commynes's *Mémoires*, the editor explained that he had taken a less interventionist approach to his text than he might otherwise have been tempted to do because his thoughts on orthography were not yet formalised: 'ie laisse l'Orthographe ainsi que ie l'ay trouuee, à peu pres, iusques à temps que i'en aye dit mon auis, respondant au Seigneur Iaques Pelettier nostre amy' ('I leave the spelling more or less as I found it until such time as I have voiced my opinion in response to our friend Mr Jacques Peletier').[18] When he came to edit his manuscript of Olivier de La Marche's *Mémoires* in 1561, Sauvage had been deliberating on matters orthographical for nearly a decade and so the fact that his transcription differs from manuscript *S* is indicative of one of three scenarios, all of which would be significant for our understanding of Sauvage as an editor of medieval manuscripts:

- Despite other indications to the contrary, Sauvage's base manuscript was not manuscript *S*. Accepting this would mean that we would have to postulate a lost manuscript of Olivier de La Marche's *Mémoires*, which was very close in its content to manuscript *S*, including some identical paratextual material such as rubrication and marginal notes.
- Sauvage's manuscript was actually manuscript *S* but he was not an exact palaeographer. Although he attempted to reproduce the medieval punctuation he saw before him, he was unable to overcome his own prejudices and therefore produced an inaccurate version of the text. A piece of evidence in favour of this hypothesis is the fact that he uses ampersands throughout his transcriptions, in line with his own typographical conventions, but where manuscripts of La Marche's *Mémoires* almost always use uncontracted 'et'.
- Sauvage's manuscript was indeed manuscript *S* but he did not take an exact record of the punctuation. He was initially unconcerned with punctuation since, as he tells his readers, he considered the manuscript to be 'en bonne & belle lettre, mais sans vraye punctuation à la mode du temps passé' ('written in good clear letters, but without any real punctuation in the manner of times gone by'.) However, he decided that an exact transcription was necessary to make precisely this point: to illustrate his skill in making something comprehensible out of a previously unpunctuated text, he needed to demonstrate just what a parlous state the text had been in prior to his intervention. He therefore added punctuation to an otherwise more or less accurate transcription of manuscript *S*, but without reference to where *S* actually had punctuation.

---

18   Sauvage, 'Advertissement aux lecteurs', in Commynes, *Mémoires*, ed. by Sauvage.

Without knowing whether manuscript *S* was Sauvage's source we cannot tell which of these scenarios we should regard as indicative of his approach to manuscript editing. However, the fact of his transcription gives us other evidence of his editorial practice, since it allows us to examine the difference between what he claims to have read and what he regards as a text worthy of presentation to his own readers. He himself alerted readers to his editorial rationale in his prologue 'Aux lecteurs' to La Marche's work. The author, he tells us was a Burgundian incapable of achieving the high style of his French counterparts:

> Touchant son stile (auquel ie luy ay laissé quelques maniéres de parler, & certains mots de son siécle, & du creu de son païs, pour difference du vray François auec le Bourguignon) ie l'ay trouué assez passable, quand il a suyui son naturel: mais le voulant farder, & agencer d'artifice, il ségaroit tellement, que l'on ne pouuoit tirer construction de ce qu'il vouloit dire: en sorte qu'il m'a souuent esté besoing de luy aider à s'expliquer.

> (Regarding his style (in which I have allowed him some turns of phrase, and certain words of his century and of his blunt native tongue, to differentiate true French from Burgundian), I found it fairly acceptable when he followed his natural disposition: but when he sought to doll it up it and embellish it with artifice, he went so far astray that one was unable to make out what he had wanted to say: with the result that I often had to help him to explain himself.)

Accordingly, most of Sauvage's changes are orthographical; he adds capital letters to proper nouns, punctuates the text, and adds diacritics according to contemporary spelling conventions. However, the 'help' offered to his author does not stop here. He rearranges parts of the text to improve its fluency, deleting phrases in some places only to reinsert them in others. For example, where he says that his manuscript had:

> Et de son [Marie de Bourgogne's] temps par guerres griefs traictiez contraires & autres violences a elle faictes & suruenues plusieurs des seigneuries dessusdictes ont este & sont tirees & distraictes de vostre main & pouuoir comme plusaplain pourrez sauoir a la croissance de voz iours/& mesmement par la poursuitte de ces presentes memoires se dieu me donne temps & grace/Et dont en augmentant le nombre de mes ans & en diminuant de corps & de vie le cœr me croit & rauiue en bon espoir que dieu se VOUS le seruez deuement vous donra grace de recouurer conquerre & vangier les torts a vous faiz a lhonneur prouffit & gloire de ceste noble vostre maison arruinee & destruicte & greuee par voz ennemis priuez & estrangiers/

> (And in her time [or his, French does not distinguish, although the context suggests that it is Marie's time that is meant] by means of grievous wars adverse treaties and other violences done to her had visited upon her many of the above-

mentioned estates have been and remain taken and removed from your hands
and your power as you will know more fully as you grow in days/and similarly
in the course of these present *mémoires* if God gives me time and grace/And by
increasing the number of my years and by diminishing my body and my life, my
heart grows and reawakens in the sure hope that God if YOU serve him loyally
will give you the grace to recover conquer and revenge the wrongs done to you
to the honour profit and glory of this your noble household ruined and destroyed
and distraught by your enemies both those familiar to you and strangers/)

he gives the text

considerant qu'au temps d'elle, par guerres, griefs, traictés contraires, & autres
violences, à elle faictes & suruenues, plusieurs des Signeuries dessusdictes ont
esté, & sont, tirees & distraictes de vostre main & pouuoir (comme plus-à-plain
pourrez sauoir, à la croissance de voz iours, & mes-mement par la poursuite
de mes Memoires, si Dieu me donne temps & grâce de les accomplir) VOVS
seruiez et priez Dieu si-deuotement, qu'il vous donne la grâce de recouurer,
conquerre, & vengier les torts à vous faicts, à l'honneur proffit, & gloire, de
cette vostre tresnoble maison: ainsi qu'en augmentant le nombre de mes ans, &
en diminuant de corps et de vie, le cueur me croist, & rauigoure en bon espoir,
que la remettrez sus: nonobstant qu'elle ayt esté tant greuee par voz ennemis,
priués & estrangers.[19]

(considering that in the time of her reign, by means of wars, grievances, adverse
treaties, and other violences, done to her and visited upon her, many of the above-
mentioned estates have been, and remain, taken and removed from your hands
and power (as you will know more fully, as you grow in days, and similarly in
the course of my *Mémoires*, if God gives me time and grace to complete them)
YOU should serve and pray to God so devoutly that he may give you the grace
to recover, conquer, and revenge the wrongs done to you, to the honour profit
and glory of this your most noble household: thus by increasing the number
of my years, and by diminishing my body and my life, my heart grows and is
reinvigorated in the sure hope that you will raise it up, notwithstanding the fact
that it has been so distraught by your enemies, both those familiar to you and
strangers.)

Here the phrase 'en augmentant le nombre de mes ans et en diminuant de corps et
de vie le cœr me croit et rauiue en bon espoir' has been moved so that it no longer
divides the ideas of God and the service due to him. Other – relatively minor –
changes can also be seen here. The ambiguity of 'son' has been resolved so that
Sauvage's reader is in no doubt as to whether the epoch referred to is indeed that
of Marie de Bourgogne or that of her father, the archaic 'ravive' is replaced by

---

[19]   La Marche, *Memoires*, ed. by Sauvage, p. 3.

the neologism 'ravigoure', and the thought implied in 'se dieu me donne temps & grace' is rendered explicit in Sauvage's edited text.

Denis Sauvage argues in his address to readers that such changes are necessary to make Olivier de La Marche comprehensible to the modern reader, but some of the editorial modifications go beyond even a broad definition of what is required for ease of understanding. As we saw above, Sauvage reproduces the opening section of his source manuscript in part to justify his decision to call this passage the author's preface and not Book One of the work, which is how the author himself referred to it. However, the incomplete nature of La Marche's *Mémoires* meant that there were two sections that had been given this latter title. In an attempt to eliminate this contradiction, Sauvage renames one of these the preface. He does so openly, devoting a large part of his own introduction to a justification of this decision. However, in the body of the text that he presents to his readers, he introduces phrases that suggest that the decision is in fact La Marche's. The current section is called 'cette Introduction', and its purpose is:

> de reueoir & recongnoistre quelques escripts, autresfois par moy recueillis des liures anciens, pour mieux vous introduire à la lecture de certains Memoires des choses, que i'ay veues moy-mesme auenir de mon temps.[20]

> (to review and survey some writings, which I have previously gathered in ancient books in order to better introduce you to the reading of certain memoires of things, which I have myself seen take place in my own time.)

None of these words is to be found in Sauvage's transcription of his manuscript source (nor in any surviving manuscript of the *Mémoires*) and yet readers who have not paid close attention to this transcription might be forgiven for thinking that they are La Marche's own. This impression is reinforced by marginal notes which Sauvage adds to his interpolated sections, such as 'Le contenu en l'Introduction suyuãte' ('The contents of the following introduction'), alongside the above text. These comments serve as signposts orientating the reader through La Marche's complex introductory structure, but much of this structure is the work of Denis Sauvage rather than his author. The ostensible distinction between the editorial paratextual material and the author's text is thus falsified to the advantage of the editor's interpretation of how the text should be constructed.

This approach to the architecture of the work persists throughout Sauvage's edition of La Marche's *Mémoires*, where it is the editor who determines the division of the text into chapters and who gives these chapters their titles. Furthermore, the editor's conception of how the work should be structured overrides clear indications to the contrary provided by his manuscript. Sauvage's edition has no smaller textual division than the chapter, and paragraphs within chapters are unknown, despite the fact that, as his transcription of his manuscript shows us,

---

[20]   La Marche, *Memoires*, ed. by Sauvage, p. 2.

paragraphs formed part of the manuscript tradition. In four instances in his edition (chapters 11, 13 and 18 of Book One and chapter 2 of Book Two), the divisions between what Sauvage identifies as chapters fall in the middle of a paragraph in every known surviving manuscript of the *Mémoires*. Of course, we cannot be sure whether Sauvage's base manuscript was indeed manuscript *S* and, if it was not, it may be that the manuscript that he used did indeed have paragraph divisions in the places that Sauvage has his chapter divisions. However, this would make his manuscript unique amongst those of La Marche's *Mémoires* and it seems more likely that Sauvage's decision not to include paragraphs in his text has led to his disregarding them as significant elements of textual architecture when deciding on how to structure his edition.

We have said that in his early editions Sauvage appears to have been working from the presupposition that it would have been desirable to present the author's original version of the text. However, as Sauvage became more competent as a historian and confident as a linguist, his interventions tended increasingly to amend the manuscript reading. A crucial turning point is his edition of Froissart where, for the first time, as well as marginal notes commenting on unfamiliar lexical items, he also included extensive notes on matters of fact and on alternate manuscript readings – notes, indeed, that were so extensive that many of them were relegated to the end of the volume. The sheer volume of notes which appear in the Froissart edition must have demanded close collaboration with Jean de Tournes, the printer, since at times all the marginal space was occupied by author's notes, which were nevertheless set out so that they either began or ended on the line featuring the annotated passage. The extent of this collaboration can be gauged by the fact that de Tournes himself added his voice to the preliminary material of the first volume in presenting his list of errata, explaining, in very similar terms to Sauvage's, that these are a consequence of the 'copie scabreuse' ('scabrous copy') with which the men have had to work and of the 'si grande corruption de Liure' ('so extensive corruption of the book'). De Tournes begs the readers to excuse us, the plural again suggesting collaboration between editor and printer and this 'nous' appears once more in Sauvage's comments whenever they refer to orthographical or lexical issues, while the singular 'je' is reserved for historical comment. Again, the high degree of collaboration between the men is suggested by the terms of the royal privilege granted to the edition which, rather than giving the printer sole control over the work, gave it to both men jointly. This had not been the case in Sauvage's previous editions and points to a growing recognition of his work as editor.[21]

Perhaps it was the experience of working so closely with a printer that led Sauvage to conclude – on no very sure foundation – that the manuscript on which

---

[21] As Elisabeth Armstrong points out, the fact that Sauvage and his printer were able to obtain a privilege for such a popular work as Froissart's chronicle at all is testimony in itself to recognition of Sauvage's pioneering work as an editor. *Before Copyright: The French Book-Privilege System 1498–1526* (Cambridge: Cambridge University Press, 1990), p. 93.

he based the next work he edited, the *Mémoires* of Olivier de La Marche, might be authorial rather than a corrupt intermediary. Alternately, perhaps it was the challenge of working with a manuscript alone that led him to rule out consideration of a possible 'escrivain', hinting instead that all infelicities of style and factual errors were the responsibility of the fifteenth-century author. Olivier de La Marche was, in any case, according to Sauvage, a lower status author than Jean Froissart. As we have seen, Sauvage viewed La Marche as a Burgundian incapable for that very reason of producing correct French. Furthermore, La Marche's ignorance was not limited in Sauvage's estimation to linguistic matters. Although Sauvage tells his readers not to hold it against the editor if the author's version of events is incorrect since 'ne doy corriger mon Auteur, que là ou il est manifestement dépraué' ('I should not correct my author except where he is manifestly corrupted'), he gives the impression that this was not in fact an infrequent occurrence and many of his notes at the end of the volume present the manuscript reading that the editor has amended in the main body of the text. To the attentive reader who takes the trouble to read and meditate upon these annotations, therefore, the manuscript is presented as a locus of error: a source of faulty information which the modern editor has been obliged to set to rights. Sauvage is reluctant, however, to pronounce definitively on whether the ultimate source of the error is the mechanism of manuscript transmission or the author's own shortcomings as a historian. In one instance, he explains that:

> nous à [sic] falu corriger & éclaircir tout ce passage d'Angleterre & de Portugal, selõ tous bons Auteurs, ou autrement il y eust eu de la corruption & de la contradiction en nostre Auteur, en cette sorte.[22]

> (we had to correct and elucidate the whole of this passage dealing with England and Portugal, according to all good authors, or otherwise there would have been corruption and contradiction in our author, with regard to this matter.)

By suggesting that the uncorrected text would have been both corrupt and a repository of author error, Sauvage raises both possibilities as potential defects of his original text. In the two annotations that follow immediately on from this one, Sauvage seems to suggest first that it is simply the manuscript that is at fault, saying 'Tout ce passage estoit vn peu scabreux, en ceste sorte .... Ce que nous pensons auoir redrecé, suyuant ce que nostre Auteur a voulu dire' ('All this passage was a bit scabrous ... which we think we have set right, according to what our author meant to say'), and then that the entire fault rests with La Marche so that 'Nous auons amendé ce passage, iusques au couronnement de Philippe de Valois, selon tous autres bons Auteurs, se brouillant & cõtrariant nostre Auteur en ceste sorte' ('We have amended this passage, up to the crowning of Philippe de Valois, according to all good authors who are in dispute and contradiction with our Author

---

    [22]   La Marche, *Memoires*, ed. by Sauvage, p. 438, annotation 11.

on this point').[23] In the first instance, the corrections are in matters of expression: Sauvage has substituted 'sous' for his manuscript's 'vous' and corrected 'estes regarde' to 'estes regardés', and it seems reasonable to assume that this does indeed arise out of the vicissitudes of scribal transmission. In the second case, the errors that Sauvage identifies are of a more factual nature, concerning as they do the transmission of the French crown. Despite his earlier declaration that La Marche is incompetent in matters pertaining to the French language, therefore, Sauvage appears to assume that simple errors of vocabulary or grammatical precision are likely to be the fault of La Marche's scribes while errors of fact are to be laid at the door of the historian.

However, this is not Sauvage's last word on the matter because, while he says that he has restored La Marche's text so that it says 'ce que nostre Auteur a voulu dire' ('what our Author meant to say'), he continues 'comme souuent il a esté besoing de luy aider à s'expliquer en autres endroits: qui emporteroyent trop de temps à tousiours les annoter' ('Since it was often necessary to help him to explain himself in certain places: so much so that it would take too much time to annotate them all'). The implication is that the errors are scribal in this instance but that in other cases the author's linguistic incapacity is at fault, and what is more, so far at fault that the editor has not been able to draw his readers' attention to every shortcoming. The expression 'voulu dire' is employed to designate not only the true meaning of the author's words but also the meaning that the author would have wanted to convey if only he had been capable of expressing himself correctly. In this reading the manuscript is far from being the authoritative means of access to the author's original text that we might assume and that Sauvage himself suggested that it was in his work on Commynes's *Mémoires*. Instead it is a doubly deficient witness: limited by the limitations of the original writer and then again by the shortcomings of the very process of manuscript transmission.

In conclusion, therefore, we can see that Denis Sauvage's career as a manuscript editor is a case of familiarity breeding contempt. The more practised he became, the less authority he was willing to concede to his authors and his manuscripts and the more he was prepared to intervene to present a reading of the text that was his rather than that of any authority that preceded him.

---

[23]   La Marche, *Memoires*, ed. by Sauvage, p. 438, annotations 12 and 13.

Chapter 8

Fictions of Authority:[1] Hélisenne de Crenne and the *Angoysses douloureuses qui procedent d'amours* (1538)

Pollie Bromilow

The circulation of the works of female authors is an aspect of the sixteenth-century book trade that has recently attracted a large amount of interest amongst scholars.[2] Many of the questions that have remained implicit since the upsurge in attention to women's writing in the 1970s are now beginning to be explicitly addressed by methodologies which combine analysis of the materiality of the book with a textual analytical approach. Whereas once the rhetorical device of the modesty topos and the appeal to a powerful female patron or anonymous community of female readers were read as the marks of a literary endeavour that may have been subject to moral censure, a growing awareness of the economic value of female-authored imprints has caused them to be seen in a new and different light that has emphasised the marketability of the female voice in sixteenth-century vernacular literatures.[3]

While an understanding of the contemporary commercial value of sixteenth-century women's writing has been enhanced by these developments in scholarship, the status of the female author has been contested as much as it has been affirmed. In one case, that of Louise Labé, the perceived desirability of female-authored works entering the print realm in the sixteenth century has even given rise to the theory that a female author might have been 'invented' by a collaborative group of male writers who were keen for their city to bask in the reflected glory of

---

[1]   I borrow this collocation from Susan Sniader Lanser, *Fictions of Authority: Women Writers and Narrative Voice* (Ithaca, NY: Cornell University Press, 1992).

[2]   See, for example, Susan Broomhall, *Women and the Print Trade in Sixteenth-Century France* (Aldershot: Ashgate, 2002).

[3]   On the marketability of female authors see Leah L. Chang, *Into Print: The Production of Female Authorship in Early Modern France* (Newark, DE: University of Delaware Press, 2009) and Diana Robin, *Publishing Women: Salons, the Presses and the Counter-Reformation in Sixteenth-Century Italy* (Chicago, IL: University of Chicago Press, 2007).

an accomplished poetess.[4] Other scholars have constructed female writers such as Hélisenne de Crenne as primarily embroiled in struggles for control over the print circulation of their texts in ways that call into question the very existence of the female author figure.[5] This essay seeks to advance an alternative hypothesis concerning the status of the female writer in print. A material and textual reading of the *Angoysses douloureuses qui procedent d'amours* reveals numerous ways in which the work constructs itself as authoritative. This authority is created partly by the text itself through its use of exemplarity to appeal to the reader and the representation of its production and reception and partly through the use of extra-textual elements such as the preface, the author's name, the title page and the use of illustrations. These different aspects together had a cumulative effect that resulted in the author's presence and prestige being promoted as much during the production of the book as in the writing of the text itself.

In order to facilitate the circulation of their works, women writers adopted numerous strategies that sought to ensure that their works were not only favourably received but also treated with the gravity that their own commitment to literary enterprise merited. As a woman writer seeking to enter the public realm of print circulation in a period where manuscript circulation might have been regarded as the more usual means of textual dissemination, Hélisenne de Crenne sought to mediate the space between, on the one hand, the rhetorical structures that professed to confine the female voice to the domestic sphere and, on the other, the potential to confirm her status as a unique and innovative new talent supported by the materiality of the printed book and the promise to her printer collaborator of making a profit.

Existing work has focussed on the importance of the preface as a privileged site within which the negotiation between private intellectual enterprise and public morality took place.[6] As an autobiographical fiction which recounts the adulterous

---

4   Mireille Huchon, *Louise Labé: Une créature de papier?* (Geneva: Droz, 2006). On the controversy that this book produced see the 'dossier de presse': Société Intérnationale pour l'Etude des Femmes de l'Ancien Régime, *Louise attaquée: Louise Labé est-elle une créature de papier?* <http://www.siefar.org/debats/louise-labe.html?lang=fr&li=art25> [accessed 17 February 2012].

5   Leah L. Chang, 'Clothing "Dame Helisenne": The staging of female authorship and the production of the 1538 *Angoysses douloureuses qui procedent d'amours*', *Romanic Review*, 92 (2001), pp. 381–403.

6   See, for example, Anne Larsen, '"Un honneste passetems": Strategies of Legitimation in French Renaissance Women's Prefaces', *Esprit Créateur*, 30 (1990), pp. 11–22; Deborah N. Losse, *Sampling the Book: Renaissance Prologues and the French Conteurs* (Lewisburg, PA: Bucknell University Press, 1994), esp. chapter 6 'Women addressing women: The differentiated text'; François Rigolot, 'La Préface à la Renaissance: Un discours sexué?', *Cahiers de L'Association internationale des études françaises*, 42 (1990), pp. 121–35. Cathleen M. Bauschatz, '"Hélisenne aux lisantes": Address of Women Readers in the *Angoisses douloureuses* and Boccaccio's *Fiammetta*', *Atlantis*, 19 (1993), pp. 59–66; '"Voyla mes dames ...": Inscribed Women Readers and Listeners in the

love affair between a young married woman and a man of low social status, one of the primary ways in which the first part of the *Angoysses douloureuses* acquires authority in the eyes of the reader is in its claim to educate through the *exemplum* of lived experience. An implicit feature of the construction of the *Angoysses douloureuses* as a first-person narrative, this claim to enable the reader to be educated by the transgressive love story is brought to the fore in the preface. In addressing her audience of 'honnestes dames' (honest women) the narrator shares her aspiration: 'qu'en voyant comme j'ay esté surprinse, vous pourrez eviter les dangereulx laqs d'amours, en y resistant du commencement, sans continuer en amoureuses pensées' ('That in seeing how I was caught, you will be able to avoid the dangerous snares of love, by resisting love from the outset, without persisting in amorous thoughts').[7] It is by participating in the story of Dame Helisenne being surprised by love that the reader will be better able to prepare herself against a similarly unexpected attack, thereby avoiding the same sinful path that befell the narrator.

Much of the efficacy of this supposedly educational project depends upon the power of the claimed lived example over the merely fictional account to move the reader to flee the path of sin. The synonymy between the author Hélisenne de Crenne and the claimed narrator of the story, Dame Helisenne, is therefore an essential aspect of the novel's authoritative claim. Indeed, although the *Angoysses douloureuses* is widely recognised to have made extensive use of existing literary models, few other contemporary texts in print circulation offer the reader the experience of a female-authored first-person love story where the narrator and author may be understood to be one and the same.[8] Gérard Genette has observed that the name of the author is important in establishing the 'generic contract' that exists between author and reader:

> The author's name fulfils a contractual function whose importance varies greatly depending on genre: slight or nonexistent in fiction, it is much greater in all kinds of referential writing, where the credibility of the testimony, or of its transmission, rests largely on the identity of the witness or the person reporting it. Thus we see very few pseudonyms or anonyms among authors of historical or

---

Heptaméron', in *Critical Tales: New Studies of the Heptaméron and Early Modern Culture* (Philadelphia, PA: University of Pennsylvania Press, 1993), pp. 104–22.

[7]   Hélisenne de Crenne, *Les Angoysses douloureuses qui procedent d'amours*, ed. by Christine de Buzon (Paris: Champion, 1997), p. 97. Hélisenne de Crenne, *The Torments of Love*, trans. by Lisa Neal and Stephen Randall (Minneapolis, MN: University of Minnesota Press, 1996), p. 7. All references are to these editions unless otherwise stated.

[8]   Buzon concurs with Paule Demats in considering that for the first part of the *Angoysses douloureuses* Crenne was inspired to use the first person by Boccaccio's *Fiammetta*. *Angoysses douloureuses*, p. 33. However, there is no attempt in this work to conflate the persona of Fiammetta with that of the author.

documentary works, and this is all the more true when the witness himself plays a part in his narrative.[9]

However, for the purposes of this discussion, it is important to acknowledge that Hélisenne de Crenne reveals the permeability of these boundaries between, on the one hand, fiction and, on the other hand, referential writing. The name 'Helisenne de Crenne' is itself a fictional construct, a pseudonym for Marguerite Briet (de Crenne). The fact that Briet chooses a pseudonym at all reveals that she is interested in manipulating her readers's expectations. Her real identity is playfully hidden behind the invented name, which is itself a marker of fiction. As Genette has reminded us, 'Clearly, using a pseudonym is already a poetic activity, and the pseudonym is already somewhat like a work. If you can change your name, you can write.'[10]

Partly because of the intrigue provoked by presenting such an audacious love story as an autobiographical fiction, the slippage between the author and the narrator has attracted a considerable amount of critical interest, as have the multiple and varied connotations of the name 'Hélisenne de Crenne' itself.[11] That the name of a female author should have attracted so much attention is not surprising. Genette has acknowledged the complexities of the interrelationships between the names of female writers and the thematic content of their works:

> In our society, the surname of a woman is not exactly a simple matter: a married woman *must* choose among her father's name, her husband's name, or some combination of the two; the first two choices – but not the third – are, in principle, opaque to the reader, who will therefore not be able to infer marital status from them; and many careers of women of letters are punctuated with these onymous variations that reveal marital, existential or ideological variations (here, I offer no example). I'm certainly forgetting other equally relevant cases, but the ones I've mentioned are no doubt enough to confirm that "keeping one's name" is not always an innocent gesture.[12]

Christine de Buzon has concluded that the intertextual qualities of the name 'Helisenne' remain an enigma to modern scholars and that it is unlikely that a single definite origin of the name will ever be apparent to critics.[13] However, it

---

[9]   Gérard Genette, *Paratexts: Thresholds of Interpretation*, trans. by Jane E. Lewin (Cambridge: Cambridge University Press, 2001), p. 41.

[10]   Genette, *Paratexts*, p. 54.

[11]   See, for example, Diane S. Wood, *Hélisenne de Crenne: At the Crossroads of Renaissance Humanism and Feminism* (London: Associated University Presses, 2000), esp. chapter 2 'Marguerite Briet'; Crenne, *Angoysses douloureuses,* esp. III 'L'Onomastique du roman'.

[12]   Genette, *Paratexts*, p. 40.

[13]   Crenne, *Angoysses douloureuses*, pp. 20–21.

would be difficult to overlook the proximity of the publication of the *Angoysses douloureuses* and another text whose female protagonist is called Elisenne: the French translation of the Spanish romance *Amadis de Gaule*, which first appeared with Denis Janot (the printer of the *Angoysses douloureuses*) in 1540. Buzon has further pointed out the onomasty of Helisenne and 'Elysian', evoking the heroine's longing for and eventual achievement of transportation to a heavenly place in the eternal company of her beloved.[14] As well as reflecting on the diegesis of the novel, this link between the two names underwrites the novel with the authority of humanist learning and erudition, perhaps giving the text a more up-to-date outlook than many contemporary reprints of medieval chivalric romance.

While the name 'Helisenne' exists to conjure up multiple literary antecedents, its fusion with 'de Crenne' offers a different type of authority to the reader. This patronymic name, similar to that of Briet's husband, ties the authorship of the *Angoysses douloureuses* to a place that could be recognised by the contemporary reader as either being real or at least seeming to be.[15] This was achieved while exploiting the nobility particle which, as Genette has asserted, was still viewed as authoritative amongst twentieth-century readers.[16] At the very least, the close relationship that the patronymic name bears to Briet's own life demonstrates that she seeks to use the illusion of involvement to add to the novel's authority. The illusion of referentiality may, of course, have been aimed at readers who knew Briet personally and were able to identify events of her life through her writing. Susan Broomhall has further remarked that:

> Crenne distinguished the social level of her intended audience. Her readers are "ladies", evidently women of the social elite, perhaps those who were most likely to be in the position of a forced, economic alliance with a much older man, but also important women who could act as patrons, to support and defend her as an independent woman writer in Paris.[17]

Under these circumstances 'de Crenne', with its aristocratic connotations, might have been chosen as a kind of 'brand name' that would help the author appeal to women readers who were from a similar background. In a first-person narrative, women readers were encouraged to see their own experience through the eyes of a female narrator whose experiences were both similar to their own and yet kept at an appropriate distance through the fictional contract.

Although central to the global meaning of the work, the relationship between the claimed and actual authorial persona in the *Angoysses douloureuses* is not straightforward. In her study of the first edition of the *Angoysses douloureuses*,

---

[14]   Crenne, *Angoysses douloureuses*, p. 28.

[15]   Buzon has identified numerous place names in the novel from the Picardy region. See Crenne, *Angoysses douloureuses*, pp. 29–31.

[16]   Genette, *Paratexts*, p. 40.

[17]   Broomhall, *Women and the Book Trade*, p. 102.

Leah Chang has commented on the rupture between the author Hélisenne de Crenne and Dame Helisenne.[18] Chang has observed that Dame Helisenne is self-evidently not the author of the work as a whole as she is unable to focalise the action throughout the novel. Chang suggests that the persona of 'de Crenne' is controlled by and competing with that of the printer, Denis Janot. She has argued that the three title pages of the *Angoysses douloureuses* stage the competitive dynamic between the two. In an age where the primacy of the author had not yet been established in the process of book production, writers were frequently unable to establish control over their text during the printing process. This meant that their authority in key spaces such as title pages was prone to being usurped by printers, translators or editors, either to offer amendments or, as in this case, to promote Janot's own work as a printer of high-quality volumes. In this sense, the printer (Janot) and the author (de Crenne) become engaged in a struggle for the textual control of the narrator's (Dame Helisenne's) story.

An analysis of the materiality of the first edition of the *Angoysses douloureuses* can also lead to the opposite conclusion, however. In this essay, I will highlight the aspects of the book that suggest that Janot and his print shop sought to promote de Crenne as an authoritative figure at least as much as they can be seen to have undermined it.

The representation of de Crenne's name is a case in point, where the author's authority can be seen to be affirmed as much as it is brought into question. The multiple title pages of the *Angoysses douloureuses*, Chang argues, expose the discontinuity between, on the one hand, 'de Crenne' and on the other 'Dame Helisenne'. Chang asserts:

> The tendency of these [modern] critics to overlook the fact that "De Crenne" never actually sits juxtaposed to "Dame Helisenne" is due, I believe, to the assumption that "Helisenne de Crenne" is the full name of the author and that the two names must necessarily signify one person. But in truth the "De Crenne" figures float by themselves on the pages on which they appear, separated from other text by punctuation and on the title pages by font size. The narrative quality of the titles further contributes to the sense that "De Crenne" and "Dame Helisenne" are two distinct entities.[19]

I would argue that this dislocation between 'Dame Helisenne' and 'Helisenne de Crenne' speaks more to sixteenth-century cultures of textual circulation than a deliberate strategy on the part of Janot to usurp the authority of the writer. The appearance of 'Dame Helisenne' on the title page may reflect the widespread appearance on contemporary title pages of romances of a brief synopsis of the action of the novel. This was frequently expressed as a narrative that revolved around the main protagonists of the adventure. As the central protagonist and

---

18   Chang, 'Clothing "Dame Helisenne"'.
19   Chang, 'Clothing "Dame Helisenne"', p. 397.

organising principle in the drama that unfolds in the *Angoysses douloureuses*, Helisenne herself would surely take centre stage in any such description. It could even be argued that, far from erasing the traces of female authorship from the title page, the attribution of the text to 'Dame Helisenne' demonstrates the extent to which the novel shifts emphasis from the love affair that is purported to be its *raison d'être*, to its recording in narrative form. Chang's reading of the status of 'de Crenne' would deny the autonomy that the author establishes for herself in the act of writing. To argue that 'de Crenne' is a construct controlled entirely by Janot because of her female gender is to overlook the ways in which the gender of the author is being exploited by both author and printer to appeal to the readership.

Furthermore, given the unreliability of the title in providing a succinct means of reference for the reader during this period, Briet may have been adopting a sophisticated strategy by aligning her pseudonym with the name of the novel's heroine.[20] She may have sought a further way in which the success of the novel could promote the longevity of her reknown as an author. Contemporary evidence for the appellation of de Crenne and her works is scant, but one reference at least to the author suggests that her identity may have been inextricably related to that of her heroine. When Marie de Romieu refers to de Crenne in her 1585 *Premières Œuvres poétiques*, for example, there is a degree of ambiguity as to what precisely she is describing:

> Venez après, Morel, Charamont, Elisenes,
> Des Roches de Poictiers, Graces Pieriennes.[21]

> (Come after, Morel, Charamont, Elisenes,/Des Roches from Poictiers, Pierian Graces.)

When one reads these lines out of context, the reference to 'Elisenes' would appear to connote the *Angoysses douloureuses*, given the practice detailed above of referring to a romance by the names of its protagonists and the fact that 'Elisenes' appears in the plural. However, it is only within the context of the list of contemporary authors that it becomes apparent that 'Elisenes' connotes the authorial identity.

It is clear that in adopting the pen name 'Hélisenne de Crenne', Marguerite Briet sought to position her authorial identity amongst the illustrious literary figures alongside which she hoped to take her place. In so doing, she was staking her claim to a right to compose and print works of fiction as a woman writer. As

---

[20]   Broomhall's view of Briet's pseudonym concurs with this reading that promotion of her status as a female author may have been the ultimate aim: 'Marguerite de [sic] Briet presented an identity as a woman author by calling both her protagonist and pseudonym Hélisenne.' *Women and the Book Trade*, p. 83.

[21]   Marie de Romieu, *Les Premières Œuvres poétiques* (1585), ed. by André Winandy (Geneva: Droz, 1972), p. 21.

Lisa Neal has pointed out, the critical attention that has been paid to the work as an autobiographical fiction of adulterous love has tended to overshadow recognition of the *Angoysses douloureuses* as a work which champions the role of the woman writer.[22] Furthermore, the part played by the material presentation of the novel in promoting Crenne's authorship has largely gone unacknowledged.

Right from the title page of the novel, the book is at pains to advertise that it has been written by a female author. The attribution of the work in the text of the title page to 'Dame Helisenne' is reinforced by the visual representation of a female author in the compartment at the bottom of the page (see Figure 8.1). According to Stephen Rawles, this compartment was first used by Janot in 1538 in the printing of Cicero's *Offices*.[23] Rawles argues that the dating of the *Angoysses douloureuses* is uncertain and it is even possible that the volume did not appear until 1539.[24] Whether or not the compartment was used for the first time in the *Angoysses douloureuses*, its appearance is sufficiently close to the publication of the novel to suggest that Janot at least had de Crenne's work in mind. The compartment depicts two lovers who are sitting side-by-side. In spatial terms, they appear to enjoy a certain amount of equality. Although the male lover might be said to enjoy a slight advantage because of the hat he is wearing, the pair are able to gaze into each other's eyes on an equal basis. While the gaze was a generic feature of the physiology of love during this period, the two lovers united by their gaze call to mind the first time that Guenelic and Helisenne set eyes on each other, when their fascination is mutual. Indeed, this moment becomes the defining feature of Helisenne's love.[25]

---

[22]   Crenne, *Torments of Love*, pp. xxvi–xxvii. A notable exception to this would be Wood's *Hélisenne de Crenne*, which views Crenne as a feminist virago and traces the development of the author across her works.

[23]   Stephen Rawles, 'Denys Janot, Parisian printer and bookseller, *fl.* 1529–1544: A bibliographical study', 2 vols (unpublished doctoral dissertation, University of Warwick, 1976), II, p. 50.

[24]   Rawles, 'Denys Janot', p. 57. More recently, Buzon has dated the appearance of the first edition of the novel to 'peu après le 11 septembre 1538'. This would indeed mean that the first use of the compartment was in the *Angoysses douloureuses*. Crenne, *Angoysses douloureuses*, p. 44.

[25]   'Et en regardant à la rue, je veis ung jeune homme, aussi regardant à sa fenestre, lequel je prins à regarder ententivement … apres l'avoir plus que trop regardé retiray ma veue: mais par force estoye contraincte retourner mes yeulx, vers luy, il me regardoit aussi, dont j'estoys fort contente: mais je prenoye admiration, en moymesmes, de me trouver ainsi subjecte, à regarder ce jeune homme, ce que d'aultres jamais ne m'estoit advenu, J'avoys accoustumé de prendre et captiver les hommes, et ne me faisoye que rire d'eulx: mais moymesmes miserablement, je fuz prise.' (Looking across the street, I saw a young man also looking out his window, and whom I began to look at attentively. … After having looked at him more than enough, I withdrew my gaze; but I could not keep from turning my eyes toward him again. He was also looking at me, which made me very happy; but I was inwardly astonished to find myself thus led to gaze at this young man; this had never

Figure 8.1   Title-page of *Les Angoysses douloureuses qui procedent d'amours*

---

happened to me with other men. I was accustomed to snaring and capturing men, and I only made sport with them; but this time I found myself wretchedly ensnared.') Crenne, *Angoysses douloureuses*, pp. 102–03; Crenne, *Torments of Love*, p. 10. On the importance of the gaze for the love intrigue at the centre of the story see Colette H. Winn, 'La Symbolique du regard dans *Les Angoysses douloureuses qui procèdent d'amours* d'Hélisenne de Crenne', *Orbis Litterarum*, 40 (1985), pp. 207–21; and Dorothea Heitsch, 'Female love-melancholy in Hélisenne de Crenne's *Les Angoysses douloureuses qui procedent d'amours* (1538)', *Renaissance Studies*, 23 (2009), pp. 335–53.

Also pictured alongside the couple is a lute. Beyond simply connoting sensory pleasures and recreation, the lute also gestures forwards to an episode early in the love affair when the playing of musical instruments acts as a powerful and supposedly covert means of Guenelic expressing his love for Helisenne:

> Je veoye mon amy quelquefoys jouer d'une fleuste, aultrefoys d'ung Luc. Je prenoye singulier plaisir à l'ouir, et à brief parler, tous ces faictz m'estoit merveilleusement aggreables.

> (I saw my beloved sometimes play a flute, other times a lute. I took singular pleasure in hearing him, and in short, I found all these things marvelously agreeable.)[26]

Music can therefore act as a means of seduction and the presence of the lute on the title page is symbolic of the way that it acts as a way of tempting the reader into the pages of the book.[27] Like the lute, the love story is diverting and pleasurable while the love itself vanishes with the protagonists' death like musical notes into thin air. In the diegesis, the lute also comes to represent the precarity of the divide between the private expression of love and public knowledge of the scandal of adultery.[28] Music is a courtly and coded communication that reveals immoral

---

[26]   Crenne, *Angoysses douloureuses*, p. 108; Crenne, *Torments of Love*, p. 13.

[27]   With reference to this passage, Buzon notes that lute-playing as a pastime became increasingly popular during the reign of François 1er, this was true as much amongst the aristocracy as the bourgeoisie. Crenne, *Angoysses douloureuses*, p. 514. In Renaissance lyric poetry the use of the lute as a metaphor for the body (gendered as either male or female) has been widely acknowledge by critics. See, for example, Carla Zecher, 'The gendering of the lute in sixteenth-century French love poetry', *Renaissance Quarterly*, 53 (2000), pp. 769–91. The lute is also used in the Renaissance as a metaphor for poetic creation. On this and its relationship to gender see *Pernette du Guillet, Complete Poems: A Bilingual Edition*, ed. by Karen Simroth James and trans. by Marta Rijn Finch (Toronto: Centre for Renaissance and Reformation Studies, 2010), p. 7.

[28]   Although intended as a private expression of love for Helisenne, the frequent sound of music playing beneath her window eventually prompts her husband to ask his neighbours what the music signifies. The neighbour's response not only confirms the existence of the love affair in the husband's mind but also reveals that Helisenne's infidelity has already become public knowledge: 'Mon mary (ce jour mesmes) s'enquist à plusieurs des voysins que signifioient telz et semblables jeux que journellement on continuoit de sonner devant nostre maison. Il luy fut respondu n'estre la coustume, s'il n'y avoit fille à marier: et incontinent la response ouye, s'en vint à nostre hoste, qui estoit homme rusticque, et de rude et obnubilé esperit, auquel il dist: Mon hoste, n'avez-vous ouy ces jours precedens par plusieurs et diverses fois la grand melodie des joueurs de flustes dont on joue devant vostre maison? Je vous asseure que, selon ma conception, je presuppose que c'est quelqu'ung qui est espris de l'amour de vostre femme, ou de la mienne.' (Fate allowed my husband – on

Figure 8.2   Woodcut of a queen and her ladies-in-waiting: *Les Angoysses douloureuses qui procedent d'amours*

secrets if correctly deciphered. In this sense, the lute can be read as a metaphor for de Crenne's text, which must construct a protective barrier between the private love affair of Helisenne and Guenelic and de Crenne's bold and public self-representation. It is interesting to note that, in this compartment, the female lover has actually set the lute to one side in order to concentrate more fully on the object she is holding: a scroll of text. This could be interpreted as an announcement that the diegesis as a whole is at least as concerned with the processes of female authorship as with the love affair itself.

Female authorship is also given authoritative status by a woodcut that is situated between the end of Helisenne's story and the beginning of her address

---

that very day – to inquire of several of the neighbours about the music that was continuing to be played in front of our lodgings. They replied that it was customary only when there was a girl of marriageable age within. As soon as he heard this, he went to our landlord, who was a rustic with a crude, limited mind, to whom he said: "My host, haven't you heard these past days, more than once and at different times, the loud music played by flute-players in front of your house? I assure you that so far as I can see, it must be someone who is in love with your wife or with mine".') Crenne, *Angoysses douloureuses*, p. 121; Crenne, *Torments of Love*, p. 20.

to the female readership at the end of the first book of the narrative (Figure 8.2). The *Angoysses douloureuses* includes over 100 woodcuts in at least five different styles and this variety makes it likely that the majority of them were reused from other projects. As was inevitable under these circumstances and common in Renaissance print culture as a whole, the woodcuts frequently did not 'match' the text that they accompanied.[29] This woodcut represents an all-female assembly at the centre of which there is a throned and crowned royal woman. Her authority is asserted in spatial terms both through her central position in the woodcut and in the fact that she occupies by far the largest volume of space of any of the women. Authority triumphs over realism in the perspective of the representation as the royal woman is the same height as her attendants, even though she is seated and they are standing. The woman further demands the viewer's attention through her left hand, which is lifted in a commanding pose. This also has the effect of emphasising that the woodcut is a snapshot of action, which is current and ongoing. The ladies-in-waiting all show their deference to the royal woman through the slight bowing of their heads and by making her the object of their gaze. Their inferiority is underscored by their partially implied representation: each of them partly obscures the view of another, while the royal woman is represented in her entirety, including her full and flowing gown. Given that the majority of the woodcuts in the *Angoysses douloureuses* can be said to be 'disjunctive' to a greater or lesser extent, the choice of this particular illustration at a moment when the narrator is explicitly addressing her 'tres chieres et honnorées Dames' (most dear and honored ladies) is significant.[30] It shows us, as does the title page, that the compilers of the *Angoysses douloureuses* were complicit in proposing an image of the author that was authoritative.

One final way in which the *Angoysses douloureuses* acquires authority is in the representation of the process of the book's production and reception.[31] At the end of the first part of the novel, Helisenne's husband imprisons her in a tower and destroys the letters that she has received from her lover. In order to comfort herself in the absence of her beloved, the heroine sets about rewriting the letters that she exchanged with Guenelic. The new narrative of their love affair is contained within the pages of a book that is shrouded in white silk. The second and third parts of the novel are narrated by Guenelic and it is only when he dies that his friend Quezinstra takes over. Fortunately for the readers of the *Angoysses douloureuses*, he is able to recover from beside Helisenne's body the white book that contains her part of the narrative, which would otherwise have perished with her.

---

[29]   Marian Rothstein has described this type of picture as 'disjunctive'. 'Disjunctive images in Renaissance books', *Renaissance and Reformation/Renaissance et Réforme*, 26 (1990), pp. 101–20, p. 101.

[30]   Crenne, *Angoysses douloureuses*, p. 221; Crenne, *Torments of Love*, p. 73.

[31]   For an analysis of this episode which argues that the novel as a whole rewrites the relationship between women's writing and desire, see Elisabeth Hodges, 'Hélisenne's purloined letters', *French Forum*, 30 (2005), pp. 1–16.

The representation of the book's editing and production is then merged with the story of the journey of the bodies of Guenelic and Helisenne to the Elysian fields.[32] Quezinstra is joined by Mercury on the journey to the underworld where the lovers' souls are judged. Mercury then takes the white book which Quezinstra had found beside Helisenne's body and takes it to the Gods, presenting it first to Minerva (Pallas):

> O déesse procréee du cerveau de l'Altitonant Juppiter, pource que certain suis que vous vous delectez souverainement aux lectures, je veulx faire present d'ung petit livre: lequel j'ay trouvé la bas en ceste region terrestre: Et à l'occasion que j'ay cogneu que bien estoit digne d'estre distinctement entendu, je lay conservé esperant qu'en voz pudicques mains lieu d'acceptation recouvrera.

> (O goddess born from the brain of thundering Jupiter, because I am well aware that you take sovereign delight in reading, I want to make you a present of a little book, which I found down there in that terrestrial region; and since I realized that it was very worthy of being heard, I kept it, hoping that it might be welcomed into your chaste hands.)[33]

Inscribed in this passage are the responses that Hélisenne de Crenne seeks to illicit from her reading public.[34] Indeed, Mercury's decription of the book as 'ung petit livre' and his account of how he found it in the lowly realm of earth echoes the tone of many Renaissance prefaces where writers, especially women writers, used the modesty topos to capture the goodwill of their readers. Furthermore, his flattery of Minerva as a superlative reader who incarnates virtues such as chastity is comparable to the compliments paid by many writers to their dedicatees. Mercury's high opinion of Minerva as an avid reader would not seem to be misplaced:

> Puis incontinent à la lecture donna principe mais ainsi comme à tel exercise s'occupoit, d'elle s'approcha Venus: laquelle estant fort curieuse de veoir choses nouvelles, voulut estre à la lecture participante. Et quand elle eut entendu et apperceu qu'il faisoit mention d'Amours, En se tournant vers Mercure ainsi luy dist: O Mercure je voys appertement que bien peu me favorisez, puis que pour

---

[32] Buzon reads this episode as a reworking of the medieval debate between Reason and Love which is evident in Helisenne's interior monologues in the opening pages of the novel. *Angoysses douloureuses*, p. 38. Chang interprets this ending as one which reverses the previous dynamic of competition between 'De Crenne' and Janot, in order to absorb Janot (as eventual printer) into the narrative of the volume's success. 'Clothing "Dame Helisenne"', p. 402.

[33] Crenne, *Angoysses douloureuses*, pp. 500–501; Crenne, *Torments of Love*, p. 198.

[34] This observation has also been made by Wood: 'Minerva thus also embodies qualities of a sixteenth-century woman reader whose elevated tastes can be readily satisfied by the volumes being published by the many printers in Paris'. *Hélisenne de Crenne*, p. 43.

gratifier à Pallas, vous m'avez frustrée de ce livre qui de soy mesmes doibt estre
dedié à ma divinité, veu que congnoissez qu'il traicte de choses amoureuses et
veneriennes.

(Then she began immediately to read it. But as she was so occupied, Venus
came up to her. Venus was very curious to see new things, and wanted to share
in the reading. When she had heard it and seen that it mentioned love, turning
to Mercury she said to him: "O Mercury, I see clearly that you have very little
regard for me, since in order to please Pallas you have deprived me of this book
which ought to be dedicated to my divinity, since you know it deals with matters
of love and sensuality".)[35]

There then follows a long exchange between the two female deities concerning
who the natural recipient of the volume should be. This has the effect both of
emphasising the desirability of the volume and underlining its multiple appeals to
the reader. Their altercations only end when Jupiter interjects with the suggestion
to Mercury:

qu'il prind la coppie de ce livre: Et que diligemment le feist imprimer, affin
de manifester au monde les peines, travaulx, et angoysses douloureuses, qui
procedent à l'occasion d'amours.

(Then he wanted him to make a copy of this book and have it immediately
printed in order to show the world the anguish, travails, and painful torments
that proceed from love.)[36]

It is clear that the only way of resolving the dispute is to disseminate the text more
widely through print publication. Indeed, Jupiter considers it to be such a useful
and learned book that he suggests that it is printed in Paris, to which Minerva
agrees, as it is a city full of an 'infinie multitude de gens merveilleusement
studieux' ('infinite mulititude of studious people').[37] The importance of the work
is emphasised by the fact that Jupiter himself gives the work its new title of the
Angoysses douloureuses qui procedent [à l'occasion] d'amours. Through this
final twist the editing, printing and place of publication of the book are themselves
inscribed into a mythology that explains the work's genesis and shapes its
reception by the reader. Above all, the *Angoysses douloureuses* anticipates its own
commercial success by projecting an image of itself as a highly desirable cultural
object.[38]

---

[35]   Crenne, *Angoysses douloureuses*, p. 501; Crenne, *Torments of Love*, p. 198.
[36]   Crenne, *Angoysses douloureuses*, p. 503; Crenne, *Torments of Love*, p. 199.
[37]   Crenne, *Angoysses douloureuses*, p. 503; Crenne, *Torments of Love*, p. 199.
[38]   As Chang has noted: 'By inscribing the printing of the book into its plot, the
producers of the work create a textual moebius strip in which the technical and imaginative

In conclusion, Hélisenne de Crenne emerges from this reading of the *Angoysses douloureuses* not as a female author whose identity was challenged and diminished by the fact of entering into print circulation, but as a woman who was able to imbue her work with authority in such a way as to ensure the success both of this work and of her future endeavours. Her relationship with Janot and the other craftsmen active in his print shop was not necessarily one of surrender to a force that sought to dominate in the struggle for textual control, however much the marks of that struggle might still be visible on the pages of the book. Hélisenne de Crenne adopted a pseudonym that helped her better express to the book-buying public the distinctive qualities of her textual output within a marketplace of cultural commodities. She developed a female authorial persona who would not only be able to 'speak from the heart' as only a woman could, but would also respond both to the traditions of supposedly female-authored love narratives and to the pro- and anti-feminist writing that Janot (and others) had printed with evident commercial success. De Crenne further inscribed the editing, publication and success of the novel in the diegesis. This protected her from criticism and created for the novel a mythology of its own origins and reception that exceeded the merely textual to encompass the material and hermeneutic aspects of its reception.

Not all of the strategies employed in the publication of the *Angoysses douloureuses* were at de Crenne's sole disposal, however. In areas such as the elaboration of the title page and the inclusion of woodcuts, for example, it is evident that Janot or one of his collaborators rather than de Crenne would have commissioned the new compartment, briefed the woodcut artist and selected the illustration to accompany the text. That a consistently authoritative view of de Crenne's authorship was presented by these different elements demonstrates the credibility that de Crenne possessed as an author even at the beginning of her career in print publication. It also hints at a certain willingness on the part of textual producers to promote the distinctive qualities offered by a female-authored text at an historical moment when its circulation in print was a speculative and pioneering project.

---

processes of book production are inextricably entwined.' 'Clothing "Dame Helisenne"', p. 403.

Chapter 9

The Early Polemics of Henry VIII's Royal Supremacy and their International Usage[1]

Tracey A. Sowerby

In 1527 Henry VIII decided that his marriage to Catherine of Aragon was not just inconvenient, but also unlawful. The failure of this marriage to produce a male heir was proof that he had contravened Levitical prohibition that a man should not carnally know his brother's wife. Over the next six years, Henry pursued an annulment. At first he sought one from the Pope, whom he sought to convince that his marriage had contravened God's law.[2] When a papal annulment did not materialise, Henry and his scholars claimed that the Pope had no jurisdiction to judge the matter, which should more appropriately be determined within England. In the process of settling his Great Matter and setting aside Catherine of Aragon, Henry repudiated papal authority and established himself as Supreme Head of the English Church. It has long been recognised by historians that these efforts were accompanied by a series of polemical tracts that outlined, exhorted and defended the king's policies to his subjects and foreign scholars. Yet a tendency to view these events in insular terms has meant that the focus has been firmly fixed on how the tracts may have been used and viewed in England and how they constructed Henry's reclaimed authority over the English Church.[3] Rex has outlined the development of the theory of obedience in these tracts and its centrality to

[1] I would like to thank the *English Historical Review* for permissions to develop material from '"All our books do be sent abroad and translated": Henrician polemic in its international context', *English Historical Review*, 121 (2006), 1271–99 (pp. 1276–82, 1292–3). This essay was written during a British Academy PostDoctoral Fellowship; I would like to thank the British Academy for their generous support.

[2] For an account of the tracts produced in pursuit of Henry's desired annulment from the papacy see Virginia Murphy, 'The literature and propaganda of Henry VIII's first divorce', in *The Reign of Henry VIII: Politics, Policy and Piety*, ed. by Diarmaid MacCulloch (London: Macmillan, 1995), pp. 135–58.

[3] The main discussions of these works are William G. Zeeveld, *Foundations of Tudor Policy* (Cambridge, MA: Harvard University Press, 1948); Geoffrey R. Elton, *Policy and Police: the Enforcement of the Reformation in the Age of Thomas Cromwell* (Cambridge: Cambridge University Press, 1972); Franklin L. van Baumer, *The Early Tudor Theory of Kingship* (New Haven, CT: Yale Historical Publications, 1940); John N. King, *Tudor Royal Iconography: Literature and Art in an Age of Religious Crisis* (Princeton, NJ: Princeton University Press, 1989).

conservative polemicists, who utilised a Tyndalian theory of obedience to push a conservative vision of the English Church.[4] There is no denying that obedience was a central theme of these polemics. Yet Henry had to convince not just his subjects of the rights of his cause, but also those foreign princes who might be, and indeed were, called upon by the Pope to remove Henry from his throne. The international context of the tracts has received relatively little attention. This essay will detail some of the means by which Henry and his government utilised polemics to try to promote a favourable image of the king outside England and justify his position as head of the English Church.

Henry VIII had sponsored the publication of a series of printed letters and tracts on the continent in the years 1512–25, but these mainly announced Henry's foreign policy and celebrated his victories on the continent.[5] In 1521, as Henry VIII's campaign against Martin Luther took shape, the King launched his most concerted propaganda effort to date: the promotion of the *Assertio Septem Sacramentorum*, his defence of papal primacy and condemnation of Luther. Further tracts against Luther followed from the pens of the king and a select group of his scholars.[6] Henry wanted to gain an international reputation as a godly scholar; he eventually fulfilled his ambition to see his work sent 'not only to Rome, but also into France and other nations'.[7]

Once Henry decided to procure an annulment of his marriage to Catherine of Aragon, he waged a concerted campaign to demonstrate the illegitimacy of his first marriage using a range of books, from the determinations of various European universities in his favour to 'king's books' compiled by English scholars.[8] In 1531 Henry turned to the printing presses to help promote his cause and a book containing the determinations of the Universities of Angers, Bologna, Bourges, Orleans, Padua, Paris and Toulouse was published first in Latin in April and then in English in November. The *Gravissimae censurae* also contained a lengthy treatise in support of the proposition that it was against divine and natural law for a man to marry his brother's widow, even if he died without children, and that the Pope had no power to dispense such cases. Indeed it was the duty of the bishops

---

    [4]   Richard Rex, 'Crisis of obedience: God's word and Henry's Reformation', *Historical Journal*, 39 (1996), pp. 863–94.

    [5]   For further details of the ways in which the policy developed over the course of Henry VIII's reign, see Sowerby, 'Henrician polemic in its international context', pp. 1271–99.

    [6]   Richard Rex, 'The English campaign against Luther in the 1520s', *Transactions of the Royal Historical Society*, 5th series, 38 (1989), pp. 85–106.

    [7]   *Letters and Papers, Foreign and Domestic of the Reign of Henry VIII*, ed. by John S. Brewer (London, 1862–1932), (hereafter *LP*), III, i, 1233. References are to document number. Where the information contained in the MS is no different from that in the calendar, I cite only the calendar reference, but I give the MS reference if the MS contains any variations.

    [8]   Murphy, 'Literature and propaganda', pp. 135–58.

to admonish the Pope should he try.[9] The *Censurae* were presented to the Pope, and circulated to some extent within Europe.[10] In the exposition that followed the determinations, emphasis was placed on the fact that the Universities whose judgements were included were those in neutral territories and could therefore be regarded as indifferent and that the argument that a man could not marry his brother's widow was firmly grounded in divine and natural law.

In 1532 Henry definitely oversaw the production of and possibly himself composed *A Glasse of the Truth*.[11] The *Glasse* was a polemical rendering of material found in the *Collectanea Satis Copiosa*, the collection of sources that provided the grounds for Henry's divorce and later the Royal Supremacy. The Glasse set the standards that later Henrician polemics would have to reach. Scripture was established as the highest possible authority, and Henry was placed directly under this. In the *Glasse* Henry was portrayed as the victim of a grave injustice: the Pope unfairly delayed Henry's rightful annulment; he exceeded his authority and contravened his own laws by refusing to allow the matter to be determined in its proper provincial setting. The matter 'ought to be determyned within this realme' and a just adjudication would be had 'if the hole heed & body of the parliament wold set their wyttes and good wylles vnto it'.[12] The choice of interlocutors also helped lend authority to the text: a lawyer and a divine, both of whom would be in a position to gauge the validity of the king's claims. Copies of the *Glasse* were distributed within England, but Henry also had international aspirations for this tract.[13] He commissioned a French translation of the *Glasse*. This may have been produced for use at the French court during Henry's visit to France in October and November 1532, as Rex has suggested, but this does not rule out the possibility that a broader Francophone audience was also intended.[14] There were further

---

[9] *Grauissimae, atq[ue] exactissimae illustrissimaru[m] totius Italiae, et Galliae academiaru[m] censurae efficacissimis etiam quorundam doctissimorum uiroru[m] argumentationibus explicatae, de ueritate illius propositionis* (London: Thomas Berthelet, 1531), STC 14286; *The determinations of the moste famous and mooste excellent vniuersities of Italy and Fraunce, that it is so vnlefull [sic] for a man to marie his brothers wyfe, that the pope hath no power to dispence therewith* (London: Thomas Berthelet, 1531), STC 14287.

[10] Murphy, 'Literature and propaganda', pp. 155–8; *LP*, V, 366.

[11] Anonymous, *A Glasse of the Truth* (London: Thomas Berthelet, 1532), STC 11918, 11919 [*LP*, V, 547]. Steven W. Haas, 'Henry VIII's *Glasse of Truthe*', *History*, 64 (1979), pp. 353–62 suggests late 1531 as the date of the first edition. Richard Rex, 'Redating Henry VIII's *A Glass of the Truthe*', *The Library*, 7th series, 4 (2003), pp. 16–27, argues that the *Glasse* was first printed in 1532. A reference by the Imperial ambassador Chapuys, suggests that the work was printed by August 1532, even if it was not yet widely available [*LP*, V, 1316].

[12] *Glasse*, F2ʳ.

[13] See for example *LP*, V, 1316, 1338.

[14] This was probably undertaken by John Palsgrave and printed by the King's printer Thomas Berthelet. It is dated 19 October 1532. National Archives: Public Record Office,

plans to disseminate the tract in the Holy Roman Empire and Italy. Consequently, Nicholas Hawkins, while serving as ambassador to the Emperor, translated the *Glasse* into Latin.[15] The Imperial ambassador in England spotted the undertones in the work, reporting that, although the tract claimed to be about Henry's marital affairs, it was also a frontal assault on the power of the papacy.[16]

The *Glasse of the Truth* was followed by several important printed works, which outlined official policy on the Divorce and provided the theoretical foundations of the Royal Supremacy, supplementing the legal changes wrought by Parliament. Shortly after Parliament passed the *Act in Restraint of Appeals*, Henry's newly appointed archbishop of Canterbury, Thomas Cranmer, pronounced in Henry's favour on 23 May 1533, four months after Henry had secretly married Anne Boleyn. The polemical works that were designed on one level to familiarise Henry's subjects with the new rhetoric of Henry's government and persuade them of its legitimacy also had to construct Henry's authority and justify his policies in such a manner as to convince a hostile international audience of the veracity of Henry's claims.

In December 1533 *ARTICLES DEVISID by the holle consent of the kynges moste honourable counsayle* were printed in London. Henry's councillors were 'honourable and elect persons' addressing his subjects with the king's consent. Their *Articles* asserted the invalidity of Henry's first marriage, and the right of the archbishop of Canterbury, Thomas Cranmer, 'beinge auctorysed by acte of parlyament' to annul it in the proper provincial setting. Papal claims to universal authority were refuted: 'by scripture, there is none auctoritie ne iurisdiction graunted more to the bysshoppe of Rome, then to anye other'; only the 'general counsel (laufully gathered) is superiour and hath power ouer al byshoppes and spiritualle powers'. The Pope was disregarding established protocols in his handling of Henry's case and had proven himself an 'vsurper of goddes lawe, an infringer of general counsels'.[17] On 26 December, copies of the *Articles* were purposely and liberally given to foreign ambassadors at the English court.[18] Meanwhile, Henry's representatives in Germany, Nicholas Heath and Christopher Mont, and in Brussels, John Hackett, were familiar with the content of the *Articles*,

State Papers 1/71, fol. 128 [*LP*, V, 1454]; John Palsgrave, *The Comedy of Acolastus translated from the Latin by John Palsgrave*, ed. by Patrick L. Carver (Oxford: Early English Texts Society, 1937), p. xlix. Anonymous, *Le myrouer de verite* (London: Thomas Berthelet, 1532), STC 11919.5. Rex, 'Glass of the Truthe', p. 24.

15   PRO, SP 1/72, fol. 154 [*LP*, V, 1660].

16   *LP*, V, 1316.

17   *ARTICLES by the holle consent of the kynges moste honourable counsayle* (London: Thomas Berthelet, 1533) STC 9177, Aiʳ–Aviiiʳ.

18   *Calendar of letters, despatches, state papers relating to the negotiations between England and Spain preserved in the archives at Vienna, Brussels Simancas and elsewhere 1531–33*, ed. by Pascual de Gayangos (London: George E. B. Eyre and William Spottiswoode, 1882), no. 1165 [*LP*, VI, 1571].

'the lityll boke that the kynges consell hath sette owt', by January 1534.[19] The diplomatic instructions of Heath and of William Paget, who was sent to Poland later that month, both contained references to 'certain books and other writings' that were to be provided for the ambassadors. It is likely that these included the *Articles*.[20] The process was not yet finessed as the *Articles* remained in English. Few foreign ambassadors and agents would have understood them in their printed form, as only a small number would have had any knowledge of the English language. Even in the later sixteenth century, English was not mentioned in a list of languages essential for the continental diplomat.[21] In 1533–34 it was left to the Imperialists and Spanish to translate the *Articles* into French and Spanish.[22]

Another work concerned with the Royal Supremacy, Edward Foxe's *De vera differentia*, was used in a similar way.[23] It drew heavily on the *Collectanea satis copiosa* and was intended for a Latinate audience. Elton described *De vera differentia* as 'an armoury of arguments'.[24] In many ways this was its strength. Foxe aimed at convincing educated, and especially foreign, opinion of the validity of Henry's repudiation of papal authority. Like Sampson, Foxe also repudiated papal claims to jurisdiction within England, asserting the independence of the provincial English Church under the authority of the King. Foxe also appealed to history to prove his case, citing Anglo-Saxon, Anglo-Norman and Old Testament kings as well as the Roman Emperors Constantine and Justinian.[25] *De vera differentia* was distributed to diplomats at the English court. Cromwell gave the Scottish ambassador a copy of a book, while the Bishop of Paris had also seen a

---

[19]   NA: PRO, SP 1/82, fols. 29–35ᵛ, fol. 117 [*LP*, VII, 21.2, 115]. By March, Philip Melanchthon had a copy of the *Articles*, on which he commented to Frederick Myconius [*LP*, VII, 318].

[20]   NA: PRO, SP 1/82 fol. 19 [*LP*, VII, 21.1]; British Library, Cotton MSS, Vitellius B IX, fol. 68; British Library, Additional MSS, 29547, fol. 1ᵛ [*LP*, VII, 148].

[21]   Ottaviano Maggi's *De legato libri duo* (1566) listed Latin, Greek, Italian, French, Spanish, German and Turkish as the essential languages of European diplomacy [Peter Burke, *Languages and Communities in Early Modern Europe* (Cambridge: Cambridge University Press, 2004), p. 115]. Joycelyne G. Russell, *Diplomats at Work: Three Renaissance Studies* (Stroud: Sutton Publishing, 1992), pp. 38–9, discusses the limited knowledge of English in Europe in the sixteenth century.

[22]   *LP*, VII, 115, 185.

[23]   Edward Foxe, *Opus eximium, de vera differentia regiae potestatis et ecclesiasticae et quae sit ipsa veritas ac virtus vtriusque* (London: Thomas Berthelet, 1534, 1538), STC 11218, 11219.

[24]   Elton, *Policy and Police*, p. 182.

[25]   John A. Guy, 'Thomas Cromwell and the intellectual origins of the Henrician revolution', in *Reassessing the Henrician Age: Humanism, Politics and Reform*, ed. by Alistair Fox and John A. Guy (Oxford: Oxford University Press, 1986), pp. 151–78.

copy, which had apparently prompted him to leave England in disgust.[26] It was deemed useful enough to be reprinted in 1538.[27]

In the following year Richard Sampson refuted papal claims to *plenitudo potestatis* in his *Oratio*.[28] Sampson appealed to Church history to argue that the early English Church had been free from papal authority. The story of the mythical King Lucius established that the early Church in England had been free from papal hegemony. Sampson argued that claims of papal supremacy had only developed following the Council of Nicea and also challenged the superiority of Peter over the other apostles, arguing for parity and thus denying the Petrine succession. Paul's Epistles to the Romans had emphasised the obligation of a Christian to obey his prince and it was this obligation that Sampson emphasised. By continuing to follow the Roman Church, England had been led into superstition and error.[29] In July 1535 Robert Barnes was sent to negotiate with the Protestant Princes in Germany. '[F]or his better remembrance and Instruction' in convincing the Schmalkaldic League that Henry's repudiation of papal authority was genuine, Barnes was given copies of 'a book made by the deane of the chaple' for reference. He was also expected to convince Philip Melanchthon to come to England to debate theology; if Melanchthon were unsure, the *Oratio* was to be proffered as evidence of Henry's sincerity. Henry's ambassador in France, Sir John Wallop, also received copies of Sampson's book to use in his audiences with Francis I. Wallop was to 'repair with the said copies to the French king' and demonstrate to Francis 'how moch it shalbe against his honour ... to give himself subject to the said bishop [of Rome]'.[30] After this initial diplomatic campaign, Sampson's *Oratio* continued to be used at foreign courts. In November 1535, 12 copies were sent to the French court for distribution. When Reginald Pole was instructed to offer his

---

[26]   *Calendar of letters, despatches, state papers relating to the negotiations between England and Spain preserved in the archives at Vienna, Brussels Simancas and elsewhere 1534–35*, ed. by Pascual de Gayangos (London: Eyre and Spottiswoode, 1886), no. 1.

[27]   As such it was the only one of the main polemics of the years 1534–36 to be considered worthy of a second edition in England. The title page of the second edition incorporated the royal arms, suggesting that it was intended primarily for foreign consumption and reinforcing its status as an officially endorsed polemic.

[28]   Richard Sampson, *Richardi Sampsonis, regii sacelliae decani oratio, qua docet, hortatur, admonet omnes potissimu[m] anglos, regiae dignitati cum primis ut obediant* (London: Thomas Berthelet, 1535), STC 21681.

[29]   Ibid., *passim*. Andrew Chibi, 'Richard Sampson, his "Oratio" and Henry VIII's Royal Supremacy', *Journal of Church and State*, 39 (1997), pp. 543–60. For a discussion of the use of the Lucius story in the English reformation see Felicity Heal, 'What can King Lucius do for you? The Reformation and the early British Church', *English Historical Review*, 120 (2005), pp. 593–614. Lucius was also mentioned in passing in Edward Foxe's *De vera differentia*.

[30]   BL, Cotton MSS, Cleopatra E VI, fols 337–8 [*LP*, VIII, 1062]. For the details surrounding Barnes' mission see Rory McEntegart, *Henry VIII, the League of Schmalkalden and the English Reformation* (Chippenham: Boydell Press, 2002), pp. 26–31.

opinion on the Royal Supremacy, he was sent one of Sampson's books to guide his judgement.[31]

Other tracts were used just as extensively in the promotion of the Henry's rediscovered authority over his Church as Sampson's *Oratio*. Stephen Gardiner's seminal justification of the Royal Supremacy, *De vera obedientia* (1535),[32] became one of the most important and most widely disseminated Latin apologetics of Henry's reign on the continent; it was also heavily utilised in Henrician diplomacy. Gardiner refuted papal claims to universal sovereignty, demonstrating that, in line with scripture, men owed obedience to their prince above all other men.[33] A list of items that were to be sent with Edward Foxe on his mission to the German princes in 1535 included 'The byshopp of Winchesters boke de obedientia'.[34] Gardiner himself, while ambassador at the French court, was sent 'a dosen of your orations'. He was to distribute these at court 'to suche personnes ther as amonges youe ye shal think convenient'.[35] Two years later, *De vera obedientia* was still being used as a diplomatic text.[36] The dissemination of *De vera obedientia* went further than that of Sampson's *Oratio*: it was published twice on the continent. One of the continental editions appeared at Strasbourg, under the auspices of Martin Bucer and his fellow reformers. It was not openly sanctioned by the English crown, probably because Bucer and his fellow editors added a Protestant gloss to the text.[37] While on embassy in January 1536, Edmund Bonner reported from Hamburg that 'they have printed there my Lord of Winchesters bok de vera obedientia and made a certin collection therof with certain additions'. Francis Rhodus, the printer of the Hamburg edition, may have obtained a copy of Gardiner's work from Bonner himself.[38] As Henry's ambassador, Bonner was his representative abroad. By writing a preface to the Hamburg edition of *De vera obedientia*, he conferred official endorsement. Bonner's preface, moreover, was designed to pique foreign interest in Gardiner's tract and its arguments against the papacy. Bonner emphasised the implications of

---

[31]   British Library, Additional MSS, 25114, fol. 110 [*LP*, IX, 848]; *LP*, X, 7.

[32]   Stephen, Gardiner, *De vera obedientia* (London: Thomas Berthelet, 1535; Strasbourg: Wendelin Rihel, 1536), STC 11584.

[33]   A modern parallel Latin-English edition of the tract can be found in Pierre Janelle, *Obedience in Church and State* (Cambridge: Cambridge University Press, 1930).

[34]   British Library, Cotton MSS, Titus B I, fol. 458 [*LP*, IX, 213.5].

[35]   Francis Brian and John Wallop, who were more established at the French court, were to advise Gardiner on the most important people to whom to give the tracts [British Library, Additional MSS, 25114, fol. 110 [*LP*, IX, 848]; *LP*, IX, 1000].

[36]   Nicholas Heath and Nicholas Wilson were told to take 'an oratyon settfurth by the bisshopp of Winchester' on embassy with them [NA: PRO, SP 1/124, fol. 149 [*LP*, XII, ii, 620]].

[37]   Strasbourg: Wendelin Rihel, 1536. Janelle, *Obedience in Church and State*, pp. xxvi–viii. For details of Foxe's mission see McEntegart, *Henry VIII*, pp. 26–76.

[38]   British Library, Cotton MSS, Nero B III, fol. 100[v] [*LP*, X, 303]; Janelle, *Obedience in Church and State*, pp. xxxi–xxxii.

Henry's troubles for other princes as earlier works such as the *Articles* had done as well as the universal invalidity of papal *plenitudo postestas*. Bonner's attempts to convert other princes to Henry's view on papal jurisdiction were common in English diplomatic efforts at this time. Emphasising the universal implications of Henry's discovery was a common theme in many of the polemical tracts envisaged as diplomatic aids.[39] In this context the 'cult of authority' which historians have often associated with these Henrician tracts may have had further importance than inculcating obedience among Henry's own subjects: it may also have been seen as a potential tool of persuasion for foreign princes who might be tempted to assert in their realms similar powers to those claimed by Henry in England.

Two other polemical works were utilised in Henrician diplomacy in 1535. Barnes, Simon Heynes, Mont and Wallop all received copies of 'the bisshopes sermons', which they were expected to use in the same way as Gardiner's *De vera obedientia*.[40] These may well have been copies of Simon Matthews's sermon in defence of the Royal Supremacy, which he had preached on 27 June.[41] The second was a tract that justified the executions of John Fisher, Bishop of Rochester, and Sir Thomas More for treason in the summer of 1535. A public statement was necessary, as the Pope had written to other European rulers to condemn Henry's actions on 26 July. Edward Foxe and Stephen Gardiner were given copies of the tract *Se sedes illa romana* so that they could 'declare and set forthe' the crimes of More and Fisher.[42]

The range of reference works English diplomats were expected to use was far greater than has been outlined above. Ambassadors' instructions often contained references to unnamed books. Many of these books and 'other writings' were undoubtedly more traditional diplomatic materials, such as copies of existing trade and peace treaties. Yet there is some evidence that even polemical works printed in England that were not connected to a specific policy were also sent abroad. Ambassadors were probably sent tracts on recent events and statements to keep them up to date. Hence Wilson and Heath were given 'a sermon lately made by the bysshopp of York' in 1537.[43] Unfortunately, full lists of the books

---

[39]   See for example *LP*, VIII, 1062; BL MS, Additional 25114, fols 96–9 [*LP*, IX, 443]; *A protestation made for the most mighty and moste redoubted kynge of Englande* (London: Thomas Berthelet, 1537), Cv^v; *An epistle of the moste myghty [and] redouted Prince Henry the viii* (London: Thomas Berthelet, 1538), Aviii^v–Biii^r.

[40]   British Library MS, Cotton Cleopatra E VI, fols 337–8 [*LP*, VIII, 1062].

[41]   If so, then either they had to wait for the books, as Matthew's sermon was not printed until 30 July, or they were given early manuscript copies of it [S. Matthew, *A sermon made in the cathedrall churche of Saynt Paule at London, the XXVII. day of June, Anno. 1535* (London: Thomas Berthelet, 1535), STC 17656].

[42]   NA: PRO, SP 1/96, fol. 24^v [*LP*, IX, 213.1]; BL MS, Cotton Titus B I, fo. 458 [*LP*, IX, 213.5]. *Se sedes illa romana* was not printed, so manuscript copies must have been taken.

[43]   NA: PRO, SP 1/124, fol. 149 [*LP*, XII, ii, 620].

and other items given to English diplomats in this period are rare. An examination of the material which has survived relating to Edward Foxe's mission to the Schmalkaldic League in 1535 is suggestive. 'A memorandum for my Lorde of herefordes despache' specified that he be given 'the boke made by my Lorde of Canterburye', 'Melanctons boke de locis communibus' and orations by Dr Adams and Epinus, as well as copies of Gardiner's *De vera obedientia* and *Se sedes illa Romana*.[44] There is evidence that Foxe was also consulting Martin Bucer's writings, although quite how he came by them is more difficult to discern. Other embassies also indicate that a wider range of books were available. In November 1537 Thomas Wyatt fell foul of Charles V for allegedly urging his fellow courtiers to read 'certain pamphlets', which the Spanish considered heretical.[45] In 1538 Wyatt, Bonner and Heynes were referred to 'suche other treatyes as have been made for the confuctacion of that pretended power' (the Papacy). This suggests that they had access to earlier works on the Royal Supremacy, such as Foxe's *De vera differentia*. In addition, they were expected to have access to 'a letter written by the bishops of Durham and London'.[46] When John Hutton died on embassy in 1538, among his possessions was a polemical work, 'a boke of the birthe of noble prynce Edwarde'.[47]

In the 1530s it was not just the theoretical relationship between Church and state that Henry VIII was changing; in the latter half of the decade the English Church witnessed doctrinal definition and attempts to reform some traditional practices. It is hardly surprising then, to find that the promotion of English works on the Continent was not restricted to government apologetics and secular propaganda. Major theological statements were also broadcast to an international audience as part of Henry's assertion of his control over his Church. In 1537 Henry's government took some care to ensure that it controlled the dissemination of the *Bishops' Book*. In September Nicholas Heath and Nicholas Wilson were sent on embassy to Flanders. They were instructed to take several texts with them, one of which was 'a book of certain thinges lately determyned here by the hole clergy'.[48] Similarly in 1543 the *King's Book* made its way to foreign courts through English diplomatic channels and Latin copies were prepared for the Imperialists.[49]

In the atmosphere of 1532–36 it was essential that English ambassadors could be seen to expound the quite complex arguments underpinning the Divorce and the Royal Supremacy. Previously ambassadors had received the texts of speeches or schedules to prepare them for negotiations. In these critical years the

---

44   British Library, Cotton MSS, Titus B I, fol. 458 [*LP*, IX, 213.5].
45   British Library, Cotton MSS, Cleopatra E VI, fols 337–8 [*LP*, VIII 1062]; *LP*, XII, ii, 1031. Wyatt probably had Henry VIII's tracts on the Council of Mantua and works such as Lorenzo Valla's *De falsa donatione Constanti*.
46   NA: PRO, SP 1/131, fols 31ᵛ–32 [*LP*, XIII, i, 695].
47   NA: PRO, SP 1/136, fol. 78 [*LP*, XIII, ii, 286.2].
48   NA: PRO, SP 1/124, fol. 149 [*LP*, XII, ii, 620].
49   See for example *LP*, XVIII, i, 364; ii, 50, 68, 98; XIX, i, 168, 216.

usage of English polemics in the international arena was extended significantly. English diplomats were also equipped with officially sanctioned printed tracts and manuscript treatises. They were expected to extract arguments from these texts and use them to frame their oratory in diplomatic audiences. On a practical level, this removed the need to recapitulate particular arguments at great length for each ambassador serving on the continent and so had the potential to reduce considerably the time spent preparing diplomatic instructions. More importantly, though, by officially endorsing polemical treatises as reference works, English diplomats were presented with a coherent, sanctioned body of work upon which to draw. Those constructing Henry's kingship in the 1530s were concerned with anything that might undermine the validity of the king's cause and so subtract from his authority. Hence problematic copies of official works were called in, as were unauthorised accounts, and errata sheets were added to many of the tracts.[50] Nicholas Hawkins' translation of the *Glasse* illustrates many of the areas of concern. He was worried about retaining passages that admitted of any weakness, asking Henry if he should translate the sections of the *Glasse* that dealt with the ungrateful complaints of Henry's subjects. Hawkins also left out quotations from sources so that they could be filled in by an expert with access to the text. Moreover he paid attention to regional variation in preference for particular styles of Latin.[51]

Understandably one of the most important issues that the government and its polemicists considered was consistency. Opponents of the king could easily criticise Henry VIII for inconsistency, as he had very publicly defended papal power against the claims of Martin Luther in 1521.[52] His subsequent *volte face* undermined his position and was used against him. In 1531 Fernando de Loazes lamented that the king whose piety had once led him to write the *Assertio septem sacramentorum* against wicked apostates now disregarded justice, law and true authority in the Church, and de Loazes did so in a printed work in favour of Catherine of Aragon.[53] Closer to home, one of the king's staunchest opponents, Thomas More, claimed that it was while reading the *Assertio* that he had been convinced that papal primacy was divinely instituted.[54] Copies of Henry's *Assertio* were circulating widely in Italy in 1536, when it was hoped that Catherine's death would see Henry return to the Roman fold.[55] The *Assertio* highlighted that Henry had to be seen to be consistent in the future. When Henry's most prolific

---

[50]   *LP*, XIII, i, 840; *Tudor Royal Proclamations*, ed. by Paul L. Hughes and James F. Larkin, 3 vols (New Haven, CT: Yale University Press, 1964–69), I, no. 229. Errata sheets were appended to John Clerk's *Oratio*, Edward Powell's *Propugnaculum*, Foxe's *De vera differentia* and Morison's *Apomaxis*, for example.

[51]   NA: PRO, SP 1/72, fo. 154 [*LP*, V, 1660].

[52]   Rex, 'English campaign against Luther', pp. 85–106.

[53]   Ferdinando de Loazes, *Tractatus in causa matrimonij Serenissimorum dominorum Henrici et Catherine Anglie Regum (Barcelona: in officina ... Caroli Amorosij, 1531)*, Aii^r.

[54]   *LP*, VII, 289.

[55]   *LP*, XI, 15.

propagandist of the late 1530s, Richard Morison, was instructed to alter a tract in 1537, he warned that changing the published opinion of the king would reduce his international credibility, declaring that 'the sentence of a prince, thanswere of an hole realme, either owght not to be printed, or els ons printed, not to be changed'.[56] Trying to ensure basic uniformity in the rhetoric used in English diplomacy abroad and at home was one means by which Henry's government could try to counter charges of inconsistency and inconstancy. Diplomats who were given fully formulated arguments were less likely to say anything that compromised the official line on a given subject, whether by accident or design.

Many of the authors of the tracts that laid the basis of the Henrician Church were themselves used in diplomatic service in the crucial years of the 1530s. In December 1533 the Imperial ambassador in England reported that Henry had 'resolved to send to the countries where there may be greater need persons of a certain rank, and fit for the task of spreading the proclamations'.[57] It is no wonder then that, as MacMahon has noted, there was a marked increase in the importance of training in civil or canon law among Henrician ambassadors in the 1530s.[58] Henry and Cromwell were concerned about the abilities of the diplomats they sent. Cranmer was asked to check Nicholas Heath's proficiency in defending the king's great matter in anticipation of Heath's embassy in 1534; he assured Cromwell that 'I knowe no man in England can defende it better than he'.[59] Moreover many of the same people were being used in diplomatic audiences at home. Thus in May 1534, Eustace Chapuys attended an audience with Henry VIII, during which Edward Foxe, Edward Lee, Richard Sampson and Cuthbert Tunstall held forth on the Divorce and Royal Supremacy.[60] This also helped to ensure that Henry's diplomats could adequately defend his recently reasserted jurisdiction over the spiritual sphere within his realm.

The arguments surrounding the Divorce and Royal Supremacy were complex. Stephen Gardiner or Edward Foxe might have had no difficulty in defending Henry's rediscovered authority over the English Church and would have been at ease rehearsing the arguments underpinning the provincial jurisdiction that allowed Henry VIII to settle his marital affairs without reference to the papacy. Other ambassadors, such as Sir Francis Bryan, appointed more for their social status and personal relationship with the king, might have more difficulty.[61] This was especially true of non-clerical ambassadors, who were often untrained in

---

[56]   British Library, Cotton MSS, Cleopatra E VI, fol. 323 [*LP*, XII, i, 1311].

[57]   *Cal. Spain 1531–33*, no. 1158.

[58]   Luke MacMahon, 'The ambassadors of Henry VIII: The personnel of English diplomacy, 1500–1550' (unpublished doctoral thesis, University of Kent, 2000), pp. 74–9.

[59]   NA: PRO, SP1/82 fol. 16 [*LP*, VII, 20].

[60]   *LP*, VII, 690.

[61]   On the importance of social status in diplomatic appointments see Matthew S. Anderson, *The Rise of Modern Diplomacy 1450–1919* (London: Longman, 1993), p. 12 and Garrett Mattingly, *Renaissance Diplomacy* (New York: Dover Publications, 1988),

theology, civil law or canon law and who made up nearly half of the diplomatic corps in Henry VIII's reign.[62] According to contemporary theory, the character and qualities of a prince could be gauged from the skills demonstrated by his chosen representative: 'the worth of a prince was seen in the men he sent to represent him abroad'.[63] The choices a king made when appointing his diplomats were therefore taken as an indication of what sort of prince he was: these could tell another court whether he was learned, interested in cultural trends, philosophically skilled, linguistically adept or militarily capable. Much of the commentary on early modern diplomacy stresses that eloquence was prized.[64] Francis Thynne expected his 'perfect ambassadour' to 'discharge his Message' 'Rhetorically by perswading eloquence, in apt words, ready tongue, sweet voice, and speedy deliverance'.[65] An ambassador might get away with having more style than substance, but eloquence could only take him so far, and another diplomatic commonplace stipulated that an ambassador should be in a position to expound fully any position his prince expected him to take. Thus Étienne Dolet thought ambassadors should 'employ a careful manner of speech, well polished and adorned by wise opinions and weighty words' and Alberico Gentili talked of 'the duty of the ambassador not merely to explain his message but to support it by arguments' in 1582.[66] This may explain why the books with which diplomats were equipped were not limited

---

pp. 184–5. For details of Bryan's missions see Gary M. Bell, *Handlist of British Diplomatic Representatives, 1509–1688* (London: Royal Historical Society, 1990), pp. 76–9.

[62]   MacMahon, 'Ambassadors of Henry VIII', pp. 116–17, states that 51 of Henry VIII's 112 ambassadors were gentlemen or nobles.

[63]   Francesco Guicciardini's paraphrase of Ludovico Sforza: *Guicciardini's Ricordi: The Counsels and Reflections of Francesco Guicciardini*, ed. by Geoff R. Berridge (Leicester: Allandale Online Publishing, 2000), p. 85. See also Ortensio Landi, *Delectable demaundes, and pleasaunt questions, with their seuerall aunswers, in matters of loue, naturall causes, with morall and politique deuises*, trans. by William Painter (London: John Cawood; 1566), STC 5059, fol. 69: 'it is commonly saide, that the prince is knowen by the Ambassador'; Walter Haddon, *Against Ierome Osorius Byshopp of Siluane in Portingall and against his slaunderous inuectiues An aunswere apologeticall* (London: John Day, 1581), STC 12594, fol. 318: 'the countenaunce of euery Ambassadour dependeth vpon the maiesty of the person whom he representeth'; Aristotle, *Thus endeth the secrete of secretes of Arystotle* (London: Robert Copland, 1528), STC770, fol. Hii[r]: 'MYghty emperour y[e] messangers alway sheweth the wysoome of hym y[t] sendeth them'.

[64]   On the importance of competent delivery, see Russell, *Diplomats at Work*, pp. 18–20.

[65]   Francis Thynne, *The perfect ambassadour treating of the antiquitie, priveledges, and behaviour of men belonging to that function* (London: printed for John Colbeck, 1652), Wing T1143, fol. 21[r–v]. Thynne presented his treatise to William, Lord Cobham in 1579.

[66]   Jesse S. Reeves, 'Étienne Dolet on the Functions of the Ambassador, 1541', *The American Journal of International Law*, 27 (1933), pp. 81–95 (p. 84). Alberico Gentili, 'The perfect ambassador', in *Diplomatic Classics: Selected Texts from Commynes to Vattel*, ed. by Geoff R. Berridge (Basingstoke: Palgrave Macmillan, 2004), p. 71.

to government polemics, but also included works by continental contemporaries and reformers, such as Melanchthon's *Loci communes*.[67] Henry VIII's policy of providing diplomats with polemical literature and printed statements of policy, as well as works by influential authors who would need to be discussed, refuted or used in support of his policies, not only promoted rhetorical uniformity, but also helped his ambassadors meet diplomatic expectations of good practice at time when he could not afford to lose face.

By the mid-1530s Henry's government was aware that it needed to produce works for continental consumption and take control of the dissemination of English polemic and statements on the Church. Henry's policies were so controversial that the need to commission works such as Gardiner's *De vera obedientia* was keenly felt and Cromwell encouraged the production of tracts for use in the international context.[68] Meanwhile, foreign diplomats at Henry's court were procuring English tracts, including many works not specifically issued in Henry's name that were considered to be the king's books.[69] English printed tracts even appeared as a matter for discussion before Charles V's council in Toledo in March 1534.[70] It soon became apparent that the Privy Council would have to take control over the distribution of Henry's printed polemic if they were to preserve the integrity of the tracts and the king. In January 1534 a French translation of the *Articles* was undertaken by a member of Charles V's court and was negatively received, while in 1537 a polemicist observed that 'all our books do be sent into other countreys and translated, somtyme, ful evyl translated'.[71] Incidents such as this demonstrated the need for Henry's government to take responsibility for the translation and distribution of their tracts outside England, to ensure that the meaning was not twisted by unfriendly translators. This undoubtedly explains why Foxe was intending to make a Latin translation of the *Bishops' Book* in 1537 and why a Latin version of the *King's Book* was prepared for the Emperor and his court in 1543.[72]

There was probably a further consideration. In 1521 Henry had written his *Assertio septem sacramentorum* against Luther and in defence of papal

---

[67] Melanchthon's 'boke de locis communibus' was specifically mentioned as a book to be taken on Foxe's embassy to Germany in 1535 [British Library, Cotton MSS, Titus B I, fol. 458 [*LP*, IX, 213.5]]. At the Diet of Schmalkalden, Foxe openly brandished texts by Melanchthon and Bucer [Janelle, *Obedience in Church and State*, p. xxvi]. Gardiner at the French court was to 'remember the declaration of the French king of tharticles sent by Melanchton/luthers epistle in the same with thother circumstances conteyned in the copies lately sent unto you' [British Library, Additional MSS, 25114, fol. 110 [*LP*, IX, 848]].

[68] See for example *LP*, VIII, 1054.

[69] *Cal. Spain 1531–3*, nos. 753, 1165 [*LP*, V, 308; VI, 1571]; *LP*, VII, 14; *LP*, IX, 965; *LP*, XIII, i, 781; *LP*, XIV, i, 72.

[70] *LP*, VII, 353.

[71] NA: PRO, SP 1/82, fols 117–18 [*LP*, VII, 115]; SP 6/6, fol. 27ᵛ.

[72] *LP*, XII, ii, 410; XIX, i, 168.

supremacy.[73] Beautifully decorated copies of the work were sent to the Pope to be distributed in the first instance among the cardinals. Once the Pope and his cardinals had authorised Henry's treatise, he had overseen its dissemination to other Christian rulers.[74] The world of polemical literature, then, was one more area where Henry had ceded the Pope jurisdiction that he now needed to reclaim. It seems likely that Henry envisaged his ambassadors facilitating the publication of some of these tracts on the continent. Nicholas Hawkins was on embassy in Italy, the country intended as the main audience for the Latin translation of the *Glasse*, when he was completing the translation. Similarly, Edmund Bonner was on embassy when he contributed to the Hamburg edition of *De vera obedientia* and may have given a copy of the original imprint to the publisher, just as Martin Bucer probably received his copy from Edward Foxe. More tracts were expected to be translated for foreign audiences or published abroad or both.[75]

Exactly how much control Henry VIII and his agents could exert over the appearance and content of government propaganda published abroad is difficult to ascertain owing to the paucity of evidence. Although there is every reason to suspect that Henrician ambassadors were instrumental in getting Gardiner's *De vera obedientia* published, this involvement did not result in the straightforward reproduction of Gardiner's text. The edition produced by the Strasbourg reformers contained paratextual material that suggested particular readings of the text. Prefacing Gardiner's work was a letter from Bucer, Capito, Hedio, and the other evangelical ministers of the city, which praised Gardiner as the author of the work as well as the evangelical efforts of Thomas Cranmer and Edward Foxe. The ministers' address to the reader also outlined how scripture was the foundation of a true Church, the importance of scripture for faith, and the necessity of rejecting superstitions. Framing the preface were two extracts. The first, from St Augustine's letter to Boniface against the Donatists, emphasised the duty of kings to punish those who contravened God's law and, like Hezekiah, Darius and Nebuchadnezzar, to remove the idols and prevent blasphemy. The second extract, taken from Justinian's *Novellae* VI.1.7–8 set out the need for a bishop to lead an honest and moral life and to be educated in sacred law.[76] The Strasbourg edition also included a small number of marginal comments that were not present in the London edition. These served to draw attention to particular points in the work, such as the assertion that moral teachings had not been abandoned in England,

---

[73]   Rex, 'English campaign against Luther', pp. 85–106.

[74]   Nello Vian, 'Le Presentazione e gli esemplari vaticani della "Assertio Septem Sacramentorum" di Enrico VIII', *Studi e Testi*, 120 (1962), pp. 355–75.

[75]   *LP*, XII, ii, 410. See also NA: PRO, SP 1/143, fol. 15 [*LP*, XIV, i, 233]; British Library, Cotton MSS Vitellius B XIII, fol. 234: 'they think [their purpose] can be by no means so well as by setting forth in print of the book my lord is now in hand with, so as the same may afterward be translated into Dutch.'

[76]   Stephen Gardiner, *Stephani Winton. episcopi de vera obecientia oratio* (Strasbourg: Wendelin Rihel, 1536), Ai^v^-vi^v^.

that all England rejoiced at their rejection of the papacy and that kings were head of the Church according to divine law.[77] In sum, this paratextual material created the impression of a more evangelical text than Gardiner's original. In contrast, the only additional material in the Hamburg edition was a short antipapal poem and a prefatory letter by Edmund Bonner that praised the work and its author. Bonner's preface outlined that, contrary to common perceptions, Henry had not broken with the Pope in order to marry Anne Boleyn, but to defend God's law and scripture. Moreover, he had done so with the consent of his subjects.[78]

Similarly, there was variation in how Henry's two tracts against the General Council, the *Protestation* (1537) and *Epistle* (1538), were published in Germany. In at least one case, the German printer did not include any of his own details, but instead claimed that the tract was printed 'IN ÆDIBUS THOMÆ BERTHLETI'.[79] Some of the imprints would undoubtedly have met with the king's approval. Peter Seitz's Latin imprint of Henry's *Epistle*, for instance, faithfully reproduced the text of the Latin original and appealed to discerning readers with a Renaissance title page border, while the first page of the text was adorned with a historiated first initial with grotesques and putti.[80] In many other instances, the finished product looked just like dozens of other vernacular cheap news pamphlets in what was probably a deliberate marketing ploy on the part of the printers. Although the basic, cheap format did little to reflect the magnificence of the English king, it did make these works affordable and, if the number of editions is any indication, helped it become a modest bestseller in southern Germany.[81]

Just how effective the polemical campaign was in winning support for Henry's cause is difficult to ascertain. Some contemporaries clearly believed that the tracts were attracting new advocates of the Supremacy and Divorce. Nicholas Hawkins

---

[77]   Gardiner, *Stephani Winton*, B6ᵛ, C1ʳ, E5ᵛ.

[78]   Stephen Gardiner, *Stephani VVintoniensis episcopi De vera obedientia, oratio: Vna cum praefatione Edmundi Boneri archidiaconi Leycestrensis ... in qua etiam ostenditur caussam controuersiæ quæ inter ... Regiam Maiestatem & Episcopum Romanum existit, longe aliter ac diuersius se habere* (Hamburg: officina Francis Rhodes, 1536), πiiʳ–ivʳ.

[79]   STC 13082.

[80]   *Serenissimi et inclyti regis Angliæ Henrici octaui &c. epistola de synodo Vincentina* (Wittenberg, Peter Seitz, 1539).

[81]   *Epistel vnd Sendbrief Henrici des viij. Künigs von Engelland vnd Franckreich ... an Kaiser Carolum ... darinn der Künig gründtlich vrsach anzaigt, warumb er nit auff das Concilium zu Vincentz ... kommen werde* (Augsburg: [s. pub.], 1538); *Der durchleuchtigsten, grosmechtigsten Herrn, herrn Heinrichs der achten ... Schrifft an keiserliche Maiestat, an alle andere christliche Könige vnd Potentaten, jnn welcher der König vrsach anzeigt, warumb er gen Vicentz zum Concilio ... nicht komen sey. Aus dem Let. verdeudtscht durch J. Jonam* (Wittenberg: Joseph Klug, 1539). These two tracts represent the two different translations of the Latin original. Neither differed significantly from the source text. Morison is the most likely author of the original tracts: Sowerby, *Renaissance and Reform in Tudor England: The Careers of Sir Richard Morison c.1513–1556* (Oxford: Oxford University Press, 2010), pp. 67–9.

believed that the French translation of the *Glasse* had done its job, informing Henry that the French were now 'defensors of youer cause', and he had little doubt that the Germans would soon follow.[82] *De vera obedientia* clearly did find enthusiastic advocates in the Strasbourg reformers, who took it upon themselves to further the tract with a more evangelical slant. Henry's campaign against a General Council summoned by the papacy in 1537–38 was apparently met with much enthusiasm in the Holy Roman Empire, causing one observer to comment that Henry's tracts were slowly turning men against the papacy.[83] In 1539 Reginald Pole was informed that an English tract that criticised him was behind the cool reception he received from Charles V.[84] Later that year John Cochleaus was equally concerned with the seeming success that Henry VIII's polemical campaigns had met with in Cologne.[85] Johann Sleidan, when writing a history of the Reformation, deemed the General Council tracts sufficiently important to warrant mention.[86]

Many of these tracts were sufficiently widely distributed and deemed significant enough to warrant a response. A Latin reply to the *Glasse* was published at Antwerp in 1533.[87] Erasmus Sarcerius penned a Lutheran critique of Gardiner's *De vera obedientia*, accusing it of cloaking popery.[88] Books I and II of Reginald Pole's anti-Supremacy *De unitate* were primarily a condemnation of Sampson's *Oratio*, and the Catholic polemicist John Cochlaeus also thought that Sampson's work warranted a full refutation.[89] Other, later tracts were also answered by Henry's continental detractors. Antonio Massa and Albertus Pighius penned responses to the tracts Henry issued against the General Council in 1537 and 1538. Richard Morison's *Apomaxis* was rebutted by Cochaleus in 1538 and his tract on the Exeter Conspiracy was critiqued in Pole's *Apologia ad Carolum Quintum*.[90] Some of Henry's ambassadors even had to defend their tracts in person. In December

---

[82]   NA: PRO, SP 1/72, fol. 154 [*LP*, V, 1660].

[83]   *LP*, XII, ii, 1001.

[84]   Thomas F. Mayer, *Reginald Pole, Prince and Prophet* (Cambridge: Cambridge University Press, 2000), p. 98.

[85]   *LP*, XIV, i, 818.

[86]   Johann Sleidan, *A famouse cronicle of oure time, called Sleidanes Commentaries concerning the state of religion and common wealth, during the raigne of the Emperour Charles the fift* (London: John Day, 1560), STC 19848a, cliij, clxvii.

[87]   Rex, 'Glass of the Truthe', p. 25; *LP*, VI, 901.

[88]   Rex, 'Crisis of obedience', pp. 886–7.

[89]   Mayer, *Reginald Pole*, p. 38; *LP*, X, 34, 420; Johannes Cochlaeus, *De matrimonio serenissimi Regis Angliae, Henrici Octavi, Congratulatio disputatoria* (Leipzig: Michael Blum, 1535).

[90]   Hubert Jedin, *History of the Council of Trent*, 4 vols (London: Nelson, 1957), I, pp. 335–6. Johannes Cochlaeus, *Scopa ... in araneas Richardi Morysini Angli* (Leipzig: Nicolaus Wolrab, 1538). Mayer, *Reginald Pole*, p. 98; Thomas Mayer, *A Reluctant Author: Cardinal Pole and his Manuscripts* (Philadelphia, PA: American Philosophical Society, 1999), pp. 52–3.

1535 Gardiner debated the arguments of his book with Friar Pallavicino at the French court, and in 1541 was again forced to defend *De vera obedientia* while at Louvain.[91]

Richard Morison's *Apomaxis* was in part an answer to the criticisms that had been printed and voiced about earlier Henrician propaganda tracts. Morison defended the earlier polemic written in favour of the Royal Supremacy and its writers, mainly because Cochlaeus had accused these authors and Henry's leading councilors of corrupting him.[92] By defending these figures, the validity of the Royal Supremacy was also defended. Morison doubted if England had 'ever had anyone more learned' than Stephen Gardiner and Edward Foxe or anyone 'as equipped to defend the cause of truth or crush the audacity, the pride, the impiety of the most arrogant popes?' Cuthbert Tunstall meanwhile, hardly needed Morison's praise: even Thomas More had admitted he was 'one of the most learned, most prudent and honest men in the world today'.[93] He attacked Cochlaeus for unfairly slandering the learned Sampson.[94] Henry was also eulogised throughout the tract. Here Morison called on independent witnesses. Thus he reproduced an Erasmian passage extolling Henry's virtues, and asserted that equally favourable opinions could be found in the works of Vives and Melanchthon.[95] The *Apomaxis* therefore underscored the consistency of Henry's polemics to date, aided no doubt by the second edition of *De vera differentia* in the following year. Although the tracts justifying Henry's Royal Supremacy were independent works, they had much in common, utilising as they did the *Collectanea satis copiosa*. This lent them an essential coherence; even if they dealt with slightly different aspects of the Royal Supremacy or its consequences, they had a large body of evidence in common. Also underpinning all of the works were the central authority of scripture, the legal authority of parliament and the burden of historical evidence against papal jurisdiction in England. The *Glasse*, for instance, invoked the decisions of the Councils of Basle, Constance, Constantinople and Nicea.[96] In addition, the *Glasse* presented the determinations of the universities as a source of authority: its readers were encouraged 'to gyue credence to so many approued vniuersities whiche affirme our allegations to be true'.[97]

---

91   *LP*, IX, 1000; XVI, 1193.

92   Cochlaeus, *De matrimonio serenissimi Regis Angliae*.

93   Richard Morison, *Apomaxis calumniarum, convitiorumque, quibus Ioannes Cocleus homo theologus exiguus artiu[m] professor* (London: Thomas Berthelet, 1537), STC 18109, Xi^r–v.

94   Morison, *Apomaxis calumniarum*, Oi^r.

95   Morison, *Apomaxis calumniarum*, Ri^v–Riii^r. The encomium from Erasmus was taken from a letter to Henry dated 15 May 1519 which was printed in his *Epistolae … ad diversos* (Basel: Johannes Froben, 1521).

96   *Glasse*, D5^r, D6^r, C1^v, D5^r, D1^v–2^r, C8^r–D1^v, D2^v–3^r, D4^v.

97   *Glasse*, A2^v. See also ibid., C2^r, C7^r, D7^v–D8^r, F3^v.

The content of the early Supremacy polemics played an important role in outlining Henry's new jurisdictional claims and establishing the central tenet of 'true' obedience due to the king. At the same time that Rex has identified an acceleration in the obedience rhetoric of the Henrician government, the usage of the tracts was also being developed.[98] A coherent body of works was deliberately presented to and targeted at an international audience, and those men writing the tracts considered a range of potential issues that might have undermined the authority of the tracts and, by association, the strength of Henry's claims. The importance which Henry's government attached to this policy is perhaps most apparent when one considers that every major embassy Henry deployed in the last four months of 1535 was given copies of Gardiner's *De vera obedientia* and Sampson's *Oratio* and probably also received Matthew's sermon and *Se sedes illa romana*. It is clear that the international strategy for using these tracts helped to reinforce the message they contained. By deploying these tracts in diplomatic situations, Henry ensured that they were not just considered to be tracts in support of the king, but the 'king's books', endorsing and at the same time endorsed by Henry's augmented authority in England.

---

98   Rex, 'Crisis of obedience', pp. 878–9.

Chapter 10
Rebuking the Princes: Erasmus Alber in Magdeburg, 1548–52

Jane Finucane

Introduction

In November 1551, Magdeburg surrendered to Electoral Prince Maurice of Saxony. Maurice's armies had besieged the city for over a year, acting on behalf of Holy Roman Emperor Charles V, who had placed Magdeburg under the Imperial Ban. Against the Emperor's will, Maurice now lifted the siege, agreeing terms so moderate that Magdeburg's endurance of the ordeal was later celebrated as a victory.[1] In one connection, Maurice refused appeals for leniency. He insisted that the Lutheran pastor Dr Erasmus Alber, who had come to Magdeburg in 1548, must be exiled. He claimed that Alber had:

> attacked [Maurice] coarsely in public and in private writings, with rhymes and
> with drawings ... he must be got rid of: he had gone too far: even a peasant
> would not bear such an attack lightly.[2]

Erasmus Alber was a reformer and poet whose translation of Aesop's fables is a German literary classic. An early, prolific collaborator in the Lutheran reformation, he helped establish the new Church in Wetterau and Brandenburg, and claimed shortly before his death in 1553 that he had 'never strayed a finger's breadth from

---

[1]   On the nuances of the settlement and negotiations, see Nathan Rein, *The Chancery of God: Protestant Print, Polemic and Propaganda against the Empire, Magdeburg 1546–1551* (Aldershot: Ashgate, 2008), pp. 177–82; on the memorialisation of the siege see Rein, *Chancery of God*, p. 182; Hans Medick, 'Historisches Ereignis und zeitgenössische Erfahrung: Die Eroberung und Zerstörung Magdeburgs 1631', in *Zwischen Alltag und Katastrophe: Der Dreissigjährige Krieg aus der Nähe*, ed. by Hans Medick and Benigna von Krusenstjern (Göttigen: Vandenhoeck und Ruprecht, 1999), pp. 307–407.

[2]   'in offentlichen unnd heimlichen Schrifften/mit Reimen und Gemählden/gröblich angegriffen ... man solte ihn aber hinweg schaffen/hette es zu grob gemacht/daß es billich kein Bawer leiden solte', Heinrich Merckel, cited by Emil Körner, *Erasmus Alber: Das Kämpferleben eines Gottesgelehrten aus Luthers Schule* (Leipzig: Heinsius, 1910), p. 129.

the teaching of Dr. Martin [Luther], that is, from the truth of the Gospel'.[3] He insisted upon his pastoral duty to admonish ungodly princes, and had clashed with local powers before coming to Magdeburg.[4] On this occasion, however, he was not alone in subjecting German princes, even the Emperor himself, to severe and public rebuke.

As tensions mounted before the siege, and during sporadic assaults on the city in 1550 and 1551, Magdeburg's inhabitants used the printing press to defend their cause throughout Germany and beyond. The dispute concerned imperial authority to implement religious reform. Charles V triumphed against the Schmalkaldic League of Protestant princes and powers in 1547. His campaign split the Lutheran powers of Northern Germany: Joachim of Brandenburg, George of Mecklenburg and Maurice of Saxony supported him. Maurice was rewarded with the electoral position after Charles deposed Maurice's cousin Elector Johann Friedrich of Saxony, commander of the Schmalkaldic League.[5] Charles then decreed that the Lutheran territories of the Empire implement a religious settlement elaborated with collaboration from his supporters among the Lutheran princes. Billed as a compromise, this settlement was popularly known as the 'Interim' because Charles and his advisers hoped that it would facilitate reunion of the Lutheran Church with Rome.[6]

---

[3]   'von D. Martini lere/das ist/von der warheit des Euangelii/nicht eins fingers breit abgewichen', Erasmus Alber, *Vom Basilisken zu Magdeburg: Item vom Hanen eyhe/daraus ein Basilisck wirt/mit seiner Bedeutung aus der heiligen Schrifft* (Hamburg: Joachim Loew, [c. 1552]), Aii.

[4]   Alber was appointed Preacher in Neustadt, Brandenburg by Elector Joachim II, on Luther's recommendation, but lost the post in 1542 after criticising Brandenburg's tax policies on the basis that they cheated the Church. He then moved to Staden, but left in 1544 after conflict with the local ruler, Philipp IV of Hanau Lichtenberg. He is the subject of two biographies. The pioneering work, including reproductions of some of Alber's unpublished writings, is Franz Schnorr von Carolsfeld, *Erasmus Alberus: Ein biographischer Beitrag zur Geschichte der Reformationszeit* (Dresden: Ehlermann, 1893). A later full-length study is Emil Körner, *Erasmus Alber: Das Kämpferleben eines Gottesgelehrten aus Luthers Schule* (Leipzig: Heinsius, 1910). Alber's activities in Magdeburg are described in Waldemar Kawerau, 'Erasmus Alber in Magdeburg', *Geschichts-blätter für Stadt und Land Magdeburg*, 28 (1893), pp. 1–62. For a useful brief introduction to Alber's life, see also Erasmus Alber, *Die Fabeln: Die erweiterte Ausgabe von 1550 mit Kommentar sowie die Erstfassung von 1534*, ed. by Wolfgang Harms and Herfried Vögel, in association with Ludger Lieb (Tübingen: Niemeyer, 1997).

[5]   See Dieter Stievermann, 'Kurfürst Johann Friedrich von Sachsen, seine hegemoniale Stellung und der Schmalkaldische Krieg' in *Johann Friedrich I – der lutherische Kurfürst*, ed. by Volker Leppin, Georg Schmidt and Sabine Wefers (Heidelberg: Hubert & Co., 2005), pp. 101–28.

[6]   This was still an interim agreement, to be applied only while the Council of Trent was in session, so that the regulation was commonly referred to as the Augsburg Interim; it was later modified in for certain territories in consultation with Wittenberg scholars to

Sixteenth-century Magdeburg was a thriving Hanseatic city, strongly fortified, with close ties to Wittenberg. Its citizens adopted Luther's reforms in 1524, consolidating the town council's gains over the increasingly marginalised Prince-Bishop of the Magdeburg archdiocese.[7] Magdeburg came to prominence after 1547 because town council and pastors alike offered open opposition to the Interim rather than wait in the hope that the balance of powers in the Empire might be altered. The Interim itself prohibited publications critical of the settlement.[8] Nonetheless, Magdeburg reacted to the edict by printing works by dissident theologians – an act that implicated the town council and clergy in illegal activity[9] – and by issuing official publications from Church and town council expounding upon their duty and intention publicly to oppose the Interim.[10] Encouraged by these developments, prominent Lutheran intellectuals sought refuge in the city. Others sent manuscripts to be published from Magdeburg, dubbed by its clergy 'the Lord God's Chancery'

---

the Leipzig Interim. See *Das Interim 1548/50*, ed. by Luise Schorn-Schütte (Heidelberg: Hubert & Co., 2005).

[7]   On the Magdeburg Reformation see Robert W. Scribner, 'Ritual and Reformation', in *Popular Culture and Popular Movements in Reformation Germany* (London: Continuum, 1983), pp. 103–22, esp. pp. 103–06; Friedrich Hulße, 'Die Einführung der Reformation in der Stadt Magdeburg', *Geschichts-blätter für Stadt und Land Magdeburg*, 1883 (18), pp. 209–369.

[8]   *Sacrae Caesareae Maiestatis Declaratio, quomodo in negocio religionis per Imperium usque ad definitionem Concilij generalis vivendum sit, in Comitijs augustanis XV. Maij anno M. D. XLVIII. proposita, et publicata et ab omnibus Imperij ordinibus recepta, è Germanica lingua in Latinam ... versa ...* (Frankfurt an der Oder, Wolrab, [1548]), foreword.

[9]   On civic authorities' responsibility for censorship, see Ruth Kästner, *Geistlicher Rauffhandel: Illustrierte Flugblätter zum Reformationsjubiläum 1617* (Frankfurt am Main: Peter Lang Verlag, 1982), pp. 132–4; Ulrich Eisenhardt, *Der kaiserliche Aufsicht über Buchdruck, Buchhandel und Presse im Heiligen Römischen Reich Deutscher Nation (1496–1806.) Ein Beitrag zur Geschichte der Bücher und Pressezensur* (Karlsruhe: C.F. Müller, 1970).

[10]   *Der Von Magdeburgk Ausschreyben Anno M.D.XLVIII. Den Ersten Augusti* (Magdeburg: Walther, 1548); Nicholas von Amsdorf, *Antwort, Glaub und Bekenntnis auff das schöne und liebliche Interim* ([Magdeburg]: [Lotter], 1548). See Thomas Kaufmann, *Das Ende der Reformation: Magdeburgs 'Herrgotts Kanzlei' (1548–1551/2)* (Tübingen: Mohr Siebeck, 2003), pp. 86–91.

for the freedom with which its defenders could print there.[11] Briefly, between 1548 and 1552, Magdeburg became an important printing centre.[12]

Two recent publications consider this phenomenon. Thomas Kaufmann has produced a valuable statistical analysis and typology of the Magdeburg's anti-Interim publications, noting the extent to which pamphlets and broadsheets alike are characterised by crude and virulent polemic. Examining representative works, he deduced that Magdeburg's publicists considered themselves to be at a new stage of eschatalogical history. God's Word had been fully revealed through the Lutheran Reformation, and now faced the final attack of the Antichrist: the End of the Reformation. This conviction drove men accustomed to acknowledge the sacral character of God-given authority to produce and circulate irreverent, unsparing representations of secular powers.[13] Nathan Rein, examining Magdeburg's German-language pamphlets, noted the criticism of Empire and Princes alike, but emphasised the essential distinction between the office of Emperor, which must be respected, and the office-holder, who may overstep the *termini prescripti* of his office. Despite the violent imagery they employed, Magdeburg's polemicists won enough sympathy and tacit support in the German lands to forestall a mustering of powerful alliances against the city.[14] Both Kaufmann and Rein see the representation of figures of authority in printed material as a vital tool in the hands of the Magdeburg publicists, providing valuable insights for historians investigating their perception of the crisis.

There are tensions in the functions which these analyses imply for such references to authority. Magdeburg's polemicists believed and sought to impress upon the public that the true Church was in mortal peril because of the depredations of particular secular powers. They had to be wary, however, in communicating this urgent truth, of jeopardising the respect due to such authorities. Caution was necessary both to safeguard the stability of Magdeburg's own community, and to impress upon outsiders that the city's stand against Emperor and Princes was

---

[11]   The first use of the epithet is perhaps in the Magdeburg Confession, *Bekandtnuss/ Unterricht und Vermahnung der Pfarrherrn und Prediger der Christlichen Kirchen zu Magdeburg/Anno M. D. L. den 13 Aprilis* (Magdeburg: Christian Rödinger, 1550). This chapter uses the German edition as reproduced in Friedrich Hortleder, *Der Römischen Keyser Und Koniglichen Maiestetē, Auch des heiligen Römischen Reichs Geistlicher und Weltlicher Stände ... Handlungen und Außschreiben ... Von Rechtmässigkeit/Anfang/Fort und endlichen Aussgang dess Teutschen Kriegs Keyser Carls dess Fuenfften*, 2nd edn, 2 vols (Gotha: Wolfgang Endters, 1645), II, pp. 1053–92, here p. 1085.

[12]   The number of editions printed per annum had rarely exceeded forty during the sixteenth century, but for 1550, it rose to 117. See Kaufmann, *Ende der Reformation*, Appendix III.

[13]   'Der existentielle Überlebenskampf im Angesicht des Endes der Reformation förderte, so scheint es, eine schonungslose, jeden sakralen Scheins beraubte Wahrnehmung der Mächte diese Äons': Kaufmann, *Ende der Reformation*, p. 489.

[14]   Nathan Rein, *The Chancery of God*, pp. 188, 190.

not an act of rebellion.[15] The fact of printing, celebrated from the early years of the Lutheran Reformation as a means of perpetuating the revelation of God's Word, complicated matters still further: references to an imminent apocalypse in the works of the polemicists lose some of their force when presented alongside the consolation that printed words, at least, will survive the present crisis to bear witness to the truth.[16]

This chapter will consider these problems, focusing in particular on Alber's portrayal of Princes and Emperor. It will identify elements in Alber's work that may have prompted Maurice's response, and consider their wider implications for the nature of the Magdeburg campaign. It will discuss some of Alber's late, rarer works, questioning received wisdom in a reformer who is frequently mentioned in scholarly works but has not been the subject of critical attention since the early twentieth century. I shall argue that Alber's collaboration in the Magdeburg campaign was not straightforward: he was to an extent isolated, in part because of the nature of his writings. Although he was by no means alone in criticising and deriding secular powers, some aspects of his works are qualitatively different from the majority produced in Magdeburg. Kaufmann's insistence that we consider the eschatalogical understanding of the Magdeburg publicists has special applicability in Alber's case. It is difficult to generalise about the stream of publications that emerged from Magdeburg in this crisis: compilations, translations, adaptations, sometimes anonymous, undated, unattributed, and sometimes stamped with the authority of city, its clergy and its chosen representatives. To characterise the relationship of individual works to the project and its coordinators is a difficult task. Alber's distinctiveness, however, highlights the existence, in the work of his contemporaries at Magdeburg, of approaches particularly adapted to the new age of print and of nuances that permit a certain reconciliation of apocalyptic expectation with diplomatic caution, incitement to arms with preservation of order. It permits us to investigate how a distinction between office-holder and office could in fact be communicated. His work thus contributes to our understanding of the nature of propaganda in the first phase of Europe's confessional conflicts and the circumstances in which early forms of Protestant resistance theory were elaborated.

Alber's expulsion after the siege cemented his reputation for intransigence, ensuring that his contribution to the Magdeburg campaign would not be forgotten. His biographers and later historians have worked on the basis that he produced a substantial contribution to the anti-Interim propaganda printed from Magdeburg and that his works may be considered representative of the broader project.

---

[15]   See Robert von Friedeberg, 'Magdeburger Argumentationen zum Recht auf Widerstand gegen die Durchsetzung des Interims (1550–1551) und ihre Stellung in der Geschichte des Widerstandsrechts im Reich, 1523–1626', in *Das Interim*, ed. by Schorn-Schütte; Robert von Friedeburg, *Self-defence and Religious Strife in Early Modern Europe: England and Germany, 1530–1680* (Aldershot: Ashgate, 2002), p. 87.

[16]   See, for example, *Bekandtnuss/Unterricht und Vermahnung*, p. 1084.

He is considered one of Magdeburg's most important contributors to print production against the Interim, and in one sense, statistics on print production from Magdeburg bear this out: he fares well in a simple ranking of numbers of editions produced per author.[17] Alber was received as an asset to the town in 1548, licensed by the town council to preach and lecture in scripture, and considered for the office of superintendent (supervisor of the city's clergy).[18] Nonetheless, Kaufmann has identified a 1549 letter from Hanns Ordtenberg to Matthias Flacius Illyricus demonstrating that Alber was perceived in some quarters as a liability. He refused to preach on request, and some thought him a man possessed. He must be integrated, Ordtenberg explained, because he might otherwise cause 'great division and trouble'.[19]

Alber was integrated to an extent: despite his tendency to denounce his enemies in print, none of his Magdeburg works or later published writings denounce the other Magdeburg publicists. With Matthias Flacius Illyricus, a rising star among the Lutheran theologians of his generation, coordinating print and propaganda in the city from 1549, Alber solicited manuscripts for publication from the city, and helped with German translations.[20] Nonetheless, there has been a tendency to overstate his original contribution to the print campaign. Much of what he wrote against the Interim remained in manuscript form;[21] his more

---

[17]   See Kaufmann, *Ende der Reformation*, Appendix III; Rein, *Chancery of God*, pp. 18–19.

[18]   Letter Alber to the Pastors of Halle [Nov?] 1548, cited in Körner, *Erasmus Alber*, p. 119.

[19]   Letter from Hanns Ordtenberg to Flacius Illyricus, 5/10/49 (Cod. Helmstad. 883, Bl. 248–57), cited in Kaufmann, *Ende der Reformation*, p. 64.

[20]   Körner, *Erasmus Alber*, p. 119. On Flacius Illyricus, see Oliver K. Olson, *Matthias Flacius and the Survival of Luther's Reform* (Wiesbaden: Harrassowitz, 2002). Heinrich Merckel reports that Flacius 'die Druckerey ... zu seinen Händen gehabt'. Heinrich Merckel, *Warhafftiger/aussführlicher und gründlicher Bericht/von der Alten Statt Magdeburg Belagerung/so die Roem Keyser ...* (Magdeburg, 1587), reproduced in Friedrich Hortleder, *Handlungen und Ausschreiben von den Ursachen des teutschen Krieges* (Frankfurt-am-Main, 1617–18), pp. 945–97, p. 970.

[21]   As well as 'A History of my Travels' (1549), written to defend himself against detractors, and now lost ('Historia peregrinationis meae', on which see Körner, *Erasmus Alber*, p. 116), he wrote and circulated a polemical letter to Johann Bugenhagen, town parson of Wittenberg, containing a refusal to recognise Maurice's authority over Electoral Saxony (Alber, 'Contra colacem, hoc est Parasithem et gnathonem maximum Ioannem Bugenhagium pomeranum D. 1.5.49', reproduced in Schnorr von Carolsfeld, *Erasmus Alberus*, pp. 210–13). There was also an 'Exhortation to the Christian Church of Saxony', warning against the Interim ('Vermanung an die Christliche Kirche in Sachsenland', on which see Schnorr von Carolsfeld, *Erasmus Alberus*, pp. 123–4, pp. 213–14), and a discussion of the concept of Adiaphora, widely used to justify Lutheran acquiescence in the agreement, in his considerations on 'Whether one should yield to the Papists even in indifferent matters' ('Ob man den Papisten, auch in mitteldingen weichen solle', on which

substantial publications from Magdeburg made little or no reference to the Interim dispute or the troubles in the Empire,[22] and his anti-Interim publications consist of broadsheets and slender collections each of two or three songs and hymns.[23] Only one of Alber's Magdeburg works, a new edition of a 1546 sermon on marriage, was published under the printer's name, advertising its association with the city.[24] None of his works gave Magdeburg as place of origin. Printers were obliged by law to advertise place of printing, but tended to neglect this stipulation when producing inflammatory publications. Alber's works are anomalous here: Magdeburg's printers became bolder in identifying the city as place of printing as the crisis developed, and emblazoned polemical publications with the city's name and shield as Magdeburg became widely associated with resistance to the Interim.[25] Alber's reputation as a significant author of anti-Interim polemics printed from Magdeburg persists in part because two substantial works often cited in this connection have been wrongly dated to his Magdeburg period. Both pamphlets are important to the reconstruction of Alber's role in the anti-Interim campaign.

Alber's *Of the Magdeburg Basilisk* (*Basilisk*) describes mysterious deaths in a Magdeburg cellar during the siege. The eponymous Basilisk proves to be illusive, but Alber extends the reference to this fabulous creature into a discussion of the problems of faith and repentance, grace and its rejection. *Basilisk* is undated, but Alber's references to events of July 1549 and use of Magdeburg's shield as

---

see Schnorr von Carolsfeld: *Erasmus Alberus*, pp. 123–4). Two of Alber's songs for the period have survived in manuscript only: 'Ein lied und vermanung an die Lantzknechte, das sie der armen Christenheyt und jhrem lieben vaterlande beystehen und die vorrether und vorherer desselben straffen woltenn, jn des Bentenawers Thon zu singenn' and 'Ein new lied von der belegerung der werden Stadt Megdeburg': see Schnorr von Carolsfeld, *Erasmus Alberus*, 101. The songs are reprinted in *Die historischen Volkslieder der Deutschen vom 13. bis 16. Jahrhundert*, ed. by Rochus von Lilienchron, 5 vols (Leipzig: Vogel, 1865–69), IV, nos 571 and 589.

[22]   Alber's printed pamphlets for this period were a brief and mild discussion of the Trinity: Erasmus Alber, *Der Holdseligen Blummen der Treifeltigkeyt bedeutung/Nutzlich zulesen/Gott dem Herrn zu ehren* ([Magdeburg], 1550]); and a reprint of a sermon on marriage: Erasmus Alber, *Ein Predigt vom Ehestand/uber das Euangelium/Es war ein Hochzeit zu Cana etc.* ([Magdeburg]: Roedinger, 1550), originally Erasmus Alber, *Ein Predigt vom Ehestand/vber das Euangelium/Es war ein Hochzeit zu Cana* (Wittenberg: Seitz, 1546). Through correspondence, Alber directed the printing of the expanded 1550 edition of his fables from Frankfurt am Main: *Das buch von der Tugent vnd Weißheit/ nemlich/Neunvnd = viertzig Fabeln/der mehrer theil auß Esopo gezogen/vnnd mit guten Rheimen verkleret/Durch Erasmum Alberum/Allen stenden n[ue]tzlich zulesen* (Frankfurt am Main: Peter Braubach, 1550).

[23]   Works which Alber had printed from Magdeburg consist of perhaps eight songs and hymns (for which see Kaufmann, *Ende der Reformation*, Appendix I and pp. 371–97).

[24]   Alber, *Ein Predigt vom Ehestand*.

[25]   See Kaufmann, *Ende der Reformation*, pp. 47–57.

frontispiece have resulted in its being listed as a 1549 Magdeburg publication.[26] Internal evidence, however, dates the pamphlet to 1552 or 1553; it was printed from Hamburg, after Alber arrived there as an exile.[27] In Hamburg, Alber used Magdeburg's crest and references to the siege to advertise his assocation with the town's struggle against the Interim as he had scarcely done from Magdeburg itself.[28] Retrospective references in *Basilisk* to the Interim and to Alber's activities in Magdeburg include a puzzling discussion of a second pamphlet, which, Alber claimed in 1552, was never printed: the *Dialogue of several people concerning the Interim (Dialogue)*: 'As soon as the Interim, with which the Devil hoped to topple the Augsburg Confession, was promulgated … in 1548, I wrote against this same horror a dialogue which was rejected by many, because nobody wished to print it, for they said it was too fierce, although one cannot attack the Devil fiercely enough.'[29]

This *Dialogue*, despite Alber's ignorance of any edition printed by 1552, exists as a pamphlet dated 1548, and is frequently treated as a Magdeburg publication.[30] *Dialogue* offers the reactions of four interlocutors (their leader a thinly disguised 'Albertus') to Charles's campaign and the Interim. As implied in *Basilisk*, Alber was unrestrained in his polemic: the pamphlet works its way through excoriation of pope, preachers and princes to a crescendo of extraordinarily vitriolic abuse of the Emperor himself. *Dialogue* articulates the widespread suspicion that Charles hopes to subsume Germany into a world-empire, and applies to him a number of highly offensive epithets. Alber undermines Charles's guarantee of imperial stability by predicting unspecified imminent misfortune, the end of the line of emperors, and, it is strongly implied, the world: Charles is a Ravager, a Herod and a Pilate, a Monster among men and a Portent of the Devil, a Murderer and Bloodhound who knows nothing about Germany, an idol to the Spanish who is Charles the fifth and last.[31]

---

[26]   Erasmus Alber, *Vom Basilisken zu Magdeburg: Item vom Hanen eyhe/daraus ein Basilisck wirt/mit seiner Bedeutung aus der heiligen Schrifft* (Hamburg: Joachim Loew, [c. 1552]). The work is dated to 1549 in Harms and Vögel, *Die Fabeln*, p. 9.

[27]   *Basilisk* places the imprisonment of former Elector Johann Friedrich in the past, which would bring the earliest possible date of completion to May 1552: Alber, *Basilisk*, Aii. Alber was in Hamburg in 1552, and died in Neubrandenburg in 1553.

[28]   Alber produced a broadsheet illustrated with Magdeburg's shield with a poem by Johann Ritzenberg: this is listed as Erasmus Alberus: [*Auslegung des Wappens der Stadt Magdeburg.*] ([Hamburg], Loew, [c. 1552]), in Werner Kayser and Claus Dehn, *Bibliographie der Hamburger Drucke des 16. Jahrhunderts* (Hamburg, Hauswedell, 1968).

[29]   Alber, *Basilisk*, Aii.

[30]   [Erasmus Alber,] *Ein Dialogus oder Gespra[e]ch etlicher personen vom Interim* ([Augsburg: Hans Gegler], 1548 [for 1557]).

[31]   [Alber,] *Dialogue*, F, E(v), Eiii(v), Qii(v), Jii. On Charles's 'world empire' see Rein, *Chancery of God*, pp. 47–89.

Alber's *Dialogue* is frequently cited to illustrate the vehemence of the Magdeburgers' attack on authority and the irreverence with which they described secular powers, even the Emperor himself.[32] This makes it all the more significant that the work was not in fact printed from Magdeburg, and appeared only after the Interim dispute was settled. The printed edition was produced in Augsburg in 1557, falsely dated 1548 as was consistent with its content. Backstreet printer Hans Gegler confessed before the Augsburg town council to printing this and other religious and anti-imperial tracts on behalf of the mystic Kaspar Schwenckfeld.[33] Alber wrote a letter from Magdeburg that indicates how Schwenkfeld may have obtained his copy of the manuscript of *Dialogue* and discusses the conditions in which work was printed from Magdeburg. He addresses Hartmann Beyer of Frankfurt, who had sent a manuscript for publication:

> Dearest brother in Christ, I have received your letter with your little book. I would have liked to see many copies of the book printed, but our printers print nothing unless they are quite certain to profit by it – which is the case for books in German and especially for those written by [Matthias Flacius] Illyricus. Now, if *he* had persuaded the printer to produce an edition of your work, the printing would not be in any doubt. I see no reason why he does not recommend it. I find it entirely satisfactory: and it certainly bears witness to your mastery of theology. Illyricus did not accept that as many as 300 copies should have been printed. I was first to write against Interim and Adiaphora, but through certain malevolent people, swine from the herd of Epicurus, it was forbidden that these writings see the light. But the *Dialogue on the Interim*, copied [by hand] more than 300 times in many passages, was sent out to Prussia, Livonia, and all parts of Germany, with my name and surname written in Greek at the end: Δαβιδ ἀκέραιος. I ask you to endeavour to print your work again, secretly. But I hope this Teutonic fear will not last much longer … if [the Germans] had a wise and brave captain *we would beat the godless Spanish to death with old rags.*[34]

---

[32] See Kaufmann, *Ende der Reformation*, pp. 211–30.

[33] On Gegler's printing of the Dialogue, see Karl Schottenloher, 'Der Augsburger Winkeldrucker Hans Gegler: Ein Beitrag zur Schwenckfeld-Bibliographie', *Gutenberg Jahrbuch*, 14 (1939), pp. 233–42.

[34] 'Tuam epistolam vna cum libello tuo accepi: frater in Chisto cariss. cuius optarim multa excusa fuisse exemplaria. Nam nostri chalcographi nullum imprimunt librum, nisi vnde certissimum sibi qu[a]estum pollicentur, pollicentur autem ex Germanicis, maxima Illyrici libris. Attamen si ille Chalcographo editionem tui libelli suauisset [!], impressus haud dubie fuisset. Cur autem non suadeat, nescio. Mihi profecto apprimé placet: et ex eo satis apparet profectus in Theologia tuus. Illyricus nolebat credere, 300 tantum exemplaria excusa fuisse. Ego primus scripsi contra Interim et Adiaphora: sed à quibusdam maleuolis, Epicuri de grege porcis ea scripta lucem videre vetita sunt. Sed dialogus contra Interim plus trecenties transcriptus multis in locis ad Prussiam, Liuoniam, omnesque Germanie partes missus est: in cuius fine nomen et cognomen meum Grecè scriptum est Δαβιδ ἀκέραιος. Sed spero hunc Teutonum timorem breui finem habiturum … si cordatum et fortem Capitaneum

Alber's letter to Beyer confirms Flacius' influence over the selection of material and implies, with the introduction of the profit motive, that Flacius also advised on distribution. Alber is too cryptic to explain the *Dialogue's* suppression: perhaps this was due to the printers' avarice, perhaps a matter of strategy, perhaps, as his dark hints about German cowardice suggest, because it was judged too dangerous to print. Whatever the cause, his letter conveys resentment at the suppression, a certain distance from Illyricus, and limited influence in the printing campaign. It suggests that the relative paucity of works printed from Magdeburg under Alber's name can be attributed to some disagreement on the message to be communicated from the beleaguered city.

How do Alber's surviving works differ from those produced by Magdeburg's other publicists? There are notable divergences in his treatment of secular powers. First, where his fellow polemicists tend not to name the figures of authority criticised, Alber identifies his targets. An anecdote in the Dialogue is one example. The anti-Interimists at Magdeburg developed a stock of tales denigrating supporters of the Interim. One described the death of Bonifacius, manservant of the Brandenburg court preacher Johann Agricola. Brandenburg's Electoral Prince Joachim allied himself with Charles V, and Agricola preached a thanksgiving sermon in Berlin after the defeat of the Schmalkaldic League and the capture of Johann Friedrich of Saxony. The sermon became notorious in evangelical circles.[35] According to the account in the *Antichrist's Bull*, printed in Magdeburg in 1550 under the name of Flacius Illyricus, the sermon was followed by:

> the death of Bonifacius, Eisleben's [Agricola's] manservant, brother-in-law of Eisleben's wife. After he had most vigorously defended our opponent, he changed utterly in the end, in his death throes, and threatened not only the opponents and the persecutors of the Gospel, but also the evil Protestants, who have helped the opponents [and] the persecutors, with terrible punishment, And threatened this not only in general, but with especial regard to particular states and princes, and most of all with regard to the traitor Eisleben.[36]

---

haberent, wir wolten die heylosen Spanier mit alten lumpen zu tod schlagen'. Letter, Alber to Hartmann Beyer, 24 August 1550, reproduced in Schnorr von Carolsfeld, *Erasmus Alberus*, as note 1, Appendix X.2, pp. 204–6. The text on Adiaphora may have been his 'Ob man den Papisten auch in mitteldingen weichen sol'.

[35]   On Lutheranism in Brandenburg see Robert Stupperich, 'Die Eigenart der Reformation in der Mark Brandenburg', in *'Dem Wort nicht entgegen...': Aspekte der Reformation in der Mark Brandenburg*, ed. by Hans-Ulrich Delius, Max-Ottokar Kunzendorf and Friedrich Winter (Berlin: Evangelische Verlagsanstalt, 1988), pp. 13–30. On Agricola's sermon, see Gustav Kawerau, *Johann Agricola von Eisleben* (Berlin: Hertz, 1881), p. 247.

[36]   'Ich halt du wissesst umb den tod Bonifacij Eislebens famulus/des Eislebens weibs schwesterman. Nach dem derselb zuvor auffs hefftigst unsere widdersacher vereindingt hatte/ist er letzlich im todkampff gantz verwandelt/und hat grewliche straff gedrawet/ nicht allein den widdersachern/den verfolgern des Evangelij. Sonder auch den bo[e]sen

The identity of these 'particular states and princes' is clear once Agricola has been named: his patron Joachim II and Joachim's allies, Maurice of Saxony among them, are obviously targets. This sort of oblique reference to figures in authority is common in the writings of the Interim's opponents, and seems unlikely to have obscured their message. Yet Alber in his *Dialogue*, recounting the same tale, leaves less to the imagination:

> Johann of Eisleben [Agricola], an Epicurean swine, had blustered and raged against the Electoral Prince Duke Johann Friedrich of Saxony, and slandered him as a Rebel, although the Prince had done him very much good: Eisleben had a Manservant, who too sang to his tune, but did not do so for long, for he became ill, and cried out continuously in his illness, Woe to you Emperor, Woe to you Eisleben, Woe to you Margrave [Joachim II of Brandenburg, as established in the reference immediately following], Woe to Duke Maurice [of Saxony], Woe to all betrayers and enemies of the Electoral Prince, and with this cry, he died. When Margrave Joachim was apprised of this, he asked Eisleben about it.[37]

As with his excoriation of Charles V in the same pamphlet, Alber names names here. He does so in both cases not simply to insult, but also to predict the abasement of these powers, now or in the next world. Magdeburg's publicists had necessarily to criticise the activities of particular authorities, but this was not a task that absolutely required explicit identification of these 'enemies of the gospel' or confident prediction of their final condemnation. An alternative to Alber's blunt delivery of this message can be found in the best-known work printed from Magdeburg during the Interim crisis, which has passed into history as its official statement on resistance, the *Confession, Instruction and Exhortation of the Pastors and Preachers of the Christian Church in Magdeburg*, the so-called *Magdeburg Confession*.

The *Magdeburg Confession* was signed in April 1550 by the town's permanent clergy and thus has the character of an official publication, produced not under

---

Evangelischen/die den widdersachen den verfolgern geholffen haben/und hat solchs nicht allein in gemein/sonder etlichen lendern und fuersten in sonderheit/und zuuoraus dem verfürer Eisleben gedrawet.' Matthias Flacius Illyricus, *Bulla des Antichrists, dadurch er das volck Gottes widderumb in den eisern ofen der Egypitishcen gefengknis denckt zuziehen/gleichstimmig mit des Meintzischen Rabsakes briefe* (Magdeburg: [Christian Rödinger], 1550), bii.

[37] 'Johanes Eyßleben/ein Epicurische saw/hat ein lange zeit daher/zu Berlin wider den Churfürsten/Herzog Johans Friderich zu Sachsen declamiert/uñ declamiert/un[d] debachiert/un[d] als einen Auffrhuriche[n] ubel gescholte[n]/der jm dooch sehr vil guts gethon hat: Es het aber Eysleben eine Famulum/deer auch seins herzen liede sang/trib es aber nich lang/dann er ward kranck/und schrey ym[m]er in seiner kranckheit/Wee dir Keyser/Wee dir Eyßleben/Wee dir Marggraff/Wir dir Hertzog Moritz/Wee allen verræthern vnnd feinden des Churfürsten: und mit solchem geschrey/starb er. Als solches für den Marggraff Joachim kame/fragt er den eyßleben drumb ...' [Alber,] *Dialogue*, Fii.

the supervision of Flacius but under Nicholas von Amsdorf, who had guided the Magdeburg reformation.[38] It was printed simultaneously in Latin and in German with the town council's support. Its first part was a confession of the Lutheran faith as practised in Magdeburg; the second an admonition indicating that armed resistance under the leadership of magistrates was a justified and necessary response to attempts to impose the Interim agreement by force. The *Confession* went beyond the traditional distinction between just ruler and tyrant to claim that any assault on Magdeburg culminating in forced imposition of the Interim would constitute the highest grade of injury that a ruler could inflict, 'something more than tyrannical'. This highest grade of injury was violent coercion of subjects who upheld and defended God's law, not conceived by the ruler in the fury of the moment but undertaken after deliberation. This, according to the *Confession*'s authors, was the threat they now faced from their authorities.[39] The *Confession* implies what Alber states directly elsewhere: that such tyrants or worse-than-tyrants face imminent judgment: 'Let the tyrants then become angrier still through this message and admonishment of ours, so that they overreach themselves sooner still, and draw God's wrath upon themselves more swift and terrible'.[40]

This passage is also a reflection on likely reactions of the authorities to the *Confession*, and is consistent with the document's explicit acknowledgement of different categories of reader: it addresses and seeks to engage with the very powers which, the reader may infer, should be identified with the devil, and with tyranny, and are at risk of attracting God's wrathful judgement. The authors of the *Confession* go so far as to address Emperor Charles V on his own terms: not as a tyrant but as a ruler faced with a fateful decision. They appeal to him directly at the beginning of their discussion of how magistrates should respond to a tyrant.

---

[38]   On Nicolaus von Amsdorf, see David Curtis Steinmetz, *Reformers in the Wings: From Geiler von Kaysersberg to Theodore Beza* (Oxford: Oxford University Press, 1976), pp. 70–76.

[39]   *Bekandtnuss/Unterricht und Vermahnung*, pp. 1076, 1085: 'Der Vierdte und hoechste Grad der Injurien/so die Obrigkeit ueben kann//ist etweas mehr dann Tyrannisch … wann die Tyrannen also toll und rasend werden/der Obrigkeit vnd den Vnterthanen in einer rechten Sachen/sondern auch in den Personen des hoechste und noetigeste Recht/ vnnd gleich vnsern Herrn Gott selbst/de ein Stiffter ist desselbigen Rechten/vnd solches nicht etwa aus Gebrechlichkeit/dass einen der Zorn moechte uber eylen/sondern mit wolbedachten Muht vnd Rath/des Vorhabens/bey allen Nachkommen das Reich zu vertilgen. Wan einer so tieff fellet/vnd wann ers gleich thut aus Vnwissenheit/vnd ist gleich der Oberste Regent/so ist er nicht allein ein Beerwolff … sondern ist der Teuffel selbst … Solches aber geschicht jetzundt von unsern Obern/dass sie mit Gewalt beyde in vns/vnnd in allen vnsern Nachkomment tilgen woellen/das rechte Erkantnuss Gottes/ohn welches Gott nicht kan geehret/auch kein Mensch selig werden.'

[40]   'Lasse auch diese Tyrannen durch diese unser Schrifft und Uermahnung noch wütender werden/damit sie Ihre Masse desto ehe uoll machen und Gottes Zorn dester schneller und grausmaer über sich führen'. *Bekandtnuss/Unterricht und Vermahnung*, p. 1085.

Acknowledging that Charles does not see Lutherans as true Christians, they argue from scripture that authorities have in the past misguidedly persecuted true believers, and that Charles should therefore tread warily.[41]

This strategy presents the crisis at Magdeburg as an instance of the devil's final attack on the Church on earth and but also as an episode susceptible of resolution if only the Emperor and the other authorities who might aptly be described as tyrannical should undergo a change of heart. The text contains frequent references to the end, but its logical emphasis is on individual judgement rather than the day of universal judgement. In situating the Interim dispute in eschatalogical history, the authors of the *Confession* in no way exclude restoration of the secular order without disruption to the Empire. They simply indicate that the Emperor and his allies are capable of taking council and choosing their path, and in order for the crisis to be resolved must – and may – repent their persecution of the Church. As a message to posterity, their work will stand regardless of the outcome of the current crisis. Alber, however, writes for the moment, excluding the possibility that the authorities in question can emerge from the crisis without dishonour. This tendency gives extra force to the references to judgement and the end of the world which abound in his works as in those of his fellow publicists: the works appear to be composed without taking into account a future for the Empire or the Church on earth.

Alber's projection of authorities' current sins into the indefinite future has strategic significance, as is apparent when he, like the authors of the *Magdeburg Confession*, considers the possibility of repentance. His verses, *Master Maurice's Confession, Repentance and Witness Statement* (1551), build on his earlier treatments of Maurice of Saxony as a Judas figure in his collection of *Three Beautiful Songs*.[42] In *Master Maurice's Confession*, he has the Electoral Prince 'confess':

> I, poor man, confess before Emperor, King and the Empire, man, woman, and young and old alike, that – as many are well aware – I have not behaved as befits a prince. I must admit openly that I have most certainly broken faith with my father. Therefore with Judas I am worthy to pay my debts in eternal pain. Who are you then, you ask me? I was Maurice, a duke … I became a traitor to him who had brought me up from my youth in a fatherly manner, and thanked him with a Judas-kiss … I repent for having forgotten the good faith shown to me by my pious cousin [Johann] Friedrich: how should I and may I do penance for this? God's Word accuses me. My body and soul must belong forever to the devil, this I know, this will most certainly be my 'amen', no Interim can help me. … Hellish Satan, console me! I have betrayed my lord, I repent it now from

---

41 *Bekandtnuss/Unterricht und Vermahnung*, p. 1073.

42 The comparison was made in the dedication of Erasmus Alber, *Drey Schöne lieder mit ihren noten* ([Magdeburg], [1549]).

my heart, but I cannot escape from it: no penance or repentance can help me: I must perish in sin.[43]

These verses, which nowhere promise the supposedly repentant Maurice forgiveness or salvation, remind the reader of Maurice's treachery through the familiar metaphor of Judas Iscariot, and reiterate the message of the Bonifacius anecdote: Protestants who persecute their co-religionists and distort their faith will suffer terrible consequences. Read in the context of Alber's career as a controversialist, the verses have more to say. Central to Luther's teaching was the question of salvation. Arguing that no man could be confident of fulfilling God's law in order to become righteous and assured of salvation on his own merits, he argued that the redemption promised in the Gospels must be based not on man's perfection according to the law but on God's free gift to the sinner. Satisfaction for sin was delivered not by the sinner's acts of penance, but through Christ's sacrifice. The sinner became open to this justification through fear of the law, expounded primarily in the Old Testament, which revealed God's wrath at human sinfulness. It prompted fear and repentance, so that the sinner turned to the Gospel and its promise of forgiveness and salvation. Faith in this promise laid the sinner open to God's grace, by which he was justified or made righteous, accepted for salvation in spite of his sins. This was the basis for Luther's assertion that faith alone justifies.

Alber, an eager defender of Luther's position, had already published on related controversies.[44] In *Dialogue*, he defended a distinction which the Interim denied: that it was proper to be pained by one's sins but that acts of penance were not

---

[43]   'ich armer man bekenne mich/vor kaiser, könig und dem rich/man, weib, auch jung und alten glich/wie meniglich wol weiss, dass ich/nit fuerstlich hab gehalten mich. An meinem vater sicherlich/hab treuw und glaub zerrissen ich/das muess ich sagen offentlich/ darumb mit Judas würdiglich/ewige pein beschuldet ich. Wer bistu dann? so fragstu mich/ Moritz, ein herzog der war ich …zü eim verräter worden ich/an dem, der doch erzogen mich/von jugend auf ganz vaeterlich/mit Judas kuss dem danket ich … Das gottes wort beklaget mich/mein seel und leib müs ewiglich/des teufels sein, das weiss ich/das würt mein amen sicherlich/kein Interim mag helfen mich. … Höllischer Sathan, tröste mich! Mein herren hab verrathen ich/das reuwet iezt von herzen mich/und kan es doch nit wenden ich/kein büss noch reuw mag helfen mich/in sünden müss verzagen ich.' *Meister herzog Moritzen beicht, reuw und bekäntnus* (Magdeburg, 1551), reproduced in Wilhelm Kühlmann, 'Magdeburg in der Zeitgeschichtlichen Verspublizistik (1551/1631)', in *Prolegomena zur Kultur- und Literaturgeschichte des Magdeburger Raumes*, ed. by Gunter Schandera and Michael Schilling in association with Dieter Schade (Magdeburg: Scriptum, 1999), pp. 79–106, here pp. 83–6. On Alber's authorship, see Kawerau, 'Erasmus Alber in Magdeburg', p. 28.

[44]   Erasmus Alber, *Das der Glaub an JESum CHRIstum alleyn gerecht und selig mach, widder Jörg Witzeln, Mamelucken vnd Ischarioten. Item von Iörg Witzels leben …* (s. l., 1539); Erasmus Alber, *Eilend aber doch wol getroffen Controfactor/da Jörg Witzel abgemalet ist/wie er dem Judas Jscharioth/so gar enhlich sicht* (s. l., 1543).

necessary – the idea of owing satisfaction for sins was a papist distortion which in fact led the sinner to reject God's freely given redeeming grace.[45] Soon after leaving Magdeburg, he published in his *Basilisk* an extended treatment of Judas's failure to win salvation despite feeling desperate regret for his treachery.[46] Tackling a perplexed question in Lutheran theology, the extent to which one could accept God's saving grace through an act of will, he engaged in some mild distortion of scripture to assert that Judas was complicit in his own downfall, having willingly avoided hearing the preaching of the Gospel.[47] *Basilisk* is probably an extended and expurgated version of Alber's treatment of the unrepentant Maurice, founded in references to Magdeburg and the Interim crisis, hinting darkly at princely targets, but – the crisis being past – nowhere divulging their names. Both works imply that certain behaviours represent an act of will in rejecting faith, so that the sinner in question could no longer recognise and accept this freely given gift, rendering his own salvation impossible. Alber uses a vocabulary on repentance and satisfaction common in Lutheran dogmatics to demonstrate that Maurice's support for the Interim has shown him to be an irredeemable sinner, incapable of repenting.[48] This is an extremely serious charge with implications for Maurice's personal authority: it may also have been calculated to affect the prospects of his diplomacy.

Maurice had spent 1551 preparing to change sides, detaching himself from Charles V's campaign and planning a new alliance of Protestant states against the Emperor. Without revealing this project, he persuaded Magdeburg's town council to surrender to him – and not to the Emperor – in return for a guarantee of religious freedom. This was not to say that Maurice renounced the Interim: the settlement still applied in his own territories. Magdeburg's clergy, who were probably excluded from the council's negotiations with Maurice, were uneasy about the settlement, but guarded in expressing their reservations.[49] *Master Maurice's Confession* should be read in this context. Maintaining his focus on

---

[45]   'Das die Buß ein Sacrament sey/hab ich nye gelseen/Das wort Poenitentia, heysset eygendlich nicht Büß/sonder Rew: Mulcta, heyst Büs: Christus hat für uns gebüßt/dz ist bezalt/uñ die straffe getragen/Esaie 53[,4] …'. [Alber,] *Dialogus*, Biii.

[46]   Alber, *Basilisken zu Magdeburg*, Bii[(v)]–Bi[v].

[47]   Alber, *Basilisken zu Magdeburg*, Biii[(v)].

[48]   Within Lutheranism, the antinomian controversies of the 1520s and late 1530s concerned problems related to sin and satisfaction. On the earlier antinomian debate see Timothy J. Wengert, *Law and Gospel: Philip Melanchthon's Dispute with John Agricola of Eisleben over Poenitentia* (Carlisle: Baker Academic, 1997). On the later dispute see Kawerau, *Johann Agricola von Eisleben* and Mark U. Edwards Jr, *Luther and the False Brethern* (Palo Alto, CA: Stanford University Press, 1975). For Luther's main discussion of this question, see his first disputation against the Antinomians, (December 1537) in *Disputationen Dr. Martin Luthers in d. J. 1535–1545 an der Universität Wittenberg gehalten*, ed. by Paul Drews (Göttingen: Vandenhoeck und Ruprecht, 1895), pp. 246–334.

[49]   Rein, *Chancery of God*, pp. 174–5.

the guilt of named individuals, persisting in his assertion that the supporters of the Interim have taken a position on which they will be judged for all time, Alber presents Maurice as incapable of true repentence or of turning his alleged regret to useful ends. The verses served to warn his readers against facile acceptance of Maurice's assurances.

Conclusion

Historians and contemporaries have noted Alber's passionate temper, but he was capable of restraint. Despite earlier clashes with authority, he adopted the tactic of openly deriding princes only in his Magdeburg years. In 1552, with the crisis past, he remained fervent in support of the deposed Johann Friedrich, but was coy about the usurper Maurice. He still argued that his 'attack on the devil' during the Interim crisis had not been unnecessarily sharp. His works of 1548–51 should not be seen as uncontrolled outpourings of rage and righteousness. Their effect was calculated, and they were distinctive in their treatment of an essential question: how could victory be imagined? Like his fellow publicists, Alber believed that he was witnessing Satan's attack on the Church, but could envisage the restoration of the Church on earth on this occasion, even if the secular order must eventually pass away: his letter to Beyer shows optimism on this point. He appears, however, to have imagined and written to facilitate a military victory. Disgraced secular powers could be expelled through the righteous wrath of the German people acting lawfully against tyranny. His works are a call to arms: exposing grotesque, doomed and wretched tyrants, provoking fear and derision, and, as Maurice bitterly noted, affording the authorities no more respect than one would show a peasant.

For the coordinators of Magdeburg's propaganda, the preferred emphasis was on choice: this was the moment at which their readers, the German people but also the authorities themselves, must decide where they stood in the light of Satan's assault on the true Church. Their decision might lead them to take arms, but might equally bring peace. Attentive to both possibilities, they produced communications, in particular the Magdeburg Confession with its elements of cautious diplomacy, which addressed readers of different estates and could function not only as polemic but also as messages to posterity. The Confession did in fact fulfil this latter function: it became the Magdeburg publicists' signal text, as well as an inspiration, a model and even a cloak for later arguments for resisting 'tyrants' on religious grounds: a resistance statement for the age of print.[50] This

---

[50] See especially Johann Sleidan, *De Statu religionis et reipublicae, Carolo quinto caesare, commentarii* ([Strasbourg: Rihel], 1555), Book 22; John Knox, *The historie of the reformatioun of religioun within the realm of Scotland, … Together with the life of Iohn Knoxe the Author, and several Curious Pieces wrote by him* (Edinburgh, 1732), p. 363. Theodore Beza advertised his work on resistance as a revision of the Magdeburg Confession: *Du Droit des Magistrats sur leurs subiets. Traitté tres necessaire en ce temps pour advertir*

was possible because Magdeburg, during and after the crisis, avoided the taint of outright rebellion and maintained the image of a city staunch and unified against the ungodly. Alber himself later lauded the city as defender of the faith;[51] the association of Magdeburg with the glorious defence of the Lutheran faith would work against any revisiting of tensions in the campaign.

Such tensions did exist, however. For the anti-Interim campaign, they presented risks, but also certain advantages. Fear of internal dissent arising from attempts to suppress material was counterbalanced by fear of losing support by failing to suppress it. The logistics of the printing campaign helped to resolve this dilemma. The publicists' favoured description of Magdeburg as the Lord God's Chancery suggests that all works emerging from the city were to be transmitted with the same urgency, but the printing press was not only a channel for the uncensored defence of the word of God: it was also the means by which certain messages were privileged. The nature of the campaign, which relied on the output of a small number of printing presses operating in wartime conditions, allowed for selection of material by financial criteria without explicitly addressing the need to modify and suppress certain tendencies. A contributor like Alber, whose independent work was marginalised even while he was integrated into the collective publishing effort, could draw on his stock of anecdotes and comparisons to enrich regulated propaganda. He could also produce on his own account material that could be reproduced more cheaply, in slighter or in manuscript format. Brief works such as Alber's songs and verses, whether printed openly or secretly or left unprinted, were ideal for further transmission by word of mouth: Maurice was distressed by 'private' as well as public works. It is thus consistent with the internal politics and the logistics of the Magdeburg project that the coordination of an official campaign to present Magdeburg's case to other states and powers may have been accompanied by less closely monitored communication with those near at hand. If Alber's independent contribution to the anti-Interim struggle was effectively confined to ephermera, he may nonetheless have encouraged the radicalisation of the citizen solider; soldiers were addressed in at least one of his unprinted songs, urged to punish traitors and those who had led their compatriots astray.

The language and range of scriptural and historical references chosen by the coordinators of Magdeburg's publicists are unlikely to strike the modern reader as moderate, but their work shows elements of careful allusion, restraint and diplomacy, and there is evidence that they excluded certain forms of verbal attack. In examining early modern propaganda and the extent to which it could incite to violence on religious pretexts, we should be attentive to attempts by civic authorities, clergy and leaders of public opinion to convince, even to polemicise, without rabble-rousing, and to absorb the fury of their collaborators without controversy. Because of the symbolic and strategic importance of unity

---

de leur devoir, tant les Magistrats que les Subiets, publié par ceux de Magdebourg l'an M. D. L. et maintenant reueu et augmentée de plusieurs raisons et exemples (s. l., 1574).

[51]   Alber, *Basilisk*, Aiii; Alber, [*Auslegung des Wappens der Stadt Magdeburg*].

among communities threatened by religious conflicts, however, we should also examine propaganda printed for wide circulation with an eye to their leaders' strenuous efforts to preserve and advertise concord, and question the extent to which such propaganda was consistent with messages received locally. Even when the coordinators of propaganda stopped short of demonising their enemies and inciting their readers to violent action, it was difficult to eradicate such publications entirely without risking division. At the same time, as an examination of Alber's reception demonstrates, the shared language, style and range of scriptural and cultural references available to publicists in a case like Magdeburg's could blur any distinction between approved and suppressed literature for both contemporaries and later readers.

Chapter 11

Religious Authority and Publishing Success in the Early Modern Jesuit Penitential Book Printing

Robert Aleksander Maryks

Juan Alfonso de Polanco's *Short Directory for Confessors* provides a fascinating insight into the interplay between personal authority, religious authority and the circulation of printed religious books in sixteenth-century Europe.[1] According to the census of the Jesuit penitential literature between 1554 and 1650, Polanco's manual was the first published Jesuit book on sacramental confession.[2] This pocket-sized booklet enjoyed considerable success and a wide geographical dissemination when it was first published. It was printed firstly in Rome and then in Leuven soon afterwards at the very beginning of 1554.[3] This was just a few years after the Council of Trent's session on penance (1551) and 14 years after the foundation of the Society of Jesus (1540).[4] The manual's preface explains that the decision to print the manuscript was fuelled by the encouragement of the papal vicar in Rome, who not only appreciated the text, but also intended to expand its circulation beyond the Society.[5] As we learn from the census, it was the only Jesuit book on sacramental confession for 20 years, until 1574, when the first

---

[1]   Juan Alfonso de Polanco, *Breve directorium ad confessarii ac confitentis munus recte obeundum* (Rome: Antonium Bladum, 1554).

[2]   Robert A. Maryks, 'Census of the books written by Jesuits on sacramental confession (1554–1650)', *Annali di Storia moderna e contemporanea*, 10 (2004), pp. 415–519.

[3]   The first editions are *in octavo*, but the majority of them were printed in 12° (37 editions) and 16° (13 editions). I use the term 'edition' in its early modern meaning that encompasses what today is understood also as reprint and translation.

[4]   It can be said, therefore, that all Jesuit writing on confession was post-Trent. As we shall see, however, the Jesuit approach to penance developed because of, but also in spite of, Trent. I disagree with Vereecke, who sees Trent as pivotal for Catholic moral theology. See, for example, Louis Vereecke, *Da Guglielmo d'Ockham a sant'Alfonso Liguori: Saggi di storia della teologia morale moderna 1300–1787* (Cinisello Balsamo: Edizioni Paoline, 1990), p. 168 and especially pp. 623–9, 643–56.

[5]   'Ita quidem [non] fecissemus, nisi Reverendissimus Archintus Summi Pontificis in alma Urbe Vicarius (qua una cum Magistro Sacri palatii de libris qui Romae imprimuntur, censuram ferre solet) nos, cum hunc tractatum vidit, ad evulgandum illum, et cum aliis etiam extra Societatem communicandum fuisset hortatus' (Polanco, *Directorium*, p. 5).

Jesuit manual for penitents only, Gaspar de Loarte's *Comfort of the tormented* was published in Rome.[6] Loarte's book was the only companion to Polanco's until 1583, when Jean Tellier's *Table* was printed.[7] The *Directory* had its editorial boom in the 1570s, which waned in the 1590s, when its popularity was overtaken by the works of two other *converso* Jesuits: Manuel Sá's *Aphorisms* (80 editions)[8] and Francisco de Toledo's *Instruction for priests and penitents* (166 editions).[9] The *Directory* was the fourth most published Jesuit guide to sacramental confession, with at least 76 editions. It had the highest number of editions in 1576 (the year of Polanco's death), when six were published, but between 1586 and 1598 it was not published more than once a year, and in some years there was no publication at all. The *Directory* was the only book translated into Illyrian and Slovenian languages, and one of the only two Jesuit confessional manuals translated into Portuguese.[10]

The superior general of the Jesuits, Ignatius of Loyola, wanted every Jesuit confessor to have a personal copy of the *Directory*. True, the manual was subsequently used in Jesuit ministries and even in lectures on cases of conscience (*lectiones casuum*),[11] and an influential *Directory to the Spiritual Exercises* (1555) by the Jesuit Juan Alonso de Vitoria recommended Polanco's *Directory*

---

[6]   Gaspar de Loarte, *Conforto de gli aflitti* (Rome: Appresso Vincentio Accolto, 1574). For more details of his life and works see *Diccionario Histórico de la Compañía de Jesús: Biográfico-Temático* [*DHCJ*], ed. by Charles E. O'Neill and Joaquin M. Dominguez, 4 vols (Rome: Institutum Historicum Societatis Iesu, 2001), pp. 2402–3.

[7]   Jean Tellier, *Tavola utilissima à confessori et penitente ... tradotta dall'originale latino da Francesco Grandi* (Rimini: Appresso Giovanni Simbeni, 1583), c. [16]. As the title indicates, this is an Italian translation of the Latin original. I was not able to find any first-edition copy, which must in any case have been printed before 1583. While Loarte's book was reprinted more than once, Tellier's one does not seem to have had the same editorial success.

[8]   Sá's *Aphorismi* were published as far away as in Nagasaki, Japan (1605). For full details of its printing history see *DHCJ*, p. 3454.

[9]   *Instructio sacerdotum ac poenitentium ... cum additionibus D. Andreae Victorelli* (Venice: apud Petrum Mariam Bertanum, 1596).

[10]   The other manual translated into Portuguese was Lucas Pinello's *Confessionario geral. Utilissimo, assi para todos os estados de penitentes se saberem bem confessar, & aparelhar, como tambem para todos os confessores exercitarem dignamente o Sacramento da Penitencia. Composto pelo P. Lucas Pinello ... traduzido da lingua Italiana em a nossa Portugueza por Antonio Vaz Duarte ...* (Lisbon: Pedro Crasbeeck, 1618).

[11]   Giancarlo Angelozzi, 'L'insegnamento dei casi di coscienza nella pratica educativa della Compagnia di Gesù', in *La 'Ratio studiorum': Modelli culturali e pratiche educative dei Gesuiti in Italia tra Cinque e Seicento*, ed. by Gian Paolo Brizzi (Rome: Bulzoni Editore, 1981), pp. 121–62, p. 147. The *Directory* was read in the Jesuit College of Vienna by 1560: Monumenta Historica Societas Iesu, *Monumenta Paedagogica*, 3 vols (Rome: Nova, 1965–), III, p. 309. It was also recommended by the synodal council of Malines (Vereecke, *Da Guglielmo d'Ockham*, p. 638).

as useful for the preparation to the general sacramental confession.[12] However, it is to be noted that the exclusivity of the *Directory* on the Jesuit penitential book market ceased after General Congregation 3 (1573) elected the new Jesuit Superior General Everard Mercurian instead of Polanco, even though the latter as elected vicar general after Francisco de Borja's death in 1572 was the most prominent figure in the Society of Jesus – he had been a senior administrator in the general curia in Rome since his appointment by Loyola in 1547 as Society's secretary. Polanco contributed also to composing the Jesuit *Constitutions*[13] and was commissioned by Loyola to translate them into Latin. He participated in the colloquy of Poissy (1562) and in the last session of the Council of Trent (1563).

Polanco was not chosen to be a new superior general, for the anti-converso Italo-Portuguese lobby strongly opposed his candidacy during the congregation because of Polanco's Jewish ancestry.[14] Indeed, he was a descendant of the *converso* Polanco and Maluenda clans of Burgos. The latter allied in the early fifteenth century with the newly converted Santa María family through the marriage of Juan Garcés de Maluenda (el Viejo) to María Nuñez (d. 1423), the sister of the chief rabbi of Burgos and later its bishop, Pablo de Santa María.[15] Some members of these affluent *converso* families – who were acquainted with Polanco – financially supported Ignatius of Loyola's studies at the University of Paris,[16] where Polanco himself studied in the mid-1530s. It is possible, thus, that the relationship between Ignatius, who sympathised with Christians of Jewish background,[17] and Juan Alfonso (or at least his family) predates the latter's joining the Jesuits in 1541.

As a result of the new superior general's 'house cleansing', Polanco was replaced as secretary of the Society of Jesus by Antonio Possevino (1533–1611) and removed from the Jesuit government along with other Jesuits of *converso*

---

[12]   *On Giving the Spiritual Exercises: The Early Jesuit Manuscript Directories and the Official Directory of 1599*, ed. by Martin E. Palmer (St Louis, MO: The Institute of Jesuit Sources, 1996), p. 23.

[13]   J. Carlos Coupeau, 'The constitutions of the Society of Jesus: The rhetorical component', *Studies in Spirituality* 14 (2004), pp. 199–208.

[14]   Maryks, 'The Jesuit Order as a "Synagogue of Jews": Discrimination of Jesuits of Jewish ancestry in the early Society of Jesus', *Archivum Historicum Societatis Iesu*, 78 (2009), pp. 339–416. *For Matters of Greater Moment: The First Thirty Jesuit General Congregations: A Brief History and a Translation of the Decrees*, ed. by John W. Padberg, Martin D. O'Keefe and John L. McCarthy (St Louis, MO: The Institute of Jesuit Sources, 1994), p. 135.

[15]   See Maryks, *The Jesuit Order as a 'Synagogue of Jews': Jesuits of Jewish Ancestry and Purity-of-Blood Laws in the Early Society of Jesus* (Leiden: Brill Academic Publishers, 2009), esp. Chapter 1.

[16]   Francisco de Borja Medina, 'Íñigo de Loyola y los mercaderes castellanos del Norte de Europa. La financiación de sus estudios en la Universidad de París', *Archivum Historicum Societatis Iesu*, 51 (1999), pp. 159–206.

[17]   Maryks, '*The Jesuit Order as a 'Synagogue of Jews'*, Chapter 2.

background.[18] It is not unreasonable to infer, then, that the publishing success of the *Directory* may well have been related to Polanco's position of authority rather than to the manual's intrinsic usefulness to confessors or students of cases of conscience. Even though it was designed to be a compendium to accommodate the needs of early Jesuits who were too busy with their ministries to dedicate much time to academic activities, the *Directory* lacked the basic awareness of important shifts operative during that century. Indeed, the official edition of the *Directory to the Spiritual Exercises*[19] from 1599 recommended instead a non-Jesuit contemporary text, namely *Enchiridion* by the Augustinian Martin Azpilcueta (1493–1586).[20] This work, known by contemporaries as the *Navarrus* after the author's birthplace, was both popular and authoritative. It was also much more comprehensive than the *Directory* and reflected important socio-economic changes taking place in the sixteenth century.

These changes can be traced, however, in the process of consultations on the text of the Jesuit pedagogical code, *Ratio Studiorum*, between the Roman editorial committee and Jesuits from different provinces before its final official edition was issued in 1599. Examining the *Ratio*'s first version (1586), the Aragonese Jesuits claimed that, during the discussion of cases of conscience students must use not any but principal works in the field, selected by the coordinator, so that from their sentences a *safer* doctrine can be advised.[21] The same tutioristic approach can be noted in the response of the Milanese Jesuits, who recommended

---

[18]   *DHCJ*, pp. 3201–3. Ironically, Possevino, who previously served the Renaissance court of the Gonzaga in Mantua, was most likely of Jewish origins too, but he probably hid his *converso* identity from his confreres. John P. Donnelly, 'Antonio Possevino and Jesuits of Jewish ancestry', *Archivum Historicum Societatis Iesu*, 109 (1986), pp. 3–29 and Alberto Castaldini, 'L'incognita marrana: Ipotesi sulle origini familiari del gesuita Antonio Possevino (1533–1611)', www.upra.org/archivio_pdf/articolouercastaldini.

[19]   Ignatius of Loyola, *Directorium exercitiorum spiritualium* (Florentiae: Apud Philippum Iunctam, 1599).

[20]   *Enchiridion sive manuale confessariorum et poenitentium* (1549 [Portuguese], 1553 [Spanish], 1573 [Latin]). Its structure may have influenced the formulation of *cursus maior* and *cursus minor* in the Jesuit *Ratio Studiorum*. See Angelozzi, 'L'insegnamento dei casi di coscienza', pp. 139, 143, 147, 150, 153 and 159; Mario Scaduto, *L'epoca di Giacomo Laínez. Il governo* (Rome: Civiltà Cattolica, 1974), p. 397; Scaduto, *L'epoca di Giacomo Laínez. L'azione* (Rome: Civiltà Cattolica, 1966), pp. 588 and 596; Turrini, *La coscienza e le leggi*, pp. 181–2. On the place of Navarrus in the history of moral theology, see Emilio Dunoyer, *L'*'Enchiridion Confessariorum' del Navarro: Dissertatio ad lauream in Facultate S. Theologiae apud Pontificium Institutum 'Angelicum' de Urbe* (Pamplona: s. l., 1957), pp. 143–54; Vereecke, *Da Guglielmo d'Ockham*, pp. 647–8; and my review of Vincenzo Lavenia's *L'infamia e il perdono: Tributi, pene e confessione nella teologia morale della prima età moderna* (Bologna: Società editrice il Mulino, 2004), *The Sixteenth Century Journal*, 38 (2007), pp. 844–5.

[21]   MHSI, *Monumenta Paedagogica*, VI, p. 246: 'Non expedit, ut his casibus student caeteri indistincte apud quoscumque voluerint doctores; sed, ut quilibet apud unum aliquem

that the coordinator should be able to judge when an opinion is to be accepted, when refused, which is just probable, and which one can be sustained *without danger* [for someone's eternal salvation].[22] The response of the Castilian Jesuits seems to be the boldest one, yet it is reflected only partially in the *Ratio*'s official version from 1599: the coordinator is expected to choose what appears just *more probable*.[23] The 1599 version reflected what the Jesuits from the Upper German Province proposed: the coordinator first has to list the *safe* classical authors and then indicate among them those who are *more probable*.[24] Interestingly, the Jesuits from the same province formulated a postulate during their provincial congregation in 1600 that the Society should indicate just one author to follow in cases of conscience, as it followed Thomas Aquinas in theology. The answer of the Superior General Claudio Acquaviva (1543–1615) was that 'the Jesuits should make every effort, as far as they can, to be uniform in their judgements, and follow the authors who are grave and approved, but it is difficult to impose generally one direction only, since there are different authors' opinions and *everybody is allowed to follow a probable opinion*' [emphasis mine].[25]

The divergence of the *Ratio* from Polanco's tutioristic *Directory* shows how the Jesuit mindset changed over the first 40 years, or so. A mere formulation of general principles, rules, commandments and laws no longer sufficed. The *Ratio* indicates a deeper understanding of the complexity of moral situations as a result of altered circumstances of the case and not only of the person, as the *Directory* seemed to suggest. No wonder, then, that the *Instruction for priests and penitents* by Francisco de Toledo – who was part of the Roman committee on the *Ratio* –

---

a praeside praestitutum; quo principalium doctorum sententiae ibi referantur, et tutior doctrina ex his colligatur, quam omnes sequi debent.'

[22] MHSI, *Monumenta Paedagogica*, VI, p. 244: 'Lector ... suum cuique opinioni momentum prudenter tribuat, sive teneatur, sive refutetur, quae tantum probabilis, quae omnino tenenda, quae reiicienda omnino, quae sine periculo sustineri potest.' The congregation of the Roman Jesuits in 1597 expressed their concern in stating which opinion is safer and which just probable, especially in dealing with economic issues (MHSI, *Monumenta Paedagogica*, VII, p. 355).

[23] MHSI, *Monumenta Paedagogica*, VI, p. 247: 'Qui praeest, deligit, quid probabilius videatur.' Is it a coincidence that this suggestion comes from the Jesuit province, to which Salamanca – where the Dominican idea of Probabilism matured – belonged?

[24] MHSI, *Monumenta Paedagogica*, VI, p. 250: 'Professor ... referat primum classicas opiniones, quarum unamquamlibet possit quis *tuto* sequi, citatis autoribus. Deinde eligat ex illis unam, quam ipse putet probabiliorem' [emphasis mine].

[25] MHSI, *Monumenta Paedagogica*, VII, p. 366: 'Difficile est, ut aliquid in universum praescribatur; cum diversae sint auctorum opiniones et probabilem cuique sequi liceat. Curandum tamen ut nostri, quoad fieri potest, uniformes sint in sententiis, et auctores graves ac probatos sequantur.' Answering the same kind of postulate by the Jesuit Province of France in 1606, Acquaviva repeated what he had said to the Germans, indicating, however, for its method and order, the manual by Francisco Toledo (MHSI, *Monumenta Paedagogica*, VII, p. 397).

rather than Polanco's *Directory*, was an answer to the new ethical perspectives.[26] Even though the Polish Jesuits would still re-print the *Directory* more than 300 years later,[27] by the end of the sixteenth century it was already outdated.

Whatever judgement is passed on the *Directory*'s helpfulness, we have to acknowledge that the information on the regularity of print editions provided by the census unmistakably indicates that the *Directory* may be considered *the* expression of the early Jesuit corporate conscience. Factors other than its helpfulness must therefore have played a dominant role in determining its print dissemination.

A closer look at the extensive correspondence emanating from the Jesuit headquarters where Polanco functioned as secretary, the Roman Curia of the Society of Jesus, reveals some intriguing information about the *Directory*'s authorship. In January 1554, shortly after the first Roman publication of the *Directory*, Polanco wrote three letters mentioning the publication of the manual commissioned by his superior Loyola. The first, in Italian and dated 13 January, was addressed to all Jesuit schools.[28] The second was written in Spanish on 17

---

[26]   For an analysis of Toledo's book, see James F. Keenan, 'The birth of Jesuit Casuistry: *Summa casuum conscientiae sive de instructione sacerdotum, libri septem*, by Francisco de Toledo (1532–1596)', in *The Mercurian Project: Forming Jesuit Culture 1573–1580*, ed. by Thomas M. McCoog (Rome: Institutum Historicum Societatis Iesu, 2004), pp. 461–82.

[27]   *Directorium breve ad confessarii et confitentis munus rite obeundum R.P. Joannis Polanci s.j. juxta modo vigentes censuras correxit Augustinus Arndt ejusd. Societ.* (Lud. Anczyc et soc.: Cracovia, 1886).

[28]   'Hauendo *N[ostro] P[adre]* ordinato si facessi in casa vn *Directorio per li confessori della Compagnia.* Acció *vniformemente*, quanto si potessi, procedessino, *alcuni Padri pigliorono questa cura*; et hauendosi a stampare, hanno voluto si mettessi il nome de chi l'haueua fatto, perché pare sia prohibito et suspetto stampar' libri sanza nome; et cossí *haueuamo messo* per titulo: 'Concinatum in domo Societatis Jesu.' *È parso a N[ostro] P[adre], che non conueneua* che si imputassi a tutta la casa, se alcuni particulari di quella auessino mancato, et cossì *si rimesse al dottor Olaue, et lui ha posto il nome mio*, et cossi lo fece stampare, quantunque *si c'è qualche cosa di buono, più presto credo sia de altri che mia*. ... Alcuni errori ch'erano della stampa si sonno adnotati al fine. Saria bono, secondo quello ch'è annotato, emendare lo estesso libro con la penna. Di qua per la fretta non si è potuto fare' Monumenta Historica Societatis Iesu, *Monumenta Ignatiana, ex autographis vel ex antiquioribus exemplis collecta. Series prima. Sancti Ignatii de Loyola ... epistolae et instructiones*, 12 vols (Madrid: Lopez del Horno, 1903–11), VI, pp. 166–7.

January to the Jesuit Diego Mirón.[29] The third was issued in Latin on 23 January to another Jesuit, Adrian Adriaensens.[30]

All three letters state that the *Directory* was compiled for Jesuit confessors on Loyola's request, the only fact confirmed in the Preface to the manual's first edition:

> Since it seemed good to explain that the priests of the Society [of Jesus] that had spread in different parts of the world should follow one and the same way in doing this ministry [of hearing confessions] – since they are moved by one and the same spirit to promote men's salvation – I have received a task from our Reverend Father Superior [Ignatius of Loyola] to compose, as far as I am able in good order, a compendium of what I had learned to be useful for both confessors and penitents, in part from lecture and in part from observation, and more so from my own personal and other people's experience.[31]

A comparison of these letters with the preface to the *Directory* reveals a striking discrepancy. From the preface we learn unequivocally that Polanco was the author of the *Directory*, whereas in all three letters Polanco discloses that the manual was

---

29 'Aqui se inbian dos *Directorios de los confessores* que se han ahora stampado, *y por orden de N.P. se tomó aquí en casa esse trabajo (y a mi me han mortificado en poner en el mi nombre)*, porque acá no parece bien estampar libro de alguna doctrina sin nombre, antes es cosa suspechosa. *Hauíase puesto* en el título "Concinnatum in domo Societatis Jesu," pero no le pareció a N.P., *y pusieron mi nombre las personas a quien se remitió*: sí que si ubiere faltas, sabrán a quien dar la culpa; de lo que ubiere bueno, a la casa, y no a mi, lo habrán de agradecer, o por mejor dezir, a Dios N.S., auctor de lo bueno, donde quiera que se halle. ... Vea V.R. por allá que manera habrá para inbiar a cada sacerdote de la Compañía el suyo, como quiere N.P. que le tenga; ... Algunos errores que auía se annotaron al fin del libro; de alli se puede corregir lo de dentro'. MHSI, *Monumenta Ignatiana*, VI, pp. 205–6).

30 'Hoc Directorium confessarii, Patris nostri iussu, domi nostrae concinnatum fuit: et quia suspectum est sine nomine quosuis libros aliquid doctrinae continentes in lucem edere, in huius titulo scripseramus nominis propri[i] loco: "Concinnatum in domo Societatis Jesu." Id tamen non probauit Pater, et ii quibus commisit hoc dubium soluendum, nomen meum, me inscio, in titulo posuerunt; quod ego sic interpretor: ut si quid male dictum deprehenderetur, mihi acceptum feratur (ut par est); si quid recte, haud dubie domui acceptum ferendum est, uel potius Deo, bonorum omnium auctori. ... Aliqua errata, quae typographo exciderunt, in fine sunt adnotata, et expediret penna emendare, quod nobis per ocium non licuit'. MHSI, *Monumenta Ignatiana*, VI, p. 233).

31 'Cum igitur visum esset expedire, ut presbyteri huius Societatis diversissimis orbis regionibus disiuncti, unam eandemque rationem in hoc ministerio gerendo sequerentur, quemadmodum uno atque eodem spiritu ad promovendam hominum salutem ducuntur. Datum fuit mihi negotium a R. P. nostro Praeposito, ut quam aptissimo ordine possem, in compendium ea redigi curarem, quae partim lectione, partim observatione, crebrisque tum meis, tum aliorum experimentis utilia esse et confessariis et confitentibus comperissem' (Polanco, *Directorium*, p. ii). Translation is mine.

composed by a *group* from the Jesuit headquarters in Rome. He does not reveal who participated in the task, but the Italian letter would suggest at least one name, that of Dr Martín Olave.[32] Further, the Latin letter states that it was Olave who took the decision to attribute the *Directory* to Polanco.[33] Olave did so because Loyola, probably with censorship requirements in mind, did not approve the idea of printing the book without expressly naming one author in particular.

If we rely on the information presented in the letters, Polanco's authorship emerges from the preface as a rhetorical device aimed at assuring the reader of the book's authority. Additionally, Miriam Turrini has observed that mentioning friends' or superiors' pressure to publish a work is a *topos* of authors' prefaces in order to avoid criticism and to ensure book's circulation.[34] In the case at hand, mentioning Loyola in the preface is a historical fact and naming Polanco as the only author of the *Directory* is all part of a plan to ensure the manual's good reception and circulation. This kind of editorial promotion is further confirmed by the title of the manual. It clearly indicates that it is intended for both confessors and penitents (*confessarii ac confitentis*). However, another letter from Polanco himself reveals something different. On 24 July 1554, Polanco advised the Jesuit Adrian Adriaensens that the manual was published just for confessors and not for the general public.[35] Indeed, the content of the manual shows that it approaches sacramental confession exclusively from the confessor's position.

The choice of Polanco's name as the only author of the manual may have been motivated by at least two reasons. Either Polanco's contribution to the work was truly significant, or the choice was made because of Polanco's authority. Perhaps both reasons were at work. Unfortunately, we can only speculate about motives, for they are veiled behind Polanco's modesty. He asserts in the quoted letters that, if there is something good in the book, it comes from others (or better still, from

---

[32]   Martín Olave (1507/8–1556) arrived at the Roman community only in September 1552 (Scaduto, *Governo*, pp. 6–7). It is hard to imagine, thus, that his contribution to the *Directory* was significant. He mainly taught theology at the Roman College. His close friendship with Polanco was renowned (see references to his name in the Index in Gonçalves da Câmara, *Remembering Iñigo: Glimpses on the Life of Saint Ignatius of Loyola. The 'Memoriale' of Luís Gonçalves da Câmara.* Translated with introduction, notes and indices by Alexander Eaglestone and Joseph A. Munitiz, S.J. (St Louis, MO: Institute of Jesuit Sources, 2004)). See also my review of the book: *The Sixteenth Century Journal*, 37 (2006), pp. 856–7.

[33]   'Hoc Directorium confessarii, Patris nostri iussu, domi nostrae concinnatum fuit: et quia suspectum est sine nomine quo suis libros aliquid doctrinae continentes in lucem edere, in huius titulo scripseramus nominis propri[i] loco: "Concinnatum in domo Societatis Jesu." Id tamen non probauit Pater, et ii quibus commisit hoc dubium soluendum, nomen meum, me inscio, in titulo posuerunt' (MHSI, *Monumenta Ignatiana*, VII, p. 299).

[34]   Turrini, *La coscienza e le leggi*, p. 36.

[35]   MHSI, *Monumenta Ignatiana*, VII, p. 299: 'Revera tamen confessariis, et non vulgo, liber ille editus fuit, et sacerdotibus, non laicis, ex usu videtur futurus'.

God) rather than from himself. He interprets his confreres' choice as a way of accepting his responsibility for any defects in the manual.

Some other letters exchanged between Polanco and his confreres may shed more light on the history of the making of the *Directory*. In his letter of 6 July 1549, Polanco wrote to his future superior, Diego Laínez, that he was planning to send him a certain 'Practice of confessing' (*Práctica del confessar*) that he had composed in a clearer and briefer fashion, but only after the Father (Ignatius of Loyola) had read it.[36] In another letter dated just two weeks later, Polanco informed the Jesuit Miguel Ochoa that he was sending him a booklet concerning the way to confess.[37] Very likely both letters mentioned the same text that would become a part of the future *Directory*.

The uneven and episodic structure of the *Directory* also gives clues as to its evolution. It consists of two unequal parts: the first and briefer is a description of the nature of the sacrament and of the requirements of the confessor; the second is a series of appendices. These appendices treat how the confessor has to perform an interrogation by reviewing the Ten Commandments and some capital vices and how to interrogate people according to *status*, or walk of life. There is also a short examination composed in verse. The appendices further contain guidance on remedies against the capital vices and on restitution, the act of commutative justice by which reparation is made for an offence. The final, longest appendix is on excommunication. The first part of the *Directory* may be what Polanco composed as the 'Practice of confessing' as far back as 1549 and the appendices might have been written by him and/or other Jesuits later at Loyola's request (especially after the Council of Trent's session on penance in 1551 and other papal documents on the issue).

In conclusion, the information in the letters allows us to suggest that the *Directory*'s publishing success was due to the religious authority of Polanco chosen by his confreres as *the* author of that manual rather than to its relatively minor usefulness to early modern confessors, who had to face the more complex, more subtle and less subjugated consciences of their numerous penitents. Indeed, the judgement that Jansen and Toulmin gave on the medieval manuals of the kind, the *Summa Silvestrina* and *Angelica*, can be also applied to the *Directory*: 'They looked to a medieval world that no longer existed: the simple lines of moral rule and precept they provided were no longer adequate.'[38]

One of the major features of the tutioristic medieval ethical mindset was the stress on the superiority of religious authority over liberty of conscience. By commissioning the exclusive and authoritative *Directory*, Loyola aimed

---

[36]   MHSI, *Monumenta Ignatiana*, II, pp. 467–8.

[37]   The letter from Polanco to Miguel Ochoa on 20 July 1549: 'Que se disponga para saber confessar, leyendo este libreto que aquí le invío muy al propósito' (MHSI, *Monumenta Ignatiana*, II, p. 486).

[38]   Albert Jonsen and Stephen Toulmin, *The Abuse of Casuistry: A History of Moral Theology* (Berkeley, CA: University of California Press, 1988), p. 146.

at preserving the unanimity of Jesuit approach to the ministry of sacramental confession. Yet the Jesuit superior general's desire was challenged by the appearance of a new ethical system of Probabilism that often undermined authority to the advantage of conscience. It was first advanced by the Dominican Bartolomé de Medina in 1577 – just one year after Polanco's death – and enthusiastically espoused by the Jesuits in the last quarter of the sixteenth century.

However, did religious authority cease to influence the dynamics of the Jesuit book market? Apparently not, for the most successful early modern Jesuit penitential manual, *Instruction for priests and penitents* (1596), was written by Francisco de Toledo, who – in spite of being of the *converso* background, as Polanco was – became the first Jesuit to be created cardinal. The history of early modern Jesuit penitential book printing, therefore, is an interesting example of how religious authority and publishing success related to each other in a complex yet intriguing way. The Society of Jesus was founded in mid-sixteenth century, at the dusk of one epoch and at the birth of another. The first Jesuits had received traditional theological medieval training but had been also affected by the early-modern movement of Renaissance Humanism, by which the second generation of Jesuits would become overwhelmingly fascinated. This explains the differences in approaches to authority that marked the *Directory*, which was rooted in tutioristic rule that conscience must be always subjugated to a higher authority of the law or an institution, and the *Ratio Studiorum* that pre-announced the shift towards Probabilism, which would give to conscience the priority over authority, and to opinion the priority over absolute truth. The second generation of Jesuits often found themselves at a difficult crossroads between their fascination with Probabilism and their being members of a religious order that stressed more than any other ecclesiastical institution their obedience to authority as an expression of obedience to God himself.

References

Manuscript Sources

British Library, Cotton MS, Vitellius B IX
British Library, Cotton MS, Vitellius B XIII
British Library, Cotton MS, Cleopatra E VI
British Library, Cotton MS, Titus B I
British Library, Cotton MS, Nero B III
British Library, Additional MS, 25114, 29547
Brussels, Bibliothèque Royale, 9466
Nagonio, Giovanni, *Ad divum Iulium II et Franciscum Mariam nepotem libri I–VIII* (1507); Rome, Biblioteca Apostolica Vaticana: ms. Vat. Lat. 1682
National Archives, Public Record Office, SP1 State Papers, Henry VIII: General Series
National Archives, Public Record Office, SP6 State Papers, Henry VIII: Theological Series
Negri, Giovan Francesco, *Annali della patria*; Bologna, Biblioteca Universitaria: MSS 1107, t. VII/1 (1500–28)
Paris, Bibliothèque nationale de France, fonds français, 2869
Paris, Bibliothèque nationale, fonds français, 12476
Ubaldini, Friano, *Cronica*, Bologna, Bologna, Biblioteca Universitaria, ms. 430, vol. III

Primary Sources before 1800

Works listed without attribution are anonymous

A Glasse of the Truth (London: Thomas Berthelet, 1532), STC 11918, 11919 [*LP* V 547]
ARTICLES by the holle consent of the kynges moste honourable counsayle (London: Thomas Berthelet, 1533) STC 9177
Barzelletta in laude de tutta l'Italia et la liberatione sua contra francesi ([n.p.]: [n. pub.], c. 1512)
The determinations of the moste famous and mooste excellent vniuersities of Italy and Fraunce, that it is so vnlefull [sic] for a man to marie his brothers wyfe, that the pope hath no power to dispence therewith (London, Thomas Berthelet, 1531), STC 14287

An epistle of the moste myghty [and] redouted Prince Henry the viii (London: Thomas Berthelet, 1538)

The Gardyners Passetaunce: Touchyng the outrage of Fraunce (London: Richard Pynson, 1512)

Grauissimae, atq[ue] exactissimae illustrissimaru[m] totius Italiae, et Galliae academiaru[m] censurae efficacissimis etiam quorundam doctissimorum uiroru[m] argumentationibus explicatae, de ueritate illius propositionis (London: Thomas Berthelet, 1531), STC 14286

Lamento di Bentivogli (Bologna: A. Lippus, 1506/1507)

Le myrouer de verite (London: Thomas Berthelet, 1532), STC 11919.5

A protestation made for the most mighty and moste redoubted kynge of Englande (London: Thomas Berthelet, 1537)

La vera nova de Bressa de punto in punto com'è andata. Novamente impressa (Venice: Alessandro Bindoni, c. 1512)

[Alber, Erasmus] *Ein Dialogus oder Gespra[e]ch etlicher personen vom Interim* ([Augsburg: Hans Gegler], 1548 [for 1557])

[Alber, Erasmus] *Das buch von der Tugent vnd Weißheit/nemlich/Neunvnd=viertzig Fabeln/der mehrer theil auß Esopo gezogen/vnnd mit guten Rheimen verkleret/ Durch Erasmum Alberum/Allen stenden n[ue]tzlich zulesen* (Frankfurt am Main: Peter Braubach, 1550)

[Alber, Erasmus] *Der Holdseligen Blummen der Treifeltigkeyt bedeutung/Nutzlich zulesen/Gott dem Herrn zu ehren* ([Magdeburg: Rödinger, 1550])

[Alber, Erasmus] *Ein Predigt vom Ehestand/uber das Euangelium/Es war ein Hochzeit zu Cana etc.* ([Magdeburg]: Rödinger, 1550)

Alber, Erasmus, *Vom Basilisken zu Magdeburg: Item vom Hanen eyhe/daraus ein Basilisck wirt/mit seiner Bedeutung aus der heiligen Schrifft* (Hamburg: Joachim Loew [c. 1552])

[Alber, Erasmus] *Vom Wintervogel Halcyon, ein herrlich Wunderwerck Gottes, mit der heiligen Schrifft assgelegt* (Hamburg: Joachim Loew, 1552)

[Alber, Erasmus] *Wider die verfluchte lehre der Carlstadder, Zwingler, Widderteüffer, Rottengeister, Sacramentläster, Eheschender, Musica verächter, Bildstürmer, Feyerfeind, und verwüster aller guten ordnung, geschreyben umb der Christen willen, fürnemlich die under den Rotten seind, fast allenthalben* (Neubrandenburg: Brenner, 1556)

Aquila, Kaspar, *Wider den spöttischen Lügner Esslebium Agricolam* (Magdeburg: Rödinger, 1548)

Aquila, Kaspar, *Ein sehr hoch nötige Ermahnung* (Magdeburg: Lotther, 1548)

Aristotle, *Thus endeth the secrete of secretes of Arystotle* (London: Robert Copland, 1528), STC770

[Beza, Theodore], *Du Droit des Magistrats sur leurs subiets. Traitté tres necessaire en ce temps pour advertir de leur devoir, tant les Magistrats que les Subiets, publié par ceux de Magdebourg l'an M. D. L. et maintenant reueu et augmentée de plusieurs raisons et exemples* (s.l., 1574)

Bighignol, *Li horrendi e magnanimi fatti de l'ilustrissimo Alfonso duca di Ferrara contra l'armata de Venetiani* (Ferrara: Baldassare Selli, 1510)

Boccaccio, Giovanni, *Il Decamerone* (Venice: per Gregorio De Gregori, 1525)

Charles V, *Sacrae Caesareae Maiestatis Declaratio, quomodo in negocio religionis per Imperium usque ad definitionem Concilij generalis vivendum sit, in Comitijs augustanis XV. Maij anno M. D. XLVIII. proposita, et publicata et ab omnibus Imperij ordinibus recepta, è Germanica lingua in Latinam ... versa ...* (Frankfurt an der Oder: Wolrab [1548])

Cochlaeus, Johannes, *De matrimonio serenissimi Regis Angliae, Henrici Octavi, Congratulatio disputatoria* (Leipzig: Michael Blum, 1535)

Cochlaeus, Johannes, *Scopa ... in araneas Richardi Morysini Angli* (Leipzig: Nicolaus Wolrab, 1538)

Commynes, Philippe de, *Les Memoires de Messire Philippe De Cõmines, Cheualier, Seigneur d'Argenton: sur les principaux faicts & gestes de Louis onziéme & de Charles huictiéme, son fils, Roys de France. Reueus & corrigez par Denis Sauvage de Fontenailles en Brie, svr vn Exemplaire pris à l'orignal de l'Auteur, & suyuant les bons Historiographes & Croniqueurs. Auec distinction de liures, selon les matieres, estans aussi les chapitres autrement distinguez que par cy deuant, & brief, le tout mieux ordonné: ainsi que les lecteurs pourront voir par l'auertissement à eux addrecé, apres l'Epistre au Roy*, ed. by Denis Sauvage (Paris: Jean de Roigny, 1552)

Cuspinian, Johannes, *Austria Ioannis Cuspiniani cum omnibus eiusdem marchionibus, ducibus, archiducibus, ac rebus preclare ad haec usque tempora ab iisdem gestis* (Frankfurt: Wechel, 1601)

Der durchleuchtigsten, grosmechtigsten Herrn, herrn Heinrichs der achten ... Schrifft an keiserliche Maiestat, an alle andere christliche Könige vnd Potentaten, jnn welcher der König vrsach anzeigt, warumb er gen Vicentz zum Concilio ... nicht komen sey. Aus dem Let. verdeudtscht durch J. Jonam (Wittenberg: Joseph Klug, 1539)

Epistel vnd Sendbrief Henrici des viij. Künigs von Engelland vnd Franckreich ... an Kaiser Carolum ... darinn der Künig gründtlich vrsach anzaigt, warumb er nit auff das Concilium zu Vincentz ... kommen werde (Augsburg: [s. pub.], 1538)

Erasmus of Rotterdam, *Epistolae ... ad diversos* (Basel: Johannes Froben, 1521)

Flacius Illyricus, Matthias, *Bulla des Antichrists, dadurch er das volck Gottes widderumb in den eisern ofen der Egypitishcen gefengknis denckt zuziehen/ gleichstimmig mit des Meintzischen Rabsakes briefe. Daraus wol zuuernemen/ was der Teufel durch seine beide tugent/das ist/durch den Moerderische krieg widder die Kirche Gottes/vnd durch seine luegen/als da sind/Concilium Interim/Mittelding/Chorrock/denckt auszurichten* (Magdeburg: [Christian Rödinger], 1550)

Foxe, Edward, *Opus eximium, de vera differentia regiae potestatis et ecclesiasticae et quae sit ipsa veritas ac virtus vtriusque* (London: Thomas Berthelet, 1534, 1538), STC 11218, 11219

Froissart, Jean, *Chronique de Froissart*, ed. by Denis Sauvage, 4 vols (Lyon: Jean de Tournes, 1559), I

Gardiner, Stephen, *De vera obedientia* (London: Thomas Berthelet, 1535; Strasbourg: Wendelin Rihel, 1536), STC 11584

Gardiner, Stephen, *Stephani Winton. episcopi de vera obecientia oratio* (Strasbourg: Wendelin Rihel, 1536)

Gardiner, Stephen, *Stephani Vintoniensis episcopi De vera obedientia, oratio: Vna cum praefatione Edmundi Boneri archidiaconi Leycestrensis ... in qua etiam ostenditur caussam controuersiæ quæ inter ... Regiam Maiestatem & Episcopum Romanum existit, longe aliter ac diuersius se habere* (Hamburg: officina Francis Rhodes, 1536)

Gaguin, Robert, *Compendium de Francorum origine et gestis* (Paris:Andreas Bocard, 1497) <http://catalogue.bnf.fr/ark:/12148/bpt6k52876x> [accessed 31 March 2009]

Gaguin, Robert, *Compendium de Francorum origine et gestis* (Lyon: [s. pub.], 1497) <http://catalogue.bnf.fr/ark:/12148/bpt6k52897w> [last accessed 31 March 2009]

Gaguin, Robert, *Compendium de Francorum origine et gestis* (Paris : Thielman Kerver,   1500)<http://diglib.hab.de/wdb.php?dir=inkunabeln/289-7-hist-2f> [accessed 31 March 2009].

Grynaeus, Simon, *Novus orbis regionum ac insularum veteribus incognitarum una cum tabella cosmographica et aliquot aliis consimilis argumenti libellis quorum omnium catalogus sequenti pagina patebit* (Basel: Herwagen, 1532)

Haddon, Walter, *Against Ierome Osorius Byshopp of Siluane in Portingall and against his slaunderous inuectiues An aunswere apologeticall* (London: John Day, 1581)

Hortleder, Friedrich, *Der Römischen Keyser Und Koniglichen Maiestetē, Auch des heiligen Römischen Reichs Geistlicher und Weltlicher Stände ... Handlungen und Außschreiben ... Von Rechtmässigkeit/Anfang/Fort und endlichen Aussgang dess Teutschen Kriegs Keyser Carls dess Fuenfften*, 2nd edn, 2 vols (Gotha, Wolfgang Endters, 1645)

Ignatius of Loyola, *Directorium exercitiorum spiritualium* (Florence: Apud Philippum Iunctam, 1599)

Inghirami, Tommaso, *Thomae Phaedri Inghirami Volaterrani orationes duae altera in funere Galeotti Franciotti Card. Vicecancellarii altera item funeris pro Julio II Pontifice Maximo*, ed. by Pietro Galletti (Rome: [s. pub.], 1777)

Knox, John, *The historie of the reformatioun of religioun within the realm of Scotland, ... Together with the life of Iohn Knoxe the Author, and several Curious Pieces wrote by him* (Edinburgh: Robert Fleming & Co., 1732)

[Labbé, Philippe (?)], *Testamentum christianum; testamentum politicum, epitaphium sorbonicum Armandi Richelii cardinalis* (Lyon: [s. pub.], 1643)

La Marche, Olivier de, *Les Memoires de Messire Olivier de La Marche, Premier Maistre d'hostel de l'archeduc Philippe d'Austriche, Comte De Flandres: Nouvellement mis en lumiére par Denis Sauvage dee Fontenailles en Brie, historiographe du Treschrestien Roy Henry, second de ce nom*, ed. by Denis Sauvage (Lyon: Guillaume Rouillé, 1561)

Landi, Ortensio, *Delectable demaundes, and pleasaunt questions, with their seuerall aunswers, in matters of loue, naturall causes, with morall and politique deuises*, trans. by William Painter (London: John Cawood; 1566)

Loarte, Gaspar de, *Conforto de gli aflitti* (Rome: Appresso Vincentio Accolto, 1574)

Loazes, Ferdinando de, *Tractatus in causa matrimonij Serenissimorum dominorum Henrici et Catherine Anglie Regum* (Barcelona: in officina ... Caroli Amorosij, 1531)

Matteo Maria da Rimini, *Barzelletta nova in laude di papa Julio II composta per frate Matheo Maria da Rimino del sacro Ordine di Servi* (Bologna: Giustiniano da Rubiera, 1506/1507)

Matthew, Simon, *A sermon made in the cathedrall churche of Saynt Paule at London, the XXVII. day of June, Anno. 1535* (London: Thomas Berthelet, 1535)

Melanchthon, Philip, *Epistola Phil. Melanthonis, in quae respondetur Flacio Illyrico* (Wittenberg: Joseph Klug, 1549)

Molinet, Jean, *Les Faictz et dictz* (Paris: Jean Longis and the widow of Jean Saint-Denis, 1531)

Morison, Richard, *Apomaxis calumniarum, convitiorumque, quibus Ioannes Cocleus homo theologus exiguus artiu[m] professor* (London: Thomas Berthelet, 1537)

Penni, Giovanni Jacopo, *Epistola di Roma a Julio pontifice maximo con la risposta del pontefice a Roma* ([Étienne Guillery(?)]: Rome, c. 1511)

Penni, Giovanni Jacopo, *La magnifica festa facta dalli Signori Romani per el carnevale MDXIII: Novamente composta per Io. Ia. De Pennis* ([Étienne Guillery(?)]: [Rome(?)], 1514)

Pinello, Lucas, *Confessionario geral. Utilissimo, assi para todos os estados de penitentes se saberem bem confessar, & aparelhar, como tambem para todos os confessores exercitarem dignamente o Sacramento da Penitencia. Composto pelo P. Lucas Pinello... traduzido da lingua Italiana em a nossa Portugueza por Antonio Vaz Duarte ...* (Lisbon: Pedro Crasbeeck, 1618)

Podio da Lugo, Giraldo, *Continentie de tutte le guerre de franzosi in Jtalia* (Rome: J. Belpin, [1510(?)])

Polanco, Juan Alfonso de, *Breve directorium ad confessarii ac confitentis munus recte obeundum* (Rome: Antonium Bladum, 1554)

Plancher, Urbain, *Histoire générale et particuliere de Bourgogne*, 4 vols (Dijon: Antoine de Fay, 1739–41)

Quadrio, Francesco Saverio, *Della storia e della ragione d'ogni poesia* (Milan: nelle stampe di Francesco Agnelli, 1741)

Rossetto, Giacomo, *Lamento de Italia diviso in capituli septe composito per Jacobo Rossetto Darthonese al beatissimo Papa Julio Secundo* ([n.p.]: before October 1512)

Sacchino da Modigliana, Francesco Maria, *Spavento de Italia* ([Venice(?)]: c. 1510)

Sampson, Richard, *Richardi Sampsonis, regii sacelliae decani oratio, qua docet, hortatur, admonet omnes potissimu[m] anglos, regiae dignitati cum primis ut obediant* (London: Thomas Berthelet, 1535)

Schiltberger, Johann, *Schiltberger. Ein wunderbarliche/und kurtzweylige/Histori/ wie Schiltberger/eyner auß der Stadt Muenchen/in Bayern/von den/Tuercken gefangen/in die Heydenschafft gefueret/unnd wider heim kommen* (Nuremberg: Johann vom Berg and Ulrich Neuber, c. 1549)

Schiltberger, Johann, *Vom Turcken und Machomet/Ein warer gruendtlicher bericht/aus dem Geschichtschreiber/Johan Schiltberger* (Frankfurt: Weigandt Han, 1595)

Schiltberger, Johann, *Narratio oder gründliche Erzehlung aller gedenkwirdigen sachen* (Vienna: Gregor Hübner, 1596)

Sleidan, Johann, *De Statu religionis et reipublicae, Carolo quinto caesare, commentarii* ([Strasbourg: Rihel], 1555)

Sleidan, Johann, *A famouse cronicle of oure time, called Sleidanes Commentaries concerning the state of religion and common wealth, during the raigne of the Emperour Charles the fift* (London: John Day, 1560)

Sorci, Giacomo de' ('il Cortonese'), *Historia come papa Iulio ha prese la città de Bologna* (Bologna: Benedetto di Ettore Faelli, 1507)

Sorci, Giacomo de' ('il Cortonese'), *Historia dele guerre, dela beatitudine de Papa Iulio secondo* (Bologna: Giustiniano da Rubiera, 1532)

Tellier, Jean, *Tavola utilissima à confessori et penitente ... tradotta dall'originale latino da Francesco Grandi* (Rimini: Appresso Giovanni Simbeni, 1583)

Thynne, Francis, *The perfect ambassadour treating of the antiquitie, priveledges, and behaviour of men belonging to that function* (London: printed for John Colbeck, 1652)

Toledo, Francisco de, *Instructio sacerdotum ac poenitentium ... cum additionibus D. Andreae Victorelli* (Venice: apud Petrum Mariam Bertanum, 1596)

Tudor, Henry, *Epistel vnd Sendbrief Henrici des viij. Künigs von Engelland vnd Franckreich ... an Kaiser Carolum ... darinn der Künig gründtlich vrsach anzaigt, warumb er nit auff das Concilium zu Vincentz ... kommen werde* (Augsburg: [s. pub.], 1538)

Tudor, Henry, Der durchleuchtigsten, grosmechtigsten Herrn, herrn Heinrichs der achten ... Schrifft an keiserliche Maiestat, an alle andere christliche Könige vnd Potentaten, jnn welcher der König vrsach anzeigt, warumb er gen Vicentz zum Concilio ... nicht komen sey. Aus dem Let. verdeudtscht durch J. Jonam (Wittenberg: [s. pub.], 1539)

Tudor, Henry, *Serenissimi et inclyti regis Angliæ Henrici octaui &c. epistola de synodo Vincentina* (Wittenberg, Peter Seitz, 1539)

Villon, François, *Le Grant Testament Villon et le Petit. Son Codicille. Le Jargon et ses Balades* (Paris: Pierre Levet, 1489)

Whytstons, James, *De iusticia & sanctitate belli per Iulium pontificem secundum in scismaticos et tirannos patrimonium Petri invadentes indicti allegationes* (London: Richard Pynson, 1512)

Zanchin, Florian and others, *Sonetti, capituli in laude de papa Iulio* (Bologna: Giovanni Antonio de'Benedetti, 1506/1507)

Primary Sources after 1800

The Gardyners Passetaunce, ed. by Franklin B. Williams (London: printed for presentation to members of the Roxburghe Club, 1985)

The Holy Bible: King James Version (Cambridge: Cambridge University Press, 1995)

Alber, Erasmus, *Die Fabeln: Die erweiterte Ausgabe von 1550 mit Kommentar sowie die Erstfassung von 1534*, ed. by Wolfgang Harms and Herfried Vögel, in association with Ludger Lieb (Tübingen: Niemeyer, 1997)

Alighieri, Dante, *Convivio*, IV. 6. 5, in *Opere minori*, vol. I, part 2, ed. by Cesare Vasoli and Domenico De Robertis (Milan and Naples: Ricciardi, 1988)

Andrić, Ivo, *The Bridge Over the Drina*, trans. by Lovette F. Edwards (London: Harvill, 1995)

Aretino, Pietro, *Lettere*, ed. by Paolo Procaccioli, 6 vols (Rome: Salerno Editrice, 1997–2002)

Beheim, Michel, *Die Gedichte des Michel Beheim*, ed. by Hans Gille and Ingeborg Spriewald, 3 vols (Berlin: Akademie-Verlag, 1968–72)

Belges, Jean Lemaire de, *La Plainte du Désiré*, ed. by Dora Yabsley (Paris: Droz, 1932)

Bembo, Pietro, *Lettere*, ed. by Ernesto Travi, 4 vols (Bologna: Commissione per i testi di lingua, 1987–93)

Bouchart, Alain, *Grandes croniques de Bretaigne: Texte établi par Marie-Louise Auger et Gustave Jeanneau sous la direction de Bernard Guenée*, 3 vols (Paris: Editions du CNRS 1986–98)

Caesar, Gaius Iulius, *C. Iuli Caesaris commentarii*, vol. I. *commentarii belli Gallici*, ed. by Alfred Klotz (Leipzig: Teubner 1921)

Calendar of letters, despatches, state papers relating to the negotiations between England and Spain preserved in the archives at Vienna, Brussels Simancas and elsewhere 1531–33, ed. by Pascual de Gayangos (London: George E.B. Eyre and William Spottiswoode, 1882)

Calendar of letters, despatches, state papers relating to the negotiations between England and Spain preserved in the archives at Vienna, Brussels Simancas and elsewhere 1534–35, ed. by Pascual de Gayangos (London: Eyre and Spottiswoode, 1886)

Câmara, Gonçalves da, *Remembering Iñigo. Glimpses on the Life of Saint Ignatius of Loyola. The 'Memoriale' of Luís Gonçalves da Câmara*. Trans.

with introduction, notes and indices by Alexander Eaglestone and Joseph A. Munitiz, S.J. (St Louis, MO: Institute of Jesuit Sources, 2004)

Castiglione, Baldesar, *Il Libro del cortegiano con una scelta delle Opere minori*, ed. by Bruno Maier, 2nd edn (Turin: UTET, 1964)

Chartier, Alain, *The Poetical Works of Alain Chartier*, ed. by James C. Laidlaw (Cambridge: Cambridge University Press, 1974)

Chartier, Jean *Chroniques de Charles VII, roi de France*, ed. by Vallet de Viriville, 3 vols (Paris: Jannet, 1858)

Crenne, Hélisenne de, *The Torments of Love*, trans. by Lisa Neal and Stephen Randall (Minneapolis, MN: University of Minnesota Press, 1996)

Crenne, Hélisenne de, *Les Angoysses douloureuses qui procedent d'amours*, ed. by Christine de Buzon (Paris: Champion, 1997)

Cuspinians, Johannes, *Johann Cuspinians Briefwechsel*, ed. by Hans Ankwicz-Kleehoven, Humanistenbriefe, 2 (Munich: Beck, 1933)

Die historischen Volkslieder der Deutschen vom 13. bis 16. Jahrhundert, ed. by Rochus von Lilienchron, 5 vols (Leipzig, Vogel: 1865–69)

Erasmus of Rotterdam, *The 'Julius Exclusus' of Erasmus*, trans. by Paul Pascal, ed. by Jesse Kelley Sowards (Bloomington, IN: Indiana University Press, 1968)

Erasmus of Rotterdam, *Iulius exclusus e coelis*, ed. by Giorgio Maselli (Bari: Palomar, 1995)

Fabri, Pierre, *Le Grand et vrai art de pleine rhétorique*, ed. by A. Héron, 3 vols (Rouen: Société des Bibliophiles Normands, 1889–90)

Fèvre, Jean le, *Chronique de Jean le Fèvre, siegneur de St-Rémy*, ed. by François Morand, 2 vols (Paris: Renouard, 1876–81)

Ficino, Marsilio, *Three Books on Life*, ed. and trans. by Carol V. Kaske and John R. Clark (Binghamton, NY: Medieval and Renaissance Texts and Studies, 1989)

Fortunio, Giovan Francesco, *Regole grammaticali della volgar lingua*, ed. by Brian Richardson (Rome and Padua: Antenore, 2001)Gentili, Alberico, 'The perfect ambassador', in *Diplomatic Classics: Selected Texts from Commynes to Vattel*, ed. by Geoff R. Berridge (Basingstoke: Palgrave Macmillan, 2004)

Gringoire, Pierre, *Œuvres polémiques rédigées sous le règne de Louis XII*, ed. by Cynthia J. Brown (Geneva: Droz, 2003)

Guicciardini's Ricordi: The Counsels and Reflections of Francesco Guicciardini, ed. by Geoff R. Berridge (Leicester: Allandale Online Publishing, 2000)

Hutten, Ulrich von, *Ulrichi Hutteni Opera*, ed. by Eduard Böcking (Leipzig: Teubner, 1862)

Inventaire sommaire des archives départementales du Nord. Série B, ed. by André Le Glay et al., 10 vols (Lille: 1863–1906)

Janelle, Pierre, *Obedience in Church and State* (Cambridge: Cambridge University Press, 1930)

La Marche, Olivier de, *Mémoires d'Olivier de La Marche*, ed. by Henri Beaune and J. d'Arbaumont, 4 vols (Paris: Renouard, 1883–88)

Le Franc, Martin, *La Complainte du livre du Champion des dames a maistre Martin Le Franc son acteur* in Gaston Paris, 'Un poème inédit de Martin Le Franc', *Romania*, 16 (1887), pp. 383–437

Le Franc, Martin, *Le Champion des dames*, ed. by Robert Deschaux, 5 vols (Paris: Champion, 1999)

Le Franc, Martin, *L'Estrif de Fortune et de Vertu*, ed. by Peter F. Dembowski (Geneva: Droz, 1999)

Luther, Martin, *Disputationen Dr. Martin Luthers in d. J. 1535–1545 an der Universität Wittenberg gehalten*, ed. by Paul Drews (Vandenhoeck und Ruprecht: Göttingen, 1895)

Marot, Clément, *Œuvres poétiques complètes*, ed. by Gérard Defaux, 2 vols (Paris: Bordas, 1990–93)

Molinet, Jean, *L'Art de Rhétorique*, in *Recueil d'arts de seconde rhétorique*, ed. by Ernest Langlois (Paris: Imprimerie Nationale, 1902)

Monstrelet, Enguerran de, *La Chronique d'Enguerran de Monstrelet en deux livres avec pieces justificatives 1400–1444*, ed. by L. Douët-d'Arcq, 6 vols (Paris: Renouard, 1857–62)

Monumenta Historica Societatis Iesu, *Monumenta Ignatiana, ex autographis vel ex antiquioribus exemplis collecta. Series prima. Sancti Ignatii de Loyola ... epistolae et instructiones*, 12 vols (Madrid: Lopez del Horno, 1903–11)

Monumenta Historica Societatis Iesu, *Monumenta Paedagogica*, 3 vols (Rome: Nova, 1965–)

Ovid, *Tristia*, in *Tristia; Ex ponto*, ed. and trans. by Arthur Leslie Wheeler (Cambridge, MA/London: Harvard University Press/Heinemann, 1965)

Palsgrave, John, *The Comedy of Acolastus translated from the Latin by John Palsgrave*, ed. by Patrick L. Carver (Oxford: Early English Texts Society, 1937)

Pizan, Christine de, *Le Chemin de Longue Étude*, ed. by Andrea Tarnowski (Paris: Librairie Générale Française, 2000)

Polanco, Juan Alfonso de, *Directorium breve ad confessarii et confitentis munus rite obeundum R.P. Joannis Polanci s.j. juxta modo vigentes censuras correxit Augustinus Arndt ejusd. Societ.* (Lud. Anczyc et soc.: Cracovia, 1886)

Rabelais, François, *Gargantua and Pantagruel*, trans. by J.M. Cohen (Harmondsworth: Penguin, 1955)

Rabelais, François, *Gargantua*, ed. by Ruth Calder and M. A. Screech (Geneva: Droz, 1970)

Reilly, Donald, *The New Yorker Collection*, <http://www.cartoonbank.com> (Image ID: 15261) [accessed 23 March 2013]

Romieu, Marie de *Les Premières Œuvres poétiques* (1585), ed. by André Winandy (Geneva: Droz, 1972)

Sanuto, Marin, *I Diarii*, 58 vols (Venice: Visentini, 1879–1903)

Schiltberger, Johann, *The Bondage and Travels of Johann Schiltberger, a native of Bavaria, in Europe, Asia, and Africa, 1396–1427*, ed. and trans. by Telfer, J. Buchan (London: Hakluyt Society, 1879)

Schiltberger, Johann, *Hans Schiltbergers Reisebuch nach der Nürnberger Handschrift herausgegeben*, ed. by Langmantel, Valentin (Tübingen: Literarischer Verein, 1885)

Stella, Erasmus, 'Erasmi Stellae Libonothani De Borussiae Antiquitatibus Libri duo', in *Scriptores Rerum Prussicarum oder Die Geschichtsquellen der preussischen Vorzei*t, 4, ed. by Theodor Hirsch and others (Leipzig: Hirzel, 1870), pp. 275–98.

Tasso, Torquato, *Le lettere*, ed. by Cesare Guasti, 5 vols (Florence: Le Monnier, 1852–55)

Tasso, Torquato, *Apologia in difesa della Gerusalemme liberata*, in *Prose*, ed. by Ettore Mazzali (Milan and Naples: Ricciardi, 1959)

Taverne, Antoine de la, *Journal de la paix d'Arras*, ed. by André Bossuat (Paris: l'Avenir, 1936)

Tudor Royal Proclamations, ed. by Paul L. Hughes & James F. Larkin 3 vols (New Haven, CT: Yale University Press, 1964–69)

Villon, François, *Poésies complètes*, ed. by Claude Thiry (Paris: Librairie Générale Française, 1991)

Secondary Sources

Adams, David and Adrian Armstrong, eds, *Print and Power in France and England, 1500–1800* (Aldershot: Ashgate, 2006)

Ady, Cecilia M., *Pius II (Aeneas Silvius Piccolomini): The Humanist Pope* (London: Methuen, 1913)

Allmand, Christopher, ed., *The New Cambridge Medieval History, Volume VII c. 1415–c. 1500* (Cambridge: CUP, 1998)

Anderson, Matthew S., *The Rise of Modern Diplomacy 1450–1919* (London: Longman, 1993)

Angelozzi, Giancarlo, 'L'insegnamento dei casi di coscienza nella pratica educativa della Compagnia di Gesù,' in *La 'Ratio studiorum': Modelli culturali e pratiche educative dei Gesuiti in Italia tra Cinque e Seicento*, ed. by Gian Paolo Brizzi (Rome: Bulzoni Editore, 1981)

Ankwicz-Kleehoven, Hans, *Der Wiener Humanist Johannes Cuspinian: Gelehrter und Diplomat zur Zeit Kaiser Maximilians I* (Graz/Cologne: Böhlau, 1959)

Armstrong, Adrian, 'La *Plainte du Désiré* de Jean Lemaire de Belges: du manuscrit illustré aux marges de l'imprimé', in *Actes du IIᵉᵐᵉ Colloque international sur la Littérature en Moyen Français (Milan, 8–10 mai 2000)*, ed. by Sergio Cigada, Anna Slerca, Giovanna Bellati, Monica Barsi, *L'Analisi linguistica e letteraria*, 8 (2000), pp. 139–56

Armstrong, Adrian, 'Paratexte et autorité(s) chez les Grands Rhétoriqueurs', in 'L'Écrivain editeur, 1: Du Moyen Age à la fin du XVIIIᵉ siecle', *Travaux de Litterature*, 14 (2000), pp. 61–89

Armstrong, Adrian, *Technique and Technology: Script, Print, and Poetics, 1470–1550* (Oxford: Clarendon Press, 2000)

Armstrong, Elisabeth, *Before Copyright: The French Book-Privilege System 1498–1526* (Cambridge: Cambridge University Press, 1990)

Arnade, Peter J., *Realms of Ritual: Burgundian Ceremony and Civic Life in Late-Medieval Ghent* (Ithaca, NY: Cornell University Press, 1996)

Baumer, Franklin L. Van, *The Early Tudor Theory of Kingship* (New Haven, CT: Yale Historical Publications, 1940)

Bauschatz, Cathleen M., '"Hélisenne aux lisantes": Address of Women Readers in the *Angoisses douloureuses* and in Boccaccio's *Fiammetta*', *Atlantis*, 19 (1993), 59-66.

Beal, Peter, *In Praise of Scribes: Manuscripts and their Makers in Seventeenth-Century England* (Oxford: Clarendon Press, 1998)

Bell, Gary M., *Handlist of British Diplomatic Representatives, 1509–1688* (London: Royal Historical Society, 1990)

Bernardi, Marco and Carlo Pulsoni, 'Primi appunti sulla rassettatura del Salviati', *Filologia italiana*, 8 (2011), pp. 167–200

Binski, Paul, *Council and Commune: The Conciliar Movement and the Fifteenth-Century Heritage* (London/Shepherdstown, W.Va: Burnes & Oates/Patmos, 1979)

Binski, Paul and Marian Biskup, 'Die herrschaftlichen Umzüge im Ordensland Preußen in den Jahren 1516 und 1518', *Jahrbuch für die Geschichte Mittel- und Ostdeutschlands*, 46 (2000), pp. 113–38

Binski, Paul and Stella Panayotova, eds, *The Cambridge Illuminations: Ten Centuries of Book Production in the Medieval West* (London: Harvey Miller, 2005)

Bondois, Paul-Martin, 'Henri II et ses historiographes', *Bulletin Philologique et historique (jusqu'à 1715) du comité des travaux historiques et scientifiques* (1925), pp. 135–49

Borja Medina, Francisco de, 'Íñigo de Loyola y los mercaderes castellanos del Norte de Europa. La financiación de sus estudios en la Universidad de París', *Archivum Historicum Societatis Iesu*, 51 (1999), pp. 159–206

Bourdieu, Pierre, *The Field of Cultural Production*, ed. by Randal Johnson (Cambridge: Polity Press, 1993)

Britnell, Jennifer, *Jean Bouchet* (Edinburgh: Edinburgh University Press, 1986)

Broomhall, Susan, *Women and the Book Trade in Sixteenth-Century France* (Aldershot: Ashgate, 2002)

Brown, Cynthia J., *Poets, Patrons, and Printers: Crisis of Authority in Late Medieval France* (Ithaca, NY: Cornell University Press, 1995)

Brown, Elizabeth A.R. 'The Trojan origins of the French: The commencement of a myth's demise, 1450–1520', in *Medieval Europeans: Studies in Ethnic Identity and National Perspectives in Medieval Europe*, ed. by Alfred P. Smyth (New York: St Martin's Press, 1998), pp. 135–79

Brunner, Otto, *Land and Lordship: Structures of Governance in Medieval Austria*, trans. by Howard Kaminsky and James van Horn Melton (Philadelphia, PA: University of Pennsylvania Press, 1992)

Brunot, Ferdinand, *Histoire de la langue française des origines à 1900: Le seizième siècle*, 2nd edn (Paris: Colin, 1922)

Buettner, Brigitte, 'Past presents: New year's gifts at the Valois courts ca. 1400', *The Art Bulletin* 83.4 (2001), pp. 598–625

Burke, Peter, *Languages and Communities in Early Modern Europe* (Cambridge: Cambridge University Press, 2004)

Burney Trapp, Joseph 'The Poet Laureate. Rome, Renovatio and Translatio Imperii', in *Rome in the Renaissance: The City and the Myth*, ed. by Paul A. Ramsey, Medieval and Renaissance Texts and Studies, 18 (Binghamton: Centre for Medieval and Renaissance Studies, 1982), pp. 93–130

Calhoun, Craig, ed., *Habermas and the Public Sphere* (Cambridge, MA: MIT Press, 1992)

Carolsfeld, Franz Schnorr von, *Erasmus Alberus: Ein biographischer Beitrag zur Geschichte der Reformationszeit* (Dresden: Ehlermann, 1893)

Carruthers, Mary J., *The Book of Memory: A Study of Memory in Medieval Culture* (Cambridge: Cambridge University Press, 1990)

Cartier, Alfred, *Bibliographie des éditions des de Tournes, imprimeurs lyonnais*, 2 vols (Paris: Editions des bibliothèques nationales de France, 1937–38; repr. Geneva: Slatkine Reprints, 1970)

Castaldini, Alberto, 'L'incognita marrana: Ipotesi sulle origini familiari del gesuita Antonio Possevino (1533–1611)', www.upra.org/archivio_pdf/articolo uercastaldini

Cave, Terence, Michel Jeanneret and François Rigolot, 'Sur la prétendue transparence de Rabelais', *Revue d'histoire littéraire de la France*, 86 (1986), pp. 709–16

Cerquiglini, Bernard, *Éloge de la variante: Histoire critique de la philologie* (Paris: Seuil, 1989)

Cerquiglini-Toulet, Jacqueline, 'L'Imaginaire du livre à la fin du moyen âge: pratiques de lecture, théorie de l'écriture', *Modern Language Notes*, 108 (1993), pp. 680–95

Chang, Leah L., 'Clothing "Dame Helisenne": The staging of female authorship and the production of the 1538 *Angoysses douloureuses qui procedent d'amours*', *Romanic Review*, 92 (2001), pp. 381–403

Chang, Leah L., *Into Print: The Production of Female Authorship in Early Modern France* (Newark, DE: University of Delaware Press, 2009)

Charron, Pascale, 'Les réceptions du *Champion des dames* de Martin Le Franc à la cour de Bourgogne: "Tres puissant et tres humain prince … veullez cest livre humainement recepvoir"', *Bulletin du bibliophile*, 2000, pp. 9–31

Chartier, Roger, *L'Ordre des livres: Lecteurs, auteurs, bibliothèques en Europe entre XIVᵉ et XVIIIᵉ siècle* (Aix-en-Provence: Alinéa, 1992)

Chartier, Roger, *The Order of Books: Readers, Authors, and Libraries in Europe between the Fourteenth and Eighteenth Centuries*, trans. by Lydia G. Cochrane (Stanford, CA: Stanford University Press, 1994)

Chibi, Andrew, 'Richard Sampson, his "Oratio" and Henry VIII's Royal Supremacy', *Journal of Church and State*, 39 (1997), pp. 543–60

Christianson, Gerald, 'Annates and Reform at the Council of Basel', in *Reformation and Renewal in the Middle Ages and the Renaissance: Studies in Honor of Louis Pascoe, S.J.*, ed. by Thomas M. Izbicki and Christopher M. Bellitto (Leiden: Brill, 2000), pp. 193–209

Cohen, Derek, *Searching Shakespeare: Studies in Culture and Authority* (Toronto: University of Toronto Press, 2003)

Collard, Franck, 'Formes du récit et langue historique dans le *Compendium de origine et gestis Francorum* de Robert Gaguin', *Bibliothèque d'Humanisme et Renaissance*, 57 (1995), pp. 67–82

Collard, Franck, *Un historien au travail à la fin du XVe siècle: Robert Gaguin* (Geneva: Droz, 1996)

Collard, Franck, 'Paulus Aemilius', *De rebus gestis Francorum*: Diffusion und Rezeption eines humanistischen Geschichtswerks in Frankreich', in *Diffusion des Humanismus: Studien zur nationalen Geschichtsschreibung europäischer Humanisten*, ed. by Johannes Helmrath, Ulrich Muhlack and Gerrit Walther (Göttingen: Wallstein Verlag, 2002), pp. 377–97

Concilium Basiliense: Studien und Quellen zur Geschichte des Concils von Basel, ed. by Johannes Haller, 8 vols (Basel: 1896–1936)

Contamine, Philippe, 'Aperçus nouveaux sur *Toison d'or*, chroniqueur de la paix d'Arras (1435)', *Revue du nord*, 88 (2006), pp. 577–96

Copley Christie, Richard, *Étienne Dolet: The Martyr of the Renaissance: A Biography* (London: Macmillan, 1880)

Coupeau, J. Carlos, 'The constitutions of the Society of Jesus: The rhetorical component', *Studies in Spirituality*, 14 (2004), pp. 199–208

Dagenais, John, 'That bothersome residue: Toward a theory of the physical text', in *Vox intexta: Orality and Textuality in the Middle Ages*, ed. by A.N. Doane and Carol Braun Pasternack (Madison, WI: University of Wisconsin Press, 1991), pp. 246–59

Damler, Daniel, 'Pars pro toto. Die juristische Erfindung der Entdeckung Amerikas', *Zeitsprünge*, 10 (2006), pp. 424–71

D'Ascia, Luca, *Erasmo e l'umanesimo romano* (Florence: Olshki, 1991)

Defaux, Gérard, 'D'un problème l'autre: herméneutique de l'*altior sensus* et *captatio lectoris* dans le prologue de *Gangantua*', *Revue d'histoire littéraire de la France*, 85 (1985), pp. 195–216

Defaux, Gérard, 'Sur la prétendue pluralité du Prologue de *Gargantua*', *Revue d'histoire littéraire de la France*, 86 (1986), pp. 716–22

Desan, Philippe, 'Nationalism and history in France during the Renaissance', *Rinascimento*, 24 (1984), pp. 261–88

Devaux, Jean, *Jean Molinet, Indiciaire bourguignon* (Paris: Champion, 1996)

212   *Authority in European Book Culture 1400–1600*

Dickinson, Joycelyne Gledhill, *The Congress of Arras 1435: A Study in Medieval Diplomacy* (Oxford: Clarendon Press, 1955)

Donnelly, John, P., 'Antonio Possevino and Jesuits of Jewish ancestry,' *Archivum Historicum Societatis Iesu*, 109 (1986), pp. 3–29

Dufournet, Jean, 'Denis Sauvage et Commynes: La Première édition critique des *Mémoires*' in *Convergences médiévales: Épopée, lyrique, roman. Mélanges offerts à Madelaine Tyssens*, ed. by Nadine Henrard, Paola Moreno and Martine Thiry-Stassin (Paris: De Boeck, 2001)

Dunoyer, Emilio, *L''Enchiridion Confessariorum' del Navarro: Dissertatio ad lauream in Facultate S. Theologiae apud Pontificium Institutum 'Angelicum' de Urbe* (Pamplona: s. l., 1957)

Duval, Edwin, 'Interpretation and the "Doctrine absconce" of Rabelais's Prologue to *Gargantua*', *Etudes Rabelaisiennes*, 18 (1985), pp. 1–17

Duval, Frédéric, 'Le Livre des commentaires Cesar sur le fait des batailles de Gaule par Robert Gaguin (1485) ou de l'art de la transposition', *La Figure de Jules César au Moyen Âge et à la Renaissance* (= *Cahier de Recherches médiévales*), 13 (2006), pp. 167–82

Edwards, Mark U. Jr, *Luther and the False Brethren* (Palo Alto, CA: Stanford University Press, 1975)

Eisenhardt, Ulrich, *Der kaiserliche Aufsicht über Buchdruck, Buchhandel und Presse im Heiligen Römischen Reich Deutscher Nation (1496–1806.) Ein Beitrag zur Geschichte der Bücher und Pressezensur* (Karlsruhe: C.F. Müller, 1970)

Emerson, Catherine, 'Five centuries of Olivier de La Marche: The rhetoric of the *Mémoires* in the hands of scribes, editors and translators', *Revue belge de philologie et d'histoire*, 83 (2005), pp. 1103–31

Fahy, Conor, *L''Orlando furioso' del 1532: Profilo di una edizione* (Milan: Vita e Pensiero, 1989)

Fish, Stanley, *Is There a Text in This Class? The Authority of Interpretive Communities* (Cambridge, MA: Harvard University Press, 1980)

Fosi, Irene, 'Court and city in the ceremony of the *Possesso*', in *Court and Politics in Papal Rome (1492–1700)*, ed. by Gianvittorio Signorotto and Maria Antonietta Visceglia (Cambridge: Cambridge University Press, 2002), pp. 31–52

Foucault, Michel, *Discipline and Punish*, trans. by Alan Sheridan (Harmondsworth: Penguin, 1979)

Foucault, Michel, *History of Sexuality*, I, trans. by Robert Hurley (Harmondsworth: Penguin, 1981)

Foucault, Michel, 'What is an author?', in *The Foucault Reader*, ed. by Paul Rabinow (Harmondsworth: Penguin, 1984), pp. 101–20

Frati, Luigi, *Delle monete gettate al popolo nel solenne ingresso in Bologna di Giulio II per la cacciata di Giovanni II Bentivoglio*, Estratto dagli Atti e memorie della R. Deputazione di storia patria per le provincie di Romagna, III serie, I, fasc. VI (Modena: Tipografia Vincenzi, 1883), pp. 1–15

Friedeburg, Robert von, *Self-Defence and Religious Strife in Early Modern Europe: England and Germany, 1530–1680* (Aldershot: Ashgate, 2002)

Friedeburg, Robert von, 'Magdeburger Argumentationen zum Recht auf Widerstand gegen die Durchsetzung des Interims (1550–1551) und ihre Stellung in der Geschichte des Widerstandsrechts im Reich, 1523–1626', in *Das Interim 1548/50*, ed. by Luise Schorn-Schütte (Heidelberg: Hubert & Co., 2005), pp. 389–437

Freeman Regalado, Nancy, 'Gathering the works: The *Oeuvres de Villon* and the intergeneric passage of the Medieval French lyric into single-author collections', *L'Esprit Créateur*, 33 (1993), pp. 87–100

Geck, Elisabeth, *Buchkundlicher Exkurs zu Herzog Ernst, Sankt Brandans Meerfahrt, Hans Schiltbergers Reisebuch* (Wiesbaden: Guido Pressler, 1969)

Geldner, Ferdinand, 'Bemerkungen zum Text des "Türkenschreis" von Balthasar Mandelreiß, des "Türkenkalenders" (1454) und der "Ermanung … wider die Türken" von Niclas Wolgemut', *Gutenberg-Jahrbuch 1983* (1983), pp. 166–71

Genette, Gérard, *Paratexts: Thresholds of Interpretation*, trans. by Jane E. Lewin (Cambridge: Cambridge University Press, 2001)

Göllner, Carl, *Turcica: die Europäischen Türkendrucke des 16. Jahrhunderts*, 3 vols (Berlin: Editura Academei and Akademie Verlag, 1961–78)

Gombrich, Ernest H., 'Renaissance and the Golden Age', *Journal of the Warburg and Courtauld Institutes*, 24 (1961), pp. 306–9

Grafton, Anthony, *Forgers and Critics: Creativity and Duplicity in Western Scholarship* (London: Collins & Brown, 1990)

Grafton, Anthony, 'Invention of traditions and tradition of invention in Renaissance Europe: The strange case of Annius of Viterbo', in *The Transmission of Culture in Early Modern Europe*, ed. by Anthony Grafton and Ann Blair (Philadelphia, PA: University of Pennsylvania Press, 1990), pp. 8–38

Greenblatt, Stephen Jay, *Marvelous Possessions: The Wonder of the New World* (Chicago, IL: University of Chicago Press, 1993)

Guy, John A., 'Thomas Cromwell and the intellectual origins of the Henrician revolution', in *Reassessing the Henrician Age: Humanism, Politics and Reform*, ed. by Alistair Fox and John A. Guy (Oxford: Oxford University Press, 1986), pp. 151–78

Gwynne, Paul, '*Tu Alter Caesar eris*: Maximilian I, Vladislav II, Johannes Michael Nagonius and the *Renovatio Imperii*', *Renaissance Studies*, 10 (1996), pp. 56–71

Haas, Steven W., 'Henry VIII's *Glasse of Truthe*', *History*, 64 (1979), pp. 353–62

Habermas, Jürgen, *The Structural Transformation of the Public Sphere: An Inquiry into a category of Bourgeois Society* (Cambridge: Polity Press, 1989)

Harris, Neil, 'Nicolò Garanta editore a Venezia 1525–30', *La Bibliofilìa*, 97 (1995), pp. 99–148

Heal, Felicity, 'What can King Lucius do for you? The Reformation and the Early British Church', *English Historical Review*, 120 (2005), pp. 593–614

Heitsch, Dorothea, 'Female love-melancholy in Hélisenne de Crenne's *Les Angoysses douloureuses qui procedent d'amours* (1538)', *Renaissance Studies*, 23 (2009), pp. 335–53

Helmrath, Johannes, Ulrich Muhlack and Gerrit Walther, eds, *Diffusion des Humanismus. Studien zur nationalen Geschichtsschreibung europäischer Humanisten* (Göttingen: Wallstein Verlag, 2002)

Helmrath, Johannes, 'Probleme und Formen nationaler und regionaler Historiographie des deutschen und europäischen Humanismus um 1500', in *Spätmittelalterliches Landesbewußtsein in Deutschland*, ed. by Matthias Werner, Vorträge und Forschungen, 61 (Stuttgart: Thorbecke, 2005), pp. 333–92

Higgins, Ian Macleod, *Writing East: The 'Travels' of Sir John Mandeville* (Philadelphia, PA: University of Pennsylvania Press, 1997)

Hirschi, Caspar, *Wettkampf der Nationen: Konstruktionen einer deutschen Ehrgemeinschaft an der Wende vom Mittelalter zur Neuzeit* (Göttingen: Wallstein Verlag, 2005)

Hodges, Elisabeth, 'Hélisenne's purloined letters', *French Forum*, 30 (2005), pp. 1–16

Housley, Norman, *Religious Warfare in Europe, 1400–1536* (Oxford: Oxford University Press, 2002)

Huesmann, Jutta, 'Hospitality at the Court of Philippe le Bon, Duke of Burgundy (c.1435–67)' (Oxford: unpublished DPhil thesis, 2001)

Hulße, Friedrich, 'Die Einführung der Reformation in der Stadt Magdeburg', *Geschichts-blätter für Stadt und Land Magdeburg*, 18 (1883), pp. 209–369

Huot, Sylvia, *The 'Romance of the Rose' and its Medieval Readers: Interpretation, Reception, Manuscript Transmission* (Cambridge: Cambridge University Press, 1993)

Hurbult, Jesse, 'The city renewed: Decorations for the *joyeuses entrées* of Philip the Good and Charles the Bold', *Fifteenth Century Studies*, 19 (1992), pp. 73–84

Index des livres interdits, ed. by J. M. Bujanda, 11 vols (Geneva: Droz, 1985–2002)

Izbicki, Thomas, *Reform, Eccesiology, and the Christian Life in the Late Middle Ages* (Aldershot: Ashgate, 2008)

Jauss, Hans R., 'Literary history as a challenge literary theory', *New Literary History*, 2.1 (1970), pp. 7–37

Jedin, Hubert, *History of the Council of Trent*, 4 vols (London: Nelson, 1957)

Jones, Ann Rosalind, *The Currency of Eros: Women's Love Lyric in Europe, 1540–1620* (Bloomington, IN: Indiana University Press, 2000)

Jonsen, Albert and Stephen Toulmin, *The Abuse of Casuistry: A History of Moral Theology* (Berkeley, CA: University of California Press, 1988)

Jouhaud, Christian, 'Nota sui manifesti e i loro lettori (secoli XVI–XVII)', *Annali della Scuola Normale Superiore di Pisa*, 23 (1993), pp. 411–26

Jung, Marc-René, 'Situation de Martin Le Franc', in *Pratiques de la culture écrite en France au XVᵉ siècle*, ed. by Monique Ornato and Nicole Pons (Louvain-la-Neuve: Fédération internationale des instituts d'études médiévales, 1995), pp. 13–30

Kastner, Ruth, *Geistlicher Rauffhandel: Illustrierte Flugblätter zum Reformationsjubiläum 1617* (Frankfurt am Main: Peter Lang, 1982)

Kaufmann, Thomas, *Das Ende der Reformation: Magdeburgs 'Herrgotts Kanzlei' (1548–1551/2)* (Tübingen: Mohr Siebeck, 2003)

Kawerau, Gustav, *Johann Agricola von Eisleben* (Berlin: Hertz, 1881)

Kawerau, Waldemar, 'Erasmus Alber in Magdeburg', *Geschichts-blätter für Stadt und Land Magdeburg* 28 (1893), pp. 1–62

Kay, Sarah, *The Place of Thought: The Complexity of One in Late Medieval French Didactic Poetry* (Philadelphia, PA: University of Pennsylvania Press, 2007)

Kayser Werner and Claus Dehn, *Bibliographie der Hamburger Drucke des 16. Jahrhunderts* (Hamburg: Hauswedell, 1968)

Keenan, James F., 'The birth of Jesuit Casuistry: *Summa casuum conscientiae sive de instructione sacerdotum, libri septem*, by Francisco de Toledo (1532–1596),' in *The Mercurian Project: Forming Jesuit Culture 1573–1580*, ed. by Thomas M. McCoog (Rome: Institutum Historicum Societatis Iesu, 2004), pp. 461–82

Kempers, Bram, 'Julius inter laudem et vituperationem: Ein Papst unter gegensätzlichen Gesichtspunkten betrachtet', in *Hoch-renaissance im Vatikan. Kunst und Kultur im Rom der Päpste I (1503–1534)*, ed. by Petra Kruse (Città del Vaticano: Biblioteca Apostolica Vaticana, 1999), pp. 15–29

Kennedy, Elspeth, 'The scribe as editor', in *Mélanges de langue et de littérature du Moyen Age et de la Renaissance offerts à Jean Frappier*, 2 vols (Geneva: Droz, 1970)

Kent, Dale V., *Cosimo de' Medici and the Florentine Renaissance: The Patron's Oeuvre* (New Haven, CT: Yale University Press, 2000)

Kerheve, Jean, 'Aux origines d'un sentiment national: Les chroniques bretons de la fin du Moyen Age', *Bulletin de la Societe Archéologique du Finistere*, 108 (1980), pp. 165–206

Kersken, Norbert,'Aspekte des preußischen Geschichtsdenkens im 16. Jahrhundert', in *Preußische Landesgeschichte: Festschrift für Bernhard Jähnig zum 60. Geburtstag*, ed. by Udo Arnold, Mario Glauert and Jürgen Sarnowsky, Einzelschriften der Historischen Kommission für ost- und westpreußische Landesforschung (Marburg: N.G. Elwart Verlag, 2001), pp. 439–56

King, John N., *Tudor Royal Iconography: Literature and Art in an Age of Religious Crisis* (Princeton, NJ: Princeton University Press, 1989)

Kingdon, Robert, 'The political resistance of the Calvinists in France and the Low Countries', *Church History*, 27 (1958), pp. 200–233

Klecker, Elisabeth,'Extant adhuc in Pannonia monumenta Severi: Historia-Augusta-Rezeption und humanistisches Selbstverständnis in Cuspinians Caesares', in *Medien und Sprachen humanistischer Geschichtsschreibung*, ed. by Johannes Helmrath, Albert Schirrmeister and Stefan Schlelein, Transformationen der Antike, 11 (Berlin: de Gruyter, 2009), pp. 77–98.

Klein, Andrea, *Der Literaturbetrieb am Münchner Hof im fünfzehnten Jahrhundert* (Göppingen: Kümmerle, 1998)

Kohl, Benjamin G., ed., *The Earthly Republic: Italian Humanists on Government and Society* (Manchester: Manchester University Press, 1978)

Körner, Emil, *Erasmus Alber: Das Kämpferleben eines Gottesgelehrten aus Luthers Schule* (Leipzig: Heinsius, 1910)

Kühlmann, Wilhelm, 'Magdeburg in der Zeitgeschichtlichen Verspublizistik (1551/1631)', in *Prolegomena zur Kultur- und Literaturgeschichte des Magdeburger Raumes*, ed. by Gunter Schandera and Michael Schilling in association with Dieter Schade (Magdeburg: Scriptum, 1999), pp. 79–106

Kümin, Beat, *Political Space in Pre-industrial Europe* (Aldershot: Ashgate, 2009)

Laidlaw, James C., 'Christine de Pizan – a publisher's progress', *Modern Language Review*, 82 (1987), pp. 35–75

Laidlaw, James C. et al., *Christine de Pizan: The Making of the Queen's Manuscript (London, British Library, Harley MS 4431)*, http://www.pizan.lib.ed.ac.uk, accessed 2 August 2010

Landi, Sandro, *Naissance de l'opinion publique dans l'Italie moderne: Sagesse du peuple et savoir de gouvernement de Machiavel aux Lumières* (Rennes: Presses Universitaires de Rennes, 2006)

Larsen, Anne, '"Un honneste passetems": Strategies of legitimation in French Renaissance women's prefaces', *Esprit Créateur*, 30 (1990), pp. 11–22

Leppin, Volker, Georg Schmidt and Sabine Wefers, eds, *Johann Friedrich I. – der lutherische Kurfürst* (Heidelberg: Gütersloher Verlagshaus, 2006)

Losse, Deborah N., *Sampling the Book: Renaissance Prologues and the French Conteurs* (Lewisburg: Bucknell University Press, 1994)

Love, Harold, *The Culture and Commerce of Texts: Scribal Publication in Seventeenth-century England* (Amherst, MA: University of Massachusetts Press, 1998)

MacMahon, Luke, 'The ambassadors of Henry VIII, the personnel of English diplomacy, 1500–1550' (unpublished doctoral thesis, University of Kent, 2000)

McEntegart, Rory, *Henry VIII, the League of Schmalkalden and the English Reformation* (Chippenham: Boydell Press, 2002)

McGrady, Deborah, *Controlling Readers: Guillaume de Machaut and His Late Medieval Audience* (Toronto: University of Toronto Press, 2006)

McKendrick, Scot, 'Reviving the past: Illustrated manuscripts of secular vernacular texts, 1476–1500', in *Illuminating the Renaissance: The Triumph of Flemish Manuscript Painting in Europe*, ed. by Thomas Kren and Scot McKendrick (Los Angeles, CA: J. Paul Getty Museum, 2003), pp. 59–78

McKenzie, Don F., *Bibliography and the Sociology of Texts* (London: British Library, 1986)

Martin Henri-Jean and Jean-Marc Chatelain, *La Naissance du livre moderne (XIVᵉ–XVIIᵉ siècles): Mise en page et mise en texte du livre français* (Paris: Éditions du Cercle de la Librairie, 2000)

Martines, Lauro, *Strong Words: Writing and Social Strain in the Italian Renaissance* (Baltimore, MD: John Hopkins University Press, 2001)

Maryks, Robert A., 'Census of the books written by Jesuits on sacramental confession (1554–1650)', *Annali di Storia moderna e contemporanea*, 10 (2004), pp. [415]–519

Maryks, Robert A., Review of Gonçalves da Câmara, *Remembering Iñigo. Glimpses on the Life of Saint Ignatius of Loyola. The 'Memoriale' of Luís Gonçalves da Câmara.* Trans. with introduction, notes and indices by Alexander Eaglestone and Joseph A. Munitiz, S.J. (St Louis, MO: Institute of Jesuit Sources, 2004), *The Sixteenth Century Journal* 37 (2006), pp. 856–7.

Maryks, Robert A., Review of Vincenzo Lavenia, *L'infamia e il perdono: Tributi, pene e confessione nella teologia morale della prima età moderna* (Bologna: Società editrice il Mulino, 2004), *The Sixteenth Century Journal* 38 (2007), pp. 844–5

Maryks, Robert A., 'The Jesuit Order as a "Synagogue of Jews": discrimination of Jesuits of Jewish ancestry in the early Society of Jesus,' *Archivum Historicum Societatis Iesu*, 78 (2009), pp. 339–416

Maryks, Robert A., *The Jesuit Order as a "Synagogue of Jews": Jesuits of Jewish Ancestry and Purity-of-Blood Laws in the Early Society of Jesus* (Leiden: Brill Academic, 2009)

Mattingly, Garrett, *Renaissance Diplomacy* (New York: Dover, 1988)

Mayer, Thomas F., *A Reluctant Author: Cardinal Pole and his Manuscripts* (Philadelphia, PA: American Philosophical Society, 1999)

Mayer, Thomas F., *Reginald Pole, Prince and Prophet* (Cambridge: Cambridge University Press, 2000)

Medick, Hans, 'Historisches Ereignis und zeitgenössische Erfahrung: Die Eroberung und Zerstörung Magdeburgs 1631', in *Zwischen Alltag und Katastrophe: Der Dreissigjährige Krieg aus der Nähe*, ed. by Hans Medick and Benigna von Krusenstjern (Göttigen: Vandenhoeck und Ruprecht, 1999), pp. 307–407

Medin, Antonio and Luigi Frati, eds, *Lamenti storici dei secoli XIV, XV, XVI*, 3 vols (Bologna: Romagnoli, 1969)

Melville, Gert, 'Die Wahrheit des Eigenen und die Wirklichkeit des Fremden: Über frühe Augenzeugen des osmanischen Reiches', in *Europa und die osmanische Expansion im ausgehenden Mittelalter*, ed. by Franz-Reiner Erkens (Berlin: Duncker & Humblot, 1997), pp. 79–101

Merkle, Gertrude H., 'Martin Le Franc's commentary on Jean Gerson's Treatise on Joan of Arc', in *Fresh Verdicts on Joan of Arc*, ed. by Bonnie Wheeler and Charles T. Wood (New York: Garland, 1996), pp. 177–88

Mertens, Dieter, 'Landeschronistik im Zeitalter des Humanismus und ihre spätmittelalterlichen Wurzeln', in *Deutsche Landesgeschichtsschreibung im Zeichen des Humanismus*, ed. by Franz Brendle et al. (Stuttgart: Steiner, 2001)

Mertens, Dieter, 'Die Instrumentalisierung der "Germania" des Tacitus durch die deutschen Humanisten', in *Zur Geschichte der Gleichung 'germanisch-*

deutsch': *Sprache und Namen, Geschichte und Institutionen*, ed. by Heinrich Beck (Berlin: De Gruyter, 2004), pp. 37–101

Meserve, Margaret, 'The news from Negroponte: Politics, popular opinion and information exchange in the first decade of the Italian press', *Renaissance Quarterly*, 59 (2006), pp. 440–80

Minnich, Nelson H., *Councils of the Catholic Reformation: Pisa I (1409) to Trent (1545–63)* (Aldershot: Ashgate, 2008)

Minnis, Alistair, J., *Medieval Theory of Authorship: Scholastic Literary Attitudes in the Later Middle Ages* (London: Scolar Press, 1984)

Miskimin, Alice, *The Renaissance Chaucer* (New Haven, CT: Yale University Press, 1975)

Moorhead, John, *Ambrose: Church and Society in the Late Roman World* (London: Longman, 1999)

Mortimer, Ruth, 'The author's image: Italian sixteenth-century printed portraits', *Harvard Library Bulletin*, n. s. 7, no. 2 (Summer 1996), pp. 1–87

Moss, Ann, *Ovid in Renaissance France: A Survey of the Latin Editions of Ovid and Commentaries Printed in France before 1600* (London: Warburg Institute, 1982)

Müller, Heribert, '"Et sembloit qu'on oÿst parler un angele de dieu": Thomas de Courcelles et le Concile de Bâle ou le secret d'une belle réussite', in *Académie des inscriptions et belles-lettres: comptes-rendus des séances*, 1 (2003), pp. 461–84

Müller, Klaus E., *Geschichte der antiken Ethnographie und ethnologischen Theoriebildung: Von den Anfängen bis auf die byzantinischen Historiographen*, 2 vols, Studien zur Kulturkunde, 29 and 52 (Wiesbaden: Steiner, 1972/1980)

Murphy, Virginia, 'The literature and propaganda of Henry VIII's first divorce', in *The Reign of Henry VIII: Politics, Policy and Piety*, ed. by Diarmaid MacCulloch (London: Macmillan, 1995), pp. 135–58

Niccoli, Ottavia, *Rinascimento anticlericale: Infamia, propaganda e satira in Italia tra Quattrocento e Cinquecento* (Rome-Bari: Laterza, 2005)

Niederkorn, Jan Paul, *Die europäischen Mächte und der 'Lange Türkenkrieg' Kaiser Rudolfs II* (Vienna: Akademie der Wissenschaften, 1993)

Noakes, Susan, 'The book market in Quattrocento Italy', *The Journal of Medieval and Renaissance Studies*, 11 (1981), pp. 23–55

Nuovo, Angela and Christian Coppens, *I Giolito e la stampa nell'Italia del XVI secolo* (Geneva: Droz, 2005)

Offenstadt, Nicolas, *Faire la paix au moyen âge: discours et gestes de paix pendant la guerre des cent ans* (Paris: Odile Jacob, 2007)

Oliver K. Olson, 'Theology of revolution', *Sixteenth Century Journal*, 3 (1972), pp. 56–79

Oliver K. Olson, *Matthias Flacius and the survival of Luther's reform* (Wiesbaden: Harrassowitz, 2002)

O'Malley, John W., 'Fulfillment of the Christian Golden Age under Julius II: Text of a discourse of Giles of Viterbo, 1507', *Traditio*, 25 (1969), pp. 265–338

O'Malley, John W., *Praise and Blame in Renaissance Rome: Rhetoric, Doctrine, and Reform in the Sacred Orators of the Papal Court, c. 1450–1521* (Durham, NC: Duke University Press, 1979)

O'Neill, Charles E. and Joaquin M. Dominguez, eds, *Diccionario Histórico de la Compañía de Jesús: Biográfico-Temático*, 4 vols (Rome: Institutum Historicum Societatis Iesu, 2001)

Padberg, John W., Martin D. O'Keefe and John L. McCarthy, eds, *For Matters of Greater Moment: The First Thirty Jesuit General Congregations: A Brief History and a Translation of the Decrees* (St Louis, MO: The Institute of Jesuit Sources, 1994)

Palmer, Martin E., ed., *On Giving the Spiritual Exercises: The Early Jesuit Manuscript Directories and the Official Directory of 1599* (St Louis, MO: The Institute of Jesuit Sources, 1996)

Peterson, Luther David, *The Philippist Theologians and the Interims of 1548: Soteriological, Ecclesiastical, and Liturgical Compromises and Controversies within German Lutheranism* (Unpublished doctoral dissertation, University of Wisconsin, 1974)

Petrucci, Armando, *Writers and Readers in Medieval Italy: Studies in the History of Written Culture*, ed. and trans. by Charles M. Radding (New Haven, CT: Yale University Press, 1995)

Pohlig, Matthias, *Zwischen Gelehrsamkeit und konfessioneller Identitätsstiftung: Lutherische Kirchen- und Universalgeschichtsschreibung 1546–1617*, Spätmittelalter und Reformation, Neue Reihe, 37 (Tübingen: Mohr Siebeck, 2007)

Premoli, Orazio, *Fra' Battista da Crema secondo documenti inediti: contributo alla storia religiosa del secolo XVI* (Rome: Desclée, 1910)

Prosperi, Adriano, 'Opere inedite o sconosciute di Giorgio Siculo', *La Bibliofilìa*, 87 (1985), pp. 137–57

Prosperi, Adriano, *L'eresia del Libro Grande: storia di Giorgio Siculo e della sua setta* (Milan: Feltrinelli, 2000)

Prodi, Paolo, *The Papal Prince. One Body and Two Souls: the Papal Monarchy in Early Modern Europe* (Cambridge: Cambridge University Press, 1988)

Quondam, Amedeo, and others, eds, *Guerre in ottava rima*, 4 vols (Modena: Panini, 1989)

Rabil, Albert, *Renaissance Humanism*, 3 vols (Philadelphia, PA: University of Pennsylvania Press, 1988)

Randall, Michael, 'On the evolution of toads in the French Renaissance', *Renaissance Quarterly*, 57 (2004), pp. 126–64

La 'Ratio studiorum': Modelli culturali e pratiche educative dei Gesuiti in Italia tra Cinque e Seicento, ed. by Gian Paolo Brizzi (Rome: Bulzoni Editore, 1981)

Rawles, Stephen P.J., 'Denis Janot, Parisian printer and bookseller (fl. 1529–1544): A bibliographical study' (unpublished doctoral thesis, University of Warwick, 1976)

Reeves, Jesse S., 'Étienne Dolet on the functions of the ambassador, 1541', *The American Journal of International Law*, 27 (1933), pp. 81–95

Rein, Nathan, *The Chancery of God: Protestant Print, Polemic and Propaganda against the Empire, Magdeburg 1546–1551*(Aldershot: Ashgate, 2008)

Reynolds, Suzanne, 'Inventing authority: Glossing, literacy and the Classical text', in *Prestige, Authority and Power in Late Medieval Manuscripts and Texts*, ed. by Felicity Riddy (Woodbridge: York Medieval Press, 2000), pp. 7–16

Rex, Richard, 'The English campaign against Luther in the 1520s', *Transactions of the Royal Historical Society*, 5th series, 38 (1989), pp. 85–106

Rex, Richard, 'Crisis of obedience: God's Word and Henry's Reformation', *Historical Journal*, 39 (1996), pp. 863–9

Rex, Richard, 'Redating Henry VIII's *A Glass of the Truthe*', *The Library*, 7th series, 4 (2003), pp. 16–27

Richardson, Brian, *Print Culture in Renaissance Italy: The Editor and the Vernacular Text, 1470–1600* (Cambridge: Cambridge University Press, 1994)

Richardson, Brian, *Manuscript Culture in Renaissance Italy* (Cambridge: Cambridge University Press, 2009)

Richardson, Brian, 'Autografia e pubblicazione manoscritta nel Rinascimento', in *'Di mano propria': gli autografi dei letterati italiani. Atti del Convegno internazionale di Forlì, 24–27 novembre 2008*, ed. by Guido Baldassarri and others (Rome: Salerno Editrice, 2010), pp. 269–85

Rigolot, François, 'La Préface à la Renaissance: Un discours sexué?', *Cahiers de L'Association internationale des études françaises*, 42 (1990), pp. 121–35

Robin, Diana, *Publishing Women: Salons, the Presses and the Counter-Reformation in Sixteenth-Century Italy* (Chicago, IL: University of Chicago Press, 2007)

Rospocher, Massimo, 'Propaganda e opinione pubblica: Giulio II nella comunicazione politica europea', *Annali dell'Istituto Storico Italo-Germanico*, 33 (2007), pp. 59–99

Rospocher, Massimo, 'Stampe e versi pericolosi: Controllo delle opinioni e ricerca del consenso durante le guerre d'Italia', in *From Florence to the Mediterranean and Beyond: Essays in Honour of Tony Molho*, ed. by Diogo Curto et al. (Florence: Olschki, 2009), pp. 381–407

Rospocher, Massimo, 'La Poesía como lenguaje de comunicación política en los espacios públicos de las ciudades italianas del Renacimiento', in *Opinión pública y espacio urbano en la Edad Moderna*, ed. by James Amelang and Antonio Castillo Gómez (Gijón: Trea, 2010), pp. 185–210

Rospocher, Massimo, '"Il passatempo del giardiniere": La giusta guerra di Enrico VIII in difesa della Chiesa cattolica,' in *Famiglia e religione nella prima età moderna. Saggi in onore di Silvana Seidel Menchi*, ed. by Giovanni Ciappelli, Serena Luzzi and Massimo Rospocher (Rome: Edizioni di Storia e Letteratura, 2011), pp. 29–44.

Rospocher, Massimo and Rosa Salzberg, 'Street singers in Italian Renaissance urban culture and communication', *Cultural and Social History*, 9 (2012), pp. 9–26

Rospocher, Massimo (ed.), *Beyond the Public Sphere: Opinions, Publics, Spaces in Early Modern Europe* (Berlin/Bologna: Dunker & Humblot/Il Mulino, 2012)

Rossi, Antonio, *Serafino Aquilano e la poesia cortigiana* (Brescia: Morcelliana, 1980)

Rowland, Ingrid D., *The Culture of the High Renaissance: Ancients and Moderns in Sixteenth-century Rome* (Cambridge: Cambridge University Press, 1998)

Russell, Joycelyne G., *Diplomats at Work: Three Renaissance Studies* (Stroud: Sutton Publishing, 1992)

Salzberg, Rosa, 'In the Mouths of Charlatans. Street Performers and the Dissemination of Pamphlets in Renaissance Italy', *Renaissance Studies*, 24 (2010), pp. 638–53

Scaduto, Mario, *L'epoca di Giacomo Laínez. L'azione* (Rome: Civiltà Cattolica, 1966)

Scaduto, Mario, *L'epoca di Giacomo Laínez: Il governo* (Rome: Civiltà Cattolica, 1974)

Schiewer, Hans-Jochen, 'Leben unter Heiden: Hans Schiltbergers türkische und tartarische Erfahrungen', *Daphnis: Zeitschrift für mittlere deutsche Literatur*, 21 (1992), pp. 159–78

Schirrmeister, Albert, *Triumph des Dichters: Gekrönte Intellektuelle im 16. Jahrhundert, Frühneuzeitstudien, NF 4* (Cologne: Böhlau, 2003)

Schoenborn, Hans Joachim, *Lebensgeschichte und Geschichtsschreibung des Erasmus Stella: Ein Beitrag zur Geschichte des gelehrten Fälschertums im 16. Jahrhundert* (Düsseldorf: Nolte, 1938)

Schottenloher, Karl, 'Der Augsburger Winkeldrucker Hans Gegler: Ein Beitrag zur Schwenckfeld-Bibliographie', *Gutenberg Jahrbuch*, 14 (1939), pp. 233–42

Scribner, Robert W., *Popular Culture and Popular Movements in Reformation Germany* (London: Continuum, 1983)

Scribner, Robert W., *For the Sake of Simple Folk: Popular Propaganda for the German Reformation*, 2nd edn (Oxford: Clarendon Press, 1994)

Sharpe, Kevin, *Reading Revolutions: The Politics of Reading in Early Modern England* (New Haven, CT: Yale University Press, 2000)

Shaw, Christine, *Julius II: The Warrior Pope* (Cambridge: Blackwell 1993)

Sherman, Michael A., 'The selling of Louis XII: Propaganda and popular culture in Renaissance France, 1498–1515' (unpublished doctoral thesis, University of Chicago, 1974)

Sherman, Michael A., 'Political propaganda and Renaissance culture: French reactions to the League of Cambrai, 1509–1510', *The Sixteenth Century Journal*, 8 (1977), Supplement, pp. 97–128

Société Intérnationale pour l'Etude des Femmes de l'Ancien Régime, *Louise attaquée: Louise Labé est-elle une créature de papier?* <http://www.siefar.org/debats/louise-labe.html?lang=fr&li=art25> [accessed 17 February 2012].

Sniader Lanser, Susan, *Fictions of Authority: Women Writers and Narrative Voice* (Ithaca, NY: Cornell University Press, 1992)

Sommé, Monique, *Isabel de Portugal, duchesse de Bourgogne: Une femme au pouvoir au quinzième siècle* (Villeneuve d'Ascq: Presses universitaires du Septentrion, 1998)

Sowerby, Tracey A., '"All our books do be sent abroad and translated": Henrician Polemic in its international context', *English Historical Review*, 121 (2006), pp. 1271–99

Speer, Mary B., 'The editorial tradition of Villon's *Testament*: From Marot to Rychner and Henry', *Romance Philology*, 31 (1977), pp. 344–61

Spitz, Lewis W., 'The course of German Humanism', in *Itinerarium Italicum: The Profile of the Italian Renaissance in the Mirror of its European Transformations. Dedicated to Paul Oskar Kristeller on the Occasion of his 70th birthday*, ed. by Heiko A. Oberman and Thomas A. Brady Jr (Leiden: Brill, 1975), pp. 371–436

Spitzbarth, Anne-Brigitte, 'De la vassalité à la sujétion: l'application du traité d'Arras (21 septembre 1435) par la couronne', *Revue du nord* 85 (2003), pp. 43–72

Stein, Henri, *Olivier de la Marche: Historien, poète et diplomate bourguignon* (Brussels: Hayez, 1888)

Stieber, Joachim W., *Pope Eugenius IV, the Council of Basel and the Secular and Ecclesiastical Authorities in the Empire: The Conflict over Supreme Authority and Power in the Church* (Leiden: Brill, 1978)

Stinger, Charles L., *The Renaissance in Rome* (Bloomington, IN: Indiana University Press, 1998)

Stupperich, Robert, 'Die Eigenart der Reformation in der Mark Brandenburg', in *'Dem Wort nicht entgegen...': Aspekte der Reformation in der Mark Brandenburg*, ed. by Hans-Ulrich Delius, Max-Ottokar Kunzendorf and Friedrich Winter (Berlin: Evangelische Verlagsanstalt, 1988)

Süßmann, Johannes, Susanne Scholz and Gisela Engel, eds, *Fallstudien: Theorie—Geschichte—Methode*, Frankfurter kulturwissenschaftliche Beiträge, 1 (Berlin: trafo Verlag, 2007)

Swift, Helen J., 'Martin Le Franc et son livre qui se plaint: une petite énigme à la cour de Philippe le Bon', in *L'écrit et le manuscrit à la fin du moyen âge*, ed. by Tania Van Hemelryck and Céline Van Hoorebeeck (Turnhout: Brepols, 2006), pp. 329–42

Swift, Helen J., *Gender, Writing and Performance: Men Defending Women in Late Medieval France* (Oxford: Oxford University Press, 2008)

Swift, Helen J., '"Des circuits de pouvoir": un modèle pour la relecture des rapports poète-mécène dans les apologies du sexe féminin de la fin du moyen âge', *Études françaises*, 47 (2011), pp. 55–69

Toschi, Paolo, *Stampe popolari italiane* (Milan: Electa, 1964)

Toussaint, Joseph, *Les relations diplomatiques de Philippe le Bon avec le Concile de Bâle (1431–1449)* (Louvain: Bibliothèque de l'Université, 1942)

Tzanaki, Rosemary, *Mandeville's Medieval Audiences: A Study in the Reception of the 'Book' of Sir John Mandeville* (Aldershot: Ashgate, 2003)

Vale, Malcolm, 'France at the end of the Hundred Years' War (*c.* 1420–1461)', in *The New Cambridge Medieval History, Volume VII c. 1415–c. 1500*, ed. by Christopher Allmand (Cambridge: Cambridge University Press, 1998), pp. 397–403

Vaughan, Richard, *Philip the Good: The Apogee of Burgundy* (Harlow: Longmans, 1970; repr. Woodbridge: Boydell, 2002)

Vereecke, Louis, *Da Guglielmo d'Ockham a sant'Alfonso Liguori: Saggi di storia della teologia morale moderna 1300–1787* (Cinisello Balsamo: Edizioni Paoline, 1990)

Verzeichnis der im deutschen Sprachberich erschienenen Drücke des XVI. Jahrhunderts (Stuttgart: Hiersemann, 1983)

Vian, Nello, 'Le Presentazione e gli esemplari vaticani della "Assertio Septem Sacramentorum" di Enrico VIII', *Studi e Testi*, 120 (1962), pp. 355–75

Völkel, Markus, 'Wie man Kirchengeschichte schreiben soll. Struktur und Erzählung als konkurrierende Modelle der Kirchengeschichtsschreibung im konfessionellen Zeitalter', in *Die Autorität der Zeit in der Frühen Neuzeit*, ed. by Arndt Brendecke, Ralf-Peter Fuchs and Edith Koller, Pluralisierung & Autorität, 10 (Berlin: LIT Verlag 2007), pp. 455–89

Walker, D. P., *Spiritual & Demonic Magic: From Ficino to Campanella* (University Park, PA: Pennsylvania State University Press, 2000)

Warner, Mark, 'The Anglo-French dual monarchy and the House of Burgundy, 1420–1435: The survival of an alliance', *French History* 11 (1997), pp. 103–30

Weber, Max, *Economy and Society: An Outline of Interpretive Sociology* (Berkeley, CA: University of Calfornia Press, 1978)

Weiss, Roberto, 'The medals of Pope Julius II (1503–1513)', *Journal of the Warburg and Courtauld Institutes*, 28 (1965), pp. 163–82

Wengert, Timothy J., *Law and Gospel: Philip Melanchthon's Dispute with John Agricola of Eisleben over Poenitentia* (Carlisle: Baker Academic, 1997)

Whitford, David M., *Tyranny and Resistance: The Magdeburg Confession and the Lutheran Tradition* (St Louis, MO: Concordia, 2001)

Winn, Colette H., 'La Symbolique du regard dans *Les Angoysses douloureuses qui procèdent d'amours* d'Hélisenne de Crenne', *Orbis Litterarum*, 40 (1985), pp. 207–21

Winn, Mary Beth, *Anthoine Vérard, Parisian Publisher, 1485–1512: Prologues, Poems, and Presentations* (Geneva: Droz, 1997)

Wittchow, Frank, 'Von Fabius Pictor zu Polydorus Vergil: Zur Transformation narrativer Modelle der antiken römischen Geschichtsschreibung in der Humanistenhistorie', in *Medien und Sprachen humanistischer Geschichtsschreibung*, ed. by Johannes Helmrath, Albert Schirrmeister and Stefan Schlelein, Transformationen der Antike, 11 (Berlin: de Gruyter, 2009), pp. 47–76

Wolgast, Eike, *Die Religionsfrage als Problem des Widerstandsrechts im 16. Jahrhundert* (Heidelberg: Winter, 1980)

Wood, Diane S. *Hélisenne de Crenne: At the Crossroads of Renaissance Humanism and Feminism* (London: Associated University Presses, 2000)

Zarri, Gabriella, 'Note su diffusione e circolazione di testi devoti (1520–1550)', in *Libri, idee e sentimenti religiosi nel Cinquecento italiano* (Modena: Panini, 1987), pp. 131–54

Zecher, Carla, 'The gendering of the lute in sixteenth-century French love poetry', *Renaissance Quarterly*, 53 (2000), pp. 769–91

Zeeveld, William G., *Foundations of Tudor Policy* (Cambridge, MA: Harvard University Press, 1948)

Zumthor, Paul, *Essai de poétique médiévale* (Paris: Seuil, 1972)

Zumthor, Paul, 'The medieval travel narrative', trans. by Catherine Peebles, *New Literary History*, 25 (1994), pp. 809–24

Index

www.ingramcontent.com/pod-product-compliance
Ingram Content Group UK Ltd.
Pitfield, Milton Keynes, MK11 3LW, UK
UKHW020355010325
455677UK00021B/465